D0733033

phonology in context

Pre-publication praise for this book

Phonology in Context brings together in one volume 11 highly informative, fresh, and readable chapters detailing the multifarious and fascinating ways in which phonology interfaces with other levels of language, as well as in the social and psychological environment surrounding verbal behaviour. In contrast to traditional approaches in which phonology is viewed as static and context-free, in this book sound patterns are studied against the background of brain and cognitive processes, first and second language acquisition, as well as cultural forces. Readers will experience the kind of intellectual excitement that comes with an academic subject being brought back to life for them. It is also a must-read for graduate students and researchers, for whom it will be an indispensable reference. – K. K. Luke, University of Hong Kong

Phonology in Context presents new research perspectives on phonology and language development, language disorder, literacy and conversation, language variation, language contact and second language learning and teaching. Martha Pennington has gathered here researchers at the cutting edge ... enabling a synthesis which marks the vibrancy, theoretical sophistication, and broad applicability of phonology as it is understood today. Common to these new understandings are realizations of how phonology is shaped by dynamic processes of usage. This book will stimulate and inform experts and novices alike. – Nick Ellis, University of Michigan

Palgrave Advances in Linguistics

Consulting Editor:
**Christopher N. Candlin,
Macquarie University, Australia**

Titles include:

Martha E. Pennington (*editor*)
PHONOLOGY IN CONTEXT

Forthcoming:

Noel Burton-Roberts (*editor*)
PRAGMATICS

Susan Foster-Cohen (*editor*)
LANGUAGE ACQUISITION

Monica Heller (*editor*)
BILINGUALISM: A SOCIAL APPROACH

Ann Weatherall (*editor*)
LANGUAGE, DISCOURSE AND SOCIAL PSYCHOLOGY

Palgrave Advances
Series Standing Order ISBN 1–4039–3512–2 (Hardback) 1–4039–3513–0 (Paperback)
(*outside North America only*)

You can receive future titles in this series as they are published by placing a standing order.
Please contact your bookseller or, in the case of difficulty, write to us at the address below
with your name and address, the title of the series and the ISBN quoted above.

Customer Services Department, Macmillan Distribution Ltd, Houndmills, Basingstoke,
Hampshire RG21 6XS, England

phonology in context

edited by
martha c. pennington

First published 2007 by
PALGRAVE MACMILLAN
Houndmills, Basingstoke, Hampshire RG21 6XS and
175 Fifth Avenue, New York, N.Y. 10010
Companies and representatives throughout the world

PALGRAVE MACMILLAN is the global academic imprint of the
Palgrave Macmillan division of St. Martin's Press, LLC and of
Palgrave Macmillan Ltd.
Macmillan® is a registered trademark in the United States,
United Kingdom and other countries. Palgrave is a registered
trademark in the European Union and other countries.

ISBN-13   978–1–4039–3536–6 hardback
ISBN-10   1–4039–3536–X hardback
ISBN-13   978–1–4039–3537–3 paperback
ISBN-10   1–4039–3537–8 paperback

This book is printed on paper suitable for recycling and
made from fully managed and sustained forest sources.

A catalogue record for this book is available
from the British Library.

Library of Congress Cataloging-in-Publication Data

10   9   8   7   6   5   4   3   2   1
16   15   14   13   12   11   10   09   08   07

Transferred to digital printing in 2009.

dedication

I dedicate this book to the wonderfully talented and inspirational people from whom and around whom I learned phonology as a graduate student at the University of Pennsylvania in the 1970s. I am most fortunate to have been taught initially by a very fine phonologist, John Fought, who set high standards, nourished a critical attitude, and patiently trained my skills of observation and transcription in classes and in independent study and supervision of my PhD research. I am fortunate as well to have had my knowledge of phonology extended and put to practical use through study and research in historical linguistics with Henry Hoenigswald and in phonetics with Leigh Lisker, both of whom also served on my dissertation committee. Finally, I am fortunate that in my second year at Penn, someone steered me to take a class with our newest professor, William Labov, whose enormous energy, unquenchable curiosity, and passion for his work and for language made learning linguistics from and around him a joyful experience. Taking a course with Labov was a life-changing event; and since that time, I have never stopped learning from him.

contents

notes on contributors

Dorothy M. Chun is Professor of German and Applied Linguistics at the University of California, Santa Barbara. She holds a PhD from the University of California, Berkeley.

Elizabeth Couper-Kuhlen holds the Chair in Present-day English Language and Linguistics at the University of Potsdam. She holds a Doctoral degree from the University of Freiburg and a Postdoctoral degree from the University of Zurich.

Paola Escudero is a Postdoctoral researcher at the Institute of Phonetic Sciences of the University of Amsterdam. She holds a PhD in Linguistics from Utrecht University.

Fiona E. Gibbon is Professor and Head of Speech and Hearing Sciences at Queen Margaret University College in Edinburgh. She is a qualified speech and language therapist and holds a PhD from the University of Luton.

Debra M. Hardison is Associate Professor of Linguistics in the MA TESOL and PhD Second Language Studies Programs at Michigan State University. She holds a PhD in Linguistics from Indiana University.

Paul Kerswill is Professor of Linguistics at Lancaster University. He holds a PhD in Linguistics from Cambridge University.

Keiko Koda is Professor of Modern Languages at Carnegie Mellon University in Pennsylvania. She holds a PhD in Education from the University of Illinois at Urbana-Champaign.

April McMahon is Forbes Professor of English Language at the University of Edinburgh. She holds a PhD in English Language/Linguistics from the University of Edinburgh.

Martha C. Pennington is Distinguished Professor of Linguistics at Elizabethtown College in Pennsylvania. She holds a PhD in Linguistics from the University of Pennsylvania.

Linda Shockey is Lecturer in Linguistics at Reading University. She holds a PhD in Linguistics from Ohio State University.

Norval Smith is Associate Professor of Linguistics at the University of Amsterdam. He holds a Doctorate in Letters from the University of Amsterdam.

Shelley L. Velleman is Associate Professor of Communication Disorders at the University of Massachusetts at Amherst. She holds a PhD in Linguistics from the University of Texas at Austin.

Marilyn M. Vihman holds the Chair in Developmental Psychology at the University of Wales, Bangor. She holds a PhD in Linguistics from the University of California, Berkeley.

series preface

christopher n. candlin

This new *Advances in Linguistics Series* is part of an overall publishing program by Palgrave Macmillan aimed at producing collections of original, commissioned articles under the invited editorship of distinguished scholars.

The books in the Series are not intended as an overall guide to the topic or to provide an exhaustive coverage of its various sub-fields. Rather, they are carefully planned to offer the informed readership a conspectus of perspectives on key themes, authored by major scholars whose work is at the boundaries of current research. What we plan the Series will do, then, is to focus on salience and influence, move fields forward, and help to chart future research development.

The Series is designed for postgraduate and research students, including advanced level undergraduates seeking to pursue research work in Linguistics, or careers engaged with language and communication study more generally, as well as for more experienced researchers and tutors seeking an awareness of what is current and in prospect in adjacent research fields to their own. We hope that some of the intellectual excitement posed by the challenges of Linguistics as a pluralistic discipline will shine through the books!

Editors of books in the Series have been particularly asked to put their own distinctive stamp on their collection, to give it a personal dimension, and to map the territory, as it were, seen through the eyes of their own research experience.

In this first book in the Series, *Phonology in Context*, Martha Pennington admirably fulfils the brief. Eschewing local and traditionally sharp distinctions (and divisions) in her subject – as for example between phonetics and phonology – she argues from a discussion of the contexts of phonological research for a strengthening of the descriptive, explanatory and predictive power of phonology within Linguistics as a core discipline central to our understanding of real-world human communicative behaviour: social, cognitive, physical and evolutionary.

Christopher N. Candlin
Senior Research Professor
Department of Linguistics
Macquarie University, Sydney

1
the context of phonology

martha c. pennington

what is phonology?

Many different answers can be given to the question, "What is phonology?" The classical definition differentiates phonology from phonetics, as in the following passage from Catford (2001):

> The study of the physiological, aerodynamic, and acoustic characteristics of speech-sounds is the central concern of *phonetics* [all emphases as in the original]. The study of how sounds are organized into systems and utilized in languages is the central concern of *phonology*. Neither of these two linguistic disciplines is independent of the other. A knowledge of what features of sound are most utilized in languages determines what aspects of sound production are most worth studying in depth. Thus phonetics depends to some extent upon phonology to indicate areas of linguistic relevance and importance. Phonology, on the other hand, is heavily dependent on phonetics, since it is phonetics that provides the insights that enable one to discover what sound features are linguistically utilized, and it is phonetics again, that supplies the terminology for the description and classification of the linguistically relevant features of sounds. (p. 177)

As this traditional delimitation of phonology and phonetics suggests, these two areas of linguistics have long been understood to be interrelated. In many approaches to phonology, the interconnection is captured in terms of levels of language or levels of analysis of language, as, for example, in Giegerich's (1992) characterization of the practice of phonology:

[A] phonological analysis entails two levels of representation – a concrete (phonetic) one and an abstract (underlying) one – as well as statements on how the units on one level are connected with corresponding units on the other level. These statements have the form of realisation rules.... (p. 31)

The distinction between phonetics as a more "concrete" level of representation contrasted with phonology as a more "abstract" level of representation is common.

Although most linguists agree that these two linguistic disciplines or levels exist and are interconnected, the focus of linguistics has generally been on phonology as an area separate from phonetics. The majority of phonologists would argue that phonology, the level at which the functional categories (e.g., phonemes) of the sound systems of spoken languages exist, is primary, and that it is acceptable (and indeed common) for phonologists to carry out their work with little or no attention to phonetics. For many phoneticians, as illustrated by the views of Catford above, phonologists disregard phonetics at their peril, since the phonetic level provides the observable and measurable basis for phonology. Yet it is fair to remark that just as phonologists often do phonology in disregard of phonetics, so phoneticians generally carry out their measurements in disregard of phonology.

For the most part, people working in these two closely related linguistic disciplines do not communicate. What's more, they tend to view their single-minded focus as justified by the demands of their work and the relative importance of their own discipline, sometimes as sharply contrasted with that of the other discipline. As Clark and Yallop (1990) observe:

Unfortunately, what may appear to be a reasonable division of labour between phoneticians and phonologists is frequently discussed in the context of assumptions about the "real" nature of speech. Thus the idea that phonetics is concerned with universal properties of speech, studied by scientific methods, may all too easily be read as a claim that phonetics deals with objective physical or concrete reality, while phonology is somewhat apologetically concerned with the linguistic organization of this reality. Or, more or less reversing the argument, phonology may be said to tackle the true mental reality behind speech, while phonetics handles "merely" the concrete outworkings of this reality. Hence the relationship between phonetics and phonology becomes controversial and it is important to understand the reasons for this, rather than to attempt an oversimplified and divisive definition of the two terms. (p. 3)

The sharp division between phonology and phonetics, and the associated debates about the practice of linguistics, are illustrative of the divisive nature of twentieth-century linguistics. This has been true both in the sense that the field of linguistics as a whole and each of its branches (phonology, syntax, etc.) have been increasingly carved up into non-intersecting areas of study and in the sense that each branch or new area tends to oppose itself theoretically, methodologically, and rhetorically to others. It may be argued that specialization and the attendant counter-positioning, which would appear to be natural processes in science and academic scholarship, accelerate research and progress in a field (in general or at certain stages of its history) by creating or helping to develop new theoretical and methodological niches. This would seem to be the case, for example, in the development of sociolinguistics and applied linguistics from the root branch of linguistics, and of Generative Phonology and later Optimality Theory as branches of phonology. However, there may be times when this dynamic of branching and differentiation from the root field becomes counterproductive, breeding excessive fragmentation, producing weaker species of theory, and slowing down or impeding progress. I believe we are at a point in linguistics where our divisions are interfering with progress and weakening our descriptive, explanatory, and predictive power. This is not the time to be reinforcing long-standing boundaries and carving up the territory further, but rather, a time when we all need to be talking to each other.

Phonology is in a period of rapid development in which branches are multiplying as phonologists seek to embrace new findings and to correct for the shortcomings of previous theories and practices. At the same time, the central role played by phonology in all aspects of language is beginning to be understood and appreciated in a way that it has not been in the last century. Among some linguists, there has recently been a recognition of the connections of phonology to higher levels of language (morphology, lexis, and syntax) and to matters of usage and performance that go beyond language per se. Consideration of phonology within these wider concerns of performance and usage – incorporating perceptual processing, cognitive organization and memory, and social behavior – is leading to new understandings of language learning and language change (see, e.g., Blevins, 2004; Bybee, 2001), and to broader generalizations about the mechanisms involved which connect phonology to other aspects of human behavior (e.g., Pennington, 2002b, 2002c). Thus is phonology being brought out of isolation and reintegrated both with other branches of linguistics and into its contexts of occurrence.

uniqueness of this volume

This is a unique volume on phonology capturing the current movement away from its formalist roots and towards new context-bound orientations for the practice of phonology that link it to phonetics, psychology, and the wider communicational and behavioral complex within which humans use language. The book's coverage repositions phonology within the real-world contexts of language development and phonological disorder, literacy and conversation, language variation and language contact, and second-language learning and teaching. The boundaries of phonology are further extended by examination of the interaction of visual and auditory information in processing speech and the connection of phonology to emotion and gesture in the evolution of human vocalization. The intended reader will have some knowledge of linguistics and of transcription but may not be a specialist in phonology.

I commissioned the chapters of this book to provide ten different perspectives on phonology in context, each a critical examination of a particular area that would provide a view of the current state of theory and methodology and would incorporate the author's own work as well as that of key researchers. The authors were selected as leading figures working at the "critical edge" of their respective areas and pushing the practice of phonology forward in new directions. In setting phonology in a context which extends beyond traditional concerns and challenges existing assumptions and practices, they all raise questions, explicitly or implicitly, about the nature of phonology and its domain of applicability.

The chapters of this volume have gone through a two-year process of development and several stages of revision, and I have worked closely with authors in evolving the content and structure of their material. In the final stage of preparation of the book, I have added references to relevant discussion in other chapters and sources, and prepared my own summaries of the chapters and discussion of the field incorporating their content. In the remainder of this introductory chapter, I first summarize the content of the other ten chapters and then follow with my own reflections that have been stimulated by them. These will I hope inspire others to read and build on the work of the scholars who contributed to this volume, and to continue creating new phonologies that place it in real-world contexts.

chapter summaries

The first two chapters offer theoretical reflections in the context of phonology in first language acquisition. Shelley L. Velleman and Marilyn M. Vihman (Chapter 2 – "Phonology in Infancy and Early Childhood: Implications for Theories of Language Learning") provide an accessible introduction to phonological theory, research, and contemporary issues through the lens of first-language acquisition. Their review identifies universal and non-universal features of child phonology and highlights those aspects that do not receive a ready explanation in phonological theory. They review studies showing that "very specific auditory traces, not only of phonetic detail but also of sociophonetic aspects such as voice quality, are retained in memory" for speech. These serve as the basis for accumulating information about the nature and the distribution of linguistic forms and functions and for acquiring the sound patterns of the native language. Based upon their examination of neurocognitive research and current phonological theories, Velleman and Vihman offer their own integrated pattern-induction model of phonological development. This model "claims no innate phonological knowledge" but "[r]ather,…specifies the learning processes by which phonological information is gathered, analyzed, and acted upon." Thus, the emphasis is placed squarely on empirical research to study the language learner's behavior and learning processes. In place of universals, their inductive model gives a central role to probabilistic learning and allows for individual variation and sociolinguistic influences on the acquisition of phonology. The learning mechanism involves "coarse-grained" (procedural) memories capturing recurrent phonological patterns in the ambient language and operating on the "fine-grained" phonetic detail in declarative memory "to differentiate systematic subphonemic variation from linguistically significant variation." As contrasted with earlier models of phonological acquisition, their model blurs "the lines between grammar and an associative cognitive system,…[reflecting] an increase in psycholinguistic reality and a deeper grounding in known brain structures and processes."

Paul Kerswill and Linda Shockey (Chapter 3 – "The Description and Acquisition of Variable Phonological Patterns: Phonology and Sociolinguistics") view traditions in phonology through the lens of variation, a topic which has not been of primary interest in the study of phonology outside sociolinguistics. They contrast "conventional" and "variationist" approaches to phonology in terms of the type of data collected and the way in which it is analyzed, noting that "typically, abstract phonologists," who have had a strong focus on theory-building, "have based their work on idealized, sometimes self-generated, and decontextualized data, in order to achieve...exceptionless regularity, or 'categoricity'." Variationists have instead concerned themselves with "how the sound units, as already posited by phonologists, vary in their phonetic shape in conjunction with and as conditioned by extra-linguistic factors, as well as by phonological and other linguistic context." Kerswill and Shockey consider a number of phonological theories in terms of how they handle variation and the acquisition of variation, noting that "[f]requency-based data...pose challenges to phonological theories in which probabilistic differences cannot be expressed." They observe that variation is a central aspect of the patterning of sound which children must acquire and that variable patterns may change throughout the lifespan of a speaker. They further note the central role of variation in language change, which is a point of convergent interest for traditional phonologists and sociolinguists, and endorse an evolutionary view of phonological change as resulting from "incomplete transmission across the generations, which may be caused by mishearing or by the signal being inherently ambiguous."

 The next two chapters focus on phonology in contexts where more than one language is spoken – contexts which are crucial for phonology since they predominate in human societies. Norval Smith (Chapter 4 – "Contact Phonology") illustrates how phonology is shaped by language contact, beginning with *loanword phonology*, in which borrowing induces change in the importing language. Phonological change also results from *areal influence* involving a group of dialects or languages which exhibit the same features. *Dialect mixing* occurs when new dialects are formed in situations of political and cultural dominance (*koiné* formation) and in situations of strong regional identity (consolidation of regional dialect features into a *regional koiné* or *regiolect*). A further type of case involves phonological influence of one dialect or variety (including a standard variety) by another. In *language mixing*, the mixed language may inherit the phonological systems of one or both contributing languages, or may exhibit a split system. In his final category, that of purported *simplification* in creole languages, Smith challenges some claims of phonological universals, such as the creole origins of properties like open syllable structure which might be traceable to a source language, and further argues that complex features of a source language may be retained rather than simplified in a creole language. In his view: "What in fact occurs in creolization might not be simplification but *negotiation* among speakers in the process of achieving phonological uniformity." Smith's chapter makes clear the dynamic nature of phonology as occurring in an ever-changing context of people and their languages coming together, noting that "the numbers of speakers of the various contributing languages and other sociohistorical factors will play a significant role in determining what the end result will look like in any given case."

Paola Escudero (Chapter 5 – "Second-Language Phonology: The Role of Perception") focuses on perception as key to understanding and modeling the acquisition of phonology in a second language. As in first-language (L1) acquisition, phonological acquistion in a second language (L2) involves "arriving at the appropriate number and type of sound categories and the appropriate mappings from the speech signal onto such categories." L2 acquisition has some unique features, including: (i) its basis in the learner's knowledge of the mother tongue and the influence of L1 transfer; (ii) constraints on development having to do with age (*maturational constraints*), the type and amount of exposure to the L2 (*input constraints*), and the cognitive mechanisms operative in learning (*learnability constraints*); and (iii) the degree of cognitive independence or interdependence of the learner's L1 and L2 systems during acquisition. Escudero reviews a number of models that have been proposed to explain perception in the acquisition of L2 phonology, then focuses on the Linguistic Perception (LP) model, which she has been involved in developing. According to the LP model, an L1 learner creates a perception grammar using a Gradual Learning Algorithm (GLA) that operates on the patterns and frequency distributions in the language input to create abstract representations of sounds and sound categories, and to continually refine these over time through increasing experience with language. According to the L2 version of this model, a *Full Copy* of the L1 perception grammar and lexical representations serves as the starting state of the new perceptual system for L2. The L2 learner has *Full Access* to all mechanisms performed by the GLA in L1 learning to create sound categories and the boundaries of those categories with respect to words. The model proposes that *Full Proficiency* (native or native-like perception) is possible in both L1 and L2 with regular usage of both. The model supports efforts to improve learners' percpetion of L2 phonology, and suggestions for training are offered.

The two chapters which follow show how phonology is linked to the larger context of communication and behavior that incorporates visual cues and affect. Debra M. Hardison (Chapter 6 – "The Visual Element in Phonological Perception and Learning") enlarges the context of phonology to include visual cues, especially lip gestures, demonstrating the intimate connection of perception of speech in the auditory channel to the visual channel. Experiments have shown that visual input from lip movements influences activity in the auditory cortex, and children develop a sensitivity to relationships between speech sounds and lip movements at an early age. In a series of her own investigations and a review of others, Hardison shows how such cues are integrated with auditory information and can aid perception and comprehension of speech in first and second language learning. Visual and auditory information reinforce each other in speech perception and interpretation, and, conversely, mismatched visual and auditory cues can cause listeners to "hear" the wrong sounds – i.e., ones which they can correctly identify visually but which are not those presented to them through recordings. From the research it emerges that interpretation of the physical appearance and movements of the lips is a component of the identification of phonemes and the interpretation of phonological information for comprehension when this information is available. Interpretation of speech is further aided by familiarity with a specific speaker's face and by access to visualizations of intonation contours. The research findings for L2 learners "are compatible with a view of speech processing involving the development of context- and speaker-dependent representations [and]…with a multiple-trace account of memory, in which all attended perceptual details of a speech event are encoded in multiple traces in memory." A variety of technologies have been designed that can help L2 learners as well as autistic and deaf children to gain visual information about speech, to highlight important cues, and to make the memory traces of speech events less ambiguous.

April McMahon (Chapter 7 – "Sounds, Brain, and Evolution: Or, Why Phonology is Plural") presents a view of phonology in phylogentic perspective, with comparisons to our primate cousins and speculations about the prehistorical development of language in a broader communicative context. McMahon raises the question of whether phonology is a unitary domain. The answer she offers is that the two different subfields and emphases of phonologists, prosodic and segmental phonology, represent different domains in more than a descriptive sense: they have different evolutionary bases and are stored in different parts of the brain. McMahon maintains that "prosody is acquired faster and earlier than segmental phonology because prosody involves a much more substantial innate component." In her view, children acquire segmental phonology from input using human capacities not specific to language but appear to "learn prosody with the assistance of innate capacities which are associated uniquely with language learning." She hypothesizes that prosody, if it is based in an innate system, "is an older system than segmental phonology, and that prosody or its precursor developed in evolutionary rather than historical time." McMahon tests this hypothesis using evidence from primate vocal communication, gesture, emotion, language disorder, and brain lateralization to show that "prosody is a classic Darwinian case of descent with modification from an earlier common system, a system that existed prior to human language as it is now." The bulk of her chapter lays out a possible evolutionary scenario in which prosody and its affective and gestural concomitants are controlled by the right hemisphere, whereas the segmental domain of phonology, which developed later in time "[a]s the brain grew in size, and began to incorporate new specializations," is controlled by the left hemisphere.

In the next two chapters, phonology is examined in the contexts of spoken discourse and written texts. Elizabeth Couper-Kuhlen (Chapter 8 – "Situated Phonologies: Patterns of Phonology in Discourse Contexts"), like McMahon, addresses the question of the domain of phonology. She notes that phonology has been too much based in written language and too much focused on contrasts in isolated forms, given that, "in the context of naturally occurring discourse – whether scripted or spontaneous, monologic or dialogic – many putative phonological distinctions disappear." Couper-Kuhlen thus advocates the study of phonology in discourse, defined as "situated language use, language deployed dynamically and in real time for communicative purposes…[and] studied in natural, real-life situations." She illustrates an approach that identifies regularities in a detailed, impressionistic description of naturally occurring conversational data and develops context-dependent functional explanations of these as *situated phonologies*. "Recurrent patterns are…sought in the impression-istic record, with careful attention being paid to factors such as lexical and syntactic structure, action type, position in the turn-constructional unit, position in the turn, position in the sequence, type of sequence or activity, and situational context – factors which have proved relevant in previous studies of interactional phonology." Functional explanations for observed patterns are developed in relation to specific contexts of action, speakers' goals and the tasks they perform in those contexts, and participants' own views of their behavior. Couper-Kuhlen observes that multiple "phonologies" will be required to describe the different ways of performing a particular action in interaction within specific goals and circumstances. "Yet despite the extreme context-sensitivity of action implementation by the speaker and of interpretation by the listener in interaction, the contribution of phonetic and prosodic cueing to the task is both patterned and systematic." Couper-Kuhlen illustrates the approach by a consideration of the phonological (prosodic and segmental) features associated with: (i) turn construction and coordination of turn-taking; (ii) linkage and separation of units of talk; (iii) accomplishing actions and action sequences; and (iv) marking speaker stance and affiliation.

Keiko Koda (Chapter 9 – "Phonology and Literacy") places phonology in the context of literacy development, elucidating how the understanding of text is built on knowledge of phonology in first- and second-language acquisition. "Learning to read can be characterized," in her words, "as learning to map between the language (phonemes and morphemes) and the writing system." Koda describes the phonological skills that underlie reading, noting that phonology is crucial for understanding the relationship of spoken to written text and that "deficiencies [in reading] are restricted primarily to the phonological domain" and not usually due to other causes. She observes that children's awareness of phonological structure in spoken language is a strong predictor of their success in learning to read, as is their ability to decode printed words into phonological components and to automate those decoding processes so that they can be performed without conscious attention, thereby freeing up cognitive capacity for the higher order processes of extracting meaning from text. Koda presents a cognitive account emphasizing the crucial role of phonology in memory, noting that "[s]ince virtually all of the sub-component processes of comprehension rely on working memory, phonological processing remains critical in text understanding at all stages of reading development." She also identifies differences in phonological processing across languages and examines the impact of learning more than one language on processing printed text. Languages are seen to have similar requirements in terms of phonological processing but to differ in their requirements for mapping between the language and the writing system, based on the linguistic unit denoted by each graphic symbol (*orthographic representation*) and the degree of regularity in symbol-to-sound correspondences (*orthographic depth*). Although "considerable variation exists in the way phonology is represented graphically in typologically diverse languages," it seems that "phonological awareness, as a major prerequisite to learning to read, once developed in one language offers substantial facilitation in literacy development in another." There are nevertheless differences in second-language decoding due to the degree of: transfer of reading skills from the L1, cross-linguistic interaction, and orthographic similiarity of L1 and L2. Koda remarks the need for additional research on L2 reading to establish "a causal linkage between decoding efficiency and higher-order operations during comprehension" and to understand the development of decoding skill over time.

The last two chapters review clinical, pedagogical, and research applications. Fiona E. Gibbon (Chapter 10 – "Research and Practice in Developmental Phonological Disorders") discusses phonological disorders in childhood from a historical perspective that shows how theory and explanation have evolved since the 1950s. She provides examples of systematic and idiosyncratic errors affecting children's speech in *functional phonological disorder*, and reviews possible causes of the condition, including poor phonological memory and poor speech motor control, as well as conditions such as structural abnormalities in the vocal tract and an early history of ear infections. However, most cases of functional phonological disorder persisting to school age cannot be attributed to any definite causes, and "there may be a number of sources underlying phonological disorders, each requiring a different approach to intervention." As in other areas of language, there has been an attempt by researchers in the previous generation to provide a unified account for developmental phonological disorders in the form of abstract linguistic processes and rules, and these accounts have yielded useful approaches to description and remediation. Yet they have failed to account for many of the observed phenomena in children with phonological disorder, in part because of an inability to correctly identify and describe some of its associated features. Many children exhibit imprecise articulation because of *undifferentiated gestures*, in which parts of the tongue (apex/blade, body, and lateral margins) move together rather than being controlled independently. They also exhibit *covert contrasts* imperceptible to a hearer but detectable by means of instrumental analysis. The discovery of these features which are not detectable by the human ear nor describable in normal place and manner terms raises fundamental questions about the classification of speech errors, the nature of developmental phonological disorders, and the methodologies used for characterizing and analyzing them. Despite these issues surrounding description and explanation, "[c]hildren with phonological disorders are a group for whom," Gibbon says, "we now have effective diagnostic and intervention procedures." Illustrated therapies are: auditory input, minimal pair contrast, maximal opposition, the traditional method of motor training, and computer-based approaches.

Dorothy M. Chun (Chapter 11 – "Technological Advances in Researching and Teaching Phonology") shows the different ways in which technology is shaping the study and teaching of phonology, phonetics, and pronunciation in a second language. Chun examines "advances and new directions in acoustic analysis and speech recognition as they relate to issues of phonology, both from a research perspective of quantifying and measuring segmental phonemes and prosody, and from the practical perspective of using technology to teach." She stresses the

increasing interest within linguistics in "authentic, spontaneous speech…
and [in] discourse-level prosody," concomitant with the availability of
digital recordings of speech, noting that "[t]hese are exciting times
for researching language with speech technology and developing
applications for teaching pronunciation, including prosody, based on
naturally occurring speech." Chun begins with a review of technological
advances within linguistics that have been used for acoustic research on
spoken language, including speech recognition, text-to-speech synthesis,
spoken dialogue systems, and speech corpora. She then turns to applied
linguistic research aiming to determine the most crucial components
of phonology, such as prosody, for listening and speaking in a second
language. In the final section, Chun examines the available hardware
and software for teaching pronunciation in a second language and the
research that has been conducted on its effectiveness. Two problems
she highlights are: (i) the limitation of automatic speech recognition to
pre-scripted speech and limited-response learning activities and (ii) the
lack of specific feedback to learners about how to remedy their errors
once these have been located. She calls for interdisciplinary cooperation
to develop software incorporating "current knowledge in computer
science, computational linguistics, and well-grounded design principles
for research and pedagogy."

the big picture

the domain of inquiry

It is inevitable that theories and models reflect the time and circumstances
in which they are born, and this is as true of linguistics in general
and phonology in particular as of any other field. Thus, twentieth-
century formal linguistics reflects a history rooted in philosophy and
mathematical logic, providing the frame as well for the development
of contrastive analysis from which descriptive phonology and later
Generative Phonology were born. In this era, the practice of phonology
involved transcription, classification, and the writing of rules based on an
inventory of discrete elements, such as phonemes or distinctive features,
seen as making up the sound systems of languages. Even after the advent
of visible speech, in sound spectography, had clearly indicated that these
discrete units did not bear much relationship to the acoustic record of
speech, linguistics largely stayed with this mode of description and its
associated theory for an additional half century.

It has become increasingly clear that this mode of discrete-item classification and description is inadequate to the characterization of the

properties of the sound systems of languages. Much has been left out in trying to map those systems to a poor analog in the written language and in trying to understand them within theoretical assumptions about autonomy, discreteness, generativity, and language universals. Within this system of description and under these assumptions, many phenomena have been ignored or marginalized (e.g., intonation, discourse-level concerns), and some have been misleadingly or incorrectly described (e.g., L1 and L2 phonological acquisition). The previous generation of linguists has perhaps been too quick to classify data in terms of familiar categories and patterns and to make generalizations in the form of phonological rules that abstract away from the details of speech data. The winnowing and simplifying assumptions seemed natural and reasonable at the time; but gradually the landscape of phonology has been shifting, to the point where the field finds its footings on quite shakey ground. It no longer seems natural or reasonable to restrict the domain of linguistics to "competence" and ignore "performance," nor to build a theory of language without attention to conversation and to infants' prelanguage communication. Nor does it seem natural for mono-lingualism to have pride of place in the field and for second-language acquisition, bilingualism, creole linguistics, and sociolinguistics to be on the periphery.

Rather than force-fitting the theory and the data to the descriptive conventions, it is time to rethink the field of phonology substantially. A number of fundamental questions can and are being raised regarding the nature of phonology, the best way to describe it, and fruitful approaches to understanding it in relation to cognitive and social domains. It may be time to re-examine our subject area, phonology, vis-à-vis not only the lower level of what we have grown used to calling phonetics, but also in relation to the higher levels of lexis and morphology, as is the current trend, as well as discourse and interactional dynamics. We also need to consider phonology in relation to the advances being made in L1 and L2 acquisition and in psychology that shed light on the nature of perception, cognition, and learning. In what follows, I present a picture of phonology in context that links perceptual, cognitive, and motor to psychological and social dimensions, drawing on the models developed by Velleman and Vihman and by Escudero for L1 and L2 acquisition, and on the contributions of the other authors.

language acquisition

In first-language acquisition, phonological patterns are discovered through sequence learning (Ellis, 1998) and other types of pattern-induction. The "coarse-grained" level accounts for the grouping together by these processes of the traces of remembered events which are close or similar in their form as well as in their associated functions. These will be classified as equivalent and thus in the same category. As I have described it elsewhere:

> Equivalence classification is a holistic, assimilative processing mode that avoids the cognitive cost of analytic processing. It is essentially a similarity (or comparison) strategy in which new input is processed by focusing on gross features and disregarding (small) differences in an effort to try to match the input to one or more exemplars of an existing category. If a "reasonable" match is found, the new input is thenceforth treated as equivalent to – "the same" as – the other exemplars. It is probably a general feature of such classification of new input that at first the new exemplar is not differentiated consistently or at all from other exemplars of the same category. (Pennington, 2000a, p. 282)

Difference between forms which perform different functions is then sorted out with reference to the finer level of phonetic detail in the context of the associated other information in declarative memory. The process of learning is driven by a basic need for cognitive economy and organization into "coarse-grained" patterns and consolidated categories. This need is balanced against a need to retain sufficient detail to be able to process new information in relation to old and to maintain sufficient distinctiveness and discriminability of patterns and categories for functionality. Children exposed to input from the same language or variety will arrive at similar though not identical systems, and will differ in their learning path as they acquire their L1 (Velleman and Vihman). As the phenomena of undifferentiated gestures and covert contrasts (Gibbon) suggest, children with phonological disorder may differ from other children in the extent to which, or the manner in which:

- they notice or process fine-grained detail;
- they operationalize phonological categories and phonetic distinctions in their articulatory behavior.

Like first-language acquisition, second-language acquisition is based on the processes of:

(i) *similarity-matching and coarse-grained pattern-induction* to organize information and manage cognitive load, balanced against

(ii) *difference-sorting and processing of fine-grained detail* to maintain discriminability and functionality.

As stressed by Kerswill and Shockey, all phonological systems have variation built in that has been acquired in childhood. This built-in variation is realized as alternate pronunciations for certain phonemes or words under certain conditions. The variability presumably results from a number of sources, including:

- *variation in the input* (exposure to non-uniform inputs under different conditions and from different speakers);
- *physiological limitations* (limitations of cognitive load, inexactness of memory traces);
- *the nature of pattern-induction* (allowance for rough equivalence and "fuzzy" boundaries).

Whatever the source, the fact that variation is part of learners' experience of language means that they can handle new forms when they are exposed to them, and will try to connect them to something they already know. Like acquisition of new variants (allophones of existing phonemes or new phonemes) in one's mother tongue, the acquisition of the new phones and sound categories of an L2 proceeds gradually on the basis of those already acquired (for discussion, see Pennington, 2000a, p. 280f). For L2 this means building the new sound system by "piggybacking" on the L1 sound system – and to a greater or lesser extent also on the other systems of the L1 – for grouping into categories and sorting differences. Whether the L2 case represents a difference in degree, massive though it may be, rather than a difference in kind in comparison to acquisition of new variants or dialect features built on the original phones and categories of the L1, is unclear.

linkages to other behaviors

If linguistic phenomena can be described as memories viewed in finer or lesser detail, or "grains," then the phonological level of language is completely tied up with the other levels, or "grainings," of the memory and processing of linguistic events. In this way, the processing of phonological information at a cognitive level connects "low-level" perceptual and motor behavior to "high-level" psychological and social behavior (Pennington, 1998a). Figure 1.1 depicts the fact that phonology cannot easily be restricted to perceptual and/or motor behavior, not even to cognitively organized perceptual and/or motor behavior, since these are contextualized in and regulated together with psychological and social behavior and organization. While the cognitive system managing all other levels of behavior can be argued to be the primary locus of the phonological system, it can also be argued that the phonological system exists at multiple levels or in multiple domains, or that there is no phonological system as such but rather an associative network linking various domains or levels at which spoken language is manifest within the cognitive system.

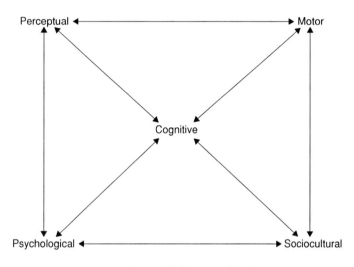

Figure 1.1   Schematic model of the domains of phonology

It should not be surprising to find that the core of all spoken language (and the basis of written language as it has evolved in connection to spoken language), which is human vocalization, is deeply embedded in human behavior at all levels. The social and psychological embedding of phonology is a reason that native-language phonology established in childhood is relatively stable and not easily altered in adulthood:

> [T]he perception-production links that are formed in L1 phonological development are complex and multi-level, and pronunciation (both segmental and suprasegmental features) comes to serve as an important indicator of temporary and permanent characteristics such as emotional state, degree of affiliation with the audience, personal identity, and social identity. (Pennington, 2000a, p. 286)

The behavioral complex within which phonology is manifest includes lip gestures, other facial characteristics, and the wider gestural complex – all factoring into listeners' processing of what speakers are saying, and what they mean by their words.

language change

The sound system of a language can be described as a relatively crystallized main or core pattern of categories and distinctions existing at a point in time. It seems to be a feature of language that such a core pattern of categories and distinctions exists, i.e., we do not define vocal behavior as language until speaker productions converge on a relatively regular set of phonological distinctions. Thus, we do not recognize that a child has mastered phonology until his/her productions have become relatively consistent and stabilized close to those of adult native speakers. Yet this core is not entirely set and so is correctly described as "relatively crystallized." It is also an important feature of language that change be possible. We can thus speak of a core pattern balanced against a periphery of different or more fluid options, such as those existing in different dialects that speakers have some familiarity with.

Phonology, like all aspects of language, is a living, changing ecosystem (Mufwene, 2001). Historical linguists and dialectologists have long understood that languages are constantly changing and fragmenting into dialects and that the pattern for lexical items and phonemes is not uniform across even one city or region. In the twentieth century it became increasingly understood that the variation extended even into the neighborhood and the family, and that social factors – such as gender, ethnicity, socioeconomic status, and situational constraints affecting speech style – were contributing to the observed patterns. Yet phonologists still tend to describe phonology as if it is a system independent of the people who speak a language, and most phonologists have not incorporated much if any social component or change potential in their systems.

A new orientation to modeling this change potential is the "A-curve" model of language change proposed by Kretzschmar and Tamasi (2003), based on distributional patterns observed from phonological and lexical data collected in the American Linguistic Atlas Project:

> Since the model predicts that any linguistic feature will exist in many variants at any time, there will always be a pool of variants, each of which may either increase or decrease in frequency. The addition of variants to the pool, linguistic innovation, may occur at any time, and

the model easily allows for innovation of variants at low frequencies. (p. 397)

Language change is defined as the changing frequencies of variants along the curve: those which increase in frequency increase their relative contribution to the pattern-induction processes by which speakers abstract the core pattern of their language.

As illustrated in the examples of Chapter 4, phonetic change or "drift" can gradually, word by word or in terms of repeated familiarization at the level of *sound* rather than words (or at the level of sound extracted from lexical exemplars), become phonological (i.e., categorical) change. Smith shows how major change may be induced by the reinterpretation of a secondary as a primary feature, such as register differences in Khmer, which are realized as "a feature of voice quality that has developed from features of formerly present consonants." Thus, language change proceeds like evolutionary change, in which secondary features gain new functionality (as noted by McMahon) and become primary, and in which the forms best fitted to the available niches and functions win out over others. Both perceptual and social factors are involved in this evolutionary change process.

The discussion by Smith of the perception by Dutch speakers of English /æ/ as equivalent to Dutch as /ɛ/, which causes English loanwords with /æ/ and /ɛ/ to fall together in Dutch as /ɛ/ (e.g., Dutch /ɛksɛs/ from English *access*) indicates that the kinds of perceptual reinterpretation identified for language change in language contact situations are essentially the same as those identified by Escudero for second language acquisition and by Blevins (2004) for first-language acquisition. It appears that we are at the beginning stages of many different perspectives tending in the same direction and converging on a grand theory of language acquisition and change.

Building on the contributions of this volume and extending the insight of Blevins (2004), sound change can be seen as the result of perceptual and cognitive processes that shape sound systems. These involve pattern-induction carried out on the regularities and irregularities of the existing phonological system. When phonological input contains deficient information, inconsistent patterns, or a diversity of forms, this will cause speakers to change their coarse-grained patterns and their estimation of where the phonetic details and boundaries of differentiating features lie within the system. The process can be extended to regular nativization processes in language contact – including creolization, bilingualism, and second-language acquisition. The same mechanism by means of which children learn language, through processes of grouping and sorting the features recalled from the ambient language, is operative in all aspects of language use, including language contact and change. There is then no need for a separate mechanism of universal grammar, or a priori universals of any kind. Rather, what appear to be universals are not: they all have exceptions and are but statistical regularities – generalizations falling out of human perceptual and cognitive abilities together with the needs of communication with other human beings. This conclusion is underscored by the findings of Port and Leary (2005) that "decades of phonetics research demonstrate that there exists no universal inventory of phonetic objects" (Abstract) and that "phonologies differ incommensurably"(ibid.). This is clearly a case in which phonology, which has been heavily vested in assumptions about language universals, cannot ignore the findings of phonetics.

This is not, however, the whole story of the basis of sound change, which also has a social dynamic, as has long been understood by sociolinguists. Phonological change can be strictly phonologically conditioned, morphologically conditioned, or lexically idiosyncratic. The different possibilities point to the different influences on phonological change in the way of perceptual, cognitive, and social factors. These might lead, on the one hand, to levelling effects that appear as consolidations, regularizations, or simplifications, or, on the other hand, to differentiation effects via acquisition or development of forms that increase variety and so allow for new distinctions. Historically, we might expect to find these different types of change occurring in innovation-adoption cycles[1] in which irregularities and idiosyncracies are introduced and then can spread and become regularized in the process. We might expect to see, for example, a lexically idiosyncratic change driven by social imitation becoming over time a more regular, phonologically conditioned change (though this is of course not the only possibility – see Bybee, 2001, for discussion).

It should be emphasized that change cycles are by no means perfect cycles but rather what we might call "leaky cycles" in the sense that probably every change occurring in language is less than 100% completed: there is always some context on the "edge" of the change – at the boundary between one word and another, one phonological category and another, one geographical area and another, or one social group and another. Moreover, the same can be said of every *stage* (however defined) of every change: at every point where some regularity seems to have occurred, there will be a ragged edge of some kind or another. This is because linguistic categories are not perfect classes but rather fuzzy ones with only roughly defined ("coarse-grained") boundaries. This is a reason that traditional phonology, which is so concerned with distinctive, non-overlapping categories, has had to idealize to such an extent, and has not been able to handle the very real effects of human nature on the nature of language – the capacities, limitations, and behaviors which result not in sharp boundaries but in the fuzzy edges and messy residues of human perceptual, motor, cognitive, psychological, and social processes.

connecting the dots: towards a unified view of phonology in context

Traditional linguistics was generally not concerned with language acquisition. However, an increasing number of researchers are working in language acquisition and making connections to issues of general theoretical interest in the field. Velleman and Vihman's chapter goes a long way to enlarging the domain of inquiry on linguistic theory to include child language acquisition, and Escudero's chapter does the same for second language acquisition. Moreover, as Escudero shows, many of the phenomena of L2 acquisition are paralleled in L1 acquisition, and there are commonalities in Gibbon's description of children with phonological disorder and descriptions of the phonological character-istics of L2 learners. The suggestions for teaching provided by Chun for L2 and by Gibbon in speech therapy are also similar. There is much to be learned about the nature of language and of language learning by more systematic comparisons of these different contexts of phonology. Too long has linguistics operated as if these different types of language acquisition were incomparable. It is important to understand the points of intersection as well as their distinctive properties.

Traditional linguistics has also not been much concerned with matters of language contact, such as bilingualism/multilingualism and pidgins and creoles. Those who have worked in these areas, who would generally classify themselves as linguists or creolists, have moreover been quite separate from those working in L2 acquisition, who classify themselves as applied linguists, second-language researchers, and/or language teachers. Yet again, there are important points of intersection and comparisons needing to be made. The description by Smith of "contact-induced change at the segmental level" as caused by "straightforward reinterpretation of foreign sounds in terms of elements of the native system" and of "foreign sounds intruding themselves into the native system, and such intrusion forcing the reallocation of allophones to phonemes" is quite similar to the phenomena observed by Escudero and others working in L2 acquisition. The primary difference is in the generality of these sorts of changes, whether they are widespread and persist into the next generation.

Work in language acquisition and language contact is providing crucial missing information and correctives to the previous generation of practice and theory in phonology and in linguistics more generally. Thus, Velleman and Vihman maintain that in L1 acquisition purported language universals are less in evidence than individual variation. Smith offers a parallel example of the supposed universalist, creole origins of open syllable structure in Saramaccan, noting that this feature is more easily explained as influence from the donor language Fon. A similar high-profile example is that of Chinese Pidgin English, many of whose features had long been assumed to be evidence of language universals but which can be shown (Pennington, 1998b; Siegel, 2000) to be transparently based in Cantonese. Source-language influence provides a more transparent and "low-inference" explanation for these phenomena than language universals and would need to be discounted before universals would seem plausible. In all three cases, the source of the mistaken imputation of universals appears to be ignorance (in both the sense of having no knowledge and of deliberately ignoring) of the facts of individual languages and of real data. Based on this discussion and that of Escudero, one can speculate that many forms attributed to universals in L2 phonology as well are actually instances of other factors – such as L1 transfer, communication strategies, stylistic factors – which could be uncovered by a careful reconsideration of the purported instances of universals in the context of other data about the languages involved and the circumstances within which the data were gathered.

Increasingly, it appears that generalizations are being missed by these separate subfields not pooling their respective areas of knowledge and data to improve linguistic theory. Thus, for example, as Smith states: "The phonological effects observed in creole languages in relation to the various other languages that were involved in their creation are not a direct result of the creolization process itself, but simply normal contact effects." Smith has captured the social dynamic of phonological simplification in pidgins and creoles by noting that it can be explained as one of negotiating a phonological compromise for communication rather than a universals-based process of creolization. In a parallel vein, Mufwene and Pargman (2003) maintain that "subject to similar ecological constraints, the same restructuring processes account for the development of both creole and non-creole English varieties in North America and elsewhere" (p. 367). In their view:

With all the restucturing going on, it is rather shocking how we could have thought that non-creole varieties have evolved differently from creole varieties, regardless of whether the latter are considered as separate languages or dialects of the same language as their non-creole kin. It is also shocking how we could have assumed that contact and external history have played a more important role in the development of creoles than in non-creole varieties.... Is the distinction between creoles and non-creoles structural or social? The above considerations suggest that the distinction is rather social.... (p. 373)

These observations, which demonstrate the value of making comparisons between research domains, point to a unity of "languaging" processes across linguistic phenomena long considered to be incomparable and to the crucial factor of social context in determining linguistic outcomes.

a look to the future

Careful research such as that of the authors contributing to this volume is providing new data raising questions about previous findings, contributing new findings, and suggesting new directions for theory and practice. In place of uniformity, these authors have found individual difference and variability; in place of static systems, they have found people changing language and interacting with each other in patterned ways; in place of innate universals, they have found observable processes and outcomes of interaction. It seems that the misconceptions of the previous era of linguistics can be remedied in part by more extensive empiricism involving compilation and analysis of valid and reliable data to extend and to continue exploring these new areas of focus and findings. Yet this may not be enough if we do not also talk across disciplines and share insights.

We are on the verge of major changes in linguistics which are impacting phonology just as they are impacting other areas of research and practice, moving the field away from static to dynamic views of language, and from highly circumscribed types of data to highly contextualized data. The focus of linguistic study is shifting in the present generation from a search for innate universals to the observation of people's social and psychological interactions through language. In the immediate future we should expect to see an increasing emphasis on empiricism, with much greater attention to detail and much greater use of full-context data, producing embedded descriptions of sound patterns and grounded theory. We can also expect to see much greater use of technology for the collection and analysis of linguistic information, and for teaching and remediating phonology in first- and second-language learners.

Most importantly, we can hope to see phonologists making greater efforts to talk to people outside their own narrow area of focus, and to learn from the practices and findings of other areas of linguistics and fields with an interest in language. All of us with an interest in phonology need to work *harder* to keep abreast of related work, data sources, and research methodologies and technologies, and to perform our analyses with attention both to detail and context. At the same time, we need to work *smarter*, by adopting a more cooperative, cross-disciplinary approach that will keep us from inventing new wheels all the time or reinventing the same wheel in our different areas of focus. If so, we can expect to see the current theoretical convergence of linguistic disciplines continuing, giving a chance for a deeper, and more correct, understanding of language in the present century than that which predominated in the previous one.

note

1. I have explored such cycles in detail in a different context (Pennington, 2004); parallels can be drawn to the work of Rogers (1995).

references

Blevins, J. (2004). *Evolutionary phonology*. Cambridge: Cambridge University Press.

Bybee, J. (2001). *Phonology and language use*. Cambridge: Cambridge University Press.

Catford, J. C. (2001). *A practical guide to phonetics*. Second edition. Oxford: Oxford Universty Press.

Clark, J., & Yallop, C. (1990). *An introduction to phonetics and phonology*. Oxford: Blackwell.

Ellis, N. C. (1988). Emergentism, connectionism and language learning. *Language Learning, 48*, 613–64.

Ellis, N. C. (1996). Sequencing in SLA: Phonological memory, chunking, and points of order. *Studies in Second Language Acquisition, 18*, 91–126.

Giegerich, H. J. (1992). *English phonology: An introduction*. Cambridge: Cambridge University Press.

Kretzschmar, W. A., & Tamasi, S. (2003). Distributional foundations for a theory of language change. *World Englishes, 22*, 377–401.

Mufwene, S. S. (2001). *The ecology of language evolution*. Cambridge: Cambridge University Press.

Mufwene, S. S., & Pargman, S. (2003). Competition and selection in the development of American Englishes. *World Englishes, 22*, 367–75.

Pennington, M. C. (1998a). The teachability of phonology in adulthood: A re-examination. *International Review of Applied Linguistics, 36*, 323–41.

Pennington, M. C. (1998b, March). From pidgin to mixed code: The social evolution of language in Hong Kong. Sociolinguistics Symposium 12. Institute of Education, University of London.

Pennington, M. C. (2002a). Equivalence classification in L2 phonology: In search of the mechanisms. In J. Leather & A. James (Ed.), *New Sounds 2000* (pp. 280–9). Klagenfurt, Austria: University of Klagenfurt.

Pennington, M. C. (2002b). Real language phonology: Optimality Theory meets sociolinguistics. *Journal of Sociolinguistics, 6,* 418–48.

Pennington, M. C. (2002c). Language learning, Relevance Theory, Optimality Theory, and sociolinguistics: Towards a new view of language in context. *Research Report 5.3.* Language Research Centre, University of Luton.

Pennington, M. C. (2004). Cycles of innovation in the adoption of information technology: A view for language teaching. *Computer-Assisted Language Learning, 17,* 7–33.

Port, R. F., & Leary, A. P. (2005). Against formal phonology. *Language, 81,* 927–64.

Rogers, E. M. (1995). *Diffusion of innovations.* Fourth edition. New York: Free Press.

Siegel, J. (2000). Substrate influence in Hawaii Creole English. *Language in Society, 29,* 197–236.

2

phonology in infancy and early childhood: implications for theories of language learning

shelley l. velleman and marilyn m. vihman

introduction

Jakobson (1941/1968) proposed that: (i) infants babble the sounds of all languages; (ii) there is discontinuity between babbling and first words; and (iii) phonemes are acquired in a universal order. Since then, all of these hypotheses have been rejected on empirical grounds and the importance of the prelinguistic foundations of phonology has been recognized. However, questions about the relationship between babble and words, the timing and extent of the impact of the ambient language on early speech perception and production, and individual differences in phonological development continue to energize research. General cognitive as well as purely linguistic foundations for phonological development, not directly addressed by Jakobson, have also been the source of fruitful recent investigations thanks to methodological advances in psycholinguistics and neurolinguistics. These issues have important implications for phonological theory, which must account for developmental as well as adult data. Claims about innate knowledge versus learning must refer to the processes by which the child develops and manifests a phonological system. Yet certain well-documented phenomena that are highly characteristic of child phonology remain to be integrated into theories of adult phonology. The goal of this chapter is to elucidate the state of the art with respect to issues and questions in child phonology, including recent findings, research methodologies and theoretical models.

In the first half of the chapter we review prelinguistic and early linguistic foundations for phonology, highlighting universal versus language-specific and child-specific aspects of phonological emergence. We then address aspects of child phonology that pose particular challenges for phonological theory. Next, neurocognitive theories are reviewed, with a focus on recent findings that shed important light on human language learning capacities. Finally, we provide brief overviews and critiques of key phonological theories. The chapter ends with a proposal for an integrated model of phonological development that embraces both neurocognitive capacities and the full range of universal, language-specific, and child-specific phenomena.

prelinguistic perceptual and vocal behaviors

Infants discriminate and produce sounds that are absent from the languages they are hearing. The non-native sounds they produce during the first six months are mainly traceable to physiological factors, such as incomplete consonantal closure and natural physiological linkages of tongue and jaw position; these effects have some impact in later stages as well (Davis and MacNeilage, 1995; Kent, 2000).[1] Physiology also has a profound effect on the sound systems that infants must learn. For example, the consonant-vowel (CV) co-occurrence patterns found in babbling have also been identified as statistical tendencies for consonant-vowel pairs in most of the world's languages (MacNeilage, Davis, Kinney, and Matyear, 2000). The most characteristic, or *unmarked*, features of phonological systems, such as labial stops [b,p], are not only more common in languages, but are also generally acquired earlier than marked ones such as interdental fricatives [θ,ð] (Locke, 1983). Unmarked features include common sound combinations (phonotactic or distributional patterns) as well as individual sounds and sound classes, such as:

- stops, nasals, glides
- coronals (dentals or alveolars)
- CV syllables
- two-syllable words

Universal markedness patterns are largely predictable based upon the principles of articulatory ease and perceptual discriminability (Liljencrants and Lindblom, 1972; Stevens, 1989). For example, voiced fricatives (e.g., [v,z]) are less common and later learned than voiceless fricatives (e.g., [f,s] because they are more difficult to produce for aerodynamic reasons

(Ohala, 1983). The interdental voiceless fricative [θ] may be rare because of its perceptual similarity to [f].

Despite similarities in their phonological systems, languages differ at the level of phonetic implementation. For example, different languages manifest different coarticulatory effects (Kingston and Diehl, 1994). Fortunately, human infants are well-equipped to learn the particulars of the language to which they are exposed. This has been established by experiments designed to elicit differential infant responses to familiarized versus novel auditory stimuli. Familiarization responses are measured either via habituation (e.g., the infant's rate of sucking a rubber nipple decreases when the same stimulus repeats) or arousal (e.g., the infant maintains a behavior, such as gazing fixedly at a visual display, upon learning that this will elicit a particular auditory stimulus). Once the infant shows familiarization, the auditory stimulus is changed (experimental condition) or not (control condition). A differential response (e.g., in sucking rate or eye gaze) to a changed stimulus indicates that the baby detected the change.

The mammalian auditory system makes it possible to discriminate many aspects of speech. Human newborns already discriminate word-like stimuli based on number of syllables. Newborns can also discriminate between languages with different rhythms, even when phonetic and intonation information is filtered out, leaving only rhythmic cues (Ramus, 2002). Newborns also discriminate between lists of grammatical (*function*) words (e.g., prepositions and articles) versus lexical (*content*) words, presumably based upon prosodic and segmental cues, such as shorter vowel durations, weaker amplitudes, and simplified syllable structures in function words (Shi, Werker, and Morgan, 1999). These capacities extend to discrimination of segmental differences. Human neonates already respond differentially to different vowels. Very young babies (1–2 months) can also discriminate many consonantal contrasts, including voicing (e.g., [d] versus [t]), place of articulation (e.g., [p] versus [t] versus [k]), and manner of articulation e.g., [m] versus [b]).

Although some discriminatory abilities are present at birth, other speech discrimination abilities may require learning. This learning occurs very early: within days of birth infants attend more to their own mother's voice, to the prosody of infant-directed speech (IDS, or "baby talk"), based on its exaggerated rhythm and pitch contours, and to the prosody of the ambient language in conversational speech. By 2 months infants respond to changes in both pitch and duration and discriminate syllables in three-syllable patterns as long as IDS prosody is used. By 4 months, infants attend more to their own name than to others (Mandel, Jusczyk, and Pisoni, 1995) and listen longer to running speech presented in IDS prosody with clauses that are phonologically coherent (not interrupted). By 6 months, infants already attend longer to word lists in their own language than in a prosodically contrasting language. In addition, 6-month-olds are able to categorize maternal utterances of different types (comforting versus approving), based upon the prosodic characteristics of each type (Moore and Spence, 1996).

In the second half of the first year of life, infants are increasingly able to recognize significant information in the language around them. Ten-month-old infants display preferences for stress patterns (Jusczyk, Cutler, and Redanz, 1993) and for consonants and sequences of consonants and vowels from their own language (Gerken and Zamuner, 2004). They also respond more to disyllabic sequences as if they were single words if the disyllables include medial consonant sequences that are common in their language – e.g., [ŋk], as in mo_nk_ey, for English-learners – than if they include less common medial consonant sequences – e.g., [pt], as in re_pt_ile – (Morgan, 1996), indicating that the babies are associating segmental phonological cues with the prosodic cues that mark word boundaries. At this age infants also prefer uninterrupted phrases and words that follow the common phonotactic patterns of the ambient language. At 11 months, babies attend longer to lists of untrained familiar over unfamiliar words (Vihman, Nakai, DePaolis, and Hallé, 2004), indicating that word learning has begun.

Prelinguistic children can segment the speech stream into word-level units despite the lack of pauses between units and the masking effects of coarticulation. Jusczyk and colleagues have used tasks in which the infant is familiarized with a word – e.g., cup cup cup cup – and then presented with a passage in which that word occurs repeatedly – e.g., The cup was bright and shiny. A clown drank from the red cup. (Jusczyk and Aslin, 1995). By 7.5 months of age English-learning babies show by their attentional responses to passages containing the trained words that they can identify the words in running speech (although neither Dutch nor French infants show the effect so early: Nazzi, Iakimova, Biertoncini, Fredonie and Alcantara, 2006). Disyllables with a trochaic (stressed-unstressed) rhythmic pattern, predominant in English, can also be picked out by infants at 7.5 months, but disyllables with the less common iambic (unstressed-stressed) rhythmic pattern are not segmented until 9 months of age (Mattys, Jusczyk, Luce, and Morgan, 1999). English infants are able to segment only in their own language or rhythmically similar languages, e.g., Dutch (Houston, Jusczyk, Kuijpers, Coolen, and Cutler, 2000) but not Chinese (Jusczyk, 1998).

How do infants segment connected speech? Both prosodic and distributional cues are likely sources of information. English-learning 9- but not 6-month-olds perceive unfamiliar pairs of syllables as belonging to a single unit only if they are trochaic (Morgan, 1996). Given that newborns are already sensitive to rhythmic differences, this role of prosody is not surprising. Distributional cues include such factors as transitional probabilities, i.e., that certain units are likely to follow one another. High transitional probabilities are exemplified in formulaic expressions: the word *pancake* has a high probability of occurrence following *flat as a* .... Transitional probabilities for within-word phoneme or syllable sequences are necessarily higher than for sequences across word boundaries. Thus, recurrent pairs of sounds or syllables are likely to form part of the same word. Adults can learn the transitional probabilities and therefore segment out the "words" of a nonsense language presented aurally with no prosodic information. Their performance improves with the addition of one prosodic cue, final syllable lengthening (Saffran, Newport, and Aslin, 1996).

In real life, both prosodic and distributional information is available to the infant. Morgan and Saffran (1995) assessed babies' use of the two types of information by comparing their performance on perceptual tasks with (i) distributional information: syllables that were consistently adjacent (e.g., [gakoti], [degako]) or not ([gakoti], [gadeko]) versus (ii) prosodic information: syllables that were consistently presented within trochaic units ([GAko] [KOga]) or not ([gaKO], [koGA]). Six-month-olds treated the syllable pairs as units whenever either distributional or prosodic cues were consistent with this conclusion. Nine-month-olds treated syllable pairs as units only when both rhythmic and distributional patterns were consistent. The older infants appear to be better at integrating the two types of cues.

These examples of infant capabilities amply demonstrate a pattern of cumulative learning based on the linguistic patterns that they have experienced. Some of the effects of the input language on the infant's developing linguistic system involve narrowing or loss of capacities that the infant had at an earlier stage. By 10–12 months infants are less able than at earlier ages to discriminate segmental contrasts not found in their own language. For example, at that age English-learning babies no longer respond differentially to velar versus uvular ejectives, two consonant types that do not occur in English. However, their differential sensitivity to familiar versus unfamiliar phonemic contrasts is neither sudden nor absolute. Infants maintain their ability to discriminate non-native contrasts at places of articulation that are less frequently used in their language longer than contrasts at more common places of articulation (Anderson, Morgan, and White, 2003). Anderson et al. argue that infants develop knowledge of the more frequently encountered contrasts earlier, leading them to disregard non-native contrasts along that dimension earlier. This implies that not only the (categorical) presence or absence of a contrasting sound or feature but also the (gradient) frequency of occurrence in the ambient language can affect children's perceptual processing. The more a child is exposed to a class of sounds, the more the child's perception becomes biased towards those sounds.

The statistical distribution of contrastive segments in input speech also has an effect on infant perception. A focus on points of maximal difference in a continuum of non-native speech sounds facilitates 8-month-old infants' learning of contrasts (Maye and Weiss, 2003). Infants whose attention is focused on the area of acoustic overlap between two speech sounds lose the ability to discriminate between them (Maye, Werker, and Gerken, 2002). Infants likely benefit from the fact that speakers' pronunciations of difficult contrasts (e.g., /f/ versus /θ/ in English) are usually distinct rather than overlapping.

Well before producing their first words children begin to tailor their vocal production to input speech patterns. From 6–12 months infants' vocalizations come to reflect ambient language prosodic patterns, vowels, and consonants. For example, as expected based upon the prosody of the ambient languages, a falling pitch contour predominates in English babies' vocalizations while falling and rising contours are equally distributed in French children's vocalizations. The vowels of 10-month-olds differ in ways that match frequencies of occurrence in their languages. Prelinguistic consonants also differ by ambient language; labials, which are more frequent in French and English than in Swedish and Japanese, are also more frequent in the vocalizations of 9–10-month-olds learning French and English. Thus, the view that babbling is a purely motoric behavior unaffected by exposure to a language (cf., e.g., Lenneberg, 1967; Locke, 1983; Petitto, 1991) cannot be accepted. Rather, children's prelinguistic vocalizations as well as their speech perception show the effects of the input language.[2]

early linguistic perception and production

Like babble, early words are largely but not exclusively characterized by unmarked elements and structures: stops, nasals, and glides; simple vowels; and simple CV syllables within two-syllable words. However, ambient language influences on production increase rapidly as the child acquires a productive vocabulary of 50–100 words. The babbling and early words of French and English-learning children show significant differences in accentual patterns (Vihman, DePaolis, and Davis, 1998), as do the vocal productions of children learning French, English, and Swedish with respect to length in syllables and frequency of use of final consonants (codas). English-learning children use shorter words and more codas, as English does. Spanish-learners produce more weak initial syllables and fewer codas than English-learners (Roark & Demuth, 2000). French, English, Swedish, and Japanese learners also display significantly different patterns of consonant use as regards both place and manner of articulation.

In some cases, what is acquired early is *not* what is more common in adult languages (i.e., unmarked). This provides an interesting type of test case, in which physiological (motor and perceptual) effects on early learning can be separated from the formal effects of markedness based on adult linguistic universals. These two factors (physiology and markedness) interact with each other and with the effects of different language environments in different ways at different points in time.

For example, "marked" long (geminate) consonants are typical of early word production regardless of the input language (Vihman and Velleman, 2000). By the time children have a 50-word vocabulary, the long consonants have disappeared in English and French due to lack of an adult model but have begun to be deployed appropriately in relation to accent in Welsh, in which consonant lengthening is part of the stress pattern (Vihman, Nakai, and DePaolis, 2006) and to be overused in Finnish and Japanese (Kunnari, Nakai, and Vihman, 2001; Vihman and Kunnari, in press). Universal ease of production factors favoring long consonants (for infants, with their slow articulation: Smith, 1978) have now yielded to ambient language patterns. In Russian, similarly, (marked) palatalized consonants are produced more successfully than their (unmarked) plain counterparts (Zharkova, 2005), arguably due to the motoric effect of the large tongue contacting the palate in the production of lingual consonants. The CV syllable is the least marked (most widely distributed) syllable type in adult languages, perhaps for physiological reasons (MacNeilage et al., 2000), yet in many languages, including Estonian, Finnish, French, Hindi, and Welsh, children have been found to omit even such early-learned initial consonants as stops in their first words (Vihman and Croft, in press). The cause may be perceptual: initial consonant omission is generally seen when, in the ambient language: (i) an unaccented initial syllable is followed by an accented final syllable (e.g., French 'baNANE') or (ii) a medial geminate consonant in the target word (e.g, Finnish /pallo/ 'ball') pulls the child's attention away from the onset consonant. In these cases, where physiological availability or perceptual salience converge with ambient language patterns but conflict with markedness as determined by adult languages generally, physiology and perceptual salience take precedence over markedness.

The picture is even more complex than this, however. Contrary to Jakobson's "discontinuity" proposal regarding the lack of connection between babbling and first words, early word productions parallel babbling in many ways. Infants do not always employ the physiologically easiest or most frequently occurring sounds and word structures. Individual children's "favorite babbles" or prelinguistic *vocal motor schemes* (McCune and Vihman, 2001) shape their early words as well as their late-stage babbles. For example, one English-speaking child, Emma, demonstrated a labial-alveolar pattern in her babble (e.g., [wedawidamenaminʌ́munim inimini]) and also in her early words: [wedi] 'raisin', [budi] 'berry, bird, booster' (Studdert-Kennedy and Goodell, 1995). Atte, a Finnish child, babbled many VCV[3] forms, and 61% of his early word forms were of the shape VCV (e.g., [ɪc̆i] *isi* 'daddy'). Similarly, by age 10 months a French baby, Laurent, was already producing variants of the consonant [l] (Vihman, 1993), which is uncommon in infant productions. This consonant persisted into his word attempts and formed the basis of one of his regular word production patterns, or *templates*. The children appear to be selecting words for production based upon a match to their own prelinguistic production experience. Both physiology and the ambient language have influenced this experience, but the children's responses are individual.

Examples such as these, combined with the findings about the prelinguistic influence of the native language on perception and production reviewed above, force a rejection of the assumption frequently made in the current Optimality Theory literature (see below) that the early word production period can be equated with the *initial state* of the child's phonology (Dinnsen, McGarrity, O'Connor, and Swanson, 1999/2000; Gnanadesikan, 2004). Rather, at the onset of word production the child's phonological development is already affected by three factors: (i) human physiological and cognitive capacities; (ii) ambient language patterns; and (iii) the child's individual response to perceptual and vocal experience (DePaolis and Vihman, 2006).

The influence of frequencies of occurrence in the ambient language on production continues throughout childhood. On a nonsense word repetition task 2-year-olds produce coda consonants more accurately if the preceding syllabic context (i.e., the CV preceding the coda) is more frequent in their language (Gerken and Zamuner, 2004; Zamuner, 2003). This influence grows with the child's linguistic system; 3-year-olds with larger vocabularies show a stronger effect of phonotactic frequency on their production than do those with smaller vocabularies (Storkel, 2001; Beckman, Munson, and Edwards, 2004).

challenges for phonological theories

Certain aspects of early phonology, such as consonant harmony and metathesis, are inconsistent with patterns seen in the world's languages. For example, consonant assimilation, in which a feature of one consonant (e.g., labialization) spreads to an adjacent consonant (as in 'in' + 'possible' = 'impossible'), is common in adult phonologies. Consonant harmony, in which such spreading occurs "across" an intervening vowel (e.g., [s] becomes [ʃ] in Chumash to agree with another [ʃ] in the word: [saxtun] 'I pay' versus [ʃaxtunitʃ] 'to be paid'; Poser, 1982), is rare and limited to certain classes of consonant sounds (Shaw, 1991; Vihman, 1978). Vowel harmony is much more common in adult phonology (e.g. in Turkish the past tense suffix is pronounced [dum] in [durdum], 'I stood', but [dim] in [geldim], 'I came').

In sharp contrast, in child phonology consonant harmony is almost universal (Smith, 1973). Children's consonant harmony occurs across vowels with all types of consonants and affects manner as well as place features (McDonough & Myers, 1991). For example, Daniel used initial and final velars in 13 of his first 50 words (e.g., [gɑk] for *clock, sock, rock, quack*: Stoel-Gammon and Cooper, 1984). "P" harmonized all consonants in a word with a nasal in any position, palatalized all of the resulting nasals (perhaps due to the "large tongue, small oral cavity" effect hypothesized above for the early emergence of Russian palatalized consonants), and also tended to harmonize vowels, resulting in forms like [njenje, njinji] for *finger (*Waterson, 1971). Jacob produced words with consonant place harmony and also vowel harmony, e.g. [gɛgo] and [dɛdo] for 'thank you', [bibi] and [bɑbɑ] for 'baby' (Menn, 1976). Overall, harmony is much more prevalent in children than in adults and can affect up to 32% of any one child's lexicon (Vihman, 1978).

Metathesis, in which two elements are reordered, also occurs relatively rarely in adult phonology, primarily as a trading of adjacent elements (e.g., *desk* as [dɛks]). Most cases involve resonants, especially liquids and vowels (Hume, 2004). In contrast, metathesis is common in children's speech. Instances of metathesis yield regular output patterns in a child's phonology (Velleman, 1996). Alice, for example, produces consonants in a front to back order in terms of articulatory place (e.g., labial before palatal or velar), regardless of their order of occurrence in the target word (Jaeger, 1997). Thus, *sheep* becomes [piç] ([ç] is a voiceless palatal fricative), *kite* [tɑʲk], and *T.V.* [piti] ([p] substitutes for /v/). Similarly, Spanish-speaking Si produces /sopa/ 'soup' as [pwᵘta] and /libro/ 'book' as [pɪtdʎ] (Macken, 1979). These apparent production constraints (or output constraints) may result from the influence of patterns familiar from prior perception and production experience, which the child overgeneralizes (Vihman and Kunnari, in press). Other child patterns involve *consonant migration* (i.e., the child changes the position of a particular consonant). For instance, a child studied by Leonard and McGregor (1991), "W", moved initial fricatives to final position ([af] 'fall', [neks] 'snake'). The frequency as well as the nature of these child patterns constitutes a significant challenge for phonological theories.

The variability of children's word forms also poses a problem for many models based upon adult phonology, in particular because of infants' *whole word processing*. Many young children appear to produce word forms holistically, maintaining the features or segments of a target word but not in the expected order (Waterson, 1971). Furthermore, multiple productions of the same word share certain characteristics but differ in detail. Some have proposed that this variability simply reflects poor "performance" or immature motor control (e.g., Hale and Reiss, 1997). We argue below that variability can only be explained on the basis of a deeper or more abstract level.

A challenge for a performance-based account of early child errors and variability is that children's lexical forms may be quite accurate initially (Ferguson and Farwell, 1975), especially the first 10–20 expressive words. Regression is then observed as the child systematizes the phonology. In many children, this systematization (phonological reorganization) takes the form of routinized patterns or production templates such as those described above for Atte, Alice, and Si. The child seemingly "selects" words for production that match the patterns that have already been mastered in babble or previously learned words (e.g., CVCV[4] forms). Generalizations of the production pattern into a more broadly applied template may initially serve to solve particular phonetic problems. As the template takes hold, however, it may be overgeneralized to include word forms unrelated to the original problem. For instance, Molly's pattern of adding a vowel to facilitate word-final consonant production (e.g., [dɑnʌʎ] 'down') was overgeneralized to words without final nasals or even final consonants, e.g., [ɪn:i] for 'Nicky' (Vihman and Velleman, 1989). Children's phonological experimentation and nonlinear progression make it evident that early phonological development is neither an automatic "unfolding" of an innate articulatory program nor a gradual increase in phonetic skill. Something has changed: Abstract patterns have begun to be induced. Such a developmental pattern cannot be accounted for within a simple performance model (Smolensky, 1996).

Because children produce highly variable and inaccurate word forms it is difficult to determine exactly how much they "know" about the words they attempt. For example, does a child who consistently uses consonant harmony nevertheless have the correct underlying representation of the word, with two distinct consonants? Word recognition studies suggest that children become increasingly focused on phonetic detail as their experience of the language increases. Seventeen-month-olds can discriminate minimal pair differences in an artificial word-learning task but 14-month-olds succeed only when word meanings are not needed. Those with larger vocabularies are better at the task (Stager and Werker, 1997; Werker, Fennell, Corcoran, and Stager, 2002). Nineteen-month-olds are worse at recognizing words with segmental substitutions – e.g., [g] for [d], as in [gɔg] for 'dog' – than words that are pronounced correctly (Swingley, 2003). Thus, at least at this age, children are listening to more than holistic word shape; they are aware of some phonetic detail.

neurocognitive theories

One of the most highly debated issues in child phonology, as in child language generally, is what knowledge the infant has about language to begin with. *Nativists* such as Chomsky (1975) and Pinker (1994) have argued that *positive evidence* alone, based on the limited and "degenerate" quality of speech input, could never suffice as a basis for learning a linguistic system. Instead, according to this view, infants are born with knowledge of universal linguistic structure, so that only details about the individual language need be learned. Acquisition is then merely a process of selecting from the linguistic options prewired into the human brain. In the *principles and parameters* version of this theory (e.g., Chomsky, 1981), certain pieces of information about the language are said to "trigger" expectations about other structures, which therefore need not be observed in order to be acquired. For example, Ramus (2002) has proposed that rhythmic cues will indicate the basic rhythm type of the ambient language (e.g., *stress-timed*, in the case of English). Each rhythm type is associated with other properties, such as syllable structure variety and complexity, and the occurrence or non-occurrence of vowel reduction

(Ramus, Nespor, and Mehler, 1999). In this view the child need not directly experience the other properties.

The "positive evidence" argument is that children are not typically corrected when they speak unless what they say is untrue. Without correction (or "negative evidence"), the argument runs, children – who clearly do produce utterances they have never heard – could be expected to produce a wide variety of universally unacceptable linguistic forms. Yet only limited types of errors actually occur. Since experimental psycholin-guistic and neurolinguistic research could not explain this surprising fact 30 years ago, Chomsky concluded that universal linguistic constraints must be innate. However, as Bates, Thal, Aram, Nass, and Trauner (1997) remark, "our belief that a structure [or a process] is inexplicable may be nothing more than a comment on our ignorance" (p. 6). The remedy for ignorance is research, and the results of neurobiological research conducted since the 1970s "underscore the extraordinarily plastic and activity-dependent nature of cortical specialization, and buttress the case for an emergentist approach to the development of higher cognitive functions" (ibid., p. 3).

New findings from experimental psychology, especially regarding implicit statistical learning and infant responses to speech in the first year of life, shed important new light on language learning mechanisms and processes and must be reflected in new theoretical models. For example, another nativist assumption was that it would be impossible for listeners to store the many details about linguistic elements and structures to which they are exposed. However, recent psycholinguistic research has provided answers to both the "no negative evidence" and the storage problems. It has been found that very specific auditory traces, not only of phonetic detail but also of sociophonetic aspects such as voice quality, are retained in memory and even impact speakers' productions (Pierrehumbert, 2001, 2003); the brain does have room for these details.

At the same time, the probabilities of occurrence of various elements and structures are tallied on an ongoing basis and this statistical information has detectable impacts upon subsequent language behavior. Even when instructed to focus on concurrent nonlinguistic events, both children and adults incidentally pick up the statistical regularities of artificial speech played in the background and – to their own surprise – are able to respond accurately to questions about whether new elements and structures are consistent with the unattended speech (Saffran, Newport, Aslin, Tunick, and Barrueco, 1997). Infants as well as adults and older children make generalizations based upon very short periods of exposure to artificial languages – as little as 2 minutes for infants, 20 minutes for adults and children (Saffran, Aslin, and Newport, 1996; Johnson and Jusczyk, 2001). Thus, "statistical underrepresentation must do the job of negative evidence" (Pierrehumbert, 2002, p. 13). That is, what is not heard is taken to be impermissible in the language.

The existence of this type of *implicit learning* can help to explain the findings described above: over the first year, infants develop familiarity with the commonly occurring prosody, consonants, vowels and consonant-vowel sequences of the ambient language. Macken (1995) argues against probabilistic (stochastic) learning of phonology because "Stochastic learning is cumulative and where paths differ, outcomes differ" (p. 695). However, differences in learning outcomes are a desired result of a learning model based on induction of patterns from statistical regularities. Outcomes do differ depending upon linguistic experience: each adult's phonological system is subtly different from that of any other. Humans are skilled at adapting their output to the sociolinguistic situation to minimize communication failures and to mark their group identity (Labov, 1966, 2001).

Further evidence against innate linguistic knowledge is provided by the recent finding that infants can implicitly learn phonologically unnatural as well as natural distributional patterns (Seidl and Buckley, 2004). Infants aged 8–9 months heard distributional patterns that either occur in some languages but not in English (i.e., intervocalic fricatives and affricates but not stops; labial consonants followed by rounded vowels only; coronals followed only by front vowels) or are unattested in any language (e.g., word-initial fricatives and affricates but not stops; labial consonants followed by high vowels only; coronals followed only by mid vowels). Subsequently, the infant participants heard novel words that did or did not follow the familiarized patterns. They learned both the natural and the unnatural patterns based upon distributional patterns. Thus, statistical learning is not limited to patterns that occur naturally. Nor is it limited to language or even to the auditory modality: infants learn visual patterns implicitly as well (Kirkham, Slemmer, and Johnson, 2002).

How does the human brain manage statistical accounting on such a grand scale? Recent research has demonstrated that neocortical (especially frontal) and basal ganglia structures are specialized for just such learning:

This system underlies the learning of new, and the computation of already-learned, rule-based procedures that govern the regularities of language – particularly those procedures related to combining items into complex structures that have precedence (sequential) and hierarchical relations. (Ullman, 2004, p. 245)

This is termed *procedural learning*. It involves the gradual induction of patterns from multiple instances of related stimuli, ranging from concrete sensorimotor procedures such as riding a bicycle to higher-level cognitive procedures such as the comprehension and production of grammar. Procedural learning is slow and implicit; the learner is typically unable to consciously recall either the process or the product. Once a pattern has been learned, however, the application of the generalizations to behavior (such as speech) is rapid and automatic (Ullman, 2004).

A complementary learning system, *declarative memory*, is responsible for *episodic learning*, "the rapid formation of comprehensive associations among the various elements of specific events and experiences, in a form sufficient to sustain an explicit...retrieval of the contents of the experience" (McClelland, McNaughton, and O'Reilly, 1995, p. 420), such as words and the contexts in which they were heard. The storage of speaker information as well as of phonetic detail that declarative memory makes possible has been shown to be operative within the first year (Houston and Jusczyk, 2000; cf. also Rovee-Collier, 1997), allowing infants to store individual linguistic experiences in toto for later analysis.

The procedural memory system processes information from declarative memory in addition to the distributional tallies that it has implicitly kept, and uses these two types of information to gradually generate abstract "rule-like relations" (Ullman, 2004, p. 237). In other words, procedural learning enables us to gradually discover relationships and regularities among events and experiences (McClelland et al., 1995). The results of procedural processing in turn influence later declarative learning, determining the salience of aspects of future linguistic experiences (Ellis, 2005).

In summary, both procedural and declarative learning are necessary: procedural generalizations are evident in the rule-governedness of many aspects of phonological behavior. Young children systematize their phonologies, suggesting abstraction away from item learning. Even 7-month-olds appear to demonstrate rule-based learning (cf. Marcus, Vijayan, Bandi Rao, and Vishton, 1999). However, declarative learning is evident in the *token effects* (based upon specific items) that have been documented as well as *type effects* (based upon generalizations) in the phonological retrieval processes of older children (Beckman, et al., 2004).

Because procedural learning includes both probabilistic and abstract processing, it is not necessary for a theory of language acquisition to choose between abstract linguistic structures (or formal grammar) and statistical learning (Pierrehumbert, 2001, 2003). In fact, several authors have proposed that probabilistic procedural learning induces more abstract procedural learning (e.g., Lotto, Kluender, and Holt, 2000; Pierrehumbert, 2001). For example, children with larger expressive vocabularies are better at repeating words that include low probability diphones (sequences of two sounds). Real words with high probability diphones (e.g., [ba]) are named more slowly, due to competition from other real words. Nonsense words are repeated more quickly if they contain high probability diphones, due to assistance from generalizations stored in procedural memory. Beckman et al. (2004) suggest that two levels of encoding are necessary to account for this: Stored fine-grained details facilitate the differentiation of systematic subphonemic variation from linguistically significant variation; this is *phonetic* learning. Coarser grained procedural generalizations about recurring phonological patterns in the words of the language constitute *phonological* learning. Phonological aspects of procedural processing may be primary for real word tasks, phonetic aspects for nonsense word tasks (Storkel & Morisette, 2002).

A two-component model of memory embraces the contradiction inherent in each individual's phonological system: the subphonemic details differ from person to person depending upon exposure while the overall patterns are shared across communities. Phonemes or other structures within individual lexical items have different production patterns depending upon the speaker's experience with that phoneme within that word. For example, as a result of many vacations in Canada the first author might tend to centralize [aʊ] in *out* and *about* but not in infrequent words like *grout* or *drought*. Individual tokens would induce stronger type as well as token effects in infants' phonologies; their limited linguistic experience affords each exposure a large impact on the whole system. Ironically, the paucity of cases in the child's declarative memory may contribute to both the relative accuracy of early word forms and their holistic nature: allophonic and sociocultural details cannot yet be filtered out; abstractions are, as yet, very gross.

The incorporation of stochastic learning into a model of phonological development as the pathway to linguistic abstractions also permits researchers to consider new perspectives on old ideas. One proposed hypothesis is that distributional data, not minimal pairs, enable children to distinguish phonemes from allophones in their languages (Peperkamp and Dupoux, 2004). Alternatively, childrens' learning of distributional allophonic patterns could be seen as evidence for a model of phonology in which the word is the primary unit of processing even for adults (Ferguson and Farwell, 1975; Vihman and Croft, in press), with distributional allophones secondarily induced from words (Pierrehumbert, 2003).

models of phonology

Given that abstract relationships are encoded in the developing phonological system, what should those relationships be called? How should we model their interactions? The models developed in the past 50 years share a focus on identifying patterns of phonological behavior rather than describing individual segments. Rules, processes, and constraints all operate at the level of feature classes rather than at the level of individual consonants and vowels.

Generative Phonology (Chomsky and Halle, 1968) was unique in its time for its rule-based account of phonology. The rules described how phonemes or classes of phonemes were produced under specified circumstances. For example, the fact that underlyingly voiced stops become voiceless in final position in German can be stated as a rule:

[+obs +voice] → [-voice] /___#   e.g., *weg* ('way') → [vɛk]

As applied to child phonology, generative rules were used to describe children's simplifications of adult phonemes, such as [+ continuant] segments (fricatives) becoming [- continuant] (stops) in certain word positions (Smith, 1973), e.g., [dɪp] 'zip'.

A problem with this approach was that it assumed that the child's underlying representations (phonemic targets) matched the adults' and were changed only to accommodate immature physiology or inappropriately organized phonology (Smith, 1973). Many authors have questioned this assumption (e.g., Menn and Matthei, 1992; see Vihman, 1996). Another problem was the focus on errors (e.g., substitutions) rather than on advances in phonological development. For example, the fact that a child could produce fricatives, although not in the appropriate contexts, could not be captured. A third problem was the difficulty of writing word-level rules within a system that was, by nature, segmental and linear. Recognition of this problem led to the application of Nonlinear Phonology to child data, which expanded the formal rule system of Generative Phonology to capture hierarchical relationships such as those between coda and syllable, syllable and word, and word and phrase (Goldsmith, 1990).

The inability of the theory of Generative Phonology as originally conceived to handle variability was seen as a further major drawback by sociolinguists as well as child phonologists. In response, *variable rules*, or generative rules with associated frequencies of occurrence, were proposed by Labov (1969). A final formal shortcoming of Generative Phonology was that it did not appropriately constrain the rules. Using the formalisms of the theory, phonological rules that are highly unnatural phonetically (neither attested in languages nor explicable based upon physiological principles) could be generated as easily as natural, commonly occurring rules.[5]

Natural Phonology (Stampe, 1972; Donegan and Stampe, 1979) was one response to this last issue. This theory was based upon the idea that perceptual and articulatory physiology constrains human phonologies in predictable ways. In order to communicate effectively, a child must overcome some of these physiological limitations – specifically, those that do not constrain the patterns of their language. A child English-learner, for example, must not apply consonant cluster simplification (or reduction) – i.e., must learn to produce consonant clusters. A Hawaiian-learner, on the other hand, need not "suppress" the process of consonant cluster reduction because the language includes no clusters.

In Natural Phonology all processes were required to have a physiological basis. However, over time this requirement was lost in practice as physiologically unnatural patterns were identified in both adult and child phonologies. Natural Phonology shared with Generative Phonology the assumption that the child's underlying representations or target forms are the same as the adult's. This theory also focuses on the child's errors (inappropriate processes) rather than on capabilities. In many cases the theory provided a label but no explanation for phonological behavior; e.g., labeling metathesis as such does not explain why it occurs. Finally, Natural Phonology, like Generative Phonology, had to deal with variability in a post hoc manner. Frequencies of occurrence could be associated with particular processes, but no mechanism predicted them.[6]

The focus of Optimality Theory (OT) is the notion that phonologies are organized in such a way as to optimize certain output forms. Rather than being process-oriented, like the models described above, OT is outcome-oriented (McCarthy and Prince, 1996; Archangeli, 1997). Thus, OT has the advantage for child phonologists of focusing on what the system does do, and on what is achieved by non-adult changes in the output, rather than on errors. In this approach, the child's phonology can be modeled as a dynamic developing system rather than as an inadequately realized adult system.

Within OT, two main forces are contrasted: *Markedness* (the preference for certain elements and structures, often but not always based upon ease of production or perception) and *Faithfulness* (the need to achieve communicative effectiveness by producing word forms that are true to the common lexicon). Faithfulness can only be judged with respect to the language of the speaker and the specific word targeted for production. Markedness occurs in both universal and language specific forms: physiologically based markedness constraints, especially, are reflected in the distributions of elements and structures in all languages, but other elements or structures are marked (avoided) in only a subset of languages. Markedness and Faithfulness are reflected in sets of *constraints* that specify, first, those output forms that are preferred or avoided and, second, the aspects of an individual word that must be maintained in production. Typical Markedness constraints identify preferred patterns such as the CV syllable, in the constraints Onset, which specifies that a word must begin with a consonant, and NoCoda, which prohibits a word final consonant. A typical example of a Faithfulness constraint is IDENT(labial), which states that if a word has a labial in the underlying representation, it must be produced with a labial.

Unlike the rules of Generative Phonology, these constraints are not present or absent ("on" or "off"). Rather, they are ranked. Those at the top of the ranking are obeyed under all conditions; lower constraints are respected only if that is possible without violating a higher ranked constraint. Because the ranking is not "all or none," it is possible to accommodate variability. Constraints may be equally ranked, yielding a variable output (e.g., 50–50, if two constraints are both relevant to the same case and are unranked with respect to each other). In more elaborated versions or modified theories built on the basic insights of OT, variability may be attributed to random ranking of mutually unranked constraints on each relevant occasion (Anttila, 1997); constraints with overlapping, normally distributed ranges of ranking values (Boersma, 1997; Boersma and Hayes, 2001); or constraints that select a set of "best" outputs that are implemented with frequencies reflecting the relative rankings of the constraints (Coetzee, 2004).

Initially, Optimality Theory assumed that all languages shared the full constraint set; the power of the theory was purported to lie in its formal simplicity and universality. In child phonology, an OT perspective has generally included the assumption that the constraints are given in the form of innate knowledge; in this view only the ranking remains to be achieved through learning. This assumption has been weakened over time as ever more language-specific constraints are identified, leaving open the question of how such a set of partially universal, partially language-specific constraints might be acquired by learners.

The neurocognitive findings discussed above suggest such a mechanism. The child's relatively systematic output patterns may result from the influence of familiar patterns (from prior perception and production experience) on the process of generalizing and inducing abstractions (Vihman and Kunnari, in press). The frequencies of occurrence of these patterns in the child's experience, possibly along with sociolinguistic factors like the status of the speaker of each exemplar (Docherty, Foulkes, Tillotson, and Watt, 2006), will determine its use by the child. The constraints may reflect abstraction over the two types of phonological data that the child gains through experience: (i) physiological (perceptual and articulatory) parameters, and (ii) the distributional characteristics and relationships of the ambient language. Implicit learning means that children will have collected, and generalized over, a great deal of data regarding the distributional frequencies found in the ambient language and in their own articulatory routines. Rule-based relations are induced from these patterns and some of these may begin to be evident in the child's productions even prelinguistically. Once a child has a minimal lexicon, it is possible to begin gathering information about the types of morphological and phonetic variability allowed within the language.[7]

Once children have productive vocabularies of about 50 words they begin to abstract away from particular target word patterns and rely instead on the production routines or templates that they have induced from experience of both target words and their own word forms. As the child not only selects words for production based on matches to the template but also adapts other words to respect the idiosyncratic constraint set reflected in that template, output forms now become less accurate.

conclusion:
towards a pattern induction model for phonology

In contrast to the theories reviewed above (Generative Phonology, Natural Phonology, and Optimality Theory), the pattern induction model proposed here claims no innate phonological knowledge. Rather, it specifies the learning processes by which phonological information is gathered, analyzed, and acted upon. The outcomes are not universal; variability both within and between speakers is expected. The means of developing a phonological system are presumed to be available to all humans by virtue of shared neurological, sensory and motor capacities. Most structures of the eventual phonological system are also shared, given their rootedness in neuromotor, perceptual, and learning capacities acting upon human experience.

Certain patterns, such as the avoidance or favoring of language-particular elements or structures and complex interactions between these constraints on output, are expected. These constraints are induced via phonologization of human language processing limitations, of patterns and associations learned implicitly and abstracted via the coarse (procedural) memory system, and of individual child responses to experience. Less fine-grained responses to phonological challenges, such as consonant harmony and metathesis, are to be expected of children whose abstract generalizations are based upon few exemplars and whose cognitive processing systems are not yet finely tuned.

In adults as well as children the constraints are gradiently influenced in their applications to particular words or contexts by grammar-external factors such as sociolinguistic variables. Thus, the lines between grammar and an associative cognitive system are substantially blurred within this model. This is a desirable result; it reflects an increase in psycholinguistic reality and a deeper grounding in known brain structures and processes.

notes

1. Editor's note: see also Chapter. 1, this volume.
2. Editor's note: Chapter 5, this volume, presents a complementary view of perception and input-driven learning for L2 acquisition.
3. Editor's note: sound sequence composed of vowel-consonant-vowel such as [ada] or [ama].
4. Editor's note: repeated sequences of consonant-vowel [dada] or [mama].
5. Editor's note: Chapter 3, this volume, includes other relevant discussions.
6. Editor's note: for another perspective on the handling of variation in Natural Phonology, see Chapter 3, this volume.
7. Editor's note: this pattern-induction model is similar to that proposed in Chapter 5, this volume, for L2 acquisition; also see Chapter 3, this volume, for further discussion of the acquisition of variable phonological patterns.

references

Anderson, J. L., Morgan, J. L., & White, K. S. (2003). A statistical basis for speech sound discrimination. *Language and Speech, 46*, 155–82.

Anttila, A. (1997). Deriving variation from grammar. In F. Hinskens, R. van Hout, & W. L. Wetzels (Eds.), *Variation, change and phonological theory* (pp. 35–68). Amsterdam: John Benjamins.

Archangeli, D. (1997). Optimality Theory: An introduction to linguistics in the 1990s. In D. Archangeli & D. T. Langendoen (Eds.), *Optimality Theory: An overview* (pp. 1–32). Malden, Massachusetts: Blackwell.

Bates, E., Thal, D., Aram, D., Nass, R., & Trauner, D. (1997). From first words to grammar in children with focal brain injury. *Developmental Neuropsychology, 13*, 239–74.

Beckman, M. E., Munson, B., & Edwards, J. (2004, June). *Vocabulary growth and developmental expansion of types of phonological knowledge.* Paper presented at LabPhon9: Change in Phonology, University of Illinois at Urbana-Champaign.

Boersma, P. (1997). How we learn variation, optionality, and probability. *Institute of Phonetic Sciences University of Amsterdam Proceedings, 21*, 43–58.

Boersma, P., & Hayes, B. (2001). Empirical tests of the gradual learning algorithm. *Linguistic Inquiry, 32*, 45–86.

Chomsky, N. (1975). *Reflections on language.* New York: Pantheon.

Chomsky, N. (1981). Principles and parameters in syntactic theory. In N. Hornstein & D. Lightfoot (Eds.), *Explanation in linguistics: The logical problem of language acquisition* (pp. 32–75). London: Longman.

Chomsky, N., & Halle, M. (1968). *The sound pattern of English.* New York: Harper and Row.

Coetzee, A. (2004). What it means to be a loser: Non-optimal candidates in Optimality Theory. Doctoral dissertation, University of Massachusetts at Amherst.

Davis, B., & MacNeilage, P. (1995). The articulatory basis of babbling. *Journal of Speech and Hearing Research, 38*, 1199–211.

DePaolis, R. A., & Vihman, M. M. (2006). The influence of production on the perception of speech. In D. Bamman, T. Magnitskaia, & C. Zaller (Eds.), *Proceedings of the 30th Annual Boston University Conference on Language Development* (pp. 43–52). Somerville, MA: Cascadilla Press.

Dinnsen, D. A., McGarrity, L. W., O'Connor, K. M., & Swanson, K. A. B. (1999/2000). On the role of sympathy in acquisition. *Language Acquisition, 8*, 321–61.

Docherty, G. J., Foulkes, P., Tillotson, J., & Watt, D. J. L. (2006). On the scope of phonological learning: Issues arising from socially structured variation. In C. T. Best, L. Goldstein, & D. H. Whalen (Eds.), *Laboratory Phonology 8.* Berlin: Mouton de Gruyter.

Donegan, P. J., & Stampe, D. (1979). The study of natural phonology. In D. A. Dinnsen (Ed.), *Current approaches to phonological theory* (pp. 126–73). Bloomington, IN: Indiana University Press.

Ellis, N. (2005). How does explicit knowledge affect implicit language learning? *Studies in Second Language Acquisition, 27*, 305–52.

Ferguson, C. A., & Farwell, C. B. (1975). Words and sounds in early language acquisition. *Language, 51*, 419–39.

Gerken, L. A., & Zamuner, T. (2004, June). *Exploring the basis for generalization in language acquisition.* Paper presented at LabPhon9: Change in Phonology, University of Illinois at Urbana-Champaign.

Gnanadesikan, A. E. (2004). Markedness and faithfulness constraints in child phonology. In R. Kager, J. Pater, & W. Zonneveld (Eds.), *Fixing priorities: Constraints in phonological acquisition* (pp. 73–108). Cambridge: Cambridge University Press. Also available from Rutgers Optimality Archive ROA-67.

Goldsmith, J. A. (1990). *Autosegmental and metrical phonology.* Cambridge: Blackwell.

Hale, M., & Reiss, C. (1997). Formal and empirical arguments concerning phonological acquisition. Unpublished manuscript. Montreal: Concordia University.

Houston, D. M., & Jusczyk, P. W. (2000). The role of talker-specific information in word segmentation by infants. *Journal of Experimental Psychology: Human Perception and Performance*, 26(5), 1570–82.

Houston, D. M., Jusczyk, P. W., Kuijpers, C., Coolen, R., & Cutler, A. (2000). Both Dutch- and English-learning 9-month-olds segment Dutch words from fluent speech. *Psychonomic Bulletin and Review*, 7(3), 504–9.

Hume, E. (2004). The indeterminacy/attestation model of metathesis. *Language*, 80, 203–37.

Jaeger, J. J. (1997). How to say "Grandma" and "Grandpa": A case study in early phonological development. *First Language*, 17(1), 1–29.

Jakobson, R. (1941/68). *Child language, aphasia, and phonological universals*. The Hague: Mouton. English translation of *Kindersprache, aphasie und allgemeine lautgesetze*. Uppsala.

Johnson, E. K., & Jusczyk, P. W. (2001). Word segmentation by 8-month-olds: When speech cues count more than statistics. *Journal of Memory and Language*, 44, 1–20.

Jusczyk, P. W. (1998). A reply to Littman and to Denenberg. *Science*, 280, 1176–77.

Jusczyk, P. W., & Aslin, R. N. (1995). Infants' detection of sound patterns of words in fluent speech. *Cognitive Psychology*, 29, 1–23.

Jusczyk, P. W., Cutler, A. & Redanz, N. (1993). Infants' preference for the predominant stress patterns of English words. *Child Development*, 64, 675–87.

Kent, R. D. (2000). Research on speech motor control and its disorders: A review and prospective. *Journal of Communication Disorders*, 33, 391–427.

Kingston, J., & Diehl, R. L. (1994). Phonetic knowledge. *Language*, 70, 419–54.

Kirkham, N. Z., Slemmer, J. A., & Johnson, S. P. (2002). Visual statistical learning in infancy: Evidence for a domain general learning mechanism. *Cognition*, 83, B35–42.

Kunnari, S., Nakai, S., & Vihman, M. M. (2001). Cross-linguistic evidence for the acquisition of geminates. *Psychology of Language and Communication*, 5, 13–24.

Labov, W. (1966). *The social stratification of English in New York City*. Washington, DC: Center for Applied Linguistics.

Labov, W. (1969). Contraction, deletion, and inherent variability of the English copula. *Language*, 45(4).

Labov, W. (2001). *Principles of linguistic change*. Volume II: *Social factors*. Malden, MA: Blackwell.

Lenneberg, E. (1967). *Biological foundations of language*. New York: Wiley.

Leonard, L. B., & McGregor, K. K. (1991). Unusual phonological patterns and their underlying representations: A case study. *Journal of Child Language*, 18, 261–72.

Liljencrants, J., & Lindblom, B. (1972). Numerical simulation of vowel quality systems: The role of perceptual contrast. *Language*, 48, 839–62.

Locke, J. L. (1983). *Phonological acquisition and change*. New York: Academic Press.

Lotto, A. J., Kluender, K. R., & Holt, L. L. (2000). Effects of language experience on organization of vowel sounds. In M. Broe & J. Pierrehumbert (Eds.), *LabPhonV: Language acquisition and the lexicon* (pp. 219–28). Cambridge: Cambridge University Press.

Macken, M. A. (1979). Developmental reorganization of phonology: A hierarchy of basic units of acquisition. *Lingua, 49*, 11–49.

Macken, M. A. (1995). Phonological acquisition. In J. A. Goldsmith (Ed.), *The handbook of phonological theory* (pp. 671–98). Oxford: Blackwell.

MacNeilage, P. F., Davis, B. L., Kinney, A., & Matyear, C. L. (2000). The motor core of speech: A comparison of serial organization patterns in infants and languages. *Child Development, 71*, 153–63.

Mandel, D. R., Jusczyk, P. W., & Pisoni, D. B. (1995). Infants' recognition of the sound patterns of their own names. *Pyschological Science, 6*, 315–18.

Marcus, G. F., Vijayan, S., Bandi Rao, S., & Vishton, P. M. (1999). Rule learning by seven-month-old infants. *Science, 283*, 77–80.

Mattys, S. L., Jusczyk, P. W., Luce, P. A., & Morgan, J. L. (1999). Phonotactic and prosodic effects on word segmentation in infants. *Cognitive Psychology, 38*(4), 465–94.

Maye, J., & Weiss, D. (2003). Statistical cues facilitate infants' discrimination of difficult phonetic contrasts. In B. Beachley, A. Brown, & F. Conlin (Eds.), *BUCLD 27: Proceedings of the 27th annual Boston University Conference on Language Development* (Vol. 2, pp. 508–18). Boston: Cascadilla Press.

Maye, J., Werker, J. F., & Gerken, L. A. (2002). Infant sensitivity to distributional information can affect phonetic discrimination. *Cognition, 82*, B101–11.

McCarthy, J. J., & Prince, A. (1996). *Prosodic morphology.* Technical Report No. 32: Rutgers University Center for Cognitive Science. (Updated version of McCarthy & Prince, 1986, unpublished ms.)

McClelland, J. L., McNaughton, B. L., & O'Reilly, R. C. (1995). Why there are complementary learning systems in the hippocampus and neocortex: Insights from the successes and failures of connectionist models of learning and memory. *Psychological Review, 102*(3), 419–57.

McCune, L., & Vihman, M. M. (2001). Early phonetic and lexical development. *Journal of Speech, Language, and Hearing Research, 44*, 670–84.

McDonough, J., & Myers, S. (1991). Consonant harmony and planar segregation in child language. Unpublished manuscript. University of California at Los Angeles and University of Texas at Austin.

Menn, L. (1976). Pattern, control, and contrast in beginning speech: A case study in the development of word form and word function. Doctoral dissertation, University of Illinois.

Menn, L., & Matthei, E. (1992). The "two-lexicon" account of child phonology: Looking back, looking ahead. In C. Ferguson, L. Menn, & C. Stoel-Gammon (Eds.), *Phonological development: Models, research, implications* (pp. 211–47). Parkton, MD: York Press, Inc.

Moore, D. S., & Spence, M. J. (1996, April). *Infants' categorization of unfiltered infant-directed utterances.* Paper presented at the International Conference on Infant Studies, Rhode Island. Abstract available in *Infant Behavior and Development* volume 19 supplement 1, p. 630.

Morgan, J. L. (1996). A rhythmic bias in preverbal speech segmentation. *Journal of Memory and Language, 35*, 666–88.

Morgan, J. L., & Saffran, J. R. (1995). Emerging integration of sequential and supra-segmental information in preverbal speech segmentation. *Child Development*, *66*, 911–36.

Nazzi, T., Iakimova, G., Bertoncini, J., Fredonie, S., & Alcantara, C. (2006). Early segmentation of fluent speech by infants acquiring French: Emerging evidence for crosslinguistic differences. *Journal of Memory and Language*, *54*, 283–99.

Ohala, J. (1983). The origin of sound patterns in vocal tract constraints. In P. MacNeilage (Ed.), *The production of speech* (pp. 189–216). New York: Springer.

Peperkamp, S., & Dupoux, E. (2004, June). *The acquisition of abstract phoneme categories*. Paper presented at LabPhon9: Change in Phonology, University of Illinois at Urbana-Champaign.

Petitto, L. A. (1991). Babbling in the manual mode: Evidence for the ontogeny of language. *Science*, *251*, 1493–6.

Pierrehumbert, J. (2001). Stochastic phonology. *GLOT*, *5*(6), 1–13.

Pierrehumbert, J. (2002) Word-specific phonetics. In C. Gussenhoven & N. Warner (Eds.), *Laboratory phonology VII* (pp. 101–40). Berlin: Mouton De Gruyter.

Pierrehumbert, J. (2003). Probabilistic phonology: Discrimination and robustness. In R. Bod, J. Hay, & S. Jannedy (Eds.), *Probability theory in linguistics* (pp. 177–228). Cambridge: MIT Press.

Pinker, S. (1994). *The language instinct*. New York: William Morrow.

Poser, W. J. (1982). Phonological representation and action-at-a-distance. In H. van der Hulst & N. Smith (Eds.), *The structure of phonological representations: Part II* (pp. 121–58). Dordrecht, Holland: Foris.

Ramus, F. (2002). Language discrimination by newborns. Teasing apart phonotactic, rhythmic, and intonational cues. *Annual Review of Language Acquisition*, *2*, 85–115.

Ramus, F., Nespor, M., & Mehler, J. (1999). Correlates of linguistic rhythm in speech. *Cognition*, *73*, 265–92.

Roark, B., & Demuth, K. (2000). Prosodic constraints and the learner's environment: A corpus study. In S. Catherine Howell, Sarah A. Fish, & Thea Keith-Lucas (Eds.) *Proceedings of the 24th Annual Boston University Conference on Language Development* (pp. 597–608). Somerville, MA: Cascadilla Press.

Rovee-Collier, C. (1997). Dissociations in infant memory. *Psychological Review*, *104*, 467–98.

Saffran, J. R., Aslin, R. N., & Newport, E. L. (1996). Statistical learning by 8-month-old infants. *Science*, *274*, 1926–8.

Saffran, J. R., Newport, E. L., & Aslin, R. N. (1996). Word segmentation: The role of distributional cues. *Journal of Memory and Language*, *35*, 606–21.

Saffran, J. R., Newport, E. L., Aslin, R. N., Tunick, R. A., & Barrueco, S. (1997). Incidental language learning: Listening (and learning) out of the corner of your ear. *Psychological Science*, *8*, 101–5.

Seidl, A., & Buckley, E. (2004). On the learning of natural and unnatural rules. Unpublished manuscript, Purdue University and University of Pennsylvania.

Shaw, P. (1991). Consonant harmony systems: The special status of coronal harmony. In C. Paradis & J.-F. Prunet (Eds.), *The special status of coronals: Internal and external evidence* (pp. 125–57). San Diego: Academic Press.

Shi, R., Werker, J. F., & Morgan, J. L. (1999). Newborn infants' sensitivity to perceptual cues to lexical and grammatical words. *Cognition*, *72*, B11–21.

Smith, B. (1978). Temporal aspects of speech production: A developmental perspective. *Journal of Phonetics, 6,* 37–67.

Smith, N. V. (1973). *The acquisition of phonology: A case study.* Cambridge: Cambridge University Press.

Smolensky, P. (1996). On the comprehension/production dilemma in child language. *Linguistic Inquiry, 27,* 720–31.

Stager, C. L., & Werker, J. F. (1997). Infants listen for more phonetic detail in speech perception than in word-learning tasks. *Nature, 388,* 381–2.

Stampe, D. (1972). A dissertation on natural phonology. Doctoral dissertation, University of Chicago.

Stevens, K. N. (1989). On the quantal nature of speech. *Journal of Phonetics, 17,* 3–46.

Stoel-Gammon, C., & Cooper, J. A. (1984). Patterns of early lexical and phonological development. *Journal of Child Language, 11,* 247–71.

Storkel, H. L. (2001). Learning new words: Phonotactic probability in language development. *Journal of Speech, Language, and Hearing Research, 44,* 1321–37.

Storkel, H. L., & Morisette, M. L. (2002). The lexicon and phonology: Interactions in language acquisition. *Language, Speech, and Hearing Services in the Schools, 33,* 22–35.

Studdert-Kennedy, M., & Goodell, E. (1995). Gestures, features and segments in early child speech. In B. deGelder & J. Morais, J. (Eds), *Speech and reading: A comparative approach* (pp. 65–88). London: Erlbaum.

Swingley, D. (2003). Phonetic detail in the developing lexicon. *Language and Speech, 46*(2–3), 265–94.

Ullman, M. T. (2004). Contributions of memory circuits to language: The declarative/procedural model. *Cognition, 92,* 231–70.

Velleman, S. L. (1996). Metathesis highlights feature-by-position constraints. In B. Bernhardt, J. Gilbert, & D. Ingram (Eds.), *Proceedings of the UBC International Conference on Phonological Acquisition* (pp. 173–86). Somerville, MA: Cascadilla Press.

Vihman, M. M. (1978). Consonant harmony: Its scope and function in child language. In J. H. Greenberg (Ed.), *Universals of human language* (pp. 281–334). Stanford, CA: Stanford University Press.

Vihman, M. M. (1993). Variable paths to early word production. *Journal of Phonetics, 21,* 61–82.

Vihman, M. M. (1996). *Phonological development: The origins of language in the child.* Cambridge: Blackwell.

Vihman, M. M. & Croft, W. (in press). Phonological development: Toward a "radical" templatic phonology. *Linguistics.*

Vihman, M. M., DePaolis, R. A., & Davis, B. L. (1998). Is there a "trochaic bias" in early word learning? Evidence from infant production in English and French. *Child Development, 69,* 933–47.

Vihman, M. M., & Kunnari, S. (in press). The sources of phonological knowledge: A cross-linguistic perspective. *Recherches Linguistiques de Vincennes.*

Vihman, M. M., Nakai, S., & DePaolis, R. A. (2006). Getting the rhythm right: A cross-linguistic study of segmental duration in babbling and first words. In L. Goldstein, D. Whalen, & C. Best (Eds.), *Lab Phon 8: Varieties of phonological competence.* New York: Mouton de Gruyter.

Vihman, M. M., Nakai, S., DePaolis, R. A., & Halle, P. (2004). The role of accentual pattern in early lexical representation. *Journal of Memory and Language, 50,* (336–53).

Vihman, M. M., & Velleman, S. L. (1989). Phonological reorganization: A case study. *Language and Speech, 32,* 149–70.

Vihman, M. M., & Velleman, S. L. (2000). The construction of a first phonology. *Phonetica, 57,* 255–66.

Waterson, N. (1971). Child phonology: A prosodic view. *Journal of Linguistics, 7,* 179–211.

Werker, J. F., Fennell, C. T., Corcoran, K. M., & Stager, C. L. (2002). Infants' ability to learn phonetically similar words: Effects of age and vocabulary size. *Infancy, 3,* 1–30.

Zamuner, T. S. (2003). *Input-based phonological acquisition.* New York: Routledge.

Zharkova, N. (2005). Strategies in the acquisition of segments and syllables in Russian-speaking children. In M. Tzakosta, C. Levelt, & J. van de Weijer (Eds.), Developmental paths in phonological acquisition. *Leiden Papers in Linguistics, 2.1,* pp. 189–213.

3

the description and acquisition
of variable phonological patterns:
phonology and sociolinguistics

paul kerswill and linda shockey

introduction

Variation is a topic that is increasingly occupying the attention of phonologists. This chapter first defines what we mean by phonological variation and explains how it is typically investigated by conventional phonologists and by sociolinguists. We suggest that the two groups differ markedly in the areas of variation that they have explored. We then look at how phonological variability is acquired by young children as part of their first language, concluding that it is acquired simultaneously with other aspects of phonology. We consider how variability in child-directed speech might affect the acquisition of phonology – and of variability. We follow the individual through childhood and adolescence to adulthood and ask how a person's phonology might change as a result of changing linguistic allegiances. The final section addresses the importance of variation to language change and asks whether sound change is predictable.

basic assumptions about phonological variation

Phonology is traditionally seen as having several components, all of which are subject to variation. Languages and to some extent varieties of a language can differ in the number and identity of phonologically significant units (*phonemes*) as well as in the possible sequences of these units (*phonotaxis*). This is one source of variation across varieties of the same language. Variation within a particular dialect is also common. Sounds can change to become more similar, and sequences can be simplified. Some changes are conditioned not by the properties of adjacent sounds, but by formative boundaries or degree of stress. The weakening of stops to fricatives (e.g., /b/ to [β]) between vowels is conditioned both by being intervocalic and by being unstressed (Shockey and Gibbon, 1992). These kinds of changes happen sporadically. Some variation reflects changes made in the past which are no longer observed, such as *goose/geese*. These are usually exceptionless. *Lexical diffusion* is another source of phonological variation (Bybee, 2002; Wang, 1977): change takes place in one word, then slowly spreads through the vocabulary. Forms where a change is complete in some variety (such as *fing* for *thing*) thus exist simultaneously with forms which do not show the change, or which only do so sporadically (**fesis* for *thesis*). Suprasegmental, or *prosodic*, variation also exists: there are cross-dialectal differences in stress and intonation (Grabe, 2002).

the domains of phonology and (variationist) sociolinguistics

Ever since the two fields have been seen as distinct, phonologists and sociolinguists have had an uneasy coexistence. Phonologists with a classical generative orientation have paid only passing attention to variation in speech style and rate which has no structural implications. For them, this type of variability was seen as being part of performance and as relatively trivial. Sociolinguists – at least those who define themselves as "variationists" – see this type of variation and its relationship to extra-linguistic factors (e.g., social class, gender, and formality) as central to their enterprise. Grammatical features and, to a limited degree, intonation figure as centrally as speech sounds and sequences.

The contrast between the "conventional" and "variationist" approaches to phonology is characterized by different attitudes towards the collection and analysis of data: typically, abstract phonologists have based their work on idealized, sometimes self-generated, and decontextualized data, in order to achieve the exceptionless regularity, or "categoricity" (Chambers, 2003, pp. 27–9), that was felt to be at the center of phonological analysis. Interest was not in the data per se, but in what light it could shine on phonological theory. (For example, what does the alternation between [ɪŋ] and [ɪn] in unstressed final -*ing* reveal about markedness?) By contrast, variationists are interested in the way the sound units, as already posited by phonologists, vary in their phonetic shape in conjunction with and as conditioned by extra-linguistic factors, as well as by phonological and other linguistic context. Central to their enterprise is the observation that phonological variability (especially where phonetic conditioning is weak) can largely be characterized as *differences in frequency* of application of a rule in a given social and linguistic context, rather than its categorical application.

Following the example of Labov (e.g., Labov, 1972, 2001; Weinreich, Labov, and Herzog, 1968), many variationists seek to derive usage-based theories of language change and variation through analysis of corpora of natural speech, collected especially to capture differences in social class and other situational context. An alternative variationist approach is that of Dressler (e.g., Dressler and Wodak, 1982), who combines Stampe's Natural Phonology (e.g., Stampe, 1979, and below) with a sociolinguistic analysis of Viennese German.

The classical phonological and sociolinguistic approaches converge in an interest in phonological change over time and whether it can be predicted. The interest of classical phonologists is largely in which theory is most effective, while sociolinguists have a greater interest in understanding the social embedding of language change (Labov, 1972, pp. 283–307).

the view from conventional phonology: theories of variation

generative phonology

Generative Phonology held that pronunciation (or surface phonetic output) is derived from applying phonological rules to a set of basic underlying forms which are information-rich, i.e., they contain all the information needed to specify the contrasts in which a particular lexical item might be expected to participate. Variation is introduced through the *optional rule*. Most phonologists did not address the issue of what causes an optional rule to apply, though some speculated that they were triggered by an increase in speaking rate, and their outputs were thought to embody different speech styles.

natural phonology

Stampe's (1979) explanation of variation in phonology is that it comes from variable success in suppressing natural processes, examples of which are "syllables have no final consonants" and "if final obstruents are allowed, they are voiceless." These natural processes always apply unless restricted from doing so. Instead of having an alternative set of procedures for casual speech, its production can be viewed as switching off some of the procedures used in formal speech. Hooper (1976, p. 114) questions whether there is a principled way to discover which forms are natural and which are suppressed. For example, with a target back consonant and a front vowel /ki/, which output is more natural, [ki] [ci] or [tʃi]?

metrical phonology

Standard Generative Phonology did not deal in syllables or other potentially sub-morphemic units, so had problems accommodating stress and rhythm. The metrical approach (Liberman, 1975; Nespor and Vogel, 1986) is oriented towards describing/explaining just these aspects of language. In English, variation can be influenced by degree of stress in a phrase, so a theory which predicts this will also predict degree of reduction, not only of vowels, but of consonants. Metrical Phonology provides a way of indicating both syllable boundaries and syllable structures, and this is important for explaining variation: syllable final (especially word-final, or *coda*) segments show much more variation than syllable-initial (or *onset*) segments. A version of metrical phonology is fully integrated into Optimality Theory (see below).

articulatory/gestural phonology

Articulatory Phonology (Browman and Goldstein, 1986, 1990, 1992), assumes that every utterance consists of a series of gestures rather than phonemes. Examples are velar opening, vocal cord approximation, and tongue-tip movement. These are produced in a language-specific timing pattern that results in sequences of vowels and consonants as well coarticulatory and assimilatory processes. A gesture always takes approximately the same amount of time, so gestures can vary only in amplitude and degree of overlap which is how different realizations come about. If one speaks faster, the gestures overlap more, hence more coarticulation is expected. If gestures overlap completely (and especially if one gesture is attenuated), it can appear that a segment has been deleted. However, Browman and Goldstein argue that no such deletion is possible: the gestures are simply indistinguishable from each other because they begin and end at the same time. Phonology in this view is not tied to segment boundaries, so can explain effects such as partial nasalization or partial devoicing of a vowel.

firthian prosodic phonology

Several linguists (Kelly and Local, 1989; Ogden, 1999; Simpson, 1992) advocate an approach which they describe as a development from the theories of J. R. Firth (1948). According to these researchers, phonology is carried out at an abstract level, and everything else is phonetics. The Firthian approach involves mapping directly from the citation form of words to their spoken, or surface, form without attributing any special significance to the phoneme or any other abstractly defined unit. Given a sequence of lexical items in citation form, it assigns phonetic features to portions of an utterance, resulting in a nasalized, labialized, or otherwise phonetically realized stretch of speech which does not necessarily correspond in any one-to-one fashion to underlying phonological units.[1] A major tenet of this theory is that contextual variation is expected – e.g., syllable-initial and syllable-final consonants are not necessarily expected to show the same type and degree of variation (as, indeed, they do not), nor are content and function words.

optimality theory

The basic principles of Optimality Theory (OT) are covered elsewhere,[2] so here we discuss only how this theory handles variation. Variation *across* varieties can be described using OT, but variation *within* one variety is (at first glance) impossible to describe because only a single mapping is allowed between the lexical input and the phonetic output, as determined by the ranked constraints. Kager (1999) suggests two possible solutions:

(i)   *variants are the result of different phonologies (phonological systems)*, such that Variant A is generated by Phonology A while Variant B is generated by Phonology B;

(ii) *variants result from variable ranking of constraints*, such that two constraints can be ranked AB on one occasion and BA on another.

Kager (1999) says of (i): "an input can be fed into two parallel co-phonologies, giving two outputs" (p. 405). This, Kager admits, is a ponderous solution to a simple problem. Nathan (1988) suggests that these co-phonologies may be speech styles, such that different speech styles have different phonologies. As regards the second option, Kager proposes that "[e]valuation of the candidate set is split into two subhier-archies, each of which selects an optimal candidate" (1999, p. 405). This is known as *free ranking* (Prince and Smolensky, 1993).

Kager opts for (ii). He points out that the notion of *preferred versus unpreferred ranking* allows the possibility of predicting which of the two outputs will be more frequent. This is a major improvement over the optional rule of Generative Phonology, which was assumed to apply randomly, but is otherwise identical to the variable rule. Nathan (1988) adds that there may be three, four, or even more casual speech outputs from the same input, which makes adequate constraint ranking a very complex business.

Boersma (1998, ch. 15) proposes an OT grammar in which constraints are ranked probabilistically rather than absolutely. This approach is subject to the same criticisms made of Labov and the Variationists (see below) with respect to whether probabilities are a valid part of grammar. Variation in OT is discussed in Shockey (2003a, 2003b).

trace/event phonology

It has been suggested (Goldinger, 1997; papers in Johnson and Mullinix, 1997; Jusczyk, 1997) that each heard token of a word (i.e., each *trace*, or event) is stored separately in the lexicon along with its context. Features such as speaking rate and voice characteristics of the speaker (sometimes referred to as *indexical* information) are included and are used to identify new instances of the same word. According to Bybee (2000a), "'Phonemes' do not exist as units [in the lexicon]; the phenomena that phonemes are intended to describe are relations of similarity among parts of the phonetic string" (p. 82). Bybee (2000b, p. 253) also notes that traces do not distinguish between phonetic and phonological forms.

Because variation is included in the lexicon, Trace Theory does not require rules for production and perception of variable forms. It is not yet clear whether it deals with variants which are conditioned by juncture and/or features of previous or subsequent lexical items, though it does allow storage of some phrases composed of several words.

variation theory

Although it is not historically the latest, we have left Variation Theory for last, since it directly informs much of the phonology done by today's sociolinguists. It is based on the ideas of Labov (1969) and is essentially a variant of Generative Phonology in which the application of a rule is governed by the linguistic, sociological, and psychological environment in which an utterance is produced. Rules are not really optional, but are almost completely deterministic, allowing for idiosyncrasies. Cedergren and Sankoff (1974) extended the theory to include probabilities: The presence or absence of a particular factor or configuration of factors affects the probability that a rule will apply. The resulting calculation can be very complex (see Fasold, 1990, pp. 244ff, for an illustration). A similar approach can be seen in Bailey (1973).

The variable rule has been criticized and, in fact, has been virtually discarded by mainstream phonologists, on two grounds:

(i) *Probabilities of application of a particular rule are a feature of a particular variety or dialect group rather than an individual.* The relationship between the language behavior of a community and the mental grammar of an individual is unknown and probably unknowable. How could an individual keep track of the percentages of rule application in their own production so as to be sure to match the group? If indeed this is possible, is it part of the grammar?

(ii) *Linguistic theories are by nature abstract and are focused on how contrast is achieved (hence meaning conveyed) in particular circumstances.* The number of outputs of a particular rule is of no interest. Pierrehumbert (1994) counterargues, however, that variation is intrinsic to the nature of language, is undoubtedly a part of our linguistic knowledge, and should therefore be intrinsic to our scientific study of language.

the view from sociolinguistics

phonetic/phonological variation

Sociolinguistics sees the domains of variability (for all linguistic levels, including phonetics/phonology, lexicon, and syntax) as the following:

- *Within a language, according to both social and geographical parameters.* Key terms are *variety*, *dialect*, and *social dialect* or *sociolect* (the variety spoken by a particular social group). Social factors include social class and sex; varieties differ geographically.
- *Between individual speakers.* The key term is *idiolect* (the variety spoken by one individual).
- *Within speakers of a language.* Key terms are *style* and *register*. *Style* is defined as referring to the amount of "attention paid to speech" (Labov, 1972), or in relation to a wider array of contextual factors, such as intended audience (Bell, 1984). *Register* is defined as usage according to "the context in which language is used" (Swann, Deumert, Lillis, and Mesthrie, 2004, p. 261), especially usage dependent on occupational or other defined social groupings. A different kind of variability involves phonetic/phonological *reduction*, *assimilation*, and *deletion* (essentially the same as casual speech processes). With some exceptions, this type of variation is rarely dealt with by sociolinguists.
- *Across time within a language.* This can result in *phonological change*, the concern of historical linguistics.

- *Across time for an individual speaker.* Initially, this refers to *first language acquisition.* Subsequently, it deals with acquisition of different dialect features as a child's social network enlarges and the person's orientation with respect to other varieties of their own language expands across the lifespan. Key terms are *second dialect acquisition* and *vernacular reorganization.*

typical areas of concentration

The major concern of variationist sociolinguists is *the fact of variability itself,* whether phonetic or phonological, and its relationship to social factors. Some phonological phenomena have been investigated very thoroughly in a sociolinguistic mode and others have not. Because sociolinguists generally address phonology only tangentially, the distinctions made earlier are rarely foregrounded. In what follows, we nevertheless attempt to categorize studies according to the area of phonology they concern, adding our own observations on phonological patterning.

A. Phonological structures
Phonological inventory:
Dialectologists have studied differences in vowel inventory across language areas. Thus, Catford (1957, cited in Francis, 1983, p. 29) maps the number of distinctive vowels in dialects in Scotland, ranging from nine to twelve, in geographically coherent steps. Southern English varieties have one more phoneme than Northern English varieties: /ʌ/ as in *cup*, where the North has /ʊ/ for *cup*. Vernacular speech in much of England lacks /h/ (e.g. *hammer* is pronounced ['æmə]; Trudgill, 1999, p. 29). Sociolinguists draw a range of conclusions from these facts. Some are concerned with the geographical spread of features (e.g., Kerswill, 2003). Others are interested in the social-class and stylistic distribution of a feature within one community (e.g., Trudgill, 1974). They speak of features like /ʊ/ in *cup* or "*h*-dropping" (lack of /h/) as being *socially stratified,* meaning that their pattern of occurrence is correlated with the social status of speakers.

   In almost all cases where there is social stratification of these features, the majority of speakers exhibit variability. The notion of "phoneme inventory" is thus challenged. Do speakers who variably produce /h/ in words like *hammer* sometimes *delete* /h/ (a unit in their inventory), or do they sometimes *insert* it as an "alien" phoneme (i.e., one that is not otherwise part of their own inventory)? Wells (1982, pp. 321–2) cites evidence that most London speakers "know" the correct distribution of the phoneme, while, by contrast, speakers of Tristan da Cunha English variably use /h/ in items which, in other varieties, have either a word-initial vowel or /h/ (Schreier, 2003). For most phonologists, a phoneme either belongs or does not belong to the inventory; sociolinguistic data often makes such a categorical statement problematic.

Phonotaxis:
Reported examples of variability in phonotaxis are rare, but although /l/ and /m/ can occur in sequence in words such as *film* and in most varieties of English, many Scottish and Irish varieties of English do not allow coda /lm/. In those varieties, *film* is pronounced ['fɪləm], i.e., with an epenthetic schwa vowel inserted between /l/ and /m/ (Dolan, 2005). As another example, most creoles do not allow a complex coda, many having a CV structure.[3] Decreolizing varieties (those which are in contact with their lexifier language) may allow the reintroduction of a final consonant, but not a consonant cluster (Holm, 2000, p. 141). Basilectal Jamaican Creole has a restriction against complex codas, leading to *guess* and *guest* being homophones (Wells, 1974). However, the mesolectal (decreolized) Jamaican variety studied by Patrick (1999, p. 130) shows variable occurrence of final *t* and *d* in clusters (e.g., in *sent*, *bend*) with great individual disparities in the deletion rate, which ranged from 56% to 95%. The higher percentage reflects a score close to that of Wells' subjects but a phonological system different from theirs because it includes a variable feature of *t/d* deletion.

Frequency-based data such as these pose challenges to phonological theories in which probabilistic differences cannot be expressed.

B. Positional variation
Segmentally conditioned variation:
Segmentally conditioned variation is a relatively well-explored marker of sociolinguistic differences. Two examples are given below.

(i)   The dialects of the Dutch province of Limburg have so-called "*Ach-Laut*" allophony: after a high front vowel, /x/ is palatalized to [ç], giving [zɪç] 'self', contrasted with [χ] after other vowels, as in [kra:χ] 'collar'. This allophony does not occur in Standard Dutch, where /x/ remains uvular or velar in all contexts (Hinskens, 1992, pp. 108, 147). Today, there is rapid loss of the feature, part of dialect leveling in Limburg. Before the change, the presence/absence of this feature was categorical: The variation was between geographical groups. Currently, there is variability both at a group level (manifested as age-related differences) and within individual speakers. Hinskens

(1992) concludes that "allophony does not necessarily preclude quantitative variation" (pp. 213–14).

(ii) *Regressive place assimilation* was examined using electropalatography (EPG) by Wright (1989) and Kerswill and Wright (1990) in order to discover whether it was a sociolinguistic marker in Cambridge speech. Electropalatograms showed an array of intermediate articulations from full alveolar closure, through partial or residual contact, to the absence of any visible contact. Some of the visibly intermediate stages were not audible and, conversely, some apparently full assimilations were still perceived as alveolar by phoneticians. The degree of assimilation could be controlled by attention paid to articulation. It was found that assimilation was not socially salient, but was instead subject to speaking rate and to suppression if the speaker was asked to pay attention to articulation. A phonetic effect in which syllable-final /l/ has little or no central tongue contact (so-called "*l*-vocalization," as in ['piːpo] for *people*), on the other hand, was socially salient (it is a dialect marker) but only weakly susceptible to speaking rate and attention (Kerswill and Wright, 1990; Wright, 1989).[4]

Phonetic variation:
Sociolinguists have largely concentrated on phonetic-level variation, in which phonological motivation is weak or absent. Few of these features have phonological consequences, with the exception of mergers. Examples from English are:

- variability in Newcastle English /t/, which can appear as [tʰ], [ʔ], [ʔt], [r], or [ɹ] (Foulkes, Docherty, and Watt, 1999);
- deletion of final –*t* and –*d* in clusters, as in [pæs], [sen] for *past, send* (Guy, 1980);
- the vowel chain shift known as the "Northern Cities Shift", which has produced effects such as raising of /æ/ in *bad* and *glad* (Labov, Yaeger, and Steiner, 1972);
- fronting of /uː/ as in *goose* [ʉ] (Bauer, 1985; Clarke, Elms, and Youssef, 1995; Kerswill and Williams, 2005);
- the merger of /θ/ and /f/ in words like *three* and *think* in British English (Kerswill, 2003);
- the merger of /ɪə/ and /eə/, as in *near* and *square*, in New Zealand English (Gordon and Maclagan, 2001).

The synchronic pattern of variation seen here is largely conditioned by sociological and/or situational factors (see, e.g., Milroy, 2002). Variationist studies reveal patterns which need to be accommodated by phonological theory, as we argued above for phonotaxis. We return to this point later.

C. Prosodic phonology: stress and intonation
Unless engaged in discourse analysis, sociolinguists have normally only *described* prosodic (or suprasegmental) variation. Thus, stress differences between American and British English are presented in lists (e.g., Trudgill and Hannah, 2002, pp. 51–2) and "typical" regional British intonations are given with few comments on social variation or change (Foulkes and Docherty, 1999, passim). A study which quantifies the natural (though elicited) speech of regionally accented speakers and which aims to improve theoretical models of intonation is the Intonational Variation in English project (e.g., Grabe, 2002). Although it does not have any avowed sociolinguistic aims, its methods are broadly variationist.[5]

acquisition of variation

All theories of first language acquisition depend on the infant (1) noticing the distribution of speech sounds and patterns in natural input and (2) learning to replicate these patterns. However, emphasis with respect to the *size* of the unit to be mastered has changed over time. Most early work in first language phonology focused on the acquisition of phonemic oppositions. Cruttenden (1979) mentions acquisition of variation, though only peripherally: English voiced plosives are realized by adults as unaspirated syllable-initially but as simply voiceless word-finally. He points out that "this may be reflected in the different treatment of the members of such pairs in some children's language" (p. 19). Another example cited by Cruttenden (from Smith, 1973), in which a child omitted /d/ in –nd clusters such as *pined* but omitted /n/ in –nt clusters such as *pint*, shows an ability to notice and to differentiate patterns above the level of the segment. Cruttenden also mentions variation which occurs in child speech but not in the adult language, such as palatalization in the vicinity of a front vowel (*finger* pronounced as [ˈfɪɲɟə]). Variation in children's speech which does not match adult variation has been observed by many researchers including Gerken (1994) and Menn and Matthei (1992), so we have evidence of non-adult patterns in dealing with positional variation, at least in the *production* (if not the underlying phonologies) of young children. These examples suggest that experimenting with variation is a stage in the acquisition of a first-language sound system.

contrast-based theories

Here we discuss theories which assume, in a traditional fashion, that acquisition of a first-language sound system is characterized by a gradually increasing phonological inventory.

natural phonology

Most agree that children's perceptual abilities far outstrip their skills in production. The auditory mechanism is fully developed even before the infant is born (Wakai, Lenthold, and Martin, 1996), and a newborn is able to recognize familiar sounds in its environment based on its experience of sound in the womb (Busnel, Granier-Deferre, and Lecanuet, 1992). Speech is not, of course, recognized entirely through hearing, but other channels of perception are also functional long before an infant has adequate peripheral motor control for articulation of speech sounds.[6]

Stampe's (1979) theory of phonological acquisition assumes that an infant's articulatory goal is to match their own output to their cognitive representation of sounds in the language, which is thought to be equivalent to that of adults in the same language environment. The young child is prevented from achieving this match because certain natural processes are in operation, such as the palatalization in the vicinity of a front vowel (*finger* pronounced as ['fɪɲɟə]) mentioned by Cruttenden (1979), and must be suppressed in order to produce the necessary sounds. Natural processes shape all languages, but to different degrees, depending on the level to which they are habitually overcome in particular languages. As mentioned above, one such process is the deletion or weakening of syllable-final consonants. As is well-documented, children tend to produce syllable-initial consonants accurately before final consonants. The naturalness of this weakening of final consonants is reflected in the facts that: (1) the most common syllable shape for languages of the world is CV; and (2) when adult speakers of a CV-type language learn a language with syllable-final consonants, at the early stage they often leave out these consonants. This can be observed, for example, in speakers of Mandarin Chinese learning English (Broselow, Chen, and Wang, 1998). The natural process of producing only open syllables is still fully operative when they learn English because it has never been suppressed. Another example is loss of voicing in final obstruents, the naturalness of which can be shown by the same arguments in terms of universal syllable types and the language learning behavior of children and adults.[7]

Variation is an integral part of this theory because it is assumed that variants of the underlying form will be produced in the course of acquisition and that variant forms are in some sense "wired into" the phonological system of any language. The theory also makes predictions about types of variation to be expected, though detail is lacking: the variation described in the papers in Foulkes and Docherty (1999), for example, could be difficult to predict.

variationists and the variable rule

Acquisition of a variable rule has been suggested as the primary mechanism for producing and perceiving variation in speech. Roberts (1994, 1997) studied [ɪŋ] and [ɪn] as realizations of final –*ing* (e.g., in *talking, interesting*, etc.) in three- and four-year-olds in Philadelphia, Pennsylvania. She discovered that the children were more likely to use [ɪn] when speaking to other children, but [ɪŋ] when speaking to adults. She further found that this type of variation was partially governed by influences normally thought to come from outside phonology: the [ɪn] forms were favored in main verbs and complements more than in nouns or adjectives (as also found by Shockey, 1974).

In her 1997 study of 146 hours of speech from 16 children, Roberts tabulated word-final –*t* and –*d* deletion. Children showed nearly the same results as adults with respect to deletion before a consonant and conformed to the adult pattern for deleting –*t* and –*d* more in one-syllable words (e.g., *mist, nest*) than in regular past tense verbs (e.g., *missed, laughed*). Their performance differed significantly in weak (i.e., irregular) past-tense verbs (e.g., *slept, left*): children's deletion pattern for irregular past tenses matched that of their pattern for single morphemes, while adults showed much less deletion in irregular verbs. There were no effects related to addressee or style.

Roberts concluded that children learn variable rules at an early age though their behavior is not identical to that of adults: children are constructing their own generalizations and abstractions about allowable forms.

between-word processes

Newton and Wells (1999) studied normal children's acquisition of (segmentally based) phonological processes across word boundaries, to establish a baseline against which to compare disordered speech. They looked at four phenomena:

- *assimilation of alveolars*, as in the production of a velar rather than an alveolar nasal (i.e., [ŋ] instead of [n]) before velar /k/, e.g., *one cloud* [wʌŋklaʊd];
- *consonant cluster reduction*, as in the loss of /t/ between consonants, e.g., *just like* [dʒʌslaɪk];
- *liaison*, where glides [j,w,r] are inserted over a word boundary between vowels, e.g., *my eyes* [maɪjaɪz];
- *correct definite article alternation* ([ði] before vowels, [ðə] before consonants).

Newton and Wells looked at 94 monolingual English children aged 3 to 7 and discovered that even the youngest behaved essentially identically to adults in the use of the first three of these features. The variant pronunciation of the definite article was learned by age 4. They conclude that arbitrary variation is actually learned while phonetically motivated variation does not have to be learned.

word-based theories

Word-based theories assume that very young children do not segment input directly into phonemes, but use some other technique for discovering linguistically meaningful units. Waterson (1987, p. 57) says that children extract features of speech which are salient to them and that their internal representation of words consists of syllable-length features such as nasality, frontness, backness, voicing, and rounding as well as more segmentally oriented features such as place and manner of articulation. These features Waterson calls "prosodies," similar or identical to those proposed by Firth (1948) for adult speech. Waterson (p. 110) assumes that children's words are represented in their mental lexicons in their full phonetic form and are the basis for the child's pronunciation.

In another attempt to describe how a child's lexicon is created, Clark (2003) summarizes the findings of Jusczyk (1997) as follows:

[I]nfants begin with approximations to word-boundaries, presumably based on information from pauses and constancy in repetitive carrier-phrases in child-directed speech. These allow them to identify certain sound sequences with strong (stress-bearing) initial syllables, and they can then use the occurrence of other strong syllables to isolate other potential word-chunks, sequences that do not appear in final position in the utterance.... The more infants discover about word boundaries, the more efficient they become at extracting words or wordlike chunks from the stream of speech as a whole. (pp. 69–70)

Trace/Event Theory is implicated in this view of the child's acquisition of phonology, on the assumption that when a child hears a word for the first time, it is stored in the lexicon as an undifferentiated acoustic event, including not only phonologically contrastive information, but also information about the circumstances under which the speech was heard (e.g., speaking rate, voice of speaker, background noise, etc.). Assuming that the child is able to recognize the subsequent tokens of the word as having the same meaning, they are stored together with the originally stored word, with the same indexical information for each token. Thus, variation is an integral part of the lexical entry.

trace or rule-based?

Foulkes, Docherty, and Watt (1999) asked when structured variation can first be found in the speech of children in Newcastle, England, aged 2 to 4, focusing particularly on /t/. They discovered that young children's pattern of variation is in most respects the same as that of adults, with three main phonological variants of /t/: initial (aspirated), medial (glottally reinforced), and final (several alternants, including glottalized and preaspirated). Where children's variants are different (e.g., they don't say [gɒɹə] for "got to" as is found in the adult community), they attribute this lack of consistency with adult forms to incomplete development of motor coordination. Foulkes et al. (1999) conclude that "sociophonetic and allophonic aspects of speech are learned alongside aspects usually considered as reflexes of the contrastive phonological system" (p. 17). Variation in the phonetic input is not simply filtered out: Children reproduce the recognizable features of the adult community. Based on these results, Foulkes and Docherty opt for a version of Trace Theory. In a similar vein, Días-Campos (2004) argues that if children were acquiring variable rules, all words of a similar sound structure would show similar variability, but in fact variability is greatest in forms which are heard most frequently.

The central question here is whether variation is produced by children in cases not previously heard. If a child from Newcastle puts *net* (which will be pronounced with a final variant of /t/) in a medial position (as in *netting*), will the intervocalic /t/ show the normal adult glottalized variant? If so, the child is abstracting from heard tokens to produce generalizations about positional variation (rules), as suggested by Roberts. If not, the episodic explanation becomes more likely, as suggested by

Días-Campos. It is also possible that these are not mutually exclusive, i.e., that children go through an episodic stage but subconsciously work out the underlying patterns eventually.

optimality theory

Working within OT, Boersma (1998) assumes that optionality of phonological processes is gradient, adding that listeners learn to match the degree of optionality in their environment in their categorization systems. He claims that Dutch children as old as four years of age pronounce /an+pa/ as [anpa], even though their parents say [ampa]. Children choose the base form, "which the learner can easily deduce from the form spoken in isolation" (Boersma, ibid., p. 332), as they have not learned to violate faithfulness constraints maintaining consistency of input and output. Later, this lesson is learned, and then the child is able to acquire the correct distribution of the two forms (with [n] and [m]). We find it surprising that Dutch 4-year-olds in failing initially to mirror the distribution of variants found in adult forms, behave so differently from English-speaking children and suggest that his assertions call for greater experimental support.[8]

acquisition of variation?

Evidence suggests that speaking of "acquisition of phonological variation" is equivalent to talking about "acquisition of windows" when buying a house: they are integral parts of the whole and are not acquired separately. Further, variation in pronunciation is used in functional ways by very young children. Anderson (1990) has found that children as young as four years old are aware of systematic variation in speech related to degree of formality and different accents and that they can use this knowledge in role-playing. Perhaps even more strikingly, 2-year-olds can take account of listener needs and modify characteristics of their speech accordingly (Berko-Gleason and Pearlmann, 1985, p. 96; cf. Shields, 1978). Child language experts thus regard acquisition of variation as one facet of acquiring communicative competence. What is not adequately understood is the degree of abstractness associated with the child's subconscious knowledge of phonological variation and whether or how this knowledge changes as the child matures.

variability in input to children

Conventional wisdom maintains that caregivers provide an exceptionally clear model of pronunciation to young children acquiring language (e.g., Gleitman, Newport, and Gleitman, 1984). A study involving pronunciation of intervocalic /t/ in Newcastle English (Watt, Docherty, and Foulkes, 2003) showed that complex sociolinguistic factors influence speech directed to children between the ages of 2 and 4. Mothers' speech to younger children showed more careful, citation-form and standard pronunciations than their speech to older children, and speech to boys showed more citation forms that that directed to girls. There is thus evidence of a tendency towards more formal or standard pronunciation in some child-directed speech.

In the Watt et al. (2003) study, child-directed speech from three male caregivers was similar to their (largely non-standard) speech to adults, suggesting that adults vary in the degree to which they accommodate their pronunciation to the age of the hearer, with possible gender differences. These results, like those of Shockey and Bond (1980), indicate that young children hear a range of phonological forms associated with different settings that may not all be directly addressed to them. Patterson (1992) concludes that children first associate variants with certain types of interactions. As noted by Patterson as well as by Labov (2001), the early stylistic uses of variants are followed by use of variation patterns associated with specific linguistic and discourse conditions and social groups.

That children adopt non-standard pronunciations as a preferred form when very young and move towards more standard forms as they become older is clearly reflected in the results of both Patterson (1992) and Díaz-Campos (2001). In the latter study, for example, Spanish final /d/ was present in only 50% of cases by children 48–53 months old, in 76% of cases by children 54–59 months old and in 90% of cases by children 60–65 months old. These figures point to patterned variation as an influential aspect of phonological input to children.

phonological change in adolescence and adulthood

The most reliable way of collecting evidence of phonological change within individual speakers is by recording them more than once over a period of time. This type of data gives a real-time view of the progression of change. Some information about the effects of changes over time can be gleaned by recording socially matched samples of speakers of different ages to gain a cross-sectional view of phonological variation. This type of data is suggestive, offering an "apparent-time" (Labov, 1972) view of phonological change. Yet there is an issue as to what is to be understood by "phonological change." Changes in frequency of a particular realization of a phoneme do not necessarily count as phonological change, as when British children increase their use of the glottal stop for /t/ as they reach adolescence, only to reduce it again by adulthood (Kerswill and Williams, 2000, p. 105; Sankoff, 2004) – most likely in response to changes in the evaluation of non-standard features of speakers of different ages. Phonological change implies the acquisition or loss of a phonemic distinction, a change in phonotaxis, or a change in the phonological conditioning of a segment. Phonetic change involves the quasi-permanent change in the realization of a segment, such as the fronting of a vowel. Change across the lifespan is referred to by Labov (2001) as *vernacular reorganization*.

There is a range of not entirely consistent evidence on what phonetic and phonological features can be changed at particular ages (reviewed in Chambers 1992; Kerswill, 1996, pp. 184–88, 200). The least restricted seem to be phonetic changes: adjustments to vowels throughout one's lifetime, usually congruent with vowel changes underway in the community or when accommodating to a new dialect area, are inferred for children aged 4–12 by Kerswill and Williams (2000) and reported for adults by Yaeger-Dror (1989) and Shockey (1984). These changes are exceptionless. Lexically unpredictable rules – phonological rules with exceptions – seem to be difficult to acquire after early childhood (Payne, 1980). The acquisition of new phonological contrasts seems restricted to children, perhaps up to the age of 7–14 (Chambers, 1992), though counterevidence is supplied by Sankoff (2004). Studying the speech of two Northern English men who were recorded for television between the ages of 7 and 35, she finds that, contrary to expectations, they were able to acquire the Southern British English contrast /ʌ/ – /ʊ/ after the age of 21. Neither speaker is consistent, however, suggesting that the acquisition of the contrast proceeds word by word (i.e., by lexical diffusion).

variation as a source of phonological change

Phonological variation is a feature of all living languages, though which variant will be found in a particular case is not always entirely predictable. This is presumably an aspect of what Weinreich, Labov, and Herzog (1968) call "orderly heterogeneity."

We know that many variants are simultaneously in use; but one variant (in a particular environment) is usually regarded as more standard than the others, and what is seen as standard can change over time. For example, pronunciation of intervocalic /b,d,g/ as [b,d,g] is standard in English and other pronunciations are regarded as non-standard. On the other hand, what are spelled *b*, *d*, and *g* and were once presumably pronounced as stop consonants are now pronounced [β, ð, ɣ] intervocalically in standard Spanish. The fact that a continuant pronunciation of voiced stops now exists intervocalically in casual English (e.g., [ˈlæɣɨŋ] "lagging") and that intervocalic weakening, or *lenition*, is a well-known change suggests that one possible path for the standard English voiced stops of tomorrow is to go in the direction of Spanish. It is however equally true that this path may not be taken: today's standard may be maintained, or another variant may become conventional. The standard of the future will, nevertheless, come from the set of today's pronunciations. It would be very surprising for a completely new variant to appear, though it could happen if a new variety is imported from outside the area and if it quickly catches on.

Predictions about the sorts of variation one might expect in a particular system are possible: phonologists call on such notions as simplicity, naturalness, or unmarkedness. As Bailey (1973) puts it, "the patterns of a language are the cumulative results of natural, unidirectional changes" (p. 32) and "the directionality of natural change is from what is more marked to what is less marked" (p. 37). Stampe (1979) argues that calling a form "marked" or "unmarked" is superficial and unrevealing and that implicational laws are nothing more than empirical generalizations. These processes, in his view, can be seen as opening avenues for sound change, but not deterministically (see also Blevins, 2004). Labov (1972, 2001) has contended that sound change in progress can be observed by studying language in its social context. He readily admits, however, that all change involves variability, but not all instances of variability involve change (Labov, 1972, 2001; Weinreich, Labov, and Herzog, 1968, p. 188).

Bybee (2002) suggests that sound change can be predicted by measuring lexical diffusion. She quotes Schuchardt (1885/1972) to the effect that "[r]arely used words lag behind; very frequently used words hurry ahead" (p. 58), i.e., once a pronunciation is found in both common and uncommon words, it can be seen as representing a (phonological or other) change. It is only recently, with the compilation of large, labeled online databases of spoken language, that such judgments have become feasible for phonetics and phonology, as written texts do not reflect variation in pronunciation (except sometimes by accident).

Predictions about which variations will lead to change remain, at best, risky. Vaissière (1998, p. 70) wryly observes that sound changes cannot be predicted, but they can almost always be given a number of more or less plausible explanations after they have been attested. The relationship

between variation and sound change is addressed insightfully by Blevins
(2004). The fundamental principle of her Evolutionary Phonology is that
sound patterns have their origin in recurrent phonetically motivated
sound change. Change over time is caused by incomplete transmission
across the generations, which may be caused by mishearing or by the
signal being inherently ambiguous. In the latter case, patterns present in a
particular language may bias the listener towards a certain interpretation.
For example, [pã] may be interpreted as a contrastively nasalized vowel
rather than a CVN (N = nasal consonant) sequence in a language where
open syllables are the rule. In a case such as this, the phonological representation may or may not change (which is why modern phonologists
argue about whether French really has phonemically nasalized vowels).
Blevins emphasizes that sound change is essentially random and non-
optimizing: it happens because of the way we produce and hear speech,
not to improve the language in any way. Her approach appears to be a
way forward in synthesizing what we know about variation, historical
linguistic processes, and the shape of sound systems.

conclusion

Phonological theory offers a large variety of ways to describe and explain
alternate pronunciations of the same lexical form within a given language.
While a significant portion of sociolinguistic research has been on these
alternates, there has not been a concerted attempt to relate findings to
linguistic principles. Variation is an integral component of the phonology
of all living languages and a working knowledge of the range of adult
variants and of the linguistic and sociological conditions under which
they are used is acquired by children along with the rest of their native
tongue. Type and degree of variation can change over the lifespan, just
as other aspects of language can. Norms of pronunciation change, and
future norms are included in the variants currently in use. Which variants
will be chosen as standard is, however, not predictable.[9]

notes

1. This approach has been used effectively in speech synthesis (Coleman, 1994;
   Coleman and Dirksen, 1995; Local and Ogden, 1997).
2. Editor's note: see Chapter 2, this volume.
3. Editor's note: see Chapter 4, this volume, for discussion of this feature in
   creoles.
4. Editor's note: for a related discussion of the technique of EPG and how it has
   been used to discover details of children's production of sound contrasts in
   cases of developmental phonological disorder, see Chapter 10, this volume.

5. Editor's note: for relevant discussion, see Chapter 8, this volume; also see the discussion of prosodic variation in chapter 4 of M. C. Pennington (1996), *Phonology in English language teaching: An international approach* (London: Addison-Wesley Longman).

6. Editor's note: Chapter 6, this volume, reviews the contribution to perception and comprehension of the visual channel; Chapter 2, this volume, describes perceptual abilities of newborns.

7. Editor's note: see Chapter 2, this volume, for another perspective on the phenomena described and on Natural Phonology in relation to child language acquisition.

8. Editor's note: for further discussion of OT in relation to child language acquisition, see Chapter 2, this volume.

9. Editor's note: a similar point is made in Chapter 4, this volume, in relation to phonological change in language contact.

references

Anderson, E. (1990). *Speaking with style: The speaking styles of children.* London: Routledge.

Bailey, C.-J. (1973). *Variation and linguistic theory.* Arlington, Virginia: Center for Applied Linguistics.

Bauer, L. (1985). Tracing phonetic change in the Received Pronunciation of British English. *Journal of Phonetics, 13,* 61–81.

Bell, A. (1984). Language style as audience design. *Language in Society, 13,* 145–204.

Berko-Gleason, J., & Pearlmann, R. Y. (1985). Acquiring social variation in speech. In H. Giles & R. St. Clair (Eds.), *Recent advances in language, communication, and social psychology* (pp. 86–111). Mahwah, NJ: Erlbaum.

Blevins, J. (2004). *Evolutionary phonology.* Cambridge: Cambridge University Press.

Boersma, P. (1998). *Functional phonology.* The Hague: Holland Academic Graphics.

Broselow, E., Chen, S-I. and Wang, C. (1998). The emergence of the unmarked in second language phonology. *Studies in Second Language Acquisition, 20,* 261–80.

Browman, C., & Goldstein, L. (1986). Towards an articulatory phonology. *Phonology Yearbook, 3,* 219–52.

Browman, C., & Goldstein, L. (1990). Tiers in Articulatory Phonology, with some implications for casual speech. In J. Kingston & M. Beckman (Eds.), *Papers in Laboratory Phonology 1* (pp. 341–376). Cambridge: Cambridge University Press.

Browman, C., & Goldstein, L. (1992). Articulatory phonology: An overview. *Phonetica, 49,* 155–80.

Busnel, M. C., Granier-Deferre, C., & Lecanuet, J. P. (1992). Fetal audition. *Annals of the New York Academy of Sciences, 662,* 118–34.

Bybee, J. (2000a). Lexicalization of sound change and alternating environments. In M. Broe & J. Pierrehumbert (Eds.), *Papers in Laboratory Phonology V* (pp. 250–68). Cambridge: Cambridge University Press.

Bybee, J., (2000b) The Phonology of the lexicon: Evidence from lexical diffusion. In M. Barlow & S. Kemmer (Eds.), *Usage-based models language* (pp. 65–85). Stanford, CA: Center for the Study of Language and Information (CSLI).

Bybee, J. (2002). Lexical diffusion in regular sound change. In D. Restle & D. Zaefferer (Eds.), *Sounds and systems: Studies in structure and change* (pp. 59–74). The Hague: Mouton.

Catford, J. C. (1957). Vowel systems of Scots dialects. *Transactions of the Philological Society 1957*, 107–17.

Cedergren, H. J., & Sankoff, D. (1974). Variable rules: Performance as a statistical reflection of competence. *Language, 50*, 333–55.

Chambers, J. K. (1992). Dialect acquisition. *Language, 68*, 673–705.

Chambers, J. K. (2003). *Sociolinguistic theory*. Second edition. Oxford: Blackwell.

Clark, E. V. (2003) *First language acquisition*. Cambridge: Cambridge University Press.

Clarke, S., Elms, F. & Youssef, A. (1995). The third dialect of English: Some Canadian evidence. *Language Variation and Change, 7*, 209–28.

Coleman, J. S. (1992). The phonetic interpretation of headed phonological structures containing overlapping constituents. *Phonology, 9*, 1–42.

Coleman, J. S. (1994). Polysyllabic words in the YorkTalk synthesis system. In P. A. Keating (Ed.), *Phonological structure and phonetic form: Papers in Laboratory Phonology III* (pp. 293–324). Cambridge: Cambridge University Press.

Coleman, J. S., & Dirksen, A. (1995). Synthesis of connected speech. In L. Shockey (Ed.) *University of Reading Speech Research Laboratory Work in Progress, 8*, 1–12.

Cruttenden, A. (1979). *Language in infancy and childhood*. Manchester: Manchester University Press.

Díaz-Campos, M. (2001). Acquisition of phonological structure and sociolinguistic variables: A quantitative analysis of Spanish consonant weakening in Venezuelan children's speech. Doctoral dissertation, Ohio State University.

Díaz-Campos, M. (2004). Acquisition of sociolinguistic variables in Spanish: Do children acquire individual lexical forms or variable rules? In T. Face (Ed.), *Laboratory approaches to Spanish phonology* (pp. 221–36). Berlin/New York: Mouton de Gruyter.

Dolan, T. P. (2005). A Hiberno-English archive. Retrieved January 22, 2006, from <www.hiberno-english.com/grammar.htm>.

Dressler, W., & Wodak, R. (1982). Sociophonological methods in the study of sociolinguistic variation in Viennese German. *Language in Society, 11*, 339–70.

Fasold, R. (1990). *The sociolinguistics of language*. Oxford: Blackwell.

Firth, J. R. (1948). Sounds and prosodies. *Transactions of the Philological Society 1948*, 127–52. Reprinted in J. R. Firth (1957) *Papers in Linguistics 1934–1951*. Oxford: Oxford University Press.

Foulkes, P., & Docherty, G. (Eds.) (1999). *Urban voices: Accent studies in the British Isles*. London: Arnold.

Foulkes, P., Docherty, G., & Watt, D. (1999). Tracking the emergence of structured variation: Realisations of (t) by Newcastle children. *Leeds Working Papers in Linguistics and Phonetics, 7*, 1–25.

Francis, W. N. (1983). *Dialectology: An introduction*. London: Longman.

Gerken, L. A. (1994). Child phonology: Past research, future directions. In M. A. Gernsbacher (Ed.), *Handbook of psycholinguistics* (pp. 781–820). New York: Academic Press.

Gleitman, L. R., Newport, E. L., & Gleitman, H. (1984). The current status of the motherese hypothesis. *Journal of Child Language*, *11*, 43–79.

Goldinger, S. (1997) Words and voices: Perception and production in an episodic lexicon. In K. Johnson & J. Mullenix (Eds.), *Talker variability in speech processing* (pp. 33–66). San Diego: Academic Press.

Gordon, E., & Maclagan, M. (2001). Capturing a sound change: A real time study over 15 years of the NEAR/SQUARE diphthong merger in New Zealand English. *Australian Journal of Linguistics*, *21*, 215–38.

Grabe, E. (2002). Variation adds to prosodic typology. In B. Bel & I. Marlin (Eds.), *Proceedings of the Speech Prosody 2002 conference* (pp. 127–32). Aix-en-Provence: Laboratoire Parole et Langage.

Guy, G. R. (1980). Variation in the group and the individual: The case of final stop deletion. In W. Labov (Ed.), *Locating language in time and space* (pp. 1–36). New York: Academic Press.

Hinskens, F. (1992). Dialect levelling in Limburg: Structural and sociolinguistic aspects. Doctoral dissertation, University of Nijmegen.

Holm, J. (2000). *An introduction to pidgins and creoles*. Cambridge: Cambridge University Press.

Hooper, J. B. (1976). *An introduction to Natural Generative Phonology*. New York: Academic Press.

Johnson, K., & Mullenix, J. W. (Eds.) (1997). *Talker variability in speech processing*. San Diego: Academic Press.

Jusczyk, P. (1997). *The discovery of spoken language*. Cambridge, Mass.: MIT.

Kager, R. (1999). *Optimality Theory*. Cambridge: Cambridge University Press.

Kelly, J., & Local, J. K. (1989). *Doing phonology*. Manchester: Manchester University Press.

Kerswill, P. (1996). Children, adolescents, and language change. *Language Variation and Change*, *8*, 177–202.

Kerswill, P. (2003). Dialect levelling and geographical diffusion in British English. In D. Britain & J. Cheshire (Eds.), *Social dialectology. In honour of Peter Trudgill* (pp. 223–43). Amsterdam: John Benjamins.

Kerswill, P., & Williams, A. (2000). Creating a new town koine: Children and language change in Milton Keynes. *Language in Society*, *29*, 65–115.

Kerswill, P., & Williams, A. (2005). New towns and koineisation: Linguistic and social correlates. *Linguistics*, *43*, 1023–48.

Kerswill, P., & Wright, S. (1990). The validity of phonetic transcription: Limitations of a sociolinguistic research tool. *Language Variation and Change*, *2*, 255–75.

Labov, W. (1969). Contraction, deletion, and inherent variability of the English copula. *Language*, *45*, 715–62.

Labov, W. (1972). *Sociolinguistic patterns*, Oxford: Blackwell.

Labov, W. (2001). *Principles of linguistic change*. Volume 2, *Social factors*. Oxford: Blackwell.

Labov, W., Yaeger, M. & Steiner, R. (1972). *The quantitative study of sound change in progress*. Philadelphia: U.S. Regional Survey.

Liberman, M. (1975). The intonation system of English. Doctoral dissertation, MIT.

Local, J., & Ogden, R. (1997). A model of timing for nonsegmental phonological structure. In R. van Santen, R. Sproat, J. Olive, & J. Hirschberg (Eds.), *Progress in speech synthesis* (pp. 109–122). New York: Springer.

Menn, L., & Matthei, E. (1992). The "two-lexicon" account of child phonology: Looking back, looking ahead. In C. A. Ferguson, L. Menn & C. Stoel-Gammon (Eds.), *Phonological Development, models, research, implications* (pp. 211–247). Timonium, MD: York Press.

Milroy, L. (2002). Introduction: Mobility, contact and language change: Working with contemporary speech communities. *Journal of Sociolinguistics, 6,* 3–15.

Nathan, G. (1988). Variability in constraint ranking as a puzzle for OT. Unpublished document. Mid-Continent Workshop on Phonology (McWOP4), Ann Arbor.

Nespor, M., & Vogel, I. (1986). *Prosodic phonology.* Dordrecht: Foris.

Ogden, R. (1999). A declarative account of strong and weak auxiliaries in English. *Phonology, 16,* 55–92.

Patterson, J. L. (1992). The development of sociolinguistic phonological variation patterns for (ing) in young children. Doctoral dissertation, University of New Mexico.

Patrick. P. L. (1999). *Urban Jamaican creole: Variation in the mesolect. (Varieties of English around the world,* G17). Amsterdam: John Benjamins.

Payne, A. (1980). Factors controlling the acquisition of the Philadelphia dialect by out-of-state children. In W. Labov (Ed.), *Locating language in time and space* (pp. 143–78). New York: Academic Press.

Pierrehumbert, J. B. (1994). Knowledge of variation. *Papers from the Parasession on Variation.* Chicago Linguistic Society, 232–56.

Prince, A., & Smolensky, P. (1993). *Optimality Theory: Constraint interaction in Generative Grammar.* Technical Report No. 2. New Brunswick/Piscataway: Rutgers University Center for Cognitive Science.

Roberts, J., (1994) Acquisition of variable rules: (t,d) deletion and (ing) production in preschool children. Doctoral dissertation, University of Pennsylvania.

Roberts, J. (1997). Acquisition of variable rules: A study of (-t, -d) deletion in preschool children. *Journal of Child Language, 24,* 351–72.

Sankoff, G. (2004). Adolescents, young adults, and the critical period: Two case studies from "Seven Up". A case study of Short A and Short U for two British speakers from age 7–35. In C. Fought (Ed.), *Sociolinguistic variation: Critical reflections* (pp. 121–39). Oxford: Oxford University Press.

Schreier, D. (2003). *Isolation and language change: Contemporary and sociohistorical evidence from Tristan da Cunha English.* Basingstoke: Palgrave Macmillan.

Schuchardt, H. (1885/1972). Über die Lautgesetze: Gegen die Junggrammatiker. Oppenheim. Reprinted and translated in T. Vennemann & T. Wilbur (1972), *Schuchardt, the Neogrammarians, and the transformational theory of phonological change* (pp. 41–72). Frankfurt: Athenäum.

Shields, M. M. (1978). The child as psychologist. Constructing the Social World. In A. Lock (Ed.), *Action, gessture and symbol* (pp. 529–56). New York: Academic Press.

Shockey, L. (1974). Phonetic and phonological properties of connected speech. *Ohio State Working Papers in Linguistics, 17,* 1–143.

Shockey, L. (1984). All in a flap: Long-term accommodation in phonology. *International Journal of the Sociology of Language, 46,* 87–95.

Shockey, L. (2003a). *Sound patterns of spoken English.* Oxford: Blackwell.

Shockey, L. (2003b). A constraint-based approach to the phonology of English accents. *Proceedings of the XVIth International Congress of Phonetic Sciences,* 2733–7.

Shockey, L., & Bond, Z. S. (1980). Phonological processes in speech addressed to children. *Phonetica, 37*, 267–74.

Shockey, L., & Gibbon, F. (1992). "Stopless stops" in connected English. *Reading Speech Research Laboratory Work in Progress, 7*, 1–7.

Simpson, A. (1992). Casual speech rules and what the phonology of connected speech might really be like. *Linguistics, 30*, 535–48.

Smith, N. V. (1973). *The acquisition of phonology: A case study*. Cambridge: Cambridge University Press.

Stampe, D. (1979). *A dissertation on Natural Phonology*. New York: Garland.

Swann, J., Deumert, A., Lillis, T., & Mesthrie, R. (2004). *A dictionary of sociolinguistics*. Edinburgh: Edinburgh University Press.

Trudgill, P. (1974). *The social differentiation on English in Norwich*. Cambridge: Cambridge University Press.

Trudgill, P. (1999). *The dialects of England*. Second edition. Oxford: Blackwell.

Trudgill, P., & Hannah, J. (2002). *International English*. Fourth edition. London: Arnold.

Vaissière, J. (1998). Synchronic variations, historical sound changes, and a suprasegmental framework. In D. Duez (Ed.), *Sound patterns of spontaneous speech* (pp. 69–82). Aix: Laboratoire Parole et Langage, CNRS.

Wakai, R. T., Lenthold, A. C., & Martin, C. B. (1996). Evoked auditory response from fetus at 34–37 weeks. *American Journal of Obstetrics and Gynecology, 174*, 1484–6.

Wang, W. S.-Y. (1977). *The lexicon in phonological change*. The Hague: Mouton.

Waterson, N. (1987). *Prosodic Phonology: The theory and its application to language acquisition and speech processing*. Newcastle upon Tyne: Grevatt and Grevatt.

Watt, D., Docherty, G. J., & Foulkes, P. (2003). First accent acquisition: A study of phonetic variation in child-directed speech. *Proceedings of the 15th International Congress of Phonetic Sciences* (pp. 1959–62). Barcelona, August.

Weinreich, U., Labov, W., & Herzog, M. (1968). Empirical foundations for a theory of language change. In W. Lehmann & Y. Malkiel (Eds), *Directions for historical linguistics* (pp. 97–195). Austin: University of Texas.

Wells, J. C. (1974). *Jamaican pronunciation in London*. Oxford: Blackwell.

Wells, J. C. (1982). *Accents of English* (3 volumes). Cambridge: Cambridge University Press.

Wright, S. (1989). The effects of style and speaking rate on /l/-vocalization in local Cambridge English. *York Papers in Linguistics, 13*, 355–65. York: Department of Language and Linguistic Science, University of York.

Yaeger-Dror, M. (1989). Real time vs. apparent time change in Montreal French. *York Papers in Linguistics, 13*, 141–51. York: Department of Language and Linguistic Science, University of York.

4
contact phonology

norval smith

introduction

The subject of *contact phonology* is a complex one. Superficially, it can be fairly simply stated as the subdiscipline of phonology that is concerned with the phonological phenomena resulting from language or dialect contact. Contact phonology is an aspect of phonology in context that is related to bilingualism and multilingualism, and to the history and development of languages and dialects. The study of contact phonology can deepen one's understanding of these areas of language while also providing theoretical perspectives on language change and the nature of phonological systems. Contact phonology is of particular interest in the current era of widespread bilingualism and adoption of English as a second language which is impacting the phonologies of many of the world's languages. However, this contact with English is only one in a long series of interactions of the phonologies of the languages of the world in the current day as well as in human history.

Phonological effects induced by contact of one language with another are a very pervasive phenomenon. Yet contact phonology has traditionally not been part of the study of phonology nor studied as a subject unto itself. This chapter represents one of the first attempts to present a unified overview of this topic.

There are two important aspects to contact phonology. The first concerns the precise nature of the linguistic contact, and the second concerns the type of phonological phenomenon that can be transferred. In this chapter, I will ignore the various types of language/dialect contact that do not result in any kind of phonological interactive effects on either of the two languages/dialects in a contact situation. The types of linguistic contact that are of interest here can be roughly divided into five types of situation:

- loanword phonology;
- areal influence;
- dialect mixing;
- language mixing;
- "simplification" due to pidginization/creolization.

Loanword phonology or *loan phonology* is concerned with the phonological strategies which make their presence felt when speakers incorporate lexical items from one language into another on a relatively large scale and in a relatively short period of time. Large-scale lexical borrowing usually takes place in situations of cultural dominance leading to adoption by the people of the dominated culture of many aspects of the ways of life and language of those of the dominating culture. Such situations may also be associated with political dominance, but are not necessarily so. Examples of situations in which large numbers of lexical items have been borrowed from one language into another are the following:

Greek > Latin	During the long period of Greek cultural influence on the Roman Empire, starting from about the second century B.C.
French > English	From the Norman Conquest in 1066 until English replaced French as the official language in 1362. At first Anglo-Norman, a form of Norman French, was the most influential; but at the end of the twelfth century Parisian French became the court language. The dominance here was in the first instance political, and secondarily cultural.
Danish > North Frisian	During the period of Danish political control of South Schleswig, up to 1864. North Frisian dialects were (and still are) spoken on the coast and islands; Danish dialects were spoken in their hinterland to the east.

Any borrowing of a word from one language to another will involve *loanword phonology* if the two languages have different phonologies. If the number of loanwords is great, this can cause lasting changes in the phonological system of the borrowing language.

Areal influence arises when a number of languages are used by people in stable and intimate contact situations in a restricted geographical area over a long period of time. Widespread intimate social contacts between speakers typically results in widespread bilingualism. The effects of such bilingualism may include increasing convergence between the phonological systems of the languages involved, eventually leading in some cases to virtual identity of the phonologies of the languages.

Dialect mixing refers to various types of mixtures. The simplest refers to the *mixing* of two local dialects, such as the dialects of two neighboring villages. This may be a local effect related to a larger scale shift, such as the *spreading* of a phonological change to new areas. Or a change in dialect may be caused by the physical *migration* of a large number of speakers of relatively uniform origin, such as the various migrations to London of speakers of East and Central Midland (Anglian) dialects which significantly altered the original Southern English (Saxon) nature of London English. A third type is *koiné* formation, where a new *standard variety* not in itself identifiable with any single dialect evolves out of a mixture of major dialects. A fourth type, related to this in that it can be described as a *regional koiné*, is due to the wearing down of local dialect features under the influence of modern communications. This is the formation of the *regiolect*, a sort of lowest common denominator of the local dialects used for regional communication and usually associated with a strong sense of regional identity. A fifth type of mixing is caused by the influence of a *standard language* on local dialects. The intense bidialectalism that often arises in cases of dialects in contact may also give rise to *hyperdialectalisms*, or pseudo-dialect forms, based on (sub-) regular phonological relationships existing across the dialects which are in contact. In dialect mixing, more than one of these situations may be involved simultaneously.

Language mixing refers to new languages that arise under conditions of bilingualism from the apparent mixture of two separate languages. The study of such languages is very recent – even more recent than the study of pidgins and creoles. Like pidgins and creoles, mixed languages were not regarded as being "proper" languages fit for scientific study. There appear to be various types (Smith, 2001), some of which are claimed to involve two separate phonological systems.

"Simplification" due to *pidginization* and/or *creolization* is a multiply tendentious topic as far as creolization is concerned. Inasmuch as creole languages are in no way simple, just different, as compared to other languages, the use of the word *simplification* is often interpreted by linguists and non-linguists alike as imputing an inferior status to these

languages. However, as we are only talking about phonology here we are on safer ground. In a recent article (Smith, forthcoming), I have argued that there is no real subdiscipline of *creole phonology* as such. The phonological effects observed in creole languages in relation to the various other languages that were involved in their creation are not a direct result of the creolization process itself, but simply normal contact effects.

With respect to the type of phonological phenomena involved, there appears to be little that cannot be affected by language/dialect contact. In the following sections, many types of contact phenomena will be illustrated with a focus on the effects on the phonological systems of the languages concerned.

loanword phonology

Loanword phonology effects vary with the number of words borrowed, and the distance between the two phonological systems concerned. Borrowing a few words from another language will not change the phonology of the borrowing language; rather, the phonology of the borrowed words will itself be adapted to fit the phonological patterns of the receiving language. If many words are borrowed, the forms of the words borrowed will likely be subject to regular *nativization processes*. This is especially likely if many speakers of the borrowing language are familiar to some degree with the donor language, without necessarily being fluent speakers of the language. It may then also be the case that the phonology of the borrowing language will be changed to some degree, depending on the number of words involved, the phonological characteristics of the two languages, and the respective status enjoyed by each of them.

english /æ/ > dutch /ɛ/

A good example, illustrating both the adaptation of borrowed words to the phonology of the importing language and phonological change induced by borrowing is Dutch, which at present has a markedly open-ended capacity for borrowing English words. The phoneme /æ/, used in both American and Southern British Standard English has no close phonetic equivalent in Dutch. Although it is functionally a low vowel in both English systems it has quite different allophones from either of the two phonologically low vowels in Dutch.

Both languages have vowel systems which are characterized by a fundamental opposition between tense and lax vowels. For the most general types of standard language in both English-speaking countries, England and America, /æ/ is a lax front vowel, pronounced between open and half-open positions. The most prestigious pronunciation of the low lax vowel in Standard Dutch, usually represented "phonetically" as an open back vowel [ɑ], is in fact closer in its phonetic value to a half-open back vowel [ʌ]. Clearly this vowel is not articulatorily or perceptually close to English /æ/. The Dutch tense low vowel /aː/, which has as its most prestigious pronunciation something approaching a cardinal low front unrounded vowel, would seem to have a more suitable quality for representing English /æ/ but is not used as a loan-equivalent. The fact that it is not a lax vowel is presumably the reason for this.

Dutch listeners are first of all confronted with English /æ/, produced not far below the roughly half-open lax mid front position of Dutch vowel /ɛ/. Secondly, they are confronted with the fact that there is another English vowel in the same area, /ɛ/, with its usual allophone in Southern English halfway between half-open and half-close positions. These two straddle the Dutch /ɛ/ phonetically, and apparently Dutch speakers cannot distinguish either of them easily from the Dutch vowel. Dutch speakers certainly have no clear insight into the place of /æ/ in the English vowel system.

English /æ/ is then borrowed into Dutch as /ɛ/, which is also used as the equivalent of English /ɛ/ itself. In other words English loans with /æ/ and /ɛ/ fall together in Dutch as /ɛ/ – e.g., the English word *access* is represented in Dutch as /ɛksɛs/. A well-known Dutch internet server is called *XS4all*, which is imagined to represent the English words *access for all*, rather than *excess for all*, which is certainly what it sounds like! Other examples of this substitution are:

(1)   *act*   εkt
         shag (tobacco)   ʃεk
         that's it (= 'that's that')   dεtsɪt

Since /ɛ/ is an existing phoneme of Dutch, no change in the Dutch phonology is implied by this substitution strategy. In the spoken English of most Dutch speakers of English as a second language, the same replacement of /æ/ by /ɛ/ also occurs, meaning that in their English phonology a contrast is lost.

english /g/ > dutch /k/

The English lax "voiced" velar stop phoneme /g/ does not occur in the native Dutch vocabulary. This represented a gap in the Dutch stop consonant system:

(2) voiceless   p   t   k
     voiced   b   d   -

Up until about 25 years ago, /g/ used to be replaced by /k/ in borrowed words, as in:

(3)   *goal*   ko:l
    game   ke:m
    gang   kɛŋ

Nowadays, the tendency is to accept /g/ into the Dutch consonant inventory as the voiced counterpart of /k/, giving the stop system:

(4)   p   t   k
    b   d   g

The above three words will now more often be realized as:

(5)   *goal*   go:l
    game   ge:m
    gang   gɛŋ

The scale of borrowing from English into Dutch, although fairly unbridled at present, will not have a major influence on the Dutch consonant system, as the languages are similar in their consonant inventories to a large extent. Apart from /g/, the only clearly new consonants are /tʃ/ and /dʒ/, and then only for some speakers. While /ʃ/ appears in English loanwords, this is familiar in Dutch as the result of the combination of /s+j/ in Dutch morphophonological processes, in addition to a number of other Frisian, French, and German loanwords.

spanish vowels > ecuadorean quechua

The situation is quite different in many languages of Latin America, where up to 40% of the vocabulary may be of Spanish origin. This massive importation of Spanish words has altered the phonology of many of these languages. The various forms of Quechua spoken in Ecuador (Stark and Muysken, 1997) provide numerous examples of Spanish loanwords and therefore the operation of loanword phonology.

One of the major differences between Spanish and Quechua concerns the vowel system. Spanish has a five-vowel system, and Quechua a three-vowel-system:

(6)   *Spanish*   *Quechua*
         i   u   i   u
         e   o
              a   a

The vowels in Spanish loans are completely "nativized" by monolingual
Quechua speakers, such that original Spanish mid vowels are changed
into the corresponding high vowels:

(7)   *Spanish*   *Quechua*   *gloss*
      celoso   siluzu   'jealous'
      compadre   cumpadri   'pal'
      convencer   cumbinsi-na   'be convinced'

spanish initial consonant clusters > ecuadorean quechua

Quechua also does not allow complex syllable onsets (initial consonant
clusters) natively. The only clusters allowed are medial ones where the
two consonants belong to different syllables. Many borrowed words
involve initial clusters, such as a liquid (/Cl-/ or /Cr-/ clusters). /Cr-/
clusters are virtually never altered in borrowed words. Whether the
greater frequency of these clusters in Spanish is responsible for this is
unclear. /Cl-/ clusters, however, are altered. Particularly in the province
of Tungurahua, the initial consonant has been dropped in various
dialects. This is also the case generally with the undoubtedly old loan
plato ('plate'), which appears in most Ecuadorean dialects as /latu/. Here
are some additional examples in which the initial consonant of a Spanish
loan has been dropped before /l/:

(8)   *Spanish*   *Tungurahua Quechua*   *gloss*
      claro   laru   'clear'
      flauta   lauta   'flute'
      floripondio   luripundiu   'Datura'
      planta   lanta   'plant'

english initial consonants > hawaiian

If the consonant system and rules of combination (the *phonotactics*) of
a language differ greatly from those of the loaning language, this can
cause the loanwords to undergo massive changes. Such effects can be

contact phonology
83

seen in nineteenth-century English loans into Hawaiian. Hawaiian only
has the following consonants:

(9) | *labial* | *coronal* | *velar* | *glottal* |
| --- | --- | --- | --- |
| p | | k | ʔ |
| | | | h |
| m | n | | |
| | l | | |
| w | j | | |

First, this system has no voiced (lax) obstruents. Any such obstruents
present in borrowed English lexical items have to be replaced in Hawaiian
by voiceless (tense) obstruents – either front (bilabial) /p/ or back (velar)
/k/. The lack of any non-front, non-back (*coronal*) obstruents has further
effects. All English coronal obstruents (/t,d,s,z,tʃ,dʒ/) are replaced by the
nearest possible obstruent, which is /k/. Additionally, no consonant
clusters or final (*coda*) consonants are allowed in Hawaiian. This
combination of prohibitions results in largescale phonological changes
in loanwords from English (Elbert and Pukui, 1979). The following
examples illustrate the substitution of /k/ for many other sounds and
changes in syllable structure to avoid consonants in clusters and in
final position:

(10) | *English spelling* | *English phonemic* | *Hawaiian* |
| --- | --- | --- |
| gasoline | /gæsəliːn/ | kakalina |
| sergeant | /sɑːdʒənt/ | kakiana |
| stocking | /stɒkɪŋ/ | kaakini |
| ticket | /tɪkɪt/ | kikiki |
| club | /klʌb/ | kalapu |
| corset | /kɔːsɪt/ | kaaliki |
| Christmas | /krɪsməs/ | kaliikimaka |

areal influence

Much of language change occurs when one dialect influences another
within a given language. Linguistic areas are created by similar dynamics
between languages as those that apply within one language between
dialects. Similar to the way that neighboring dialects influence each
other by *bidialectalism*, neighboring languages influence each other by
bilingualism.

east tucanoan sibilants > tariana

Aikhenvald (2002) illustrates the operation of areal influence in phonology from East Tucanoan languages on the Tariana language or languages (Arawak family) in the Vaupes area of Amazonia, in the Brazilian-Colombian border region. Aikhenvald describes the custom in this area that one should marry someone from a different language group. Marrying within one's own language group is regarded as incestuous. Many linguistic and cultural features of the inhabitants of this area are shared, and we can therefore speak of a Vaupes linguistic area.

Lexical borrowing is not the route by which phonological influence spread in this area. In fact, Aikhenvald states that there is a strong inhibition against borrowing forms from other languages. Widespread bilingualism among women is the explanation for the resemblances among the phonological systems of these languages in contact, as the wife learns the husband's language after marriage.

Most Tariana languages have been replaced by Tucano (East Tucanoan). Most of the remaining active speakers belong to the Wamiarikune group, with its two dialects of Santa Rosa and Periquitos. These two dialects contrast with respect to the influence of Tucano. Northern Arawakan languages (the family to which the Tariana languages belong) tend to have at least two sibilant consonants, "usually a fricative s and an affricate tʃ" (Aikhenvald, 2002, p. 37). The Santa Rosa dialect of Wamiarikune Tariana has this property too, as in the following contrasting Santa Rosa words:

(11)   ísa   'smoke'   ítʃa   'hair'
       ísi   'oil, fat'   ítʃi   'howler monkey'

Most East Tucanoan languages, in contrast, have only one fricative sibilant, s (though with affricate allophones). The Periquitos dialect shares this East Tucanoan feature, due to widespread bilingualism with East Tucanoan languages. The sibilant distinction present in Santa Rosa has been neutralized in Periquitos to /s/.

east tucanoan nasal harmony > tariana

A second feature of East Tucanoan influence on Tariana described by Aikhenvald (2002) concerns *nasal harmony*. East Tucanoan languages are famed for this feature. Once again, the Periquitos dialect parallels these features to a markedly greater degree than the Santa Rosa dialect. In the Periquitos dialect, the presence in a Tariana word of a nasal consonant or a nasalized vowel will cause all vowels to become nasalized, while /d/ and /ɽ/ are replaced by /n/ and /y/ by /ɲ/. Examples provided by Aikhenvald include the following:

(12) -tõnéta   >   tõnḛ́tã   'roll dough'
      kenõwa-na   >   kẽnõwã-nã   'a tree-like plant'
      di-yṹ   >   nĩ-ɲ ṹ   'he goes up'

western kalasha retroflex vowels

A third case of areal influence concerns phonologically retroflex vowels. Retroflex vowel phonemes are very rare among the languages of the world, but do occur in the western dialects of Kalasha, an Indo-Aryan language belonging to the so-called Dardic subgroup spoken in northwest Pakistan (Heegård & Mørch, 2004). Kalasha possesses four types of vowels – plain, nasalized, retroflexed, and nasalized retroflexed. For no other language has this last type been proven to be a separate set of phonemes, although the neighboring language of Waigali at least possesses these types phonetically. Other langues with a series of distictive retroflex vowels include the Dravidian language Badaga (Emmeneau, 1939), and the Amerindian languages Serrano (Hill, 1967) and Yurok (Robins, 1958). In Kalasha, these types of vowels are only found in the western Rumbur-Bumburet, Birir-Jinjiret and Urtsun dialects. The following table gives examples of these vowels in the western Kalasha dialects of Rumbur and Urtsun, contrasting these with the eastern Kalasha dialect of Kakatak and Kati, which is from the Nuristani language area. These dialect forms are contrasted with their historical Indo-Aryan (IA) source:

(13) Retroflex vowels in Dardic and Nuristani (V˞ = retroflex vowel)

Old IA	Rumbur	Urtsun	Kalkatak	Kati	gloss
pāṇí-	pḛ̃˞	as'pḛ̃˞	pha(:)n	duʃ'pḛ̃˞	'palm of the hand'
kilāṭa-	ki'la˞			ki'la˞:ṭ	'kind of cheese'
āṣāɖɦiya-	a'za˞i	a'za˞:i	a'za:ṛi		'apricot'
maṇí-	mã˞'(fi)ĩ˞k	'maˤĩ˞k	ma'ṛi:k		'beads'

From (13) it is clear that the retroflex vowels in the Western Kalasha dialect area derive from lost retroflex consonants in Old Indo-Aryan. The eastern dialects like Kalkatak have no retroflex vowels at all, displaying instead a variety of reflexes including retroflex consonants. To the east are languages lacking retroflex vowels, while to the west there are other languages apparently possessing retroflex vowels, such as Kati (see table) and Waigali (not shown), belonging to the Nuristani group of Indo-Aryan languages. Note that Kalasha does not belong to the same subgroup of Indo-Aryan as Kati and Waigali. This suggests that the presence of retroflex vowels is a feature that has diffused across a subfamily boundary.

the east asian linguistic area: register, tone, and monosyllabicity

In Southeast Asia we find a vast area of contact between languages and language families stretching from Southern China through Vietnam, Cambodia, Thailand, and Laos. Three examples of areal features are the development of *register systems* (involving contrasting voice quality), *tonogenesis* (development of contrasting pitch levels or contours), and a tendency to *monosyllabicity* (words of one syllable only). We can take as an illustration a case in which examples of all three can be found, the Chamic languages. These languages are Austronesian languages spoken on the Asian mainland, in Cambodia, Vietnam, and on Hainan Island in southeast China, as well as in Atjeh province on Sumatra. I will mention three Chamic languages which display phonological contact phenomena of these types.

Old Cham was the language of the former *Champa* kingdom lasting from the sixth to the seventeenth centuries. This kingdom was squeezed between various Khmer and the Vietnamese kingdoms, and, as we shall see, this has not been without linguistic consequences.

register in western cham

Western Cham is spoken in Cambodia, where its speakers are in contact with various languages belonging to the Austroasiatic family. Khmer, the main language of Cambodia, is a member of this family, and possesses a phonological feature referred to under the term *register*. *Register* in the context of this language family refers to a feature of voice quality that has developed from features of formerly present consonants and has clear phonetic similarities to aspects of *tongue root harmony* as found in many African languages. Historically, register distinctions have arisen due to a merger of voiced and voiceless initial consonants. The former voiced consonants have induced a lax, breathy *voice quality* in the following vowel, while the former (and still) voiceless consonants are associated with a tense, clear voice quality. In tandem with this, the vowels themselves are more closed in their articulation following former voiced consonants, as against more open in their articulation following former voiceless consonants. (This is similar to the situation with the feature of *advanced tongue root*, which is associated with a more closed vowel position and often with a lax voice quality.) Finally, in contrast to the voiceless consonants, the former voiced consonants are associated with a lower pitch and a lowered larynx (Henderson, 1952).

Edmondson and Gregerson (1993) identify at least the vowel height aspect as holding for Western Cham, and also the pitch difference (ignoring preglottalized voiced consonants, which retain their voicing). Tenseness differences may also exist. It seems fairly certain that this type of contrast, illustrated in (14), is due to Khmer influence:

(14)   *Western Cham* (*V* = lax, breathy vowel)
        paw   [paw]   'tobacco pouch'
        baw   [paw]   'snail'
        ʔbaw   [(ʔ)baw]   'bag'

tonogenesis in eastern cham

Eastern Cham (Phan Rang dialect; Thurgood, 1993) has moved a step further than Western Cham in the phonological effects of loss of a former voiced/voiceless consonant contrast. The phonation effect associated with original voiced stops, and seen in Western Cham, is only partially present in CV-syllables in Eastern Cham. However, there is a consistent tone opposition on the stressed syllable (the last syllable in a polysyllabic stem) between low and high tones.

If the stressed syllable began historically with a voiced stop, this syllable now has a low tone. If the stressed syllable began historically with a voiceless stop or /s/, this syllable now has a high tone. If a *presyllable* (a syllable preceding the stressed syllable) began with a voiced stop, and the stressed syllable began with a liquid or /h/, then the lowering effect of the originally voiced stop has been transferred to the stressed syllable, giving it a low tone. In addition, glottal stop finals have a pitch-raising allophonic effect, especially noticeable in the low tone, which has a rising component. Eastern Cham is in contact with Vietnamese, like Khmer an Austroasiatic language. Vietnamese has a well-developed tone system of six tones (also involving *creaky voice* or constricted vibration of the vocal cords in some cases). Thus, it can be assumed that the development of tone in Eastern Cham has occurred under the areal influence of Vietnamese.

I illustrate these tonogenetic phenomena in (15), where grave accents mark the low tones. Stressed (second) syllables with no marking have high tone. The first two examples (a) illustrate what happens when the stressed syllable was historically preceded by a voiced stop. The voicing is lost and the following vowel has a low tone. The following two examples (b) have a Proto-Chamic voiceless stop in the onset of the stressed syllable, so the tone is high. The next two examples (c) illustrate presyllables with voiced stop onsets followed by liquid onsets in the stressed syllable. Here the initial voiced stops once again cause low tones on the stressed syllable. The last example (d) has an initial voiceless stop, so has a high-toned stressed syllable.

(15)   *Proto-Chamic*   *Eastern Cham*   *gloss*
     (a)   ʔuduŋ   ʔatùŋ   'nose'
           dada   tətà   'chest'
     (b)   bituk   pətuk   'cough'
           mata   məta   'eye'
     (c)   bara   pərà   'shoulder'
           biləu   pələw   'body-hair'
     (d)   kuliːt   kəliʔ   'skin'

Note that many unstressed vowels in this language reduce to [ə]. This is also an areal tendency in Southeast Asia in general. Complete loss of such vowels is found in Rade, another Chamic language of Vietnam (Maddieson and Pang, 1993). This leads us on to the third Chamic language I want to examine here – Utsat (Thurgood, 1993).

monosyllabicity in utsat

Utsat is spoken on Hainan Island in southeast China by a small Moslem community. The other languages of Hainan are uniformly monosyllabic as to their lexical stems. These are: Southern Min Chinese; the Li, the major minority group, whose languages are distantly related to Thai; Be, another relative of Thai; and so-called "Miao-speakers" – a Yao language, part of the Miao-Yao family, whose further relationships are controversial.

Utsat is no exception to this monosyllabic tendency. Generally, the stressed syllable of the Proto-Chamic form comprises the main portion of the surviving Utsat syllable. If the Proto-Chamic form has a medial liquid and an initial stop, this has developed in Utsat to an aspirated stop (usually pronounced as a fricative; Maddieson and Pang, 1993), if the original initial stop was voiced (e.g., *phia[11]*), and as a plain stop if the initial stop was voiceless (e.g., *piu[55]*), illustrated in (16).[1] Note that there is still a partial correlation with tone such as we saw in the Eastern Cham example (15).

(16)   *Proto-Chamic*   *Utsat*   *gloss*
        mata   ta[33]   'eye'

maɲak	ɲa^{24}	'oil'
tanah	na^{55}	'earth'
basah	sa^{55}	'wet'
tikus	ku^{55}	'rat'
dada	tha^{11}	'chest'
əbus	phu^{55}	'ransom, rescue'
ʔiduŋ	thuŋ^{11}	'nose'
digəi	xai^{11}	'tooth'
labuh	phu^{55}	'fall down'
laɡah	xe^{55}	'tired'
bras	phia^{11}	'rice'
bara	phia^{11}	'shoulder'
biləu	phiə^{11}	'body hair'
bahrəu	phiə^{11}	'new'
ɡlay	xiaiʔ^{42}	'forest'
pluh	piu^{55}	'ten'

dialect mixing

Under *dialect mixing* we can distinguish four types of process. These are *koiné formation*, the similar *regiolect formation* (the formation of regional koinés), *dialect shift* (the influencing of one dialect by another), and the *influencing of standard varieties by dialect(s)*.

koiné formation

Koiné formation occurs when a new dialect is formed on the basis of a group of existing dialects, possibly with most features deriving from the politically or culturally most important dialect(s). The original Hellenistic (Greek) koiné was the first-known case of this process. The new dialect was based mainly on the Attic dialect of Athens, but combined with the phonology of the closely related dialects of Ionia (the central western coast of Asia Minor and the offshore islands). Attic Greek already had considerable status, due to the far-reaching political influence of Athens, a major player among the Greek city-states, although it was by no means always on the winning side in the frequent internecine strife in Greece, Asia Minor, and southern Italy. As far as culture is concerned, nearly all of the known Greek literature is in either Attic or Ionic. The writings of Homer, the greatest poetic work in Greek, are for example largely in Ionic. According to Joseph (1999), Athens may well have had a population of 300,000 at the height of its power in the fifth to fourth centuries B.C. Joseph estimates the total Greek-speaking population then to have been of the order of 800,000 people. If this is at all accurate, the number of speakers could also have been a factor in the dominance of Attic in later days. King Philip of Macedonia adopted Attic-Ionic Greek as the language of his court in the fourth century B.C. His son Alexander the Great continued this practice, and carried the Greek language with him in his extensive conquests in the east, using Greek as the administrative language of his new empire.

This Greek koiné, underpinning all forms of Greek spoken at the present day with the exception of Tsakonian,[2] gained in strength with the expansion of the Roman Empire eastwards starting in the first century B.C. Another factor was the growth of the Eastern Church, with Greek as its liturgical language, where Asia Minor soon became one of the main strongholds of Christianity. The emperor Diocletian divided the Roman Empire into two parts in 285 A.D. The official language of the Western Empire was Latin, while in the Eastern Empire the de facto official language was Greek, which replaced the native languages of Asia Minor, such as Lydian, Lycian, Carian, Phrygian, Galatian, and others. The koiné won out over the dialects of the old small independent Greek states, such as Thebes, Corinth, Boetia, and Lesbos, among others. The great diversity in dialects that had previously existed was eliminated, only to be replaced by a new diversity as the koiné broke up under the Ottoman Empire to the point of where dialect intercomprehensibility no longer existed in all cases.

The large number of speakers and the widespread use of Attic(-Ionic) as an administrative language enabled the markedness of the Attic (monophthongal) vowel system in the classical period to triumph over the more symmetrical vowel systems of the other dialects. The following is the koiné vowel system:

(17)   i iː   y yː   uː
        e eː   o
        ɛː   ɔː
                  a aː

There are two marked features here. The first is the occurrence of front rounded vowels /y,yː/ where all other Greek dialects except for Ionic had back rounded vowels. The second is the remarkably unbalanced nature of the system as regards long and short vowels. The monophthongization of the old diphthongs /ei/ and /ou/ had disturbed the symmetry of the earlier vowel system, giving the new long vowels /eː/ and /uː/.[3] This complex system did not last long, undergoing a wholesale realignment, and resulting eventually in the following much simpler system by the end of the Hellenistic period (Joseph, 1999):

(18)   i   y   u
        ɛ   ɔ
              a

regiolect formation

The term *regiolect* refers to a similar situation linguistically to koiné formation, but differs sociolinguistically. Hinskens (1993) suggests restricting this term to cases where the locally distinctive features of dialects are given up but where wider common regional features are preserved. In this sense, one could also speak of a *regional koiné*. Regiolects arise only in cases of strong regional identity. Hinskens discusses the case of Limburg (the Netherlands), where dialect use is widespread in informal contexts.

Hinskens (2004) also provides a smaller-scale example of such a phenomenon from the municipality of Ubach-over-Worms in south Limburg. The dialect of the larger part of the municipality belongs to the so-called "transitional zone" between the East Limburg dialects and the Ripuarian dialects.[4] In this zone, diminutives formed on stems ending in a velar consonant are realized as /-ʃkə/. In the Ripuarian dialect of Rimburg spoken in the eastern part of the municipality, the normal equivalent would involve the variant /-skə/. However, the Rimburgers are now moving towards using /-ʃkə/, like the other inhabitants of the municipality.

(19)   *Rimburg (older) Rimburg (newer) Ubach-over-Worms gloss*
        kʏkskə   kʏkʃkə   kʏkʃkə   'little biscuit'

In this case, it would probably be more fitting to describe this as a "municipiolect" rather than a regiolect, as Ubach-over-Worms is hardly to be described as a region.

dialect shift

The following discussion of German[5] dialect dynamics refers, unless specified otherwise, to a situation that reached its endpoint around the beginning of the twentieth century. The situation since then has changed vastly with the rapid expansion of Standard German through all levels of society. The viability of the numerous traditional local dialects varies; some have practically disappeared, while others remain in widespread use – for example, those spoken in Switzerland. In what follows, I make extensive use of Schirmunski (1962).

The old local dialects of Germany are divided traditionally into three groups, (i) Low German (Low Saxon, Platt(deutsch)) or *Niederdeutsch*; (ii) Middle German or *Mitteldeutsch*; and (iii) High German or *Oberdeutsch*. An equally frequent division is into Low and High, depending on whether the *High German consonant shift*, in which stops became affricates and/or fricatives, has *regularly* applied. I will return to Middle German below. The boundary between Low and High German is a very complex affair. In the central area, there is a fairly clear boundary running from west to east, but at the west end there is the famous *Rhenish Fan*, where the *phonological isoglosses*, or boundaries between different pronunciations, *fan* out to cover a large area.

Up to a point in the eastern Sauerland where all of these separate isoglosses essentially converge in their spread eastwards, the various isoglosses fan out westwards to the end of German-speaking territory. This so-called fan runs from north to south – from a point on the German/ Dutch border near Venlo in the north, to the upper reaches of the River Saar in French Alsace in the south. From north to south some of the more well-known isoglosses distinguished by German dialectologists are: the *ik/ich*-isogloss, the *maken/machen*-isogloss, the *dorp/dorf*-isogloss, the *dat/das*-isogloss, and the *appel/apfel*-isogloss.

At the eastern end of the boundary, things become much less clear. The dialects in this area are sometimes referred to as *settlers' dialects* (*Siedlungs- dialecten*). Germans of mixed dialectal origin settled in Slavic language territory (Pomeranian, Sorbian, Kassubian, Slovincian, Polish, etc.). The mixture of High and Low German dialect speakers is one reason for the sometimes less clearcut nature of the eastern German dialects.

Precisely because of this difficulty in determining the boundary between Low and High the term Middle German was devised. Middle German can be defined as those dialects in Germany between the *ik/ich*-isogloss and the *appel/apfel*-isogloss. According to Schirmunski, Middle German is basically High German on a Low German base, or *substrate*. It is largely an area that was Low German-speaking in the early Middle Ages, but in which various High German consonant-shift isoglosses have been moving northwards ever since, as is known from the historical record.

dialect shift in the halbmundart of berlin

One feature of the shifting dialect situation for German is the atypical pronunciation of the High German affricate phonemes /pf/ and /ts/ in significant portions of the Middle German area. The old city dialect (Halbmundart) of Berlin formed a High German peninsula in an otherwise Low German area of the Brandenburg region. Berlin previously had a Low German dialect. In the old city dialect, the pronunciation of the two unfamiliar High German affricates (spelled *pf* and *z*) in initial position had been as fricatives /f/ and /s/, and this substrate feature was retained.

(20)

Old Berlin dialect	German orthography	gloss
feniç	Pfennig	'penny'
flantsən	pflanzen	'to plant'
sait	Zeit	'time'
seːn	zehn	'ten'

Such fricative rather than affricate pronunciations used to be typical of Low German first-language speakers' High German generally, and this is clearly the origin of these pronunciations in the dialects in which they later occur. Furthermore, there were Low German "relic" words in this dialect, as was typical in the whole Middle German area, such as:

(21)

Berlin city dialect	German orthography	gloss
ik/ikə	ich	'I'
wat	was	'what'
et	es	'it'
ʃiːtən	scheißen	'to shit'

We know now that sound changes do not operate overnight. It is not the case that whole communities discover when they get out of bed one morning that during the night they have replaced one sound with another across the board. Sound changes operate first on some words and later on others. The changes proceed at different rates through styles of speech, age groups, and social groups, and are ultimately transmitted at a personal level through the various social networks in which speakers participate (Milroy, 1980). A sound change may lose its force before it has progressed through all the members of the relevant group of words. To judge by the relic words in numerous German dialects, extremely common function words such as pronouns are more resistant to change than the rest of the vocabulary.

dialect shift in the german dialect of wermelskirchen, rhineland

Another interesting case of what can happen near the High German consonant-shift boundary is illustrated by the dialect of Wermelskirchen near Remscheid in the Rhineland (Schirmunski 1962, pp. 287–8). In this dialect are found the shifted variant of the voiceless stops (i.e., fricatives) following short vowels and the unshifted variant (i.e., stops) following long vowels. This applies even within paradigms:

(22)	*Infinitive*	*1st Singular Present*	*1st/3rd Plural Past*	*Past Participle*	*gloss*
	ʃmiːtən	ʃmiːt	ʃmesən	jəʃmesən	'smite'
	brɛçən	brɛç	brɔːkən	jəbrɔxən	'break'

Note that the conditioning is purely phonological – depending on the length of the vowel and not on the morphological slot in the paradigm. In the first case we have an unshifted /t/ in the 1st Singular Present, and a shifted /s/ in the 1st/3rd Plural Past, while in the second case things are the other way round. Such a strict regularization occurred nowhere else in the Rhineland according to Schirmunski. Initial voiceless stops are not shifted at all, apart from a few literary loanwords:

(23)	*Wermelskirchen*	*orthography*	*gloss*
	taŋk	Zahn	'tooth'

dialect-influenced standard

The difference between dialect-shifting, or the influencing of one dialect by another, and the occurrence of a dialect-influenced standard language is a matter of degree. The perceived social status of language varieties can cause dialect shift. It was not chance that caused the isogloss between High and Low German to move continually north for hundreds of years. The fact that the High German dialects resemble Standard German phonologically to a greater degree than do Low German dialects undoubtedly was a factor. There is also only a difference of degree between a dialect-influenced standard and a regiolect as Hinskens (2004) points out.

scots > scottish standard english

A striking case of a dialect-influenced standard language is that of Scottish Standard English (SSE). This is exemplified by the native speech of the author, a middle class Glaswegian (native of Glasgow). The phonology of SSE is radically different in one aspect from all other forms of first-language Standard English spoken in Great Britain, the U.S.A., Canada, Australia, New Zealand, and South Africa.[6]

These other Standard Englishes share in general very similar vowel systems where two classes of vowels – "tense" and "lax" – are opposed to each other.

(24)

	Tense	Lax
Duration	long	short [longer before voiced consonant]
Relative height	higher	lower
Peripherality	peripheral	high vowels centralized
Homogeneity	diphthongal	monophthongal

In SSE, the oppositions of "tense" and "lax" vowels are realized partly in a different fashion (as indicated by boldface type):

(25)

	Class A	Class B
Duration	**short** [long before r,v,ð,z,ʒ,#]	**short**
Relative height	higher	lower
Peripherality	peripheral	high vowels centralized
Homogeneity	**monophthongal**	monophthongal

This gives the following differences between the Southern British Standard English (Received Pronunication – RP) and SSE:

(26)

	RP	SSE		
greet	/griːt/	[grɪit]	**/grit/**	**[grit]**
greed	/griːd/	[grɪid]	**/grid/**	**[grid]**
agree	/əgriː/	[əgrɪi]	/əgriː/	[əgriː]
agreed	/əgriːd/	[əgrɪid]	/əgriːd/	[əgriːd]
grief	/griːf/	[grɪif]	**/grif/**	**[grif]**
grieve	/griːv/	[grɪiv]	/griv/	[griːv]
grit	/grɪt/	[grɪt]	/grɪt/	[grët]
grid	/grɪd/	[grɪʴd][7]	/grɪd/	**[grëd]**

The SSE forms given in boldface type represent some of the major differences between the phonetic realizations of SSE and RP. Specifically, I have singled out the lack of phonological lengthening (or diphthongization) of tense vowels in the context before stops and voiceless fricatives, and the lack of phonetic lengthening of lax vowels before "voiced" stops. Now we have to consider why we have these differences. Let us compare the realizations of high front vowels in a number of Scots dialects located to the south of Glasgow, in Renfrewshire (R), Lanarkshire (L), and Ayrshire (A). These vowels do not in all cases correspond to high front vowels in SSE.

(27)		SSE	Eaglesham (R)	Newbigging (L)	Newmilns (A)
	beet	/bit/ [bit]	/bit/ [bit]	/bit/ [bit]	/bit/ [bit]
	dead	(/dɛd/)	/did/ [did]	/did/ [did]	/did/ [did]
	eye	(/ae/)	/ iː/ [iː]	/ iː/ [iː]	/ iː/ [iː]
	beef	/bif/ [bif]	/bif/ [bif]	/bif/ [bif]	/bif/ [bif]
	nieve (fist)	–	/niv/ [niːv]	/niv/ [niːv]	/niv/ [niːv]
	bit	/bɪt/ [bët]	/bët/ [bët]	/bët/ [bët]	/bët/ [bët]
	bid	/bɪd/ [bëd]	/bëd/ [bëd]	/bëd/ [bëd]	/bëd/ [bëd]

The small amount of data given here is sufficient to identify the Glasgow SSE vocalic system as possibly deriving from a substrate pattern similar to that found in this group of dialects. Stem-final vowels and certain "tense" vowels preceding voiced fricatives are long. All other high vowels are short. This is precisely the pattern encountered in the SSE of Glasgow (and other places). The boldface forms illustrate the lack of lengthening of tense vowels before stops and voiceless fricatives, and the lack of a voicing effect in lax vowels before voiced stops, i.e., the features of the SSE vowel system that diverge from those of other standard varieties of English.[8]

language mixing

Mixed languages are of distinct types as far as phonology is concerned. Some have inherited two phonological systems, while others clearly have a single phonology – that of one of the two contributing languages. In cases where a present-day language has inherited two phonological systems, a theoretical question is whether the language should be described in terms of two phonological systems or in terms of a split segmental phonology. This has been done in a number of Meso-American language descriptions in the past, largely for practical ease of description. The question is whether the proper way of dealing with these split systems is to distinguish strata in the lexicon parallel to those operating in English with regard to Germanic and Latinate morpheme classes, with their differing effects (e.g., on stress assignment to syllables). Or do we need parallel phonologies in some cases?[9]

two phonologies – michif

One case illustrating a mixed language with two phonologies is Michif, a language spoken in the Canadian and American border prairie provinces by members of the Métis ethnic group. The Métis are a mixed population descended from French fur traders and travelers and American Indian women. The Métis were bilingual or multilingual. Bakker and Papen (1997) presume that French and Cree were spoken by many Métis, and that there was much code-mixing. Although Michif can only be proved to have existed by 1930, the authors believe that it has existed since the early 1800s.

Michif is not directly derived from a mixture of French and Cree, but from two varieties of those languages, Métis French and a lingua franca form of Plains Cree. Métis French itself exhibits the influence of Cree or some other Algonquian language. One possible sign of Cree influence is that it has no high mid vowels /e/ and /o/. These are raised to high vowels and fall together with /i/ and /u/. Métis French also has sibilant harmony: if two sibilants are present in a word, they must be the same (either /ʃ – ʃ/ or /s – s/). For more information on Métis French, see references in Bakker and Papen (1997).

At present, a third of Michif speakers know Métis French, and only a small percentage speak Cree. Cree phonology is evidenced in Michif words of Cree origin, notably in verb forms, while French phonology is evidenced in words of French origin, notably in the noun forms.

The split phonologies present in Michif differ in both the consonant and vowel systems. The Michif-Cree consonant system is fairly minimal, with a voiceless stop-affricate series (/p,t,tʃ,k/), one sibilant and an h-sound as fricatives, two nasals, and two glides. The Michif-French consonant system is much more complex, being very similar to Standard French. It has the same four voiceless stops as the Michif-Cree part (/p,t,tʃ,k/); a full set of voiced counterparts to these; two voiceless sibilants (a "hissing" /s/ and a "hushing" /ʃ/), a voiceless labiodental (/f/), and /h/; the voiced counterparts of the fricatives (/v,z,ʒ/); four nasals (/m,n,ɲ,ŋ/); two liquids (/l,r/); and two glides (/w,j/). The Michif-Cree consonant system is a subset of the Michif-French one. We can indicate the relationships as follows, where the Michif-French consonant system is shown with consonants present in both subsystems given in boldface type:

(28)   **p**   **t**   **tʃ**   **k**
        b   d   dʒ   g
        f   s   ʃ   **h**

v	z	ʒ	
m	**n**	ɲ	ŋ
	l, r		
w		**j**	

A feature of Michif phonology derived from Métis French is sibilant harmony, as in the following words of French origin:

(29) ʃɛʃ   'dry'   < sèche
      ʃavaʒ   'Indian'   < sauvage
      zezy   'Jesus'   < Jésus
      riʃɛʃ   'wealth'   < richesse

The vowel systems of the two portions of Michif phonology (Michif-Cree and Michif-French) are not so neatly related as is the case with the consonant systems. The Michif-Cree system distinguishes long and short vowels. The long vowel system I interpret as:

(30) ii   uu
      εε   aa

The short vowel system has only one low vowel:

(31) i   u
          a

Bakker and Papen mention three nasalized vowels, but the underlying status of their [æ̃] is unclear, as they indicate that this varies with /εεn/. Clearer is the status of the other two nasalized vowels, /ĩ, ũ/.

The Michif-French vowel system is different. I interpret the oral vowel subsystem as follows (overlap with the Michif-Cree system is represented by boldface):

(32) **i**   y   (ə)   **u**
      ε   œ   **a**   ɔ

The long vowels of Standard French are absent, increasing the contrast with the Michif-Cree system.

Both the Michif-Cree and the Michif-French subsystems involve a fairly broad range of allophony. Bakker and Papen do not discuss this in any detail, so that it is not clear whether personal variation, intra-speaker variation, or variation between Michif-speaking communities is involved. With regard to the vowel /i/, Baker and Papen list both [ɪ] and [i] allophones for both Michif-French and Michif-Cree subsystems, but with a different distribution.

The status of the /ə/-like vowel is unclear, and it is uncertain to what extent it resembles its French counterpart. The nasalized vowels are as follows:

(33)   ũ

        ɛ̃   œ̃   ã

Here the relationships cannot be indicated in terms of proper inclusion. The /ũ/, which is both the only high back nasalized vowel of Michif, can be considered part of both systems. In Michif-French, it represents the back nasalized vowel of Standard French, /ɔ̃/. Michif-Cree also has a high front nasalized vowel /ĩ/, which does not form part of the Michif-French system.

one phonology – media lengua

The scond case of a mixed language that I will briefly discuss is Media Lengua (ML), a mixed language spoken in Ecuador. The component languages are Quechua and Spanish. It can be described in brief as a system with Spanish lexical items borrowed and adapted (*relexified*) into Quechua grammatical structures. Muysken (1996) puts the date of formation of Media Lengua at between 1920 and 1940. It is spoken according to him by "acculturated Indian peasants, craftsmen, and construction workers" (Muysken, 1996, p. 374). Media Lengua is spoken in villages that "are socially and geographically intermediate" (ibid.) between the Quechua-speaking rural world in high-altitude Andian settlements, and the Spanish-speaking towns on the valley floor. While some older ML speakers speak Quechua, and some young children may speak Spanish (Muysken's fieldwork is from the late 1970s), ML is not intelligible to either Quechua speakers or Spanish speakers.

Let us consider the two cases we examined previously (pp. 81–2) with reference to Ecuadorean Quechua:

(34)   The raising of Spanish /e,o/ to /i,u/ in Quechua; and
        The representation of /Cl-/ clusters.

In the first case, we find mixed reflexes, with a greater tendency for original Spanish /e,o/ to be retained in ML if the vowels are accented, as seen in the following examples:

(35)

Spanish	Media Lengua	gloss
querer	kiri	'want'
relój	reloxo	'watch'
conocer	konozi	'know'
por qué	purki	'why'
por qué	porke	'because'

In the second case, /f/, a non-native phoneme which has been borrowed from Spanish into some forms of Quechua (e.g., Imbabura Quechua, sometimes occurs in ML in onset clusters, as in /flor/ 'flower' (< Spanish flor). This is despite the fact that /f/ is often replaced by /pʰ/, as is usual in Ecuadorean Quechua, cf. ML /pʰruta/ 'fruit' (< Spanish *fruta*).

We can see that when new Spanish phonemes such as /e,o,f/ are imported into the Quechua and then the ML sound system, new phonotactic possibilities are introduced. In fact, however, these phonological innovations do not go beyond what bilingual speakers of Quechua do in any case. This is unsurprising as ML was formed by a group of bilingual speakers.

split prosody – saramaccan

Another interesting case concerns a number of aspects of the phonology of Saramaccan, a creole language spoken by maroons (descendants of runaway slaves) in Surinam, the former Dutch Guiana, in South America. This is sometimes regarded as a mixed creole, as it has two main sources of its basic vocabulary, English and Portuguese, English being the most important. However, it is mixed in more ways than one as we will see.

Saramaccan makes extensive use of tone, but it is not a straightforward case of a tone language. As has been most clearly stated by Good (2004a, 2004b), Saramaccan involves a split prosodic system. On the one hand, there are numerous words of European origin, from English, Portuguese, and Dutch.[10] On the other hand, there are two major sources of African vocabulary in Saramaccan: first, Fon, a Gbe language of Benin in West Africa; and second, probably the (Ki)Ntandu form of Kikongo, hailing from Zaire in western Central Africa.

All three European languages are stress-accent languages. This means that each word has one syllable bearing the accent. This accent, whose position is partly predictable in all three languages, is realized largely in terms of relative length and amplitude. With an intonation contour, these syllables are the ones that are aligned with the high tones of the contour. This fact will be seen to have significance in the light of the reinterpretation of the European prosody in Saramaccan.

Both of the African source languages for Saramaccan are tone languages which can be fully described in terms of two tones, high and low. Both of these languages have contributed significantly to the Saramaccan lexicon. Around 150 lexical items in Saramaccan have been identified as derived from each language, and it is certain that there are in fact more.[11]

European-derived lexical items appear in Saramaccan generally with a high tone corresponding to the position of the stress in the European language. Examples (with high tone indicated by the acute accent over the vowel) are:

(36)

Saramaccan	European language	gloss
náki	*knock* (English)	'hit'
kulé	*correr* (Portuguese)	'run'
sipéi	*espelho* (Portuguese)	'mirror'

The only general type of exception to the rule that the high tone indicates the position of the original stressed vowel are cases like the following, where an epenthetic vowel has been inserted to break up a cluster following a stressed vowel:

(37)

Saramaccan	European language	gloss
síkìsi	six (English)	'six'
wólúku	wolk (Dutch)	'cloud'

The other vowels in these words have variable tone-assignment according to their phrasal environment, but are represented as toneless in the lexicon. These words contrast significantly with predominantly (but not solely) African-derived words, which have specific tones on every vowel (mora). In the following examples, high tone is indicated by an acute accent over a vowel and low tone by a grave accent:

(38)

Saramaccan	Original language	gloss
pùkùsù	lu-mpukusu (Kikongo)	'bat'
bàndjà	mbaansya (Kikongo)	'side'
màtùtù	ma-tutu (pl.) (Kikongo)	'small rat'
zònká	zòkán (Fon)	'charcoal'

The two types of words – those which are derived from European or non-European (largely African) sources – differ in their behavior in several ways, as further explored in Good (2004a, 2004b).

simplification (or not) in creole languages

It has often been claimed that pidgin and creole languages are simpler than other languages. The term *pidgin* covers such a wide range of communication systems that it is doubtful whether any generalizations can be made about them. Moreover, the phonological changes associated with creoles by no means paint a consistent picture. Many of the so-called simplifications associated with creole languages are probably to be associated with phonological patterns present in substrate languages.

open syllable structures in saramaccan

For example, creolists have pointed out that Saramaccan favors an open syllable structure, adding a vowel to words with English final consonants, as in the following examples:

(39)	*English*	*Saramaccan*	*gloss*
	back	ɓáka	'back'
	love	lóɓi	'love'
	bed	ɓédi	'bed'

This is sometimes assumed to result from the imposition of an unmarked syllable structure on English lexical items. In fact, it more likely represents the major Fon substrate present in Saramaccan, as Fon allows only open syllables. At the same time, it cannot be denied that Fon syllable structure is unmarked, but the process of creolization does not need to be invoked to explain this fact.

complex fon labial-velar stops > saramaccan

Another illustration of the Fon influence on Saramaccan is the presence of numerous lexical items of Fon origin. Some of these preserve so-called *labial-velar* stops. These are stops with a complex articulation involving simultaneous closure at the labial and velar places of articulation. In the following examples, labio-velar articulation is indicated by /gb/ and /kp/ (acute and grave accents indicate high and low tone, respectively, as before; and a rising tone is indicated by a combination of the two):

(40)
Fon	Saramaccan	gloss
àgbàdʒá	àgbàdjá	'cartridge pouch'
àgbǎn	àgbán[12]	'dish, pot'
dénkpè	dèkpè	'dagger'

The retention of these complex sounds in Saramaccan can certainly not be regarded as representing any kind of *simplification*. The Saramaccan people were isolated from major external influences for a long period of time. This may be a contributing factor. Compare the facts in the following section.

complex fon labial-velar stops > sranan labials

Sranan is the coastal creole of Suriname. It represents the language of the former slave population in this ex-Dutch colony. Here too Fon must be assumed to have been an important substrate language. What happens to Fon labial-velar stops in Sranan? The following examples show that the complex labial-velar stops of Fon are replaced by simpler labial stops in Sranan:

(41)
Fon	Sranan	gloss
kpédʒèlùkún	pegrekú[13]	'Xylopia'
gbɔ̀ xèén[14]	bohén[15]	'cough'
lògbózò	lobóso	'rheumatism'

Is this replacement not a type of simplification? Once again, there is no reason to assume that this is the case. The explanation is surely that unlike the Saramaccans, who have a 300-year history of isolation, the language of the coastal creoles was exposed to constant influence from Dutch, which lacks labial-velar stops. Therefore, these doubly articulated stops were replaced by (plain) labials. Here we observe a case of superstrate influence, which may represent a normal or common state of affairs for a creole language.

creolization/pidginization in the southern sudan

An interesting case of pidginization/creolization concerns a number of related languages that have their common origin in Southern Sudan. Three Arabic-based contact languages are involved: (i) Juba Arabic, the lingua franca of Southern Sudan – nowadays both a pidgin and a creole; (ii) KiNubi, a creole spoken in Kenya and Uganda; and (iii) Turku, a pidgin of French colonial Chad (Owens, 1997). The basis for all three was trading camps in Southern Sudan, with the following components: Arab and Nile Nubian traders from Northern Sudan, locally recruited soldiers, numerous slaves, and other camp followers. The formative period lasted from only 1854 to about 1880, i.e., approximately one generation. Owens estimates the number of native Arabic speakers at between 10% and 25% of the population at the formative period. The population of the camps was estimated to be nearly 60,000 in 1870, of which more than two-thirds were slaves. This compares to an indigenous population in the area of about 190,000.

The *Turku*-using community was created when a traders' rebellion was defeated by the expansionistic Egyptians, who were attempting to extend their authority over the region. A group of rebel soldiers moved to present-day Chad, then attacked and took over the Kingdom of Bornu. In 1888, the Egyptian governor abandoned Southern Sudan in the face of the Mahdist uprising and crossed into Uganda with his soldiers and their camp-followers. These formed the ancestors of the present *KiNubi*. From 1893, these soldiers were co-opted into the British East Africa Company. *Juba Arabic* represents the pidgin spoken by those soldiers and camp-followers that remained behind in Southern Sudan. By 1985, Juba Arabic had become the native language of 40% of the population of the town of Juba (population 200,000), the capital of Southern Sudan.

A comparison of the phonology of KiNubi with that of Arabic reveals major differences. One of the major substrate languages is Bari, together with other Nilotic languages, but little Nilotic influence can be traced in KiNubi. As we saw above, under normal circumstances it is not usual for creoles/expanded pidgins to inherit much in the way of substrate phonology.

Among the more important deviations from Arabic are the following:

(42)   (a) KiNubi lacks the Arabic pharyngeals and pharyngealized consonants (the so-called *emphatics*).
(b) KiNubi lacks the geminate consonants of Arabic.
(c) KiNubi has a typical 5-vowel system, with only a marginal length distinction in the low vowel /a/. Nilotic languages tend to have very large vowel systems, with additional distinctions of length and tongue-root advancement.
(d) Whereas Arabic makes use of the pan-Semetic triconsonantal lexical root system, there is no sign of such a system in KiNubi. KiNubi has fully specified consonants and vowels in its lexical representations for nouns and verbs, e.g.:

kalám	'word'
bágara	'cow'
bíyo	'to buy'
áʃrubu	'to drink'

(e) The position of the accent is variable, whereas most forms of Arabic have predictable stress.

KiNubi is of special interest as a more recent case of creolization. What we see here in fact appears to be not so much simplification as the removal of the most marked phonological features of both Arabic *and* the Nilotic languages – reduction to the lowest common denominator, as it were. What in fact occurs in creolization might not be simplification but *negotiation* among speakers in the process of achieving phonological uniformity. Clearly, the numbers of speakers of the various contributing languages and other sociohistorical factors will play a significant role in determining what the end result will look like in any given case.

conclusion

Few aspects of phonology are immune from change under conditions of language contact. For this reason, it is pointless to try to list every phenomenon that is susceptible to change under contact. Nevertheless, it is worthwhile to review the types of cases described in this chapter.

We have observed contact-induced change at the segmental level. These cases included straightforward reinterpretation of foreign sounds in terms of elements of the native system, foreign sounds intruding themselves into the native system, and such intrusion forcing the reallocation of allophones to particular phonemes. We have observed the phonotactics of the native system being changed, but also native systems resisting such change, either by deleting elements or by epenthesizing them. We have observed changes such as neutralization of voicing distinctions taking place on the one hand while on the other hand new phonological distinctions of register or tone are created by promoting allophony to distinctive status. Finally, we have observed more drastic changes in phonological structure like the tendency to monosyllabicity in Southeast Asian languages.

As these many and varied cases demonstrate, language contact is the driving force behind much phonological change. It would therefore appear that the various types of linguistic contact, which have largely been ignored in mainstream linguistics in general and phonology in particular, deserve to take a more prominent place in a view of phonology geared to describing and explaining language in the real-life contexts of human interaction.

acknowledgements

I am extremely grateful to the editor for her insightful comments and critical nudgings, also to Klaske van Leyden for her assistance with the revision of the manuscript.

notes

1. The tone numbers 55 indicate a high tone, 33 a mid tone, and 11 a low tone. A rising tone starting relatively low and rising to a relatively high point is indicated by 24; a falling tone starting relatively high and falling to a relatively low point is indicated by 42. Tonal deviations, not addressed here, can also be observed.
2. Descended from the Laconian dialect of classical times, a member of the Doric group of dialects.
3. Raised from /oː/.
4. These represent a restricted extension of the German Ripuarian dialects into a strip of eastern Limburg in the Netherlands (the Kerkrade, Vaals, Bocholtz, and Rimburg area).
5. By dialects of German, I refer both to dialects of what is called High German, as well as dialects of Low German, recognized in both the Netherlands and Germany in terms of the European Treaty on Regional and Minority Languages under the name of *Low Saxon* (Nedersaksisch/Niedersachsisch).
6. Editor's note: note the discussion in Chapter 5, this volume, of the differential acquisition of Scottish English versus Southern British English vowels by second-language learners.
7. The raised single length mark indicates the longer pronunciation of the vowel before a voiced obstruent.
8. In fact, most Scots dialects do not exemplify the SSE patterns to this extent. In particular, they possess a number of unchangeable long vowels in the Class A ("tense") group. This actually makes it easier to begin to identify the geographical source of these phenomena. This has not, to my knowledge, been attempted so far.
9. A good illustration of the use of strata in theoretical work is Ito and Mester (1995).
10. Suriname was an English colony from 1651 to 1667. Portuguese Jewish planters were brought in 1665 and 1667 from Cayenne (French Guiana) to Suriname, where they acquired a large group of plantations on the middle reaches of the Suriname River. Suriname became a Dutch colony in 1667. These historical influences are the main factors explaining the presence of the various European lexical strata in Saramaccan. For more on the formation of the Saramaccan tribe, see Price (1983).

11. A recent cursory examination by the present writer of the extensive list of plant names in various languages of Suriname in van 't Klooster, Lindeman, and Jansen-Jacobs (2003) has emphasized this fact.
12. In both Fon and Saramaccan, a final *n* in the spelling indicates a nasalized vowel.
13. Sranan is basically a stress-accent language; the acute accent mark indicates the position of the stress.
14. This form is from the Gun language, and is an ideophone referring to breathing. Gun is closely related to Fon.
15. This form is from a nineteenth-century dictionary.

references

Aikhenwald, A. Y. (2002). *Language contact in Amazonia*. Oxford: Oxford University Press.

Bakker, P., & Papen, R. A. (1997). Michif: A mixed language based on Cree and French. In S. G. Thomason (Ed.), *Contact languages: A wider perspective* (pp. 295–363). Amsterdam: John Benjamins.

Edmondson, J. A., & Gregerson, K. J. (1993). Western Cham as a register language. In *Tonality in Austronesian linguistics* (pp. 61–74) Honolulu: University of Hawaii Press.

Elbert, S. H., & Pukui, M. K. (1979). *Hawaiian grammar*. Honolulu: University of Hawaii Press.

Emmeneau, M. B. (1939). The vowels of the Badaga language. *Language, 15 (1)*, 43–7.

Good, J. (2004a). Tone and accent in Saramaccan: Charting a deep split in the phonology of a language. *Lingua, 114*, 575–619.

Good, J. (2004b). Split prosody and creole simplicity: The case of Saramaccan. *Journal of Portuguese Linguistics, 11–30*.

Heegård, J., & Mørch, I. E. (2004). Retroflex vowels and other peculiarities in the Kalasha sound system. In A. Saxena (Ed.), *Himalayan languages: Past and present* (pp. 57–76). Trends in Linguistics, Studies and Monographs 149. Berlin/New York: Mouton de Gruyter.

Henderson, E. J. A. (1952). The main features of Cambodian pronunciation. *Bulletin of the School of Oriental and African Studies, 14 (1)*, 149–74.

Hill, K. C. (1967). A grammar of the Serrano language. Doctoral dissertation, University of California Los Angeles.

Hinskens, F. (1993). Dialect levelling in Limburg: Structural and sociolinguistic aspects. Doctoral dissertation. University of Nijmegen.

Hinskens, F. (2004). Nieuwe regenboogkleuren: Jonge typen niet-standaardtaal en hun taalkundig belang ('New colours of the rainbow: New types of non-standard language and their linguistic importance'). Inaugural lecture, Department of Linguistics. Amsterdam: Vrije Universiteit.

Ito, J., & Mester, A. (1995). The core–periphery structure of the lexicon and constraints on reranking. In J. Beckman, S. Urbanczyk, & L. Walsh (Eds.), *Papers in Optimality Theory* (pp. 181–210). Amherst: Graduate Linguistic Student Association.

Joseph, B. D. (1999). Ancient Greek. In J. Garry & A. Faber (Eds.), *Encyclopedia of the world's major languages, past and present* (pp. 256–62). New York/Dublin: H. W. Wilson Publishers.

Maddieson I., & Pang, K.-F. (1993). Tone in Utsat. In *Tonality in Austronesian linguistics* (pp. 71–89). Honolulu: University of Hawaii Press.

Milroy, L, (1980). *Language and social networks*. Oxford: Blackwell.

Muysken, P. C. (1997). Media Lengua. In S. G. Thomason (Ed.), *Contact languages: A wider perspective* (pp. 365–426). Amsterdam: John Benjamins.

Owens, J. (1997). Arabic-based pidgins and creoles. In S. G. Thomason (Ed.), *Contact languages: A wider perspective* (pp. 125–172). Amsterdam: John Benjamins.

Price, R. (1983). *First-time: The historical vision of an Afro-American people*. Baltimore: Johns Hopkins University Press.

Robins, R. H. (1958). *The Yurok language: Grammar, texts, and lexicon*. Berkeley: University of California Press.

Schirmunski, V. M. (1962). *Deutsche Mundartkunde: Vergleichende Laut- und Formenlehre der deutschen Mundarten*. Berlin: Akademie-Verlag.

Smith, N. (2001). Younger languages: Genetically modified. Unpublished manuscript. University of Amsterdam.

Smith, N. (forthcoming). Creole phonology. In J. V. Singler & S. Kouwenberg (Eds.), *Handbook of pidgin and creole linguistics*. Oxford: Blackwell.

Stark, L. & P.C. Muysken (1977). *Diccionario español quichua, quichua español*. Quito: Publ. de los Museos del Banco Central del Ecuador.

Thurgood, G. (1993). Phan Rang Cham and Utsat: Tonogenetic themes and variants. In *Tonality in Austronesian linguistics* (pp. 91–106). Honolulu: University of Hawaii Press.

van 't Klooster, C. I. E. A., Lindeman, J. C., & Jansen-Jacobs, M. J. (2003). Index of vernacular plant names of Suriname. *Blumea (Journal of Plant Taxonomy and Plant Geography)*, Supplement 15.

5
second-language phonology: the role of perception

paola escudero

introduction

It is well known that adult learners have great difficulty when attempting to learn the sounds of a second language (L2), as observed in the phenomenon commonly known as "foreign-accented speech." Despite the fact that adults have well-developed cognitive capabilities and have superior abilities for many complex learning and problem solving tasks, if the task is to learn the sound system of a language, adults are generally outperformed by children. How can we explain this paradox? This chapter builds a case to show that the explanation crucially involves perception.

In early phonological theory, the role of perception in explaining the performance of L2 speakers was taken seriously, as shown by the writings of Polivanov and Trubetzkoy in the first half of the twentieth century. Polivanov (1931/1964) claimed that the consonant and vowel phonemes of an L2 are perceived through the first language (L1) sound system, so that difficulties in the production of L2 sounds were viewed as a consequence of the influence of the L1 in perception. Likewise, Trubetzkoy (1939/1969) believed that inadequate production of L2 sounds had a perceptual basis, suggesting that the L1 system acted as a "phonological filter" through which L2 sounds were perceived and classified. Despite these early perception-based proposals, in the second half of the twentieth century, the focus of much research and theorizing in L2 phonology was on the production of sounds (see, e.g., Lado, 1957; Eckman, 1977, 1981; Major, 1987).

109

Increasingly, however, L2 phonologists have recognized the contribution of perception to "foreign accent," and a growing cross-linguistic speech perception literature has shown that L2 learners also have "perceptual foreign accents," i.e., the way they perceive the L2 is based on their L1 perceptual system (for a review of these studies, see Strange, 1995). As I will argue in this chapter, the origin of a foreign accent is the use of language-specific perceptual strategies that are entrenched in the learner and that cannot be avoided when encountering the sounds of a second language. Therefore, the chapter concentrates on critically discussing the issues and explanations regarding L2 perception as well as on the implications of such explanations for language teaching.

evidence for the priority of perception in phonological production

A growing body of literature supports the proposition that in both L1 and L2 phonological acquisition, perception precedes production chronologically and is a prerequisite for the development of productive control of individual sounds.[1] Within L2 phonology, a number of studies support the argument that in L2 development, perception precedes production and that a perceptual difficulty is likely to underlie the widely observed difficulty adults have in producing L2 sounds (Leather, 1999; Llisterri, 1995). Borden, Gerber, and Milsark (1983), for example, demonstrated that Korean learners' ability to identify and discriminate phonemes developed earlier and was more accurate than their ability to successfully produce L2 phonemes, thus suggesting that perceptual abilities might be a prerequisite for accurate production. Neufeld (1988) described a "phonological asymmetry" whereby learners were often much better able to perceptually detect sound errors than to avoid producing them. The same asymmetry was found for Chinese and German learners of English (Flege, 1993). In addition, a study of Brazilian and English learners of Canadian French (Rochet, 1995) established that L2 production errors were correlated with their identification errors in a perceptual task. Moreover, Barry (1989) and Grasseger (1991) reported that learners who had "well-established perceptual categories" also showed accurate production of L2 sounds, concluding that accurate perception needs to be established before accurate production takes place and, further, suggesting that perceptual tests can predict difficulties in L2 production.

Despite a large body of evidence establishing perception as the basis of production in a second language, other studies (e.g., Caramazza, Yeni-Komishian, Zurif, and Carbone, 1973; Flege and Eefting, 1987; Goto,

1971; Sheldon and Strange, 1982) have challenged the precedence of perception in L2 phonology and provided evidence that perceptual mastery does not necessarily precede, and may in fact lag behind, accurate production in L2 learners. However, these findings can be contested on the basis of a number of methodological shortcomings such as the controlled nature of the production tasks and the articulatory training undergone by the learners, which elicit highly monitored and unnatural L2 production, as well as the problematic nature of their data analyses. Furthermore, most of these studies report on perceptual findings that were conducted within a bilingual language setting, which, according to psycholinguistic evidence (Dijkstra, Grainger, and Van Heuven, 1999; Grosjean, 2001; Jared and Kroll, 2001), results in the activation of two languages and, consequently, in performance patterns intermediate between the speaker's L1 and L2 that would have not been found had the learners been in a monolingual L2 setting.

Given the number of studies showing the priority of perception in L2 phonology and the questionable nature of the studies purporting to provide counterevidence, the weight of the evidence suggests that in the acquisition of L2 phonology: (i) perception develops first and needs to be in place before production can develop, and (ii) the difficulty adult learners experience producing L2 sounds has a perceptual basis, such that incorrect perception leads to incorrect production. L2 phonologists should therefore increasingly incorporate perception into their models of learning, and give a central place to the assumption that the learner's ability to perceive non-native sounds plays a crucial role in the acquisition of L2 phonology.

learning to perceive sounds in a second language

As in learning the sounds of the mother tongue, learning to perceive sounds in a second language involves arriving at the appropriate number and type of sound categories and the appropriate mappings from the speech signal onto such categories. However, L2 acquisition differs from L1 acquisition in a number of respects, including:

(i)   The staring point, or initial state, at the onset of learning a language;
(ii) The developmental constraints affecting mature learners; and
(iii) The cognitive interplay of two language systems during acquisition.

Each of these features of L2 acquisition needs to be considered in the description and explanation of L2 sound perception.

initial state

It has been widely observed that L2 sound perception is highly constrained by linguistic experience, i.e., by the sounds and perceptual processes of the native language, and it has been standard practice to describe, predict, and explain L2 perception by referring to the already-in-place L1. For instance, Trubetzkoy and Polivanov observed that L2 learners tend to associate the sounds of the new language to the sounds of their own L1 system, and they regarded this association as the cause of the learners' divergence from native speakers of the L2. In the field of second-language acquisition, the strong role of the L1 in L2 learning has been considered an important explanatory factor underlying L2 performance. The observed phenomena have typically been described and explained through the widely used concepts of *transfer* (or *interference*) and *cross-linguistic influence*, which, in general, refer to the fact that learners will make use of their L1 to cope with the L2 learning task. However, these terms, as they stand, do not specify how much or to what extent the learner will make use of the L1. Yet the assumed degree of transfer is crucial to the explanation of L2 acquisition.

In the realm of segmental phonology, a transfer explanation is especially attractive, given that there is nowhere else in the learner's L2 where L1 influence is more obvious. Yet the specific degree and nature of L1 transfer in L2 phonology remains, to date, a controversy, as acknowledged by Archibald and Young-Scholten (2003). Assumptions about the level of L1 transfer (namely, no transfer, partial transfer or full transfer) that best represents the initial state of L2 learners will influence the assumptions that can be made about the L2 learning task and L2 development. It is important to notice that the concept of transfer can have different meanings as suggested by Hammarberg (1997), so that it could refer to a learner "*strategy*" (either conscious or unconscious), to the "*process*" of transferring L1 knowledge onto the learning of L2 phenomena, or to the "*result*" of such a process. However, most L2 proposals seem to combine all three possible interpretations in their use of the concept of L1 transfer.

developmental constraints

The most common constraints that have been claimed to apply to L2 acquisition are *maturational constraints*, referring to physiological changes taking place – particularly, in the brain – as one matures. Most proponents of these constraints point at the fact that adults are not nearly as efficient language learners as children and explain the lack of efficiency in adults on biological and neurological grounds. For example, Penfield and Roberts (1959) claimed that an innate, *biological clock* for language learning allowed direct learning from the input until approximately the age of 9, with later ages of learning resulting in progressively poorer attainment levels. Lenneberg (1967) suggested that this loss of predisposition for language learning was due to the completion around puberty of *hemispheric lateralization*, the specialization in most humans of the two hemispheres of the brain for different functions. Lenneberg labeled the period between two years of age and puberty a *critical period* for language acquisition. This idea led him to formulate the *critical period hypothesis* (CPH), which claims that only before puberty can learners acquire a language automatically from mere exposure to the linguistic input around them. Other scholars have spoken of a *sensitive period or periods* (e.g. Long, 1990) for language acquisition.

Despite the obvious need for postulating age-related constraints on language acquisition, it seems controversial to claim that biological or neurological constraints act alone, as social, psychological, input, and language use factors are correlated with the observed decline in language acquisition capabilities. Moreover, there may be no categorical loss of language acquisition abilities at a specific age, but rather a continuous decrease in the probability of mastering an L2 at a native level of proficiency. This is in fact what is suggested in a recent review and proposal on maturational constraints in L2 acquisition by Hyltenstam and Abrahamsson (2003), who claim that there is a continuous *maturational period* which predicts that acquisition will be increasingly difficult with increasing maturation. However, they remain neutral with respect to the exact levels of L2 attainment that are possible after puberty because other non-maturational constraints can influence the end result (ibid., pp. 575–6).

Input constraints constitute an important type of non-maturational constraint, which is the linguistic evidence needed for language learning to occur. It seems that L1 learners need only *positive evidence*, i.e., exposure to speech around them (*ambient language*), in order to learn their native language, while L2 learners seem to need *negative evidence*, i.e., corrections or specific instruction, in order to learn a second language. In the area of input, other important issues need to be considered, such as the type of positive evidence given to an adult L2 learner, the relative use by and around the learner of L1 and L2, and the relative amount of exposure to the two languages – all of which may be crucial in determining level of proficiency in an L2.

Learnability constraints are at the core of the question of how L2 learners develop from an L1 transfer initial state to more closely approximate native-level knowledge and performance in a second language. Whether or not a native level of knowledge and performance are achieved, in order to learn a second language, some kind of a learning mechanism must be in place. Following a generativist perspective on language learning, some L2 researchers have proposed that L2 learning may or may not be guided by the set of principles or mechanisms that compose *universal grammar* (UG), which are universal, innate, and specific to the faculty of language. Several researchers have proposed that learners have *full access* to UG in L2 acquisition (see, e.g., Schwartz & Sprouse, 1996). However, as White (2003) rightly points out, the learner needs both a set of universal restrictions or principles defining possible grammars and a learning device. From a UG (*nativist* or *innatist*) perspective, such a device will function as a triggering or accessing device to select among the possible types of grammars.

In current phonological theory, learning devices have been proposed in the form of algorithms which analyze and modify the rules or constraints that constitute the developing grammar. An example of such a learning algorithm within a nativist or UG perspective is Tesar and Smolensky's (2000) *Constraint Demotion Algorithm*, which works within a description of phonological knowledge as developed in *Optimality Theory* (for an introduction, see Kager 1999). Alternatively, an *emergentist* account (for a review see MacWhinney, 1999) proposes that learning occurs in a bottom-up fashion, i.e., the learner's knowledge of an L2 changes with environmental input, by means of a general cognitive learning device, i.e., an algorithm or mechanism that is not specific to language.

the cognitive interplay of two language systems

If both L1 and L2 sound categories and perceptual processes are represented as knowledge in the learner's mind, the next natural question is how these two systems relate to each other. Presumably, they both belong to the linguistic faculty, but do L2 learners have a single perceptual system or two systems? The amount of separation or integration assumed between the L2 learner's phonological systems influences the level of perceptual proficiency that a learner can have in both languages. This type of constraint can be termed a *representational constraint*. Cook (2002) proposes that there are three logical possibilities for the representational status of two or more language systems. Figure 5.1 is an adapted version of a figure from Cook (2002, p. 11), which shows the possibilities of separated or connected L1 and L2 representations and includes an additional possibility of *mixed representations* as *merged* (or *integrated*, in Francis' terminology).

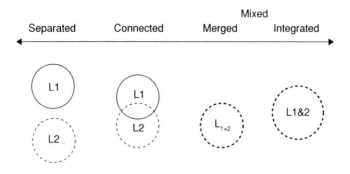

Figure 5.1 Possible cognitive status of sound categories and perceptual processes in L2 learners and
bilingual speakers (adapted from Cook, 2002, p. 11)

It is a matter of debate which of these possibilities best describes the
knowledge or performance of L2 and bilingual speakers; and we will see
that assuming one of these possibilities crucially shapes the explanations
of L2 perception discussed in the next section. In a *separated* systems
view, L1 and L2 sound categories would be seen as belonging to distinct,
autonomous systems. On the other hand, the *mixed* view advocates that
L1 and L2 sound systems are, in fact, a single representational system.
This perspective has, in turn, two possibilities – namely, *merged* or
integrated systems. Merged representations imply no language differentiation, whereas integrated representations imply language specification
within a single combined system. Within a less extreme perspective, such
as the *connected* view, L1 and L2 representations are mostly distinct but
may share some elements or properties, as shown by the intersection in
the figure.

explaining L2 sound perception

In this section, I review six different models that aim to explain non-
native or L2 sound perception, among which a new phonological
proposal that incorporates phonetic and psycholinguistic insights. For
each model, I critically discuss the view of perception, the proposal for
the L2 learning task, the interpretation of the L2 learning constraints
just reviewed, and the predictions and supporting evidence for the initial
state and development over time.

the ontogeny model

Roy Major's Ontogeny Phylogeny Model (OPM; Major, 2001, 2002)
attempts to describe the principles involved in the formation of L2

phonological systems, the change in L1 that results from exposure to L2, as well as language contact phenomena such as bilingualism and multilingualism. Major (2002, p. 88) states that the model is purposely not described in terms of the mechanisms of any linguistic framework so that its claims can survive beyond the life of any specific theory. Major explicitly states that the model makes very general claims without any details concerning specific phenomena such as fine-grained phonetics. He argues that this is a virtue of his model rather than a weakness because the model provides a macroscopic framework for testing individual phenomena. However, since the main input to the phenomenon of L2 perception that interests us here is the fine-grained phonetic information in the speech signal, it seems of importance to provide a more explicit proposal regarding the role of perception in the development of phonological competence.

In Major's model, one of the main tenants is the involvement of universal principles in the formation of phonological systems. It is proposed that L1 and L2 acquisition are aided by a set of innate linguistic universals which provide the L1 learner with a head start. These comprise: a universal grammar (UG), as well as learnability principles, markedness, underlying representations, rules, processes, constraints, and stylistic universals (all of them presumably specific to the faculty of language). For perception, it seems that markedness may not play a role, unless some auditory events could be described as more marked than others. If so, such events would perhaps be better described in terms of frequency and/or saliency. In general, representations as well as processes would need to be considered components of a possible explicit proposal for the knowledge underlying perception.

Although almost all of the supporting evidence comes from production data, the model also addresses L2 phonological competence for the perception of L2 sounds. Major's explanation for the finding of phoneme boundaries in bilingual perception that are intermediate between monolingual L1 and L2 boundaries, as reported in Caramazza et al. (1973) and in Williams (1977), provides a starting point for a proposal about L2 perception. According to Major, this intermediate performance in perception can be explained by the OPM's proposal of partially merged L1 and L2 systems (Major, 2002, p. 82): each of the bilingual's phonological systems is proposed to have a component of the other system (but see the Linguistic Perception model below).

With respect to L2 development, Major proposes that the development over time of the three components of the L2 phonological system – i.e., the L1 system, the L2 system, and the universal system (U) – will be different for different learning scenarios. It is proposed that L2 learners could be faced with three learning scenarios, namely "normal", "similar," and marked, depending on the nature of the linguistic phenomenon to be learned. If the L2 phenomena to be learned are "normal," i.e., dissimilar to L1 phenomena and not typologically rare, acquisition is guaranteed and L2 development will occur through:

(i)   the declining influence over time of the L1 component;
(ii)   an increase followed by a later decrease in influence of the U component over time; and
(iii) the increasing influence of the L2 component.

Relative to this "normal" scenario, L2 phenomena that are either "similar" to L1 phenomena or "marked," i.e., relatively rare linguistically (Major, 2002, p. 76), are predicted to be acquired more slowly. At the stage at which L2 "normal" phenomena would have been acquired, the learner's system for "similar" and "marked" phenomena would still be developing under the control of not only the L2 but also the L1 and U.

Despite the clear predictions for the different L2 scenarios, the learning mechanisms that trigger the decrease and increase in influence of the three components are not proposed, nor is there a proposal for the role of input in development. In addition, the "similar" scenario may not be more difficult or demand more time than the "normal" scenario, if acquisition of a typologically similar language item demands only the adjustment of already existing structures, while acquisition of a typologically distant language item implies the formation of new knowledge, which takes considerable time.

the phonological interference model

Unlike Major's theory-free and rather general proposal, Cynthia Brown's Phonological Interference Model (PIM; Brown, 1998) addresses speech perception through the formal means of phonological theory. The model aims to explain the origin of the influence of L1 phonology on the acquisition of L2 segments as well as to identify the level of phonological knowledge involved in such L1 influence. In the non-linear phonological framework of the model, that of *feature geometry* (Clements, 1985), it is assumed that phonemes have an internal structure composed of a hierarchy of phonological features which are contained in the phonological component of UG. In addition, Brown's model considers a two level process of mapping and categorization of speech sounds, in which the phonological structure mediates the perception of speech sounds, as shown in Figure 5.2.

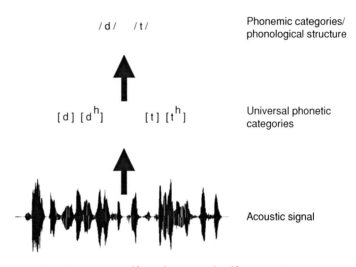

Figure 5.2 Brown's proposal for speech perception (adapted from Brown, 1998, p. 148)

As can be seen, Brown suggests that the acoustic signal is first broken down into universal phonetic categories by means of an auditory discrimination mapping (represented by the lower arrow). Then, these phonetic stimuli are processed at the second level (upper arrow), which consists of the speaker's feature geometry, or phonological structure. Within this proposal, the first mapping – that of auditory discrimination – is considered non-linguistic and non-cognitive, i.e., it is a general auditory process of discriminating sounds, whereas the second mapping is considered linguistic, i.e., it is language-specific.

With respect to the acquisition of perception, Brown and Matthews (1997) argue that the child starts out with a universal feature geometry, provided by UG, which is expanded over the course of acquisition until the adult feature geometry for the particular language is attained. It is argued that L1 development is guided by the particular dependency and constituency relations encoded in UG (Brown, 1998, p. 144) and by the child's detection of contrastive use of segments in the input. However, it is not clear how exactly the child would "detect" a contrast in the input so that additional structure can be incorporated into the developing phonological grammar. Regarding L2 perception, Brown argues that the L1 feature geometry, or phonological grammar, maps the L2 input onto existing L1 phonological categories and consequently eliminates the ability to perceive cues in the acoustic signal that could trigger L2 acquisition. Brown further proposes that if the distinguishing feature of a non-native contrast exists in the L1 grammar as a feature used for other L1 contrasts, then the L2 contrast will be perceivable and so will not be merged into the L1 category.

As an example, Brown compares the perception of English /r/ and /l/ by Chinese and Japanese learners. The English contrast is signalled by a difference in the place of articulation for /r/ but not /l/ as retroflex and thus coronal. Unlike Japanese, Chinese has a contrast that is also specified by the feature of retroflex versus non-retroflex (or coronal), i.e., alveolar versus retroflex sibilants. It is therefore predicted that Chinese but not Japanese learners should acquire the non-native (English) contrast of /r/ and /l/, based on the contrastive feature of retroflexion or coronality shared with the native language. Brown's results showed that indeed only Chinese learners were able to accurately discriminate the English contrast (Brown, 1998, pp. 155–70). However, Brown's results could still be interpreted as showing that Chinese learners map the two English consonants onto two different L1 categories, whereas the Japanese map them onto a single one. Additional experiments in the cross-language perception of monolingual Chinese and Japanese listeners would help to decide the issue.

Within Brown's model, no explicit proposal for the interplay between the L1 feature geometry and the developing L2 geometry has been made, and it is not clear whether L1 structures would be modified as they are redeployed to constitute L2 representations. In addition, Brown suggests that L2 phonologists should concentrate on non-native contrasts in which one of the members of the contrast is a phoneme in the learner's L1 because they provide a window to explaining how L1 features can enable L2 development. This would mean that the model could not account for the learning of new L2 features, such as the acquisition of vowel length categories in speakers of languages which do not distinguish between the duration of vowel sounds (e.g., Spanish, Polish, and Portuguese).

the perceptual assimilation model

Catherine Best's Perceptual Assimilation Model (PAM; Best, 1995) attempts to account for the observed performance in the perception of diverse non-native contrasts. Based on the frameworks of *Articulatory Phonology* (Browman and Goldstein 1989) and the *ecological approach* to speech perception, also called *direct realism* (Fowler, 1986), it is argued that an adult listener has no mental representations for perceiving speech, but rather directly seeks and extracts the patterns of articulatory gestures and gestural constellations from the speech signal. This direct realist, non-mentalist proposal contrasts with the mentalist and abstract speech

---

perception proposals of the OPM and Brown's phonological interference model. Unlike Major's and Brown's model, the PAM explicitly proposes that perceptual learning in infants and children leads to language-specific perception, as the child automatically recognizes the pattern of articulatory gestures in the language environment. With respect to cross-language or non-native perception, the language-specific organization of articulatory events is proposed to lead to a lack of similar efficiency in finding familiar gestural patterns in non-native speech.

The model's central premise is that listeners tend to *assimilate* non-native sounds to the native sounds that they perceive as most similar. The model defines "perceptual similarity" in terms of dynamic articulatory information, i.e., in terms of the ways in which articulatory gestures shape the speech signal. Thus, regarding cross-language and L2 perception, the PAM proposes that accuracy in the discrimination of non-native sounds depends on the way they are assimilated to L1 sounds. It can be interpreted from this proposal that successful L2 sound discrimination is the basis for L2 perceptual success. With respect to cross-language perception, it is predicted that different degrees of sound discrimination will be found depending on which of the patterns of assimilation has been applied. Thus, for instance, if two foreign speech sounds are assimilated to two different native sounds, or phonemes, discrimination is predicted to be excellent, whereas if two sounds are assimilated to a single native category, discrimination will be poor.

The Perceptual Assimilation Model does not provide a clear mechanism for L2 development since its main aim is to predict and document cross-language perception, although Best and Strange (1992) suggest that exposure to L2 input (i.e., experience with the L2) may lead to the reorganization of perceptual assimilation patterns. However, neither the mechanism of such L2 reorganization nor its effect on L1 perception are addressed, and, crucially, a proposal for the extraction of the articulatory features for two languages is not considered.

the native language magnet model

Patricia Kuhl's Native Language Magnet model (NLM; Kuhl, 1991, 2000) aims at explaining the development of speech perception from infancy to adulthood. It is proposed that complex neural perceptual maps underlie the perception of auditory events, and that such neural mappings result in a set of abstract phonetic categories. Adult perception is seen as a language-specific process because infants learn the perceptual mappings of their ambient language (Kuhl, 2000, p. 11854). Kuhl's NLM proposes that, as a result of the emergence of neural maps to perceive the speech signal, perceptual representations are stored in memory, and these are the basis of the learner's development of sound production. Because perceptual mappings differ substantially for speakers of different languages, the perception of one's primary language is completely different from that required by other languages (Iverson and Kuhl, 1996). Kuhl (2000) emphasizes the language-specific nature of perception, further claiming that "no speaker of any language perceives acoustic reality; in each case, perception is altered in service of language" (p. 11852).

With respect to L1 acquisition, unlike the PAM, Kuhl's proposal considers the mechanisms underlying the learning of language-specific perception. It is proposed that the child engages in learning processes that lead to the emergence of a speech perception system and perceptual representations. Kuhl puts forward a body of evidence (e.g., Saffran, Aslin, and Newport, 1996) showing that infants acquire sophisticated information from the signal through the detection of the distributional and probabilistic properties of the ambient language as they seek to identify higher order units and categories. It is proposed that infants' perception becomes language-specific through the categorization, statistical processing, and resulting perceptual reorganization of the acoustic dimensions of speech that take place between the ages of 6 and 12 months. However, no formal proposal for the underlying mechanisms of these learning processes is offered.

With respect to L2 perception, the learning task within the NLM is to create a new perceptual system that can map the new language onto the appropriate phonetic categories. In Kuhl's view, the existence of an L1 language-specific perceptual filter will make learning an L2 difficult because later learning is constrained by the initial mental mappings that have shaped neural structure. That is, the model proposes that perceptual experience constrains future perceptual learning (e.g., L2 learning) independent of a strictly timed period. This argument gives an alternative explanation to "maturational constraints," i.e., the existence of a "critical period" for language learning, which have been commonly proposed to underlie the fact that adults do not learn languages as naturally and efficiently as children, as mentioned above. However, Kuhl (2000) also suggests that early in life, interference effects are minimal and two different mappings of the acoustic signal to different languages can be acquired, whereas when a second language is learned later in life (after puberty) separation between the two perceptual systems may be required to avoid interference. This difference has been shown in brain imaging studies demonstrating that only adult bilinguals who acquire both languages early in life activate overlapping regions of the brain when processing the two languages (Kim, Relkin, Lee, and Hirsch, 1997).

Despite its enlightening proposals, the NLM does not address the learning mechanism by which L2 experience can create new mappings appropriate for the L2. It may be reasonable to assume that L2 learning would occur through similar mechanisms to those found in L1. However, since Kuhl's proposal suggests that creation of new L2 mappings is more difficult after puberty and may require additional mechanisms (Kuhl, 2000, p. 11856), a more explicit proposal for L2 learning is needed. In addition, the model does not consider how the separation of perceptual mappings for two languages and the activation of overlapping regions of the brain are achieved, nor how these may be influenced by different levels of L2 proficiency.

the speech learning model

James Flege's Speech Learning Model (SLM) has been primarily concerned with ultimate attainment in L2 production (Flege, 1995, p. 238) and, more recently, with ultimate attainment in L2 perception (Flege, 2003). Flege has therefore concentrated on bilinguals who have spoken their L2 for many years and not on beginning learners. For him, sound perception is defined as the discerning of the phonetic features or properties in the signal that make it possible to identify the appropriate "positional-defined allophones" or "phonetic categories" of the language. In the SLM proposal, just as in Brown's model, there is no explicit proposal for how phonetic discerning or processing (i.e., the extraction of phonetic information for categorization) works. Neither does it propose how the degree of *perceived phonetic distance* can be measured, although the SLM suggests possibilities such as auditory, gestural, and phonological metrics for such perceived distance. In agreement with the PAM and the NLM models, Flege assumes that perception is language-specific and that therefore L2 perception problems do not have a general auditory basis (Flege, 1995, p. 266).

With respect to L1 acquisition, the model seems to assume the same learning processes and mechanisms proposed by the NLM model, namely, the ability to accurately perceive featural patterns in the input and to categorize a wide range of segments (Flege, 2003). However, no formal proposal for the mechanisms behind the learning of L1 perception is associated with the model, apart from the claim that perception is dominated by "equivalence classification," a mechanism that leads to the categorization of acoustically different tokens into the same abstract category (Flege, 1987, 1995). With respect to the proposal for L2 learning, the SLM has a strong perceptual component. Its basic tenant is that L2 production errors result from inaccurate L2 perceptual "targets," which, in turn, result from a failure to discern the phonetic differences between pairs of distinct L2 sounds or between non-identical L2 and L1 sounds. It is argued that learners relate L2 sounds to L1 positional allophones, and L2 perceptual failure occurs when the L1 phonological system filters out the distinctive features or properties of L2 sounds. However, the exact workings of such perceptual filtering are not discussed.

The SLM proposes that adults retain the capacity which infants and children make use of in acquiring their L1, including the learning of accurate perception of the properties of L2 speech sounds and the formation of new phonetic categories (see Flege and MacKay, 2004, for recent supporting evidence). L2 development is, however, constrained by four main factors: perceived cross-language similarity, age of arrival, L1 use, and the storage of L1 and L2 categories in a common phonological space. The first factor deals with the ability to discern the phonetic differences among L2 sounds or between L2 and L1 sounds depending on the degree of perceived cross-language phonetic similarity. The greater the perceived phonetic dissimilarity of an L2 sound from the closest L1 sound, the more likely it is that a new category will be created for an L2 sound (Flege, 2003). In support of this contention, Flege (1987) showed that native English learners of French could produce French /y/ more accurately that French /u/ because French /y/ is perceptually more distant from the closest English vowel than is the French /u/, which has a near (but not identical) counterpart in English /u/. However, no cross-language perceptual data was gathered to support Flege's interpretation of the L2 production data.

The second factor, age of arrival (AOA), predicts that native-like L2 perception will be more likely in learners who have an early (normally before puberty) AOA in the L2 community than in learners with a late AOA (after puberty) AOA (see Flege and MacKay, 2004, for recent supporting evidence). The state of development of L1 sound categories at the time of arrival in the L2 environment will influence the accuracy of L2 perception: the more developed the learner's L1 categories are, the more likely they are to block the formation of new categories for L2 sounds. With respect to the third factor, L1 use, it is predicted that learners who frequently use their L1 will be less likely than those learners who rarely use their L1 to attain a native level of L2 perception. Flege and colleagues (Flege and MacKay, 2004; Piske, MacKay, and Flege, 2001) found that learners who frequently used their L1, in contrast to those who infrequently used their L1, differed from native speakers in their perception of the L2.

Finally, the SLM proposes that L1 and L2 phonetic categories are represented cognitively in a common phonological space so that both systems will mutually influence one another. As a consequence, it is predicted that when a new phonetic category is established for an L2 sound that is close to an L1 sound, *dissimilation* will occur (Flege, 2002, 2003), causing the bilingual's L1 and L2 phonological categories and their L1 and L2 perception to be different from those of native speakers of each of the two languages (Flege, Schirru, and MacKay, 2003). Also, if a new category is not established for an L2 sound which differs audibly from the closest L1 sound, an experienced L2 learner will develop a "composite" (i.e., merged) category as a result of *assimilation* (Flege, 1987; MacKay, Flege, Piske, and Schirru, 2001). Flege (1995, 2002) argues that the principles of assimilation and dissimilation and the existence of a common L1-L2 phonological system may underlie Grosjean's (1999) claims that there can be no "perfect" bilingual, i.e., one who performs like a monolingual in both of their languages. Rather, since the bilingual's two systems are always both engaged at the same time, the "mixing" of L1 and L2 is inevitable. However, Grosjean's claims clearly refer to online performance rather than cognitive representation of the two languages. Therefore, concluding that bilinguals have a single cognitive representation for L1 and L2 phonetic systems seems rather extreme.

the linguistic perception model

The model of Linguistic Perception (LP) aims at describing, explaining, and predicting the knowledge underlying speech perception and the acquisition of this knowledge in learning a first or a second language. The LP model is embedded in the theoretical framework of *Functional Phonology* (Boersma, 1998), which claims that cognitive linguistic knowledge underlies speech perception. According to the LP model, the language-specific knowledge underlying speech perception comprises (i) a linguistic and grammatical processor, i.e., a *perception grammar*, which maps (i.e., categorizes) the variable and continuous acoustic signal; and (ii) perceptual representations or perceptual input, depicted in Figure 5.3. The perception grammar embraces psycholinguistics, phonetics, and phonology since it:

- incorporates "processing" into linguistic knowledge (*psycholinguistics*);
- contains "cue constraints" which are expressed in phonetic terms (*phonetics*); and

- expresses language-specific phenomena through formal linguistic means (*phonology*).

Within the LP model, the representations of sounds could vary in nature and degree of abstraction depending on the acoustic properties and feature combinations of auditory events in the language environment (Boersma, 1999). In addition, it is assumed that perception is a process mediating between (i) the acoustic-phonetic input in the outside world and (ii) the perceptual representation of language sounds, which, in turn, act as the input to (iii) the recognition system, which is responsible for accessing words in the mental lexicon, as shown in Figure 5.3.

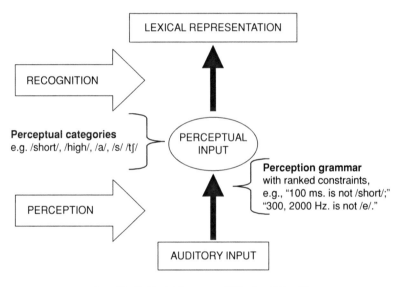

Figure 5.3   The Linguistic Perception model (Escudero 2005, p. 43)

According to the model, the acoustic signal is linguistically analyzed bottom-up without top-down application of lexical knowledge, which is compatible with many psycholinguistic models (e.g., Norris, 1994; models in McQueen, 2004). With respect to the workings of the perception grammar, it is proposed that an *optimal listener* will construct the perceptual categories that are most likely to have been intended by the speaker and thus will pay attention to the acoustic cues that are most reliable in the environment when perceiving sound segments (Escudero and Boersma, 2003). For example, Scottish English (SE) speakers pronounce the vowels /i/ and /ɪ/ with almost the same duration and with a very different vowel height, whereas Southern British English (SBE) speakers make a large duration distinction and a smaller height distinction between the two vowels (Escudero and Boersma, 2003). Therefore, the model predicts that SE will rely almost exclusively on height and hardly at all on duration when distinguishing the two vowels, whereas SBE listeners will rely more on duration and less on the spectral cue, which is confirmed by findings reported in Escudero (2001). According to Escudero and Boersma (2003), a perception grammar contains *cue constraints* that implement optimal perception and integrate multiple language-specific acoustic dimensions into phonological categories.

With respect to L1 acquisition, Boersma, Escudero, and Hayes (2003) extended the Linguistic Perception (LP) model to account for the developmental path that an infant follows when learning to perceive sound categories. It is assumed that sound categories and linguistic perception emerge from the learner's interaction with adult speakers and are not innately given to the newborn. Thus, a child needs to construct abstract representations of the sounds of the native language by creating a perception grammar, a process that is achieved through two learning mechanisms that are implemented sequentially by the Gradual Learning Algorithm (GLA; Boersma and Hayes, 2001). That is, the GLA acts initially as an identity matching and distributional learning device fed by the patterns and frequency distributions of the acoustic events in the linguistic input. This auditory-driven learning, based strictly on the patterns of sound in the ambient language, results in the "warping" of the infant's perceptual space so that F1 values of the acoustic input will be mapped onto the closest values of distributional peaks.[2] Second, once an abstract lexicon is in place in the learner's cognitive system, it can act as a reference system for achieving a more accurate perception grammar. This is achieved through the re-ranking of perception grammar constraints performed by the GLA.[3]

With respect to L2 learning, Escudero and Boersma (2004) and Escudero (2005) propose an L2 version of the Linguistic Perception model (L2LP) which involves the three[4] components of:

(i)   *Full Copying* of the L1 perception grammar and lexical representations as the basis for a new perceptual system for L2;
(ii) *Full Access* to all mechanisms of L1 learning;
(iii) *Full Proficiency* in both L1 and L2 under conditions of high usage of both.

For the L2 initial state, it is proposed that the learner automatically creates a "copy" of the L1 perception grammar and the L1 representations when starting to learn an L2. This means that the L2 perception is handled from the beginning by a separate perceptual system which began as a copy of the L1 system but evolves with experience with the L2. With respect to L2 development, it is proposed that L2 learners have access to the same learning mechanisms, performed by the GLA, that were available for L1 learning – namely, auditory-guided category formation and lexicon-guided boundary shifting for phonological categories. With respect to ultimate attainment in the L2, it is proposed that native or native-like perception in a learner's two languages is possible because L1 and L2 constitute two separate systems (i.e., two separate sets of perceptual categories and two perception grammars). Both L2 development and L1 stability are predicted provided that the two languages are each used on a regular basis.

In support of Full Copying, Escudero (2001) showed that Spanish learners of Scottish English (SE) had native-like perception of SE /i/ and /ɪ/, while Spanish learners of Southern British English (SBE) used only duration differences to identify the SBE versions of these same vowels. These findings suggest that these learners reuse their Spanish perception grammar and therefore perceive the SE vowels as the two Spanish vowels /i/ and /e/ but perceive the SBE vowels as Spanish /i/, as proposed in Escudero (2001) and Escudero and Boersma (2004). The PAM describes these different L2 patterns as two-category and single-category assimilations, while the SLMs refers to them as "similar" sounds and "new" sounds, respectively. In addition to giving a definition for them, the L2LP model provides the mechanism and the formalization for the different developmental paths in learners faced with these two different scenarios. Furthermore, the model considers the case of Dutch learners of Spanish as a different (i.e., a third) L2 learning scenario (see Escudero, 2005, for a detailed description of the three learning scenarios for L2 sound perception).

Regarding Full Access and Full Proficiency, Escudero and Boersma (2002) showed that the /i/-/e/ category boundaries of Dutch learners of Spanish shift to a native-like location in advanced learners. In addition, Escudero (under review) shows that in a "similar" scenario, advanced Canadian English learners of Canadian French shift their initial L1 category boundaries to match those of native listeners. These studies suggest that previous findings (see, e.g., Caramazza et al., 1973; and Flege and Eefting, 1987) of non-native performance in the same scenario can be disputed. Escudero and Boersma (2002) and Escudero (under review) also tested the L1 perception of the L2 learners and found that they had monolingual-like category boundaries. The reason why these two studies find Full Proficiency in the learners' L1 and L2 is because they controlled for "language modes" (Grosjean, 2001): the learners were conditioned to think that the only language they were hearing was either their L1 or their L2 but never both (see Escudero, 2005, for a discussion). Thus, the L2LP model's three hypotheses are born out because: (i) L1 and L2 constitute two separate systems given that the learner's L1 does not get affected (*Full Copying*); (ii) L2 learners develop through the same mechanisms observed in L1 acquisition (*Full Access*); and (iii) both L1 and L2 can be optimal (*Full Proficiency*).

the role of linguistic perception in teaching and training l2 phonology

It has been shown that training L2 listeners with tokens that have been acoustically manipulated in order to display exaggerated properties results in successful L2 perceptual processing (McClelland, Thomas, McCandliss, and Fiez, 1999). Furthermore, presenting L2 listeners with multiple instances of L2 sounds produced by different talkers and in different contexts also leads to effective perceptual training (Pisoni, Lively, and Logan, 1994). From this evidence, Kuhl (2000, p. 11855) argues that feedback and reinforcement are not necessary in learning to perceive L2 sounds, but rather that non-native listeners simply need the "right" kind of perceptual input, i.e., exaggerated acoustic cues, multiple instances of the same sound, and a mass listening experience – which are the features of child-directed speech (also called "motherese"). This suggestion is compatible with the Linguistic Perception model, which proposes that the GLA will act upon auditory inputs to gradually re-rank constraints; the more frequent an auditory input is, the faster the algorithm will reach the optimal perception of such input. Thus, L2 perception accuracy would benefit from perception training to enhance L2 input, both its acoustic properties and its frequency.

Another important skill that could be trained is "language control," the ability to activate one language system and inhibit the other based on linguistic and non-linguistic evidence. Kroll and Sunderman (2003, pp. 122–4) suggest that L2 teaching should incorporate a component of language activation and control, perhaps through the use of the L2 only and the avoidance of the L1 in the classroom, in order for beginning learners to modulate the cross-linguistic activation of the two languages in a manner similar to proficient bilinguals. The L2 version of the LP model is compatible with this training paradigm because it argues that L2 learners and bilinguals have two separate linguistic systems and that online activation of the two systems could lead to inaccurate L2 responses which do not represent the state of L2 development nor the stability of the L1 system. Therefore, it would be important to investigate whether listeners' performance accuracy could improve, if a language setting that inhibits more than one language is provided and if language control is learned, as seems to be suggested by the findings of Escudero and Boersma (2002) and Escudero (under review).

conclusion

The focus on production of much research and discussion in L2 phonology and language teaching has meant that until recently, the essential role of perception has been underappreciated. Research examining perception is leading to a greater understanding of the mechanisms underlying language learning and learning in general, as well as the nature of bilingualism. The L2LP model, which is consistent with a large body of research and consolidated theory in both L1 and L2 learning, differs from most previous approaches to modeling L2 phenomena in having perceptual processes at its core. In assuming the mechanisms of Full Copying and Full Access, and in describing them in formal terms, it goes considerably beyond previous work that attempted to explain L2 phonological data. Moreover, in assuming the possibility of Full Proficiency in both L1 and L2 as determined by usage factors, it provides new perspectives for understanding the causes of both "foreign accent" and the native or native-like behavior of highly bilingual speakers. In addition, its theoretical basis supports the learnability of phonology and offers directions for approaches to pedagogy to improve perception and to develop effective bilingual learning strategies. The L2LP model would thus appear to provide promising directions for current and future work in L2 phonology, and it is hoped that others in applied linguistics will continue to develop this model and its implications, theoretical as well as practical.

notes

1. Editor's note: see Chapter 2, this volume, for a review of the literature for L1 acquisition; see Chapter 10, this volume, for a discussion of speech perception in developmental phonological disorder.
2. This view is compatible with Kuhl's NLM as well as with the recent findings of distributional learning in infants (Maye, Werker, and Gerken, 2002).

3. These types of perceptual adjustments have been shown to occur developmentally in infants and children (Gerrits, 2001; Nittrouer and Miller, 1997).
4. The first two components of the model are an interpretation of the formal hypothesis of Full Transfer/Full Access as proposed by Schwartz and Sprouse (1996).

references

Archibald, J., & M. Young-Scholten (2003). The second language segment revisited. *Second Language Research, 19*, 163–7.

Barry, W. (1989). Perception and production of English vowels by German learners: Instrumental-phonetic support in language teaching. *Phonetica, 46*, 155–68.

Best, C.T. (1995). A direct realist view of cross-language speech perception. In W. Strange (Ed.), *Speech perception and linguistic experience: Theoretical and methodological issues* (pp. 171–203). Baltimore: York Press.

Best, C. T., & Strange, W. (1992). Effects of phonological and phonetic factors on cross-language perception of approximants. *Journal of Phonetics, 20*, 305–31.

Boersma, P. (1998). Functional phonology. Doctoral dissertation, University of Amsterdam. The Hague: Holland Academic Graphics.

Boersma, P. (1999). On the need for a separate perception grammar. *Rutgers Optimality Archive, 358*.

Boersma, P., Escudero, P., & Hayes, R. (2003). Learning abstract phonological from auditory phonetic categories: An integrated model for the acquisition of language-specific sound categories. *Proceedings of the 15th International Congress of Phonetic Sciences*, 1013–16.

Boersma, P., & Hayes, B. (2001). Empirical tests of the Gradual Learning Algorithm. *Linguistic Inquiry, 21*, 45–86.

Borden, G., Gerber, A., Milsark, G. (1983). Production and perception of the /r/-/l/ contrast in Korean adults learning English. *Language Learning, 33*, 499–526.

Browman, C. P. & L. Goldstein (1989). Articulatory gestures as phonological units. *Phonology, 6*, 201–51.

Brown, C. (1998). The role of the L1 grammar in the L2 acquisition of segmental structure. *Second Language Research, 14*, 136–93.

Brown, C., & Matthews, J. (1997). The role of feature geometry in the development of phonemic contrasts. In S. J. Hannahs & M. Young-Scholten (Eds.), *Focus on phonological acquisition* (pp. 67–112). Amsterdam: John Benjamins.

Caramazza, A., Yeni-Komshian, G., Zurif, E. & Carbone, E. (1973). The acquisition of a new phonological contrast: The case of stop consonants in French-English bilinguals. *Journal of the Acoustical Society of America, 5*, 421–28.

Clements, J. N. (1985). The geometry of phonological features. *Phonology, 2*, 223–52.

Cook, V. J. (2002). Background to the L2 user. In V. J. Cook (Ed.), *Portraits of the L2 user* (pp. 1–28). Clevedon: Multilingual Matters.

Dijkstra, A., Graingeer, J., & Van Heuven, W. J. B. (1999). Recognition of cognates and interlingual homographs: The neglected role of phonology. *Journal of Memory and Language, 41*, 496–518.

Eckman, F. R. (1977). Markedness and the Contrastive Analysis Hypothesis. *Language Learning 27*, 315–30.

Escudero, P. (2001). The role of the input in the development of L1 and L2 sound contrasts: Language-specific cue weighting for vowels. *Proceedings of the 25th annual Boston University Conference on Language Development*, (pp. 250–61). Somerville, MA: Cascadilla Press.

Escudero, P. (2005). Linguistic perception and second language acquisition: Explaining the attainment of optimal phonological categorization. Doctoral dissertation, University of Utrecht.

Escudero, P. (under review). Evidence for perceptual boundary shifts in L2 acquisition: The case of Canadian English learners of Canadian French.

Escudero P., & Boersma, P. (2002). The subset problem in L2 perceptual development: Multiple-category assimilation by Dutch learners of Spanish. In B. Skarabela, S. Fish, & A. H.-J. Do (Eds.), *Proceedings of the 26th annual Boston University Conference on Language Development* (pp. 208–19). Somerville, MA: Cascadilla Press.

Escudero, P., & Boersma, P. (2003). Modeling the perceptual development of phonological contrasts with Optimality Theory and the Gradual Learning Algorithm. In S. Arunachalam, E. Kaiser, & A. Williams (Eds.), *Proceedings of the 25th Annual Penn Linguistics Colloquium, Penn Working Papers in Linguistics, 8*, 71–85.

Escudero, P., & Boersma, P. (2004). Bridging the gap between L2 speech perception research and phonological theory. *Studies in Second Language Acquisition, 26*, 551–85.

Flege, J. E. (1987). The production of "new" and "similar" phones in a foreign language: Evidence for the effect of equivalence classification. *Journal of Phonetics, 15*, 47–65.

Flege, J. E. (1993). Production and perception of a novel, second-language phonetic contrast. *Journal of the Acoustical Society of America, 93*, 1589–608.

Flege, J. E. (1995). Second language speech learning theory, findings, and problems. In W. Strange (Ed.), *Speech perception and linguistic experience: Issues in cross-language research* (pp. 233–77). Baltimore: York Press.

Flege, J. (2002). Interactions between the native and second-language phonetic systems. In H. Burmeister, T. Piske, & A. Rohde (Eds.), *An integrated view of language development: Papers in honor of Henning Wode* (pp. 217–44). Trier: Wissenschaftlicher Verlag Trier.

Flege, J. (2003). Assessing constraints on second-language segmental production and perception. In A. Meyer & Schiller, N. (Eds.), *Phonetics and phonology in language comprehension and production: Differences and similarities*. Berlin: Mouton de Gruyter.

Flege, J., & Eefting, W. (1987). Cross-language switching in stop consonant production and perception by Dutch speakers of English. *Speech Communication, 6*, 185–202.

Flege, J. E., & MacKay, I. (2004). Perceiving vowels in a second language. *Studies in Second Language Acquisition, 26*, 1–34.

Flege, J., Schirru, C., & MacKay, I. (2003). Interaction between the native and second language phonetic subsystems. *Speech Communication, 40*, 467–91.

Fowler, C. A. (1986). An event approach to the study of speech perception from a direct-realist perspective. *Journal of Phonetics, 14*, 1–38.

Gerrits, E. (2001). The categorisation of speech sounds by adults and children. Doctoral dissertation, University of Utrecht.

Goto, H. (1971). Auditory perception by normal Japanese adults of the sounds "l" and "r." *Neuropsychologia, 9*, 317–23.

Grasseger, H. (1991). Perception and production of Italian plosives by Italian learners. *Actes du XIIème Congrès International des Sciences Phonétique, 5*, 290–3.

Grosjean, F. (1999). Studying bilinguals: Methodological and conceptual issues. *Bilingualism: Language and Cognition, 1*, 117–130.

Grosjean, F. (2001). The bilingual's language modes. *One mind, Two languages: Bilingual language processing* (pp. 1–22). Oxford: Blackwell.

Hammarberg, B. (1997). Conditions on transfer in phonology. In A. James & J. Leather (Eds.), *Second language speech: Structure and process* (pp. 161–80). Berlin: Mouton de Gruyter.

Hyltenstam, K., & Abrahamsson, N. (2003). Maturational constraints in SLA. In C. Doughty & M. Long (Eds.), *Handbook of second language acquisition* (pp. 104–29). Oxford: Blackwell.

Iverson, P., & Kuhl, P. K. (1996). Influences of phonetic identification and category goodness on American listeners' perception of /r/ and /l/. *Journal of the Acoustical Society of America, 99*, 1130–40.

Jared, D., & Kroll, J. F. (2001). Do bilinguals activate phonological representations in one or both of their languages when naming words? *Journal of Memory and Language, 44*, 2–31.

Kager, R. (1999). *Optimality Theory*. Cambridge: Cambridge University Press.

Kim, K., Relkin, N., Lee, K., and Hirsch, J. (1997). Distinct cortical areas associated with native and second languages. *Nature, 388*, 171–4.

Kroll, J. F., & Sunderman, G. (2003). Cognitive processes in second language acquisition: The development of lexical and conceptual representations. In C. Doughty & M. Long (Eds.), *Handbook of second language acquisition* (pp. 104–29). Cambridge: Blackwell.

Kuhl, P. K. (1991). Human adults and human infants show a "perceptual magnetic effect" for the prototypes of speech categories, monkeys do not. *Perception and Psychophysics 50*, 93–107.

Kuhl, P. K. (2000). A new view of language acquisition. *Proceedings of the National Academy of Sciences USA, 97*, 11850–57.

Lado, R. (1957). Linguistics across cultures. In *Language transfer in language learning* (pp. 21–32). Rowley, MA: Newbury House Publishers.

Leather, J. (1999). Second-language speech research: An introduction. In J. Leather (Ed.), *Phonological issues in language learning* (pp. 1–58). Oxford: Blackwell.

Lenneberg, E. (1967). *Biological foundations of language*. New York: Wiley.

Llisterri, J. (1995) Relationships between speech production and speech perception in a second language. In K. Elenius & P. Branderud (Eds.), *Proceedings of the 13th International Congress of Phonetic Sciences* (pp. 92–9). Stockholm: KTH/Stockholm University.

Long, M. H. (1990). Maturational constraints on language development. *Studies in Second Language Acquisition, 12*, 251–85.

MacKay, I. R. A., Flege, J. E., Piske, T., & Schirru, C. (2001). Category restructuring during second-language speech acquistion. *Journal of the Acoustical Society of America, 110(1)*, 516–28.

MacWhinney, B. (1999). Models of the emergence of language. *Annual Review of Psychology, 49*, 199–227.

Major, R. C. (1987). Phonological similarity, markedness, and rate of L2 acquisition. *Studies in Second Language Acquisition, 9*, 63–82.

Major, R. C. (2001). *Foreign accent*. Mahwah, NJ: Erlbaum.

Major, R. C. (2002). The phonology of the L2 user. In V. Cook (Ed.), *Portraits of the L2 user* (pp. 65–92). Clevedon: Multilingual Matters.

Maye, J., Werker, J. F., & Gerken, L. A. (2002). Infant sensitivity to distributional information can affect phonetic discrimination. *Cognition, 82*, B101–11.

McClelland, J., Thomas, A., McCandliss, B., and Fiez, J. (1999). Understanding failures of learning: Hebbian Learning, competition for representational space, and some preliminary experimental data. In J. Reggia, E. Ruppin, & D. Glanzman (Eds.), *Progress in brain research*, Volume 121: *Disorders of brain, behavior and cognition: The neurocomputational perspective* (pp. 75–80). Amsterdam: Elsevier.

McQueen, J. M. (2004). Speech perception. In K. Lamberts & R. Goldstone (Eds.), *The handbook of cognition* (pp. 255–75). London: Sage Publications.

Neufeld, G. G. (1988). Phonological asymmetry in second language learning and performance, *Language Learning, 38*, 531–59.

Nittrouer, S., & Miller, M. E. (1997). Developmental weighting shifts for noise components of fricative-vowel syllables. *Journal of the Acoustical Society of America, 102*, 572–80.

Norris, D. (1994). Shortlist: A connectionist model of continuous speech recognition. *Cognition 52*, 189–234.

Penfield, W., & Roberts, L. (1959). *Speech and brain mechanisms*. Princeton: Princeton University Press.

Piske, T., Mackay, I., & Flege, J. (2001). Factors affecting degree of foreign accent in an L2: A review. *Journal of Phonetics, 29*, 191–215.

Pisoni, D. B., Lively, S. E, & Logan, J. S. (1994). Perceptual learning of nonnative speech contrasts: Implications for theories of speech perception. In J. Goodman & H. C. Nusbaum (Eds.), *Development of speech perception: The transition from recognizing speech sounds to spoken words* (pp. 121–66). Cambridge: MIT Press.

Polivanov, E. D. (1931/1964). La perception des sons d'une langue étrangère [The perception of the sounds of a foreign language]. *Travaux du Cercle Linguistique de Prague 4*, 79–96.

Rochet, B. (1995). Perception and production of second-language speech sounds by adults. In W. Strange (Ed.), *Speech perception and linguistic experience* (pp. 379–410). Timonium, MD: York Press.

Saffran, J. R., Aslin, R. N., & Newport, E. L. (1996). Statistical learning by 8-month old infants. *Science 274*, 1926–8.

Schwartz, B., & Sprouse, R. (1996). L2 cognitive states and the Full Transfer/Full Access model. *Second Language Research 12*, 40–72.

Sheldon, A., &. Strange, W. (1982). The acquisition of /r/ and /l/ by Japanese learners of English: Evidence that speech production can precede speech perception. *Applied Psycholinguistics, 3*, 243–61.

Strange, W. (1995). Cross-language study of speech perception: A historical review. In W. Strange (Ed.), *Speech perception and linguistic experience: Issues in cross-language research* (pp. 3–45). Baltimore: York Press.

Tesar, B., & Smolensky, P. (2000). *Learnability in Optimality Theory*. Cambridge: MIT Press.

Trubetzkoy, N. S. (1939/1969) *Grundzüge der Phonologie*. Travaux du Cercle Linguistique de Prague, 7. [Translator C. A. M. Baltaxe, *Principles of phonology*. Berkeley: University of California Press, 1969.]

White L. (2003). On the nature of interlanguage representation: Universal grammar in the second language. In C. Doughty & M. Long (Eds.), *Handbook of second language acquisition* (pp. 104–29). Malden, MA: Blackwell.

Williams, L. (1977). The perception of consonant voicing by Spanish English bilinguals. *Perception & Psychophysics, 21*, 289–97.

6
the visual element in phonological perception and learning
debra m. hardison

introduction

Research in the field of phonology has long been dominated by a focus on only one source or modality of input – auditory (i.e., what we hear). However, in face-to-face communication, a significant source of information about the sounds a speaker is producing comes from visual cues such as the lip movements associated with these sounds. Studies on the contribution of these cues to the understanding of individual speech sounds by native listeners including the hearing impaired date back several decades. Only recently has this source of input been explored for its value to second-language (L2) learners.

This chapter provides an overview of the contribution of facial cues to spoken language processing, and the current knowledge of when, where, and how auditory and visual cues are integrated. We then take a look at the applications of these cues to perceptual learning by L2 learners, followed by a discussion of the contributions of recent advances in technology for the understanding of both the auditory and visual modalities of speech. For example, software programs are available that combine audio recordings with visual displays of features of speech such as the contour created by the pitch of the voice. Improvements in computer-animated faces show some promise in perception and production training for learners because they can display a detailed view of how sounds are produced in the mouth in contrast to viewing the face of a natural speaker. Auditory-visual web-based tools are now available that expand the scope of inquiry from individual sounds and facial linguistic cues to include other components of a speech event such as hand-arm gestures. Such tools facilitate analysis of the integration of facial expressions, intonation, and gestures. The chapter concludes with a discussion of directions for future research.

distinguishing visual speech cues

Fifty years ago, Miller and Nicely (1955) suggested that lip movements could facilitate a listener's perception of consonants by providing visual cues as to where the sounds are being articulated (i.e., produced) in the mouth. This is especially helpful in noisy environments. However, not every visible articulatory movement identifies one and only one speech sound. There is no consensus in the speechreading (lipreading) literature on the consonants that are visually distinguishable from one another. This lack of agreement has resulted from the variation across studies in important factors such as the speakers, influence of adjacent sounds, and testing conditions (e.g., lighting). Demorest, Bernstein, and DeHaven (1996) suggested the following groups, each containing consonants considered to be visually indistinguishable from one another when produced in a syllable with a vowel that has an open-mouth position (e.g., *ba*). These groups are /p,b,m/, /f,v/, /θ,ð/ (e.g., *think, the*), /w,r/, /t,d,s,z/, /k,g,n,l,h/, plus a category of consonants that generally involve substantial protrusion of the lips as shown by the underlined letters in the following examples: /ʃ/ *shoe*, /ʒ/ *measure*, /tʃ/ *chip*, and /dʒ/ *jump*. As one might imagine, the vowel in a syllable can have considerable influence on how easily the preceding consonant is identified based on lip movements alone. Identification accuracy is highest when the adjacent vowel is produced with a relatively open-mouth position (e.g., /a/, *father*). In general, a speaker's lip position for a rounded vowel such as /u/ (e.g., *true*) virtually obliterates the movements associated with producing the preceding consonants unless they are also produced with substantial lip involvement (e.g., /p/ or /f/). This anticipatory rounding of the lips is responsible for most consonant errors in speechreading experiments (Benguerel and Pichora-Fuller, 1982), and may extend over as many as four preceding consonants (Daniloff and Moll, 1968). The distinctiveness of a consonant's production also varies according to the speaker (Kricos and Lesner, 1982).

The above discussion points out the considerable variability a listener faces in the identification of speech sounds. Research on variability in speech in recent years has raised our awareness of the important role of speaker variability in auditory speech perception (see e.g., Johnson and Mullennix, 1997). Bradlow, Torretta, and Pisoni (1996) reported several characteristics that define an individual producing highly intelligible speech: female, use of a wide pitch range, and precise articulation of vowels making full use of the movement potential of the mouth and jaw. For auditory-visual speech intelligibility, there are additional criteria for greatest discernibility of visual speech: absence of facial hair that can obscure lip movements, the number of changes in facial movement during the production of a word, total elapsed time from the beginning of the word to each of the changes in movement, intensity of facial movement, and total duration of the word (Berger, 1972). What is amazing is that despite variability across the multiple dimensions of speech production, listeners are able to make use of visual cues from a speaker's face on a daily basis whether compensating for noise, impaired hearing ability (e.g., Summerfield, 1979), or language differences in the case of a second-language speaker (e.g., Hardison, 1999, 2003).

the power of visible speech

Although less information may be communicated visually versus auditorily (unless a factor such as hearing loss or significant noise interferes with comprehension), the visual channel of speech provides some powerful input. In 1976, a short paper appeared in the journal *Nature* describing a perceptual illusion involving conflicting visual and auditory information (McGurk and MacDonald, 1976). Observers were shown videotaped recordings of a woman producing consonant-vowel syllables in which the visual and auditory cues for the initial consonants did not match. When asked to identify the consonant they heard, typically, the observers heard something that combined the characteristics of both the visual and auditory cues. For example, an auditory cue of /ba/ presented with a visual cue of /ga/ often produced the response "da"; an auditory /ga/ combined with a visual /ba/ could produce the response "bga". In the first type of case, the observer perceived an initial consonant that is intermediate in its articulation between the two consonants presented, one in the auditory and one in the visual channel. In the second type of case, the observer perceived the two consonants presented as occurring in a combination or sequence. These types of illusions were discovered accidentally while Harry McGurk was reviewing dubbed videotapes of matched and mismatched auditory and visual /ba/-/ga/ pairs (Burnham, 1998; McGurk, 1998).[1] This phenomenon came to be known as the "McGurk effect" and the 1976 paper is now a classic in the field. It served as the springboard for subsequent decades of research on auditory-visual speech processing.

This apparently simple combination of mismatched syllables represents a valuable tool allowing a researcher to determine the relative contributions of the visual and auditory channels of speech input to the percept (Welch and Warren, 1980). Results from numerous experiments have revealed variability in the strength with which individuals experience the McGurk effect. In fact, findings from MacDonald and McGurk (1978) showed a different pattern of responses than those from their first study (McGurk and MacDonald, 1976). For example, in the second study, the combination of visual /ka/ and auditory /pa/ produced 70 per cent correct "pa" responses rather than the compromise responses (in this case, of "ta") as in the initial study. This difference may have been the result of the set of materials or stimuli used in the second experiment, which included auditory-visual combinations of a greater variety of sounds. When listener-observers integrate auditory and visual information, they do so in the context of perceiving a single speech event. The similarity of the two cues determines the degree to which an observer is able to integrate them into a single perceptual event. However, even if the cues are out of synchrony by ± 180 milliseconds (ms), an observer's perceptual system still attempts to organize this input as a single experience for analysis (e.g., Remez, Pardo, Piorkowski, and Rubin, 2001). In addition, a speaker's exposure to a second language and aural proficiency affect identification of the cues and their subsequent integration. Visual influence also varies according to the salience of the cue for a specific sound in its phonetic context. As noted earlier, rounded vowels can obscure lip movements associated with consonant production, which in turn, results in an almost non-existent McGurk effect for a syllable with /u/. Familiarity with a person's face also determines the effect of a speaker's lip movements independent of the familiarity of the voice. When participants in one study (Walker, Bruce, and O'Malley, 1995) were shown matched face–voice pairs (from the same speaker) and mismatched pairs (from different speakers), those who were familiar with the faces, and thus, with the association between the speaker's articulations and speech sounds, were less susceptible to McGurk effects than those who were not.

Several studies have reported weak McGurk effects for native speakers of languages other than English. For Japanese speakers, the occurrence of the illusion depended on the intelligibility of the auditory cue: in a background of noise, visual cues had a greater effect (Sekiyama and Tohkura, 1991). A similar weak effect was found for Chinese speakers living in Japan who were presented with syllables produced by a Japanese speaker and by an American (Sekiyama, 1997). The participants' length of stay in Japan ranged from four months to six years. Generally, those who had been in the language environment longer showed a stronger influence of visual cues. In experimental research using a computer-animated face combined with synthetic speech, Massaro, Cohen, Gesi, Heredia, and Tsuzaki (1993) found that visual cues influenced the interpretation of the synthetic speech by native speakers of Japanese, Spanish, and American English.

These studies demonstrate that the human perceptual system can unite information from both the auditory and visual modalities and further process these two types of input as components of a single event. The integration process is influenced by the observers' familiarity with the speaker's articulations, ability to identify the cues, and the degree to which they perceive them to be related.

perspectives on auditory-visual integration: when, where, and how it occurs

Findings from various studies have suggested the existence of a neuro-cognitive mechanism, structure, or level of representation common to the processing of visual and auditory input. Campbell (1987) found that observers dealt with lipread information as if it had been heard rather than seen. After being presented with color names which they either heard, lipread or read, participants were able to recall which items had been read, but could not distinguish between those they had heard and those they had lipread. This finding suggested that lipreading and hearing draw on similar memory storage mechanisms. Watson, Qui, Chamberlain, and Li (1996) found that native speakers of English (normal-hearing adults) have similar lipreading and speech recognition abilities. These results suggest that speech processing involves the interaction of visual and auditory inputs at some level. This integration of visual and auditory information appears to occur early in processing, before a sound is identified by a listener-observer, and then to strongly influence that identification. Evidence for the integration of visual and auditory information prior to linguistic identification is provided by the responses found in the McGurk effect that do not match either cue (e.g., a "da" response to a mismatched visual /ga/ and auditory /ba/ combination).

Several neurological studies using magnetoencephalographic (MEG) recordings have documented the effects of visual input from lip movements on the area of the brain, the auditory cortex, that primarily processes sound (e.g., Sams, Aulanko, Hämäläinen, Hari, Lounasmaa, Lu, and Simola, 1991). In one experiment, a Finnish female was recorded articulating /pa/ and /ka/. Using these syllables, two types of stimuli were created: congruent (i.e., auditory and visual cues were the same) and incongruent (i.e., auditory and visual cues were different). Participants were then presented with a higher percentage of either the congruent or incongruent stimuli. Neuromagnetic measurements differed significantly between the frequently and infrequently presented stimuli. However, substituting lights as visual cues instead of lip movements did not show the same effect of frequency of presentation. Sams et al. concluded that the visual input specifically from the lip movements influenced activity in the auditory cortex. In addition, cues from one modality can alter judgments about stimulus intensity in another modality. In another study, participants were asked to use a scale to rate the intensity of a light emitted diode (LED) presented under different experimental conditions. When a brief broad-band auditory stimulus was presented along with the LED, participants rated the visual cue as more intense (Stein, London, Wilkinson, and Price, 1996). This finding supports the presence of neurons (nerve cells) influenced by more than one sensory modality.

A sensitivity to relationships between lip movements and speech sounds appears to develop early in life and may be useful in the acquisition of speech perception and production by young children (e.g., Dodd, 1987; Meltzoff and Kuhl, 1994). Blind infants are reported to babble less than sighted ones after the first six months of life (Mills, 1987), suggesting that lipread or other facial cues might be an important source of stimulation in language development. Infants only 12–21 days old imitate adult mouth movements such as tongue protrusion, mouth opening, and lip protrusion (Meltzoff and Moore, 1993). Dodd (1979) found that infants as young as three months were aware of the association between lip movements and speech sounds. They preferred to watch a video presentation of nursery rhymes when the auditory and visual cues were synchronous. Infants between four and twelve months of age produced more and longer utterances containing consonants after receiving auditory-visual versus auditory-only speech input; some silently imitated the lip movements (Dodd, 1987). Dodd suggested that by 19 months of age, lipread information appears to serve a linguistic purpose for toddlers who can lipread familiar words.

Studies measuring the direction and duration of infants' eye gaze have shown that they develop auditory-visual correspondences quite early. Infants show a preference for matched visual and auditory speech cues. For example, 4-month-old infants were shown two visual images side-by-side of a speaker appearing to produce the vowels /i/ (e.g., be) and /u/ (e.g., true) while they heard a sound that matched only one of the vowels. The infants looked longer at the face that matched the sound (Kuhl and

Meltzoff, 1984). In this case, the lip movements needed to produce these vowel sounds are quite visually distinctive. Walton and Bower (1993) presented 6–8-month-old infants with a face that appeared to be producing /u/, and paired this visual cue with each of the following sounds: /u/ (creating a matched, familiar combination), a French vowel produced with more rounding of the lips than the English vowel (an unfamiliar sound to the infants but a possible auditory-visual combination), and /i/ (a mismatched, "impossible" combination). Results revealed a preference for the matched and possible pairs over the impossible one. Even though the infants had not been exposed to French, the rounding of the lips was an important characteristic, which the unfamiliar French vowel shared with the correct English vowel.

Infants also prefer to imitate auditory-visual stimuli that match. Legerstee (1990) presented matched and mismatched auditory and visual cues to different groups of infants 3–4 months of age. Only those who were exposed to the matched cues for the sounds /a/ and /u/ imitated the vowels. In recent studies, Lewkowicz (e.g., 2002) noted that infants' responsiveness to various features of faces and voices changes throughout their early development. Integration of these features depends on the nature of the information and the infant's developmental age.

Children's exposure to matched auditory-visual perceptual events appears to play a role in normal attentional development. Deaf children performed much more poorly than hearing children when they were asked to respond to some visual signals and not others (Quittner, Smith, Osberger, Mitchell, and Katz, 1994). This finding suggested that focused visual attention may develop with associated auditory experience. For the deaf children, significant improvement was noted in their attentional development within two years following cochlear implant surgery. The procedure involves insertion of an electronic device into the inner ear to stimulate nerve fibers to produce signals recognized as sounds by the brain.

Investigating the issue of where integration of auditory and visual information takes place in the brain has been facilitated by recent technological developments. Functional magnetic resonance imaging (fMRI) studies have been conducted to localize the neural processes involved in the visual aspects of speech perception. Some research suggests that speech motor areas of the brain, including Broca's area known to be active during auditory speech perception, are also involved in the recognition of a speaker's lip movements when speech is presented in noise (Callan, Callan, and Vatikiotis-Bateson, 2001). These findings are consistent with the proposal that a particular system of neurons underlies both the auditory perception of speech and visual observation of the associated lip movements (Rizzolatti and Arbib, 1998).

Visual and auditory information can be related through feedback pathways from areas of the cortex that integrate input from different sensory areas (see Rolls, 1989). De Sa and Ballard (1997) conducted computational studies using a labeling algorithm designed to model biologically plausible computations that might be involved in a high level cognitive task such as the human observer's integration of auditory and visual speech cues. The investigation used a dataset comprised of the acoustic and visual patterns taken from recordings of English consonant-vowel syllables (e.g., /da/). The computation involved two artificial modalities analogous to the human visual and auditory modalities representing independent networks of co-occurring information (input patterns) from the same source (e.g., a speech signal). Results indicated that when both modalities were simultaneously trained to classify the acoustic and visual patterns, and provided mutual feedback, they reached a greater performance level than when they were trained independently. Separate modalities independently processing different sets of input were able to "teach each other" (p. 342) through integration (i.e., access to each other's output) at a higher level and through mutual feedback.

To capture the process of integrating auditory and visual information in a single memory representation, Massaro (e.g., 1987) proposed a fuzzy logical model of perceptual recognition (FLMP). FLMP consists of three stages: feature evaluation, integration, and pattern classification. In the initial stage of this model, information from the visual and auditory modalities is evaluated independently in the early stages of processing in terms of the degree to which each feature in the stimulus matches the auditory and visual features in each stored representation in memory. The goal is to determine which representation is the best match for the stimulus. The evaluation of features may be influenced by the cue's intelligibility, and in the case of an L2 learner, the first language (L1), and L2 linguistic experience (Hardison, 1999). The second stage is integration of the cues from both modalities. Here the more informative cue contributes the most to the process, which is influenced by the observer's assumptions of the degree to which the auditory and visual cues represent a single perceptual event. Pattern classification, the third stage, is the perceptual outcome.

Issues of when, where, and how auditory-visual speech integration occurs are questions motivating continued research. Some researchers have proposed that the primary mode of speech perception is auditory-visual (e.g., Rosenblum, 2002). This position is supported by the findings from research on the McGurk effect, speech perception by infants, and neurological perspectives on speech processing.

clinical and pedagogical applications of multimodal speech

Perhaps the most commonly known role for visual cues has been with regard to facilitating speech comprehension by the hearing impaired. In a recent study, two groups with cochlear implants – children deafened before they acquired language and adults deafened after language acquisition – were better able to identify words with auditory-visual versus auditory-only input (Kirk, Pisoni, and Lachs, 2002). For the children, exposure to visible speech cues also resulted in more intelligible speech production.

Several reports indicate that the information value of visual cues can be improved with training. Hearing-impaired adults trained in visual consonant recognition showed dramatic improvement in the recognition of /r/ (presented in a syllable with /a/), which was the most improved of all of the consonants trained. Accuracy increased from 36.1% to 88.6% after a total of 14 hours of speechreading training although maximum improvement for most consonants (at a lower level of accuracy) was reached during the first five hours (Walden, Prosek, Montgomery, Scherr, and Jones, 1977). A subsequent study revealed that separate visual-only training and auditory-only training using syllables resulted in improvement in auditory-visual sentence recognition (Walden, Erdman, Montgomery, Schwartz, and Prosek, 1981). In other research with normal-hearing adults, improvement in lipreading facilitated auditory-visual speech perception (Massaro, Cohen, and Gesi, 1993).

Research on the potential benefits of auditory-visual speech training for L2 learners has been a more recent development though attention to lip shapes has long been a practice in teaching English as a second language, and was noted over 30 years ago by a native Japanese-speaking researcher (Goto, 1971) as valuable in understanding L2 speech. In the discussion of Japanese speakers' difficulty in identifying American English /r/ and /l/, Goto concluded that in the auditory presentation of sounds, "there was the disadvantage of not being able to read the lips of the speaker" (p. 321). Many years later, Hardison (1999) investigated the McGurk effect in L2 learners of English to assess the contribution of auditory and visual speech cues to the perception of English /p,f,w,r,t,k/ in syllables with a following vowel /a/. This study included auditory and visual cues that matched and those that did not. Data from a total of 120 advanced learners of

English from four L1 backgrounds (Japanese, Korean, Spanish, and Malay) revealed a significant increase in identification accuracy of English /r/ and /f/ for the Japanese and Korean speakers when the corresponding visual cues were available. For mismatched pairs, the visual cues of /t,k/ influenced the learners' perception of sounds such as /p/. Responses indicated that they thought they had heard /t/ or /k/. However, when /t/ and /k/ represented the auditory cues and were paired with visual /p/, the auditory cues /t/ and /k/ were correctly identified. Unlike /r/ and /f/, the sounds /t/ and /k/ are generally not problematic for L2 learners of English. These examples thus demonstrate that the more informative cue contributed the most to what the learner perceived.

The benefit of visual cues for sounds such as /r/ and /f/ which learners of English find difficult suggested a need for further research on how the information value of visible speech cues might be enhanced for L2 learners. Previous studies (e.g., Bradlow, Pisoni, Yamada, and Tohkura, 1997; Homa and Cultice, 1984; Lively, Logan, and Pisoni, 1993) that had focused on the auditory training of Japanese speakers to identify /r/ and /l/ established the following criteria for successful training:

(i)   multiple natural exemplars to demonstrate both similarities in the production of a single sound in different phonetic contexts and differences between sounds;
(ii)   variability in the training materials and the speakers used to produce them in order to mirror the variability found in the natural language environment; and
(iii) feedback during training.

A subsequent study (Hardison, 2003) compared auditory-visual and auditory-only training of intermediate-level Japanese and Korean learners of English to identify American English /r/, /l/, /f/ (versus /p/), and /θ/ (versus /s/). Participants were enrolled in an intensive English program in the U.S. and had been in the country for one to seven weeks prior to the study. None were receiving pronunciation training. Learners were given three weeks (15 sessions each 45 minutes) of perceptual training using multiple words produced by several native speakers of American English and recorded on videotape. These minimal pairs allowed the above sounds to be contrasted in various word positions with different adjacent vowels. For both Japanese and Korean learners, auditory-visual training resulted in significantly greater improvement in identification accuracy than auditory-only training. With regard to /r/ and /l/, visual input contributed the most to perceptual accuracy for the phonetic environments that were the most difficult for the learners based on native-language phonology (i.e., initial word position for the Japanese and final word position for the Koreans). Accurate perception of /r/ and /l/ was influenced significantly by the speaker producing the words in training, the position of the sound in the word, and the adjacent vowel. Learners were able to generalize their improved abilities to the perception of new words, and both new and familiar words produced by a new speaker. In addition, production of all sounds improved significantly as a result of perceptual training. These findings emphasized the power of visible speech cues for language learners, and their value in modifying adult perceptual categories to incorporate the variability found in natural speech.

Articulatory movements in the production of speech naturally precede the associated auditory signal. For example, the production of the consonant sound /b/ involves the closure of both lips followed by the release that creates the speech sound. The visual cue associated with the lip closure precedes the auditory cue to the sound. This precedence serves a priming role for a listener (Munhall and Tohkura, 1998) and results in earlier identification of words by native and non-native speakers of English in auditory-visual versus auditory-only presentation (Hardison, 2005c). Essentially, the listener-observer has a head start because visual cues are available to some degree before the associated auditory cue is detected. For example, Sekiyama and Sugita (2002) reported that in their study, the lip closure for the sound /b/ in the syllable /ba/ was completed 600 ms before the auditory signal started.

A subsequent study investigated whether this priming role of visual speech cues could be enhanced for L2 learners through focused training using minimal pairs contrasting /r/, /l/, /p/ and /f/ and result in earlier identification of words beginning with these sounds (Hardison, 2005b). For this purpose, a gating paradigm was used (e.g., Grosjean, 1980) with modifications for auditory-visual speech. Gating involves the successive presentation of increasing amounts of a target word. After each presentation, participants write down the word they think is being produced. For example, if the word is *singer*, the first presentation provides the following information: visually, the lips are apart and unrounded, and the teeth are close together; auditorily, there is a hissing sound typical of /s/. With each subsequent presentation, more of the word is presented until the participant hears the entire word. The initial two sounds of a word play an important role in determining the set of potential candidates for the word identification process (Marslen-Wilson and Welsh, 1978). A salient identifiable visual cue can enhance this process.

In the Hardison (2005b) study, participants were the same learners of English as a second language that participated in the perceptual training study. The target words were familiar two-syllable nouns that were presented in two-frame increments (approximately 66 ms). The word-identification task was administered before and after the above perceptual training. Results revealed that auditory-visual versus auditory-only speech facilitated identification of words both before and after perceptual training with some variation according to the word's initial two sounds (i.e., a consonant-vowel sequence). This variation was sensitive to influence from L1 phonology. For the Japanese speakers, identification of words beginning with /r/ and /l/ showed greater accentuation of the advantage of auditory-visual versus auditory-only input following training compared to other word-initial consonants. For the Koreans, although visual cues resulted in significantly earlier identification of words, especially those beginning with /r/ and /l/, the benefit provided by visual cues did not change significantly with training.

This contrast between the two groups of learners may be attributable to the differences in L1 phonology and the important role of a word's first two sounds in the identification process. Japanese has a flap (e.g., the medial sound in *butter*) in initial word position; Korean has no word-initial /r/ or /l/ sound. During perceptual training, the Japanese had lower accuracy scores for word-initial /r/ and /l/ (Hardison, 2003) compared to the Koreans, for whom these sounds in word-final position were more difficult to identify. As noted earlier, the first two sounds in a word are crucial to the word identification process as these activate all stored representations in memory of words having this initial sequence suggesting potential word candidates (Marslen-Wilson and Welsh, 1978). As additional information is presented, the initial pool of candidates, or cohort of possible words is reduced in size. Although semantic context facilitates processing when available and comprehensible, initial activation is based on acoustic-phonetic input (Tyler and Wessels, 1985). In a situation where visual cues are also present, activation begins even earlier. This priming role for visual speech cues can be enhanced through training to facilitate word identification. This was particularly helpful for the Japanese speakers in the above study whose perception difficulties with /r/ and /l/ were greatest in word-initial position. The combined contributions of (i) visual cues in input and (ii) successful perceptual training reduced the set of potential candidates to the process of identifying a word presented in an auditory-visual context.

One study suggests that there may be further variation across languages and types of training in the extent to which visual cues assist learning and identification of L2 phonemes. Hazan, Sennema, and Faulkner (2002) did not find an advantage for visual speech cues for Spanish speakers trying to identify British English /p,b,v/ embedded in nonsense words. In their study, participants' mean identification accuracy in auditory-visual perception (78.1%) was very similar to auditory-only (77.3%). Those participants who performed poorly in distinguishing /b/ and /v/ did so whether visual information was present or not, and those who were able to distinguish the sounds did so using either auditory or visual information. There are several factors that may account, at least in part, for the lack of parellelism to Hardison's findings and those of the prior studies referred to above on which that investigation was based. Among the possible relevant factors are differences in (i) discernibility of the visual cues of lip gestures in the learners' L1 (Spanish versus Japanese or Korean) and/or the target language variety (British English versus American English); (ii) the learners' linguistic experience, motivation, and attention to critical stimulus features to encode them in memory traces; and (iii) the designs of the investigations (e.g., the period of training, type of feedback, size of video screen, and the use in the Hazan et al. study of nonsense words, which are not obviously identifiable in terms of the phonemes of a specific language or variety). Further investigations are needed to determine whether, for example, the visual dimension is less salient and discernible for British than American English, for Spanish speakers than for Japanese or Korean speakers, or for a certain set of phonemes for a particular speaker group or combination of first and second languages (e.g., the labial obstruents for Spanish learners of British English).

Taken together, the findings of spoken language processing studies by L2 learners are compatible with a view of speech processing involving the development of context- and speaker-dependent representations. This view is in turn consistent with a multiple-trace account of memory, in which all attended perceptual details of a speech event are encoded in multiple traces in memory. Brown (1990) suggests that the trace of an event is not a single entity with psychological or physiological localization, but entails a series of changes that have taken place over the various levels of cognitive processing through which a representation has developed. Following multiple-trace memory theory, signals processed in primary (short-term or working) memory constitute probes or retrieval cues that activate, in parallel, stored traces in long-term memory (e.g., Hintzman, 1986). The contribution of each of these traces in working memory is weighted according to its similarity to the features of the probe. Ultimately, the probe returns an *echo* to primary memory. The features that comprise the perceptual representations that probe long-term memory depend on the attention given to the acoustic and visual attributes of the stimulus relevant to the particular task. In focused perceptual training, multiple exemplars of a phoneme or phonemic contrast along with feedback and repetition allow learners to attend to those stimulus features that provide useful input in identification decisions. Such training increases the salience and information value of important auditory and visual characteristics. In learning, the features of an experience are represented in a trace. Previously stored traces are not altered; instead, new ones are added. As a consequence of training, new L2 traces should be less ambiguous in content, and less confusable with, or at greater psychological distance from, existing L1 traces. Successful L2 perceptual learning limits the activation of spurious word candidates by creating a situation in which the echo from a collection of L2 traces acting together in response to a probe overrides the echo from L1 traces, resulting in earlier identification of L2 words. This process is enhanced further by the temporal precedence of identifiable visual speech cues.

In identifying a spoken word – a process that extends over time – echo intensities are obtained and perhaps modified over a period of time until a decision is reached. For L2 learners, one of the challenges is the assessment of similarity between stimulus and stored memory representation, which influences the rate at which initial word candidates can be reduced to a small set – and ultimately one choice – as increasing amounts of the word are heard and/or seen. Therefore, increasing the information value for learners of the auditory and visual cues to speech sounds, in the context of the priming role of visible speech, facilitates L2 spoken language processing (see Hardison, 2000, for a detailed discussion).

technological advances, applications, and new directions

Looking back on the speechreading literature, it is evident that lip movements have long been considered the source of linguistic information on a speaker's face. Yet, recent studies suggest that lip movements may not be the sole source. Two questions have motivated these investigations: what areas of the face impart linguistic information to observers, and is this information encoded in long-term memory traces to facilitate later processing of speech by the same speaker? To address the question of where observers gaze in auditory-visual speech perception, Vatikiotis-Bateson, Eigsti, Yano, and Munhall (1998) used special equipment mounted on goggles to monitor eye positions and movements in order to determine where native speakers of American English and Japanese were looking while observing two persons on videotape speaking in their respective first languages. The speaker produced a series of 35–45-second monologues in four different levels of background noise. The participants were asked to respond to multiple-choice comprehension questions. For analysis, eye-position data were assigned to different facial regions. For example, each eye and the surrounding upper cheek area and lower forehead area comprised a region with the vertical boundary extending about two-thirds of the way down the middle of the nose. The lower edge of the nose, mouth, jaw, and lower cheek areas comprised another region. Results indicated that both groups gazed more at the speaker's mouth as noise levels increased; however, 45–70% of each presentation was spent gazing at the speaker's eyes (i.e., more than 65% of the time at the lowest noise levels). The most common areas on the faces that drew the observers' attention were the eyes and mouth, not in-between points such as the nose. Therefore, Vatikiotis-Bateson et al. proposed that phonetically relevant information was distributed on the face beyond the area around the mouth as a result of changes in the facial muscles, in conjunction with changes in the vocal tract that accompany movement of the lips and jaw to produce speech sounds. They speculated that observers detect "well-learned, phonetically correlated events" (Vatikiotis-Bateson et al., 1998, p. 938). Because these are well-learned, detection of information is possible at some physical distance from the immediate target of an observer's gaze.

In contrast, Lansing and McConkie (1999) proposed that when observers look at objects such as faces, their eyes tend to go to the center (e.g., the nose). In a speechreading experiment with native speakers of English, they found eye gaze was directed towards the mouth for information about specific speech sounds. Of course, a speechreading task with no auditory information would necessitate greater attention to the speaker's mouth. However, the authors suggested that the difference in findings between their study and that of Vatikiotis-Bateson et al. (1998) could also be due to the way the facial regions were divided for analysis. In the Lansing and McConkie study, data were summarized using three facial regions: upper (forehead and eyes), middle (cheeks and nose), and lower (mouth plus chin). Gazes towards the forehead, cheeks or chin of the speaker were infrequent and brief. Gazes in the middle region of the face (i.e., the cheeks and nose) accounted for 37% of the data – gazes that would have been assigned to one of the eye regions following the division of regions in the study by Vatikiotis-Bateson et al. (1998). Lansing and McConkie suggested that gaze directed toward the nose as a central feature might represent visual attention to the face as a whole. Following Massaro's (1998) argument that speech information can be acquired without direct fixation of one's gaze, information beyond the mouth would still be available. Therefore, observers might use this strategy of looking at the middle of a speaker's face to establish a more global facial image. This would serve as a general framework of interpretation, especially when initially presented with an unfamiliar speaker; and then, subsequent shifts in the direction of eye gaze would be in response to focused attention to specific areas of the face.

A recent study addressed both the information value of various areas of the face as well as the question of what may be encoded in long-term memory by adult L2 learners of English (Hardison, 2006). Specifically, the study investigated the role of familiarity with a speaker's voice and areas of the face on the identification of spoken words in auditory-visual and auditory-only conditions. Participants were assigned to two groups. One group viewed videotaped presentations over a nine-day period (i.e., study sessions) of twelve female native speakers of English producing a series of words from a database. The participants were asked to learn to recognize the voices and faces. In the subsequent test session, they were asked to identify words (from the study sessions as well as new words) produced by four of these familiar speakers and four unfamiliar ones in two different levels of background noise. The control group participated only in the test session. Videotaped recordings were edited to produce four conditions: three auditory-visual and one auditory-only. The three auditory-visual conditions were based on findings from the above eye-tracking studies and included: (i) a full view of the speaker's head, (ii) the mouth and jaw area only, and (iii) the eye and upper cheek areas. Results indicated that accuracy in identifying the spoken words was higher when there was less noise, and higher for words produced by familiar speakers. Accuracy was also better with visual cues, especially with a full view of the head, or the mouth and jaw area only. The advantage of familiarity with the speaker's face and voice was particularly noticeable in the worst noise condition when only the mouth or eye areas were visible. These findings suggest that the mouth area was the primary source of linguistic information, but the eyes and upper cheeks of a familiar speaker were significantly more informative than auditory-only input. The results also suggest that learners preserve details of a speaker's face and voice in long-term memory, and that this facilitates subsequent processing of that person's speech.

The development of new technologies in speech science has included three-dimensional computer-animated talking heads as conversational agents with associated synthesized or natural speech. One of the best known is *Baldi* (e.g., Massaro, 1998), which now has an Italian-speaking counterpart, *Baldini* (Cosi, Cohen, and Massaro, 2002). These animated agents provide acoustic and visual speech cues based on measurements from human faces. They represent potential benefits for such segments of the population as hearing-impaired individuals, autistic children, and perhaps L2 learners, in facilitating the development of face-to-face communication skills. Unlike a human model, animated talking heads can display internal details of how sounds are produced in the mouth by making the skin on the face transparent. Baldi continues to undergo improvement of its structures and the naturalness of its appearance. One goal is to produce animated conversational agents that are capable of appropriate interactive language-specific behaviors including emotional expressions, head nods, eye contact, and upper body gestures (Cosi et al., 2002).

In a recent study using an animated talking head, Japanese participants identified Japanese syllables more accurately when head movements (i.e., rhythmic head movements that accompany speech) were present. Manipulation of head motion was controlled independently of other visual or acoustic speech characteristics (Munhall, Jones, Callan, Kuratate, and Vatikiotis-Bateson, 2004). The head movements had been based on a human speaker and were found to correlate strongly with the pitch and loudness of the speaker's voice.

The Munhall et al. (2004) study is indicative of the expanding direction of speech research towards a consideration of the coordination of various components of a speech event in context including visual information of the head and face as well as gestures of various kinds and their influence on spoken language processing. Sueyoshi and Hardison (2005) conducted a study to compare the relative contributions to listening comprehension of lip movements and hand–arm gestures for high and low proficiency learners of English as a second language. Learners at both proficiency levels were assigned to one of three conditions: auditory-visual with presentation of hand gestures and facial cues, auditory-visual with facial cues only, and auditory-only. Results indicated significantly greater accuracy on a multiple-choice listening task when visual cues were present than in the auditory-only condition. Comprehension scores for the lower proficiency learners were highest for the condition in which both hand gestures and facial cues were visible. However, the higher proficiency learners performed best when they saw only facial cues, suggesting that hand gestures facilitate comprehension at lower proficiency levels but more linguistic experience enhances the information value of facial speech cues such as lip movements.

Questionnaire responses from all learners showed they found visual cues to be very helpful in listening comprehension.

Capturing the larger picture of the speech event that portrays language in context has also been aided by technological innovations that provide visual input for language learners, for example, in the form of visualizations of pitch contours (Chun, Hardison, and Pennington, 2004; Hardison, 2004).[2] Multimodal tools such as Anvil (Kipp, 2001),[3] an annotation tool originally developed for the analysis of gesture, allows a researcher to align the display of the pitch contour of a speaker's voice with the associated video of the speech event. Anvil and the Real-Time Pitch (RTP) program of Kay Elemetrics Computerized Speech Lab were used in a recent study to investigate two types of contextualized input in prosody training for 28 advanced second-language learners of English whose first language was Mandarin Chinese (Hardison, 2005a). Their recorded oral presentations served as training materials to provide more meaningful input for them. Two groups received training input using Anvil with integrated video of their presentations and visual displays of associated pitch contours, and practiced prosody with RTP. The RTP allowed the learners to see the pitch contour of a native speaker producing the same sentence. Two groups used only the RTP to view their pitch contours and practiced with the same feedback. Within each of these pairs, one group received discourse-level input and the other individual sentences. Results indicated that all groups improved based on global prosody ratings provided by native speakers of English. Those who had practiced with discourse-level input were better able to transfer this improvement to subsequent natural discourse, and the presence of video was more helpful with discourse-level input than with individual sentences. From these results, it would appear that meaningful contextualized speech input that includes visual information is especially valuable in prosody training.[4]

Future research in auditory-visual speech has several paths to follow in addition to exploring the various components of speech events in context. These include neurophysiological studies of speech processing using techniques such as functional imaging, which have expanded the traditional focus from Broca's and Wernicke's areas in the brain toward a consideration of other regions associated with a more complex neural system (e.g., Scott, 2003). The field of facial animation is introducing virtual agents capable of interacting with the user in man–machine communication systems (e.g., Massaro, Cohen, Beskow, and Cole, 2000). Web-based technological tools are now accessible and hold promise for language teachers and researchers as we continue to explore our perceptions of the visual and auditory components of speech events.

conclusion

This chapter has focused attention on the under-explored visual modality of speech input, emphasizing its substantial role in determining the perceptual outcome when visual cues are available as in face-to-face communication. Both the hearing-impaired and various L2 learner populations benefit from training that can increase the information value of these cues. Studies clearly indicate that the benefits of visual cues extend beyond perception of a single phoneme in a syllable to the earlier identification of words in natural speech. With the advent of technological tools, it has become increasingly apparent that sounds and lip movements are only some of the components of a speech event. A speaker's coordination of head movements, facial expression, speech production including individual sounds and prosody, and gestures offer a fruitful direction for further studies. Such studies can increase our understanding of phonological perception and production as part of integrated communicative events and provide practical applications for analyzing, modeling, and mastering the phonological component of these events.

notes

1. The proceedings of the Conference on Auditory-Visual Speech Processing held in 1998 include video files of Harry McGurk producing a sequence of syllables in which the acoustic cue is always /ba/ but the visual cue varies (e.g., /ba/, /va/, /θa/, /da/, /ga/). These are available from the ISCA (International Speech Communication Association) Archive at <http://www.isca-speech.org/archive/avsp98> (retrieved January 20, 2006).
2. Editor's note: see also Chapter 11, this volume.
3. For information on Anvil, see http://www.dfki.de/~kipp/anvil (retrieved January 20, 2006). Directions are given for those who wish to obtain the address for downloading the files.
4. Editor's note: the use of video with computer-based tools in training L2 discourse-level phonology is an area in rapid development (see Chapter 11, this volume).

references

Benguerel, A.-P., & Pichora-Fuller, M. K. (1982). Coarticulation effects in lipreading. *Journal of Speech and Hearing Research, 25,* 600–7.
Berger, K. W. (1972). *Speechreading: Principles and methods.* Baltimore: National Education Press.

Bradlow, A. R., Pisoni, D. B., Yamada, R. A., & Tohkura, Y. (1997). Training Japanese listeners to identify English /r/ and /l/: IV. Some effects of perceptual learning on speech production. *Journal of the Acoustical Society of America, 101,* 2299–310.

Bradlow, A. R., Torretta, G. M., & Pisoni, D. B. (1996). Intelligibility of normal speech I: Global and fine-grained acoustic-phonetic talker characteristics. *Speech Communication, 20,* 255–72.

Brown, J. W. (1990). Overview. In A. B. Scheibel, & A. F. Wechsler (Eds.), *Neurobiology of higher cognitive function* (pp. 357–65). New York: The Guilford Press.

Burnham, D. (1998). Harry McGurk and the McGurk effect. In D. Burnham, J. Robert-Ribes, & E. Vatikiotis-Bateson (Eds.), *Proceedings of Auditory-Visual Speech Processing '98* (pp. 1–2). Sydney, Australia: Causal Productions PTY, Ltd.

Callan, D., Callan, A., & Vatikiotis-Bateson, E. (2001). Neural areas underlying the processing of visual speech information under conditions of degraded auditory information. In D. W. Massaro, J. Light, & K. Geraci (Eds.), *Proceedings of Auditory-Visual Speech Processing 2001* (pp. 45–9). Sydney, Australia: Causal Productions PTY, Ltd.

Campbell, R. (1987). Lip-reading and immediate memory processes or on thinking impure thoughts. In B. Dodd, & R. Campbell (Eds.), *Hearing by eye: The psychology of lipreading* (pp. 243–55). London: Erlbaum.

Chun, D. M., Hardison, D. M., & Pennington, M. C. (2004, May). Technologies for prosody in context: Past and future of L2 research and practice. Paper presented in the Colloquium on the State-of-the-Art in L2 Phonology Research at the annual conference of American Association for Applied Linguistics. Portland, Oregon.

Cosi, P., Cohen, M. A., & Massaro, D. W. (2002). Baldini: Baldi speaks Italian! In J. H. L. Hansen, & B. Pellom (Eds.), *International Conference on Spoken Language Processing 2002* (pp. 2349–52). Sydney, Australia: Causal Productions PTY, Ltd.

Daniloff, R. G., & Moll, K. (1968). Coarticulation of lip rounding. *Journal of Speech and Hearing Research, 11,* 707–21.

Demorest, M. E., Bernstein, L. E., & DeHaven, G. P. (1996). Generalizability of speechreading performance on nonsense syllables, words, and sentences: Subjects with normal hearing. *Journal of Speech and Hearing Research, 39,* 697–713.

de Sa, V., & Ballard, D. H. (1997). Perceptual learning from cross-modal feedback. In R. L. Goldstone, P. G. Schyns, & D. L. Medin (Eds.), *The Psychology of Learning and Motivation* (Vol. 36, pp. 309–51). San Diego, CA: Academic Press.

Dodd, B. (1979). Lip-reading in infants: Attention to speech presented in-and out-of-synchrony. *Cognitive Psychology, 11,* 478–84.

Dodd, B. (1987). The acquisition of lip-reading skills by normally hearing children. In B. Dodd, & R. Campbell (Eds.), *Hearing by eye: The psychology of lip-reading* (pp. 163–75). London: Erlbaum.

Goto, H. (1971). Auditory perception by normal Japanese adults of the sounds "l" and "r." *Neuropsychologia, 9,* 317–23.

Grosjean, F. (1980). Spoken word recognition processes and the gating paradigm. *Perception & Psychophysics, 28,* 267–83.

Hardison, D. M. (1999). Bimodal speech perception by native and nonnative speakers of English: Factors influencing the McGurk effect. *Language Learning, 49,* 213–83.

Hardison, D. M. (2000). The neurocognitive foundation of second-language speech: A proposed scenario of bimodal development. In B. Swierzbin, F. Morris, M. E. Anderson, C. A. Klee, & E. Tarone (Eds.), *Social and cognitive factors in second language acquisition* (pp. 312–25). Somerville, MA: Cascadilla Press.

Hardison, D. M. (2003). Acquisition of second-language speech: Effects of visual cues, context, and talker variability. *Applied Psycholinguistics, 24,* 495–522.

Hardison, D. M. (2004). Generalization of computer-assisted prosody training: Quantitative and qualitative findings. *Language Learning & Technology, 8,* 34–52. Available at <http://llt.msu.edu/vol8num1/hardison>.

Hardison, D. M. (2005a). Contextualized computer-based L2 prosody training: Evaluating the effects of discourse context and video input. *CALICO Journal, 22,* 175–90.

Hardison, D. M. (2005b) Second-language spoken word identification: Effects of perceptual training, visual cues, and phonetic environment. *Applied Psycholinguistics, 26,* 579–96.

Hardison, D. M. (2005c). Variability in bimodal spoken language processing by native and nonnative speakers of English: A closer look at effects of speech style. *Speech Communication, 46,* 73–93.

Hardison, D. M. (2006). Effects of familiarity with faces and voices on L2 spoken language processing: Components of memory traces. Paper presented at Interspeech 2006 – International Conference on Spoken Language Processing, Pittsburgh, PA.

Hazan, V., Sennema, A., & Faulkner, A. (2002). Audiovisual perception in L2 learners. In J. H. L. Hansen, & B. Pellom (Eds.), *International Conference on Spoken Language Processing 2002* (pp. 1685–8). Sydney, Australia: Causal Productions PTY, Ltd.

Hintzman, D. L. (1986). "Schema abstraction" in a multiple-trace memory model. *Psychological Review, 93,* 411–28.

Homa, D., & Cultice, J. (1984). Role of feedback, category size, and stimulus distortion on the acquisition and utilization of ill-defined categories. *Journal of Experimental Psychology: Learning, Memory, and Cognition, 10,* 83–94.

Johnson, K., & Mullennix, J. W. (Eds.) (1997). *Talker variability in speech processing.* San Diego, CA: Academic Press.

Kipp, M. (2001). Anvil – A generic annotation tool for multimodal dialogue. In *Proceedings of the 7th European Conference on Speech Communication and Technology* (pp. 1367–70). Aalborg, Denmark: Eurospeech.

Kirk, K. I., Pisoni, D. B., & Lachs, L. (2002). Audiovisual integration of speech by children and adults with cochlear implants. In J. H. L. Hansen, & B. Pellom (Eds.), *International Conference on Spoken Language Processing 2002* (pp. 1689–92). Sydney, Australia: Causal Productions PTY, Ltd.

Kricos, P. B., & Lesner, S. A. (1982). Differences in visual intelligibility across talkers. *Volta Review, 84,* 219–25.

Kuhl, P. K., & Meltzoff, A. N. (1984). The intermodal representation of speech in infants. *Infant Behavior & Development, 7,* 361–81.

Lansing, C. R., & McConkie, G. W. (1999). Attention to facial regions in segmental and prosodic visual speech perception tasks. *Journal of Speech, Language, and Hearing Research, 24,* 526–39.

Legerstee, M. (1990). Infants use multimodal information to imitate speech sounds. *Infant Behavior & Development, 1,* 343–54.

Lewkowicz, D. J. (2002). Perception and integration of audiovisual speech in human infants. In J. H. L. Hansen, & B. Pellom (Eds.), *International Conference on Spoken Language Processing 2002* (pp. 1701–4). Sydney, Australia: Causal Productions PTY, Ltd.

Lively, S. E., Logan, J. S., & Pisoni, D. B. (1993). Training Japanese listeners to identify English /r/ and /l/. II: The role of phonetic environment and talker variability in learning new perceptual categories. *Journal of the Acoustical Society of America, 94,* 1242–55.

MacDonald, J., & McGurk, H. (1978). Visual influences on speech perception processes. *Perception & Psychophysics, 24,* 253–7.

Marslen-Wilson, W., & Welsh, A. (1978). Processing interactions and lexical access during word recognition in continuous speech. *Cognitive Psychology, 10,* 29–63.

Massaro, D. W. (1987). *Speech perception by ear and eye: A paradigm for psychological inquiry.* Hillsdale, NJ: Erlbaum.

Massaro, D. W. (1998). *Perceiving talking faces: From speech perception to a behavioral principle.* Cambridge: MIT Press.

Massaro, D. W., Cohen, M. M., Beskow, J., & Cole, R. A. (2000). Developing and evaluating conversational agents. In J. Cassell, J. Sullivan, S. Prevost, & E. Churchill (Eds.), *Embodied conversational agents* (pp. 287–318). Cambridge: MIT Press.

Massaro, D. W., Cohen, M. M. & Gesi, A. T. (1993). Long-term training, transfer, and retention in learning to lipread. *Perception & Psychophysics, 53,* 549–62.

Massaro, D. W., Cohen, M. M., Gesi, A., Heredia, R., & Tsuzaki, M. (1993). Bimodal speech perception: An examination across languages. *Journal of Phonetics, 21,* 445–78.

McGurk, H. (1998). Developmental psychology and the vision of speech: Inaugural lecture by Professor Harry McGurk, 2nd March 1988. In D. Burnham, J. Robert-Ribes, & E. Vatikiotis-Bateson (Eds.), *Proceedings of Auditory-Visual Speech Processing '98* (pp. 3–20). Sydney, Australia: Causal Productions PTY Ltd.

McGurk, H., & MacDonald, J. (1976). Hearing lips and seeing voices. *Nature, 264,* 746–8.

Meltzoff, A. N., & Kuhl, P. K. (1994). Faces and speech: Intermodal processing of biologically relevant signals in infants and adults. In D. J. Lewkowicz, & R. Lickliter (Eds.), *The development of intersensory perception: Comparative perspectives* (pp. 335–69). Hillsdale, NJ: Erlbaum.

Meltzoff, A. N., & Moore, M. K. (1993). Why faces are special to infants – On connecting the attraction of faces and infants' ability for imitation and cross-modal processing. In B. de Boysson-Bardies, S. de Schonen, P. Jusczyk, P. McNeilage, & J. Morton (Eds.), *Developmental neurocognition: Speech and face processing in the first year of life* (pp. 211–25). Dordrecht: Kluwer Academic.

Miller, G. A., & Nicely, P. E. (1955). An analysis of perceptual confusions among some English consonants. *Journal of the Acoustical Society of America, 27,* 338–52.

Mills, A. E. (1987). The development of phonology in the blind child. In B. Dodd & R. Campbell (Eds.), *Hearing by eye: The psychology of lip-reading* (pp. 145–61). London: Erlbaum.

Munhall, K. G., Jones, J. A., Callan, D. E., Kuratate, T., & Vatikiotis-Bateson, E. (2004). Visual prosody and speech intelligibility. *Psychological Science, 15,* 133–7.

Munhall, K. G., & Tohkura, Y. (1998). Audiovisual gating and the time course of speech perception. *Journal of the Acoustical Society of America, 104*, 530–9.

Quittner, A., Smith L., Osberger, M., Mitchell, T., & Katz, D. (1994). The impact of audition on the development of visual attention. *Psychological Science, 5*, 347–53.

Remez, R. E., Pardo, J. S., Piorkowski, R. L., & Rubin, P. E. (2001). On the bistability of sine wave analogues of speech. *Psychological Science, 12*, 24–29.

Rizzolatti, G., & Arbib, M. (1998). Language within our grasp. *Trends in Neurosciences, 21*, 188–94.

Rolls, E. (1989). The representation and storage of information in neuronal networks in the primate cerebral cortex and hippocampus. In R. Durbin, C. Miall, & G. Mitchison (Eds.), *The computing neuron* (pp. 125–59). Reading, MA: Addison-Wesley.

Rosenblum, L. D. (2002). The perceptual basis for audiovisual speech integration. In J. H. L. Hansen, & B. Pellom (Eds.), *International Conference on Spoken Language Processing 2002* (pp. 1461–4). Sydney, Australia: Causal Productions PTY, Ltd.

Sams, M., Aulanko, R., Hämäläinen, M., Hari, R., Lounasmaa, O. V., Lu, S.-T., & Simola, J. (1991). Seeing speech: Visual information from lip movements modifies activity in the human auditory cortex. *Neuroscience Letters, 127*, 141–5.

Scott, S. K. (2003). How might we conceptualize speech perception? The view from neurobiology. *Journal of Phonetics, 31*, 417–22.

Sekiyama, K. (1997). Cultural and linguistic factors in audiovisual speech processing: The McGurk effect in Chinese subjects. *Perception & Psychophysics, 59*, 73–80.

Sekiyama, K., & Sugita, Y. (2002). Auditory-visual speech perception examined by brain imaging and reaction time. In J. H. L. Hansen, & B. Pellom (Eds.), *International Conference on Spoken Language Processing 2002* (pp. 1693–6). Sydney, Australia: Causal Productions PTY, Ltd.

Sekiyama, K., & Tohkura, Y. (1991). McGurk effect in non-English listeners: Few visual effects for Japanese subjects hearing Japanese syllables of high auditory intelligibility. *Journal of the Acoustical Society of America, 90*, 1797–805.

Stein, B. E., London, N., Wilkinson, L. K., & Price, D. D. (1996). Enhancement of perceived visual intensity by auditory stimuli: A psychophysical analysis. *Journal of Cognitive Neuroscience, 8*, 497–506.

Sueyoshi, A., & Hardison, D. M. (2005). The role of gestures as visual cues in listening comprehension by second-language learners. *Language Learning, 55*, 671–709.

Summerfield, Q. (1979). Use of visual information for phonetic perception. *Phonetica, 36*, 314–31.

Tyler, L., & Wessels, J. (1985). Is gating an on-line task? Evidence from naming latency data. *Perception & Psychophysics, 38*, 217–222.

Vatikiotis-Bateson, E., Eigsti, I-M., Yano, S., & Munhall, K. G. (1998). Eye movement of perceivers during audiovisual speech perception. *Perception & Psychophysics, 60*, 926–40.

Walden, B. E., Erdman, S. A., Montgomery, A. A., Schwartz, D. M., & Prosek, R. A. (1981). Some effects of training on speech recognition by hearing-impaired adults. *Journal of Speech and Hearing Research, 24*, 207–16.

Walden, B. E., Prosek, R. A., Montgomery, A. A., Scherr, C. K., & Jones, C. J. (1977). Effects of training on the visual recognition of consonants. *Journal of Speech and Hearing Research, 20,* 130–45.

Walker, S., Bruce, V., & O'Malley, C. (1995). Facial identity and facial speech processing: Familiar faces and voices in the McGurk effect. *Perception & Psychophysics, 57,* 1124–33.

Walton, G. E., & Bower, T. G. R. (1993). Amodal representation of speech in infants. *Infant Behavior & Development, 16,* 233–43.

Watson, C. S., Qiu, W. W., Chamberlain, M. M., & Li, X. (1996). Auditory and visual speech perception: Confirmation of a modality-independent source of individual differences in speech recognition. *Journal of the Acoustical Society of America, 100,* 1153–62.

Welch, R. B., & Warren, D. H. (1980). Immediate perceptual response to intersensory discrepancy. *Psychological Bulletin, 88,* 638–67.

7

sounds, brain, and evolution:
or, why phonology is plural[1]

april mcmahon

what is phonology?

phonology and its neighbors

If we were giving prizes for most frequently set examination questions in
undergraduate linguistics, one extremely good candidate would be "What
is the difference between phonetics and phonology?" More ambitious
versions of this question might ask about the interface between the two
domains, or introduce an argumentative statement such as "There is no
difference between phonology and phonetics. Discuss."

The assumption is that there are two domains of inquiry, phonetics and
phonology, but that the exact location of the boundary between them
is uncertain – or alternatively, that there might really be only a single
domain of inquiry, and that we might legitimately and productively
argue about this. At a rather more advanced level of study, similar
questions may arise about the distinction between phonology and
morphology.

In this chapter, I pursue a rather different question, though some
of the arguments are reminiscent of those about whether phonology
is different from morphology or the same as phonetics. Rather than
considering uniting phonology with another adjacent linguistic level,
I suggest that phonologists might have to reconsider their domain of
inquiry for another reason. Evidence from a range of different sources
suggests that the essential question here is whether *phonology*, as it is con-
ventionally presented, studied and taught, is a unitary domain at all.

different emphases within phonology

The most elementary experience of phonology indicates that there are two rather different things going on inside this allegedly single subject area. Typically, phonologists and phonology courses note that phonology has *segmental* and *suprasegmental* (or *prosodic*) subcomponents; but the usual practice of phonologists and the preferred territory of theories is not neutral or even-handed between the two. Phonologists have a strong tendency to work on either segmental issues (properties of vowels and consonants, phoneme systems, feature theory, and morphophonological alternations), or on prosodic ones (stress, intonation, and syllables). This can be observed very clearly when we contrast recent textbooks, all intended for first-year undergraduates. Carr (1999) devotes 66 pages out of 148 to syllables, stress, rhythm, connected speech, and intonation, while Davenport and Hannahs (1998) focus all but 24 pages out of 187 on segments, features, phonemes, and rules; and in McMahon (2001), only two chapters out of ten involve anything above the level of the segment.

When we turn to phonological theories, we can observe the same preferences and the same division of labor. *Articulatory Phonology* (Browman and Goldstein, 1989, 1992) is primarily concerned with segments – or more accurately, with the individual movements or gestures (e.g., of the lips, tongue, and vocal folds) which speakers make to form what phonologists have typically analyzed as segments. Higher-level units are outside the domain of this model; there is, for instance, no real account of the syllable. *Lexical Phonology* (Giegerich, 1999; McMahon, 2000a; Mohanan, 1986) is also essentially segmental, though it focuses on interactions with morphology, while Articulatory Phonology is concerned with the relationship of phonology to phonetics. In contrast, *Metrical Phonology* (Giegerich, 1985; Hogg and McCully, 1998) is primarily about stress, syllables, and rhythm, and is almost completely focused on the organization of segments into higher-level units. In the same way, *Optimality Theory* (Kager, 1999; McCarthy, 2002; Prince and Smolensky, 2004), which has become the dominant paradigm in phonology over the past ten years, has a strong bias towards syllables and stress. Extensions of Optimality Theory (OT) from prosodic to segmental phenomena have caused a gradual dilution of the early strong OT principles of innateness and universality of constraints, along with an explosion in abstract and specialized phonological mechanisms to account for exceptional cases and irregular phenomena.

The emphasis on stress and syllabification which is characteristic of OT is a relatively recent innovation in the field of phonology, and the still pervasive assumption that "segmental phonology" and "phonology" are synonymous can be particularly infuriating for prosodic phonologists. Phonologists writing on stress, and to an even greater extent, intonation, often seem to feel they must justify the place of prosody in phonetics and phonology. As Cruttenden (1986) observes:

> Phonetics, in the mind of the "man in the street", nurtured on *Pygmalion* and *My Fair Lady*, generally consists of sounds and the transcription of sounds: he thinks, for example, of the word *nice* being transcribed as /naɪs/.... But there are clearly other features involved in the way a word is said which are not indicated in a segmental transcription. (p. 1)

Later in the same passage, Cruttenden explicitly discusses pitch and voice quality as two of these "other features." Ladd (1996), introducing the theme of his book, explains that

> the heart of this theory is the idea that intonation, and pitch in particular, has a phonological organisation. This idea requires some justification, since pitch seems to pose problems for phonology. (p. 1)

Ladd goes on to recognize that his concerns are rather different from the main emphases of current phonology:

> The conception of "phonology" underlying this book is fairly elementary, and most of the theoretical issues discussed here are remote from current debates in phonological theory. The reader who wishes to know more about the relevance of intonational phenomena for Optimality Theory, for instance, will find little of direct interest here. (p. 4)

This emphasis on segmental phonology is also strongly characteristic of studies of phonological variation and change. It is, of course, particularly difficult to work on the history of prosody, since stress, intonation, and even length are often not consistently marked in spelling. Colantoni and Gurlekian (2004), in a relatively rare recent exception to this tendency to focus in variationist work on segmental phonology, consider the possible role of contact in changes in Buenos Aires Spanish intonation. They note the intrinsic difficulties of making historical hypotheses on intonation, when even our knowledge of present-day variation in the field is so limited and so relatively unsupported by experimental studies. Much more research is needed on prosodic variation, from which we might be able to generalize to hypotheses about prosodic change. At present, there is still a considerable imbalance towards segmental comparisons in descriptions of accent variation (see, e.g., Giegerich, 1992; McMahon, 2001).

prosodic versus segmental phonology

Underlying these different emphases is a puzzle. Linguists usually regard phonology as a single domain, and while we might expect individual theories to be rather better at analyzing certain areas within that domain, and individual phonologists to develop a preference for phenomena of one kind rather than another, we might not automatically expect these biases and preferences to fall into such neat sets. Over and over again, we find that theories and individuals work for, and on, either: (a) features and segments; or (b) syllables, rhythm, and pitch. We find a repeatable, almost predictable tendency for phonology to be interpreted primarily as either an overarching system of organization involving syllables, feet, and utterances, or as the characteristics and interactions of the individual segment-sized elements that fit into those higher-level structures.

This *might* be a coincidence; or it might be telling us that what we have been calling "phonology" for the last hundred or so years is not a single domain at all, but two. Phonologists talk as if their subject area is a single domain of inquiry, but behave as if it were really two areas, from which we may choose one on which to focus (without necessarily admitting that we are making a choice at all). Perhaps it would be both more honest, and more enlightening, to accept that "phonology" is really two interacting but separate domains, which both happen to involve the systematic patterning of sound. There are many cases where an area once accepted as a single domain is subsequently separated into two; indeed, phonetics and phonology were not distinguished by many linguists in the nineteenth century. Outside phonology, recent progress in physics has been characterized by the development of two very differently oriented theories, namely General Relativity and Quantum Physics (Davies and Brown, 1988).

If we accept that there are two kinds of phonology, or that what we have grown used to calling phonology in fact covers two domains, what should we call these two domains, and what belongs in each one? The terminological issue is less central, but arguably thornier. As Harris, Watson, and Bates (1999) note, "It is now widely accepted in the theoretical literature that phonological representations combine two quite distinct organizational subsystems, PROSODY and MELODY"(p. 493), where prosody is, for the moment, the area including stress, intonation, and syllables, and melody is vowels and consonants. The terms *prosody* and *melody* are also used in McMahon (2005); but they are not ideal, since "melody" immediately brings to mind tunes and singing, which, as we shall see below, connect with the clearly prosodic intonation. Harris, Watson and Bates (1999) relate their prosody-melody dichotomy to Jakobson's (1971) distinction between *framework* and *content*. These might be better terminological candidates, though again not perfect: why should stress, in languages where it is not predictable, be classified as "framework" rather than "content?" Largely on the grounds of familiarity rather than absolute transparency or appropriateness, I use the terms *prosody* (or *prosodic phonology*) and *segmentals* (or *segmental phonology*).[2]

What phenomena should we then expect to find in the domains we have agreed, at least provisionally, to call *prosody* and *segmentals*? Harris et al. (1999) provide a particularly helpful outline of the scope of the two areas, as follows:

a) Prosodic structure...comprises a hierarchy of domains which define relations between segments within phonological strings. The terminal nodes of this hierarchy are skeletal syllabic positions, which are gathered into syllabic constituents (onsets, nuclei and rhymes).... Syllabic constituents themselves are grouped into larger domains, including the foot and the prosodic word. Relations defined at these levels are implicated in such matters as metrical structure (responsible for word stress, amongst other things), vowel syncope and the scope of long-distance harmonic assimilation.

b) Melody...codes those characteristics of a segment's make-up that are manifested as phonetic quality, including such properties as labiality, palatality, occlusion, friction and voicing. These categories are assumed to be deployed on separate autosegmental tiers, in recognition of the fact that each is independently accessible by phonological processes. (The use of the term MELODY acknowledges the similarity between tonal and non-tonal categories in this respect (Halle & Vergnaud 1980)). (Harris et al., 1999, p. 493)

In other words, prosody involves stress and intonation: both use the same features of fundamental frequency, intensity, and duration, though at different levels (lexical versus utterance). Stress and intonation are also interdependent. As Cruttenden (1986) notes, "we have to know which syllables are accented in utterances because accented syllables form the framework for intonation" (p. 19). However, prosody as defined here includes issues of hierarchy, syllable membership, and quantity.

According to Harris et al. (1999), it would also include positional effects (*phonotactics*), and some aspects of *harmony*.

Logically, this must be right: the phonotactic fact that in English /h/ can appear initially, in syllable onsets, but not finally, in codas, is obviously about more than a single segment; so is the fact that /s/ can precede /t/ but not /d/. Likewise, if we are dealing with a language which has vowel harmony, where the quality of the first vowel in a word or other unit determines aspects of the quality of all other vowels in the same unit, we are clearly dealing with more than the individual segments. However, I would take issue with the assessment of Harris et al. (1999) that phonotactics and harmony are necessarily prosodic; instead, they might be indications that prosody and segmentals interact with and condition one another.[3] Perhaps the dividing line between prosody and segmentals is whether we are dealing with elements within a larger unit, as opposed to individual sounds and their interactions.

In this as in other cases, we need to determine what fits into each category on the basis of evidence and patterning, not by following traditional labels. On the one hand, as we have seen, prosody here includes syllables and syllabification, which would not traditionally be included in this class. On the other hand, Harris et al. see tone as melodic, or segmental; and this follows from the fact that tone is contrastive and that it typically develops historically from segmental sources (Hock, 1986).[4]

It is one thing to observe that phonologists behave as if there is a difference between prosody and melody, and quite another to explain it. I argue in the rest of this chapter that the division between prosody and segmentals runs deeper than we might suppose, and that this depth is time depth: in other words, the differential development and characterization of the two phonologies is a function of the evolution of human language.

acquisition, prosody, and evolution

Most linguists would agree that our remit is not only to strive to describe and understand what speakers *do*, but also what they *know*. And whenever we consider knowledge, we must necessarily concern ourselves with where that knowledge comes from: is it innate, or is it learned? Since prosody varies between languages, and indeed dialects, there must be a learned component; but it would appear that children learn prosodic phonology rather early in normal acquisition (Bloom, 1973; Snow, 1994; Vihman, 1996). Vihman (1996) concludes that "prosodic features are salient to infants from early in life and also appear to be available relatively early for voluntary manipulation in production" (p. 205). Cruttenden (1986, p. 172) notes that babies will mimic adult pitch patterns from approximately 8 months of age; Crystal (1979) asserts that even 2–3-month-old babies may be aware of prosodic contrasts. In general, "control of pitch increases and stabilizes throughout the first year of life" (Vihman, 1996, p. 212); segmental phonology is acquired more slowly.

I argue that prosody is acquired faster and earlier than segmental phonology because prosody involves a much more substantial innate component. In brief, segmental phonology can be learned from only the primary linguistic data the child hears; but prosody cannot, because it involves crucial, hidden structure (see McMahon, 2005). In the case of segmentals, as Carr (2000) argues, "there are, if anything, more data available to the neonate than is strictly required for phonological acquisition" (p. 93). Insofar as any internal help is needed in this learning process, it will involve capacities and capabilities which are not specific to language, like our ability to make vocal sounds, and to recognize patterns.[5] Of course, this does not mean that segmental phonology can vary without limit; humans are shaped by genetics and by evolution, and only certain possibilities can be accommodated within those evolved structures. But limits on vocal tracts, ears, and brains are not specific to language.

Prosodic structure appears to be manifested only partially in, and thus *underdetermined* by, the phonetic signal. Children can only learn a stress system, for instance, with the assistance of information which cannot be heard directly in the input they receive. Most obviously, as noted by Dresher and Kaye (1990), the placement of stress depends on syllabification; but syllable boundaries are not audible. Children therefore are highly likely to learn prosody with the assistance of innate capacities which are associated uniquely with language learning. This need not be so for segmentals; the child can hear everything needed to learn the system of vowels and consonants appropriate for a particular language or language variety. It is thus not accidental that theories of phonological learning which rely on innate capacities controlled by a set of universal *parameters* (Dresher and Kaye, 1990) or *constraints* (Tesar and Smolensky, 2000) are concerned with stress systems rather than consonant or vowel systems, which are more variable and also more amenable to learning from experience.

If some innate, universal grammar or other inborn apparatus is required for the acquisition of prosody but not for segmental phonology, we might also assume that prosody, though not segmentals, can appropriately be analyzed by means of innate constraints or parameters in adult grammars.

If we extend our view to include not only acquisition but evolution, we may go further towards understanding why innate mechanisms are not only inappropriate for segmental phonology, but also quite clearly unavailable to the child.

If we assume that modern humans evolved in Africa approximately 200,000–100,000 years BP (Before Present) and subsequently radiated out of Africa from around 100,000 years ago (Stringer and McKie, 1997), then there are straightforward physical limitations on how much difference could have developed between human sub-populations in the time available; 84% of total human variation can be found within any single human population (Barbujani, Magagni, Minch, and Cavalli-Sforza, 1997), reflecting the fact that genetic mutations take a very considerable period of time to spread through populations. There has been plenty of evolutionary time for modern humans to have evolved differences from our other primate relatives, since the chimp–human split is usually dated at approximately 5–7 million years BP, but very little time on an evolutionary timescale for modern humans to have developed differences from one another.

What this means is that anything innate must be shared among all human languages: language-specific differences cannot be innate, because the main radiations of *Homo sapiens* out of Africa are relatively recent, later than 100,000 years BP. Even under active selection pressure on a particular linguistic feature, the mutation responsible could not develop and spread to fixation in all and only the speakers of a single language during the entire lifetime of that language, let alone in the period since some critical change such as the Great Vowel Shift of Middle English (see McMahon, 2000b).

The conclusion from the foregoing discussion is that the development of specific patterns of segmental phonology, and of quirky and language-specific interactions of melody and morphology, cannot be attributed to universal, innate factors. General physical and neurological structures are shared across the species and are reasonable candidates for evolved systems. In segmental phonology, however, variation within the anatomical limits set by the vocal tract is a matter for the specific language and community, and is learned by members of that community by exposure to spoken data.

If prosody does rely on an innate system, then it can be hypothesized that prosody is an older system than segmental phonology, and that prosody or its precursor developed in evolutionary rather than historical time. How might we test this hypothesis? First, we would expect that universals should be more plentiful in the prosodic component of language than in the segmental component. We might also expect closer affinities between human prosodic systems and non-human communication systems, on the one hand, indicating residual features of the common ancestral state of humans and other primates, and between prosody and non-linguistic systems (such as gesture and emotion), on the other. If such evidence is forthcoming, we can conclude that prosody is a classic Darwinian case of descent with modification from an earlier common system, a system that existed prior to human language as it is now. In the following sections, I consider evidence to this effect from non-human primate vocal communication, gesture, emotion, language disorder, and brain lateralization.

prosody and non-human primate vocal communication

Non-human primates typically communicate in a number of modalities – auditory, olfactory, visual, and tactile. The first of these offers the most immediate connections with prosody in human spoken language, though Locke (1998, p. 194) notes that comparisons between human and non-human primate vocalizations can be difficult to make. Most work on vocal signaling in other primates has concentrated on alarm calls, as these are the easiest to elicit and record, and their meaning is generally relatively clear. Quieter vocalizations in small groups are harder to record, and much more difficult to assess in terms of meaning (Corballis, 1992), though as discussed below, these social uses of vocal signals are key to a number of theories of language evolution.

Most observed affinities between human language and non-human primate vocal communication involve human suprasegmentals. Hauser and Fowler (1992) observe that a gradual decrease (*declination*) of fundamental frequency (perceived as pitch) across an utterance, along with a rapid final fall at the end of an utterance, are sufficiently common in human languages to have been proposed as universals. Declination in particular results from the fact that pressure below the vocal folds (*subglottal pressure*) will typically fall progressively through expiration, and subglottal pressure in turn causes the vocal folds to vibrate more slowly, unless the speaker actively counteracts this natural effect. Consequently, Hauser and Fowler (1992) argue that declination and the utterance-final fall in fundamental frequency "reflect dispositional features of the vocal-tract – that is, regularities that are easier to allow to occur than they are to inhibit or to offset" (p. 363). This natural tendency has now become conventionalized, in that these prosodic characteristics frequently mark utterance boundaries and may therefore have a language-use function in acting as cues to the end of a speaker's conversational turn.

Hauser and Fowler (1992) investigated the vocalizations of six groups of vervet monkeys and one group of rhesus macaques in order to ascertain whether these primates like humans exhibited declination and a final fall in fundamental frequency during two-call or three-call communicative signals (*bouts*). Adult vervets showed a significant decrease in fundamental frequency from call one to call two, and a further, additional decrease from call two to call three, providing some evidence for both declination and a final fall. Young vervets did not yet seem to have full command of this pattern. In the case of rhesus macaques, there was clear evidence for declination, though less evidence for the final fall, with only 60% of bouts showing a greater fall between calls two and three than between calls one and two. Hauser and Fowler also investigated interruptions of call bouts by other animals, and found that young vervets, who showed no consistent pattern of fundamental frequency in long call bouts, were interrupted far more frequently than adults. Furthermore, "five out of the six interrupted bouts showed precipitous falls...to a near-terminal value between the first two calls of a three-call bout" (Hauser and Fowler, 1992, p. 368). The implication is that a sharp fall in pitch is perceived as a signal of completion of the call even by other animals. It would appear that declination and, to a lesser extent, a final fall, in pitch are natural and follow from the structure of the respiratory system and larynx in both humans and other primates as used in vocalization. Humans and vervets both also use these prosodic patterns as a guide to turn-taking in conversation.

prosody, gesture, and emotion

As Corballis (1992) observes:

> Chimpanzees in the wild...use gestures quite extensively to communicate with one another. For example, they extend hands in greeting, signal to another to halt, gesture for food or grooming, beckon for approach; moreover the stages in which gestures emerge in young chimpanzees parallel quite closely those observed in human children. (p. 214)

Goodall (1986) refers to certain chimpanzee facial expressions as "vocalization-bound" (p. 119), indicating that they appear only in combination with a particular call. This strong link between physical and vocal signals is also characteristic of human prosody.[6]

Bolinger is one of the strongest advocates of an indivisible union between intonation and gesture. He argues that, whereas segmental phonology involves the concatenation of inherently meaningless units, "intonation – meaning strictly the rise and fall of pitch as it occurs along the speech chain – has its symbolizing power thanks to a primitive drive mechanism that raises pitch as tension rises and lowers it as tension falls" (Bolinger, 1983, p. 156). That is, general bodily tension involves increasing subglottal pressure and potentially vocal fold tension, and hence a rise in fundamental frequency. Bolinger outlines a large number of cases in which pitch and gestures move in parallel, so that a shift upwards in pitch is mirrored in upward movements of the head, jaw, arms, hands, shoulders, and corners of the mouth, and a downward movement of any or all of these accompanies a drop in pitch.

These connections of gesture and intonation recall Hauser and Fowler's (1992) arguments, reviewed in the previous section, that declination is a direct consequence of physical structures and movements in the respiratory and phonatory systems. However, just as declination can be brought under the speaker's control and can acquire particular meanings in the linguistic system (notably its correlation with boundaries and completion of a speech event or turn), so gestures and intonation can be consciously controlled by speakers and can also develop different usage in the systems of particular cultures and languages. Gestures can, to an extent, be "read" universally, and we share many automatic and universal gestures with our primate relations. Yet there will be culture-specific cases when our universal fall-back positions let us down. In the same way, intonational variation has developed cross-linguistically, although there are strong and generally reliable universal strategies for interpreting intonational contours.

Bolinger (1983) connects rises and falls in pitch to rises and falls in tension both literally, in the sense of vocal tract and respiratory mechanics, and metaphorically, or emotionally. Rising tension in an emotional sense may mean anger, fear, or strong commitment to the message being conveyed; lower tension may signal lack of commitment, boredom, or an attempt to calm an interlocutor, for instance. The same is true for primates in general: the quality of vocal signs in both humans and chimpanzees, for example, will vary, depending in part on the muscular setting and facial expression in force when they are produced. Since our expression and the tenseness of our facial musculature often reflect our feelings, there is an automatic link with emotion.

According to Goodall (1986):

> Chimpanzee vocalizations are closely bound to emotion. The production of a sound in the *absence* of the appropriate emotional state seems to be an almost impossible task for a chimpanzee. (p. 125)

Conversely, chimpanzees find it extremely difficult to suppress their calls, which seem to follow naturally when the "appropriate emotional state" is engendered, although they can learn to do so to some extent. Goodall (ibid.) reports the case of the adolescent male chimpanzee, Figan, later a dominant member of his group, to whom she gave some bananas. He immediately produced a series of excited food calls, and the other members of the group rushed back and stole his present.

> A few days later he waited behind again, and once more received his bananas. He made no loud sounds, but the calls could be heard deep in his throat, almost causing him to gag. (p. 125)

In Goodall's (ibid., p. 127) list of the chimpanzee calls she observed, each is associated with a particular emotional state: the *wraaa* alarm call, signaling fear (of strangers or strangeness); the *huu* indicating puzzlement; various barks, *waa*-barks, and tantrum screams showing anger or rage; and laughs, pants, lip smacks, and tooth clacks suggesting pleasure at being groomed. Humans have developed the means to vocalize or suppress vocalization, and to initiate or end conversation at will, regardless of the presence of a particular stimulus; but we appear to retain the close connection of prosody with emotion.

This close association of intonation in particular with emotion contributes to the greater ease of identifying universals in prosody than in segmental phonology. As Hirst and Di Cristo (1998) observe:

> Intonation is universal first of all because every language possesses intonation.... Intonation is universal also because many of the linguistic and paralinguistic functions of intonation systems seem to be shared by languages of widely different origins. (p. 1)

Hirst and Di Cristo's own study of intonation in 20 languages supports earlier surveys which indicate universal patterns of pitch distribution. Ultan (1978), for instance, considered 53 languages, and reports the following data for *yes–no* questions:

- 71.7% languages had a terminal rise;
- 34% had higher pitch during the contour, typically towards the end;
- 5.7% had falling and rising alternatives;
- 5.7% had a terminal fall or low pitch.

Only 5.7%, or three, of Ultan's 53 languages had a consistent fall rather than a rise in *yes–no* questions. Two of these, Fanti and Grebo, are tone languages (which complicate the picture by introducing a further, segmental use of pitch); and the other, Chitimacha, was reported in 1946 as having a single remaining speaker, raising the question of whether the data obtained were characteristic of earlier stages of the language or a peculiarity of the one speaker. Thirty-two of 36 languages surveyed by Bolinger (1978) had a rise or higher pitch in questions. Conversely, as Cruttenden (1986) observes: "It is…a nearly absolute linguistic universal that unmarked declaratives have a final falling pitch" (p. 158). Ultan (1978) himself draws a conclusion in terms of emotional meaning, referring to

> the widespread contrast between a terminal falling and a terminal rising contour representing a meaningful distinction between an attitude of finality or conclusiveness and one of suspension, incompleteness, doubt, questioning, or the like on the part of the speaker. (p. 219)

Ladd (1996) argues that intonation has a linguistic, phonological organization, and cannot be analyzed as purely encoding emotion or tension. He is also careful to note that claims for universality must be specific enough to be meaningful: simply requiring questions to have a high or rising pitch at some point would include virtually every utterance, question and non-question alike. Ladd nonetheless concludes that intonational variation is generally extremely circumscribed, and so can appropriately be analyzed parametrically, as has also been suggested for stress systems. Ladd also accepts that intonation carries paralinguistic, or affective, as well as linguistic, messages: "Sometimes against our will, it signals or helps signal information about our sex, our age, and our emotional state, as part of a parallel communicative channel that can be interpreted by listeners (even some non-human ones) who do not understand the linguistic message" (ibid., p. 1). Thus, intonation can be interpreted quite reliably even when the segmental phonology is not understood, either because the hearer does not share the speaker's language, or because the segmental content has been experimentally removed by acoustic filtering. As Ladd concludes, paralinguistic messages "are non-propositional and difficult to paraphrase precisely, and yet in many circumstances they communicate powerfully and effectively" (p. 33).

This is not to say that intonation is invariant: on the contrary, intonational change can and does take place in particular groups, and prosody may vary dialectally. As Cruttenden (1986) points out:

> There are certain areas which are particularly susceptible to idiosyncratic uses of tones. Greetings, farewells, and social formulas are one such area: the conventional way of intoning the equivalent of *Good morning* will vary from language to language; moreover variation within one language in such areas will be sensitive to very subtle social conventions. (p. 169)

We return to a possible evolutionary account of such variation below.

prosody and language disorder

If studies of children with disordered language development show that prosodic and segmental phonology are always affected together, then it will be harder to justify the idea that they are essentially independent. On the other hand, if segmental phonology is subject to disorder or delay while prosody develops normally, or vice versa, then the argument for independence is strengthened. Several recent papers suggest that prosody and segmentals are not necessarily implicated together in language disorder.

Harris et al. (1999) discuss a case "in which the prosodic subsystem is the primary site of disturbance (admittedly with melodic side-effects)" (p. 495). The child "PS" was recorded between ages 4;11 (years; months) and 6;07. His short vowel system was essentially identical to the Standard Southern British English adult system, though he collapsed /ɪ/ *lick* and /ʊ/ *book* as /ɪ/. However, PS showed more dramatic divergence from the adult system in the long vowels and diphthongs, with the three consistent patterns shown below.

(i)   Shortening and monophthongization: *weed* [wɪd], *tube* [tɪb], *class* [kwæs];
(ii) Hardening: *cow* [kab], *know* [nəb], *you* [jɪb], *see* [sɪɟ], *day* [dɛɟ], *eye* [aɟ];
(iii) Adult in-gliding vowels treated as bisyllabic: *tire* [tɔjə], *here* [hɪjə]; the two resulting vowels are separated by a glide or a hardened stop.

Harris et al. (1999) argue that all three innovations are reactions to the same prosodic deficit: for PS, a single vowel (V) is an acceptable nucleus, but a double vowel (VV) is not. In consequence, the target vowel may be shortened or monophthongized. Alternatively, it may be subjected to "hardening," which "results in an adult up-gliding vowel being rendered as a short vowel followed by an oral stop" (Harris et al., 1999, p. 506). All of these processes alter the adult form to make it compatible with PS's highly constrained syllable template. As Harris et al. (1999) conclude, "the case study provides external confirmation of the independence of the prosodic and melodic facets of phonological representation" (p. 523).

More commonly, we find reports of impaired segmentals but unaffected prosody. These cases typically involve intonation. A case in point is Wells and Peppé (2003), who report work with eighteen 8-year-olds, each 1.5 standard deviations below the mean on one of two standard tests. These children were matched to control groups by both language age (i.e., the age their performance on standard tests corresponded to for children without language impairment) and chronological age.

Wells and Peppé developed a series of tasks to test performance of language-impaired children in terms of prosodic usage and comprehension. The overall results for the language-impaired children were below those of their language age controls on only two out of sixteen tasks, providing very little evidence for a specific prosody impairment. The language-impaired children scored significantly below those of their chronological age on nine out of sixteen tests, including all those involving performance rather than comprehension. However, in tasks which tested the ability to convey or comprehend the difference between confirming and checking understanding using prosody,[7] the language-impaired children behaved very similarly to other children of their chronological age. Wells and Peppé conclude that prosodic imitation is weak for language-impaired children, but that there seems to be no association of prosody beyond the word level with other areas of language impairment. Indeed, areas of prosodic strength are a potential functional resource for language-impaired children, who can assess emotional, affective, or attitudinal meaning from prosodic resources, providing additional contextual knowledge which aids their understanding.

These conclusions are strongly supported by van der Meulen, Janssen, and Den Os (1997), who tested imitation of intonation patterns and recognition of emotional meaning for 30 normally-developing and 30 language-impaired 4–6-year-olds. They found that the language-impaired children experienced greater difficulty with the imitation task, but that there was no statistically significant difference between the performances of the two groups on the emotion-identification task. The relative weakness in imitation does not, however, necessarily indicate a specific prosodic deficit, since the language-impaired children might have experienced quite independent problems in processing the sentences to be imitated (van der Meulen, Janssen, and Den Os, 1997, p. 166).

Snow (1998) similarly argues that developmental disorders of morphosyntax do not appear to predict prosodic impairment, showing "that 4-year-old children with specific language impairment...demonstrate a normal expressive control of prosodic boundary features" (p. 1167). In fact, Snow suggests that "prosody may be a residual strength for many children with [specific language impairment]" (ibid.). In later work, Snow (2001) further demonstrates, even more appositely from the point of view of the prosody-segmentals distinction, that 4-year-old children with developmental language impairment exhibited a dissociation between their performance in intonation and in segmental phonology. Snow (1998) concludes that "lexical and prosodic levels of phonology are independent and dissociable" (p. 582) and "many children with [language impairment] who have poor intelligibility can partly compensate for deficits in articulation by emphasizing their prosodic strengths" (p. 583).[8]

prosody and brain lateralization

This evidence of differential involvement of prosody and melody in language impairment might further predict neurological differences between the two domains. Evidence from aphasia and selective brain stimulation in neurosurgery patients indicates considerable human neurological specialization for language. Furthermore, there is clear evidence of a strong asymmetry in the modern human brain: for right-handed speakers, many language functions correlate with left-hemisphere brain activity, while left-hemisphere damage disrupts language production and/or perception (Altmann, 1997; Deacon, 1997; Locke, 1998; Pinker, 1994). There is strong experimental support for this conclusion; for instance, Pinker (1994) notes that patients can continue to talk with a temporarily paralyzed right, but not left, hemisphere. Blumstein and Cooper (1974) report that in dichotic listening experiments, where a different auditory stimulus is presented to each ear: "Right-handed subjects typically show a right ear superiority for verbal stimuli such as real words, real or synthetic nonsense syllables, and even backwards speech" (p. 146).[9]

More recently, Sininger and Cone-Wesson (2004) presented stimuli composed of either tones or clicks to more than 1500 infants and measured the resulting activity in the cochlea, or inner ear. They found greater activity in right ears in response to clicks, and greater activity in left ears in response to tones. This finding supports the apparent specialization of the left hemisphere for segmental speech processing and of the right hemisphere for prosody, but suggests that the two inner ears may also be specialized for processing of different sound types.

It should not be assumed, however, that the left hemisphere in humans is only associated with language. More generally, "the left hemisphere dominates in linguistic function and manual control, whereas the right hemisphere dominates in spatial reasoning, emotional perception, and face recognition" (Hauser, 1993, p. 476). There also seem to be hemispheric differences in the manner in which information is perceived and processed: "the left hemisphere is specialized for prepositional, analytic, and serial processing of incoming information, while the right hemisphere is more adapted for the perception of appositional, holistic, and synthetic relations" (Bever and Chiarello, 1974, p. 537). Bever and Chiarello provide some supporting evidence from the perception of music, showing that "musically naïve" informants had a left-ear superiority for the recognition of melodies, whereas trained musicians had a right-ear superiority. They attribute the difference to the fact that "musically experienced listeners have learned to perceive a melody as an articulated set of relations among components" (Bever & Chiarello, 1974, p. 538), making the analytic left hemisphere appropriate, while untrained listeners simply hear the tune as a whole.

Bever and Chiarello's (1974) experiment indicates that the right hemisphere is involved in processing music and other non-linguistic environmental noise. However, as Deacon notes (1997), "the right hemisphere is not the non-language hemisphere" (p. 311), but is involved in the processing of narrative, including ideas and arguments, as well as prosody. Blumstein and Cooper (1974), for instance, review evidence showing that "the acoustic correlates of intonation contours, i.e., fundamental frequency, and to some extent, amplitude, [are] lateralized in the right hemisphere" (p. 147). They also note that speakers of tone languages show a right-ear (and hence left-hemisphere) advantage when pitch is used to distinguish lexical items, supporting our assessment that tone is segmental rather than prosodic. Blumstein and Cooper's experiments involved acoustic filtering of the segmental content of utterances, with the intonation contour left intact; participants were presented with a pair of these filtered utterances dichotically (one to each ear), then asked to say whether a single subsequent example matched either member of that pair. Participants showed an extremely consistent left ear advantage, indicating that "when intonation contours are extracted from the phonetic medium, they are processed more efficiently by the right hemisphere" (ibid., p. 151). This left-ear advantage was maintained in a second experiment, in which informants were presented with a dichotic pair involving nonsense syllables with particular intonation contours, and then asked whether an acoustically filtered utterance (with the nonsense syllables obscured, but the intonation contour remaining) matched either member of the pair. The right hemisphere clearly has a dominant role in processing intonation, regardless of whether the segmental signal is comprehensible or not.

These results are strongly supported by evidence from aphasia and differential hemispheric damage. Schirmer, Alter, Kotz, and Friederici (2001) conclude that patients with right-hemisphere lesions experienced greater difficulty in producing intonation patterns than those with left-hemisphere lesions, and argue that there is particularly strong evidence for the right-hemisphere lateralization of affective or emotional prosody. Blumstein and Cooper (1974) report that aphasics with left-hemisphere damage who cannot process sentences semantically can nonetheless frequently distinguish the function of such sentences as commands, questions, or statements, presumably on the basis of the intonation contour. In addition, they note that "the comprehension of stress contrasts, another component of language prosody, is remarkably well preserved in aphasia" (ibid., p. 156). On the other hand, "right-hemisphere damaged patients may fail to recognise whether a speaker is happy, sad, surprised, or angry on the basis of his or her tone of voice" (Altmann, 1997, p. 183), supporting both the connection of the right hemisphere with emotion, and of emotion with intonation. These findings support those reported above, by Wells and Peppé (2003), Snow (1998, 2001) and others, that language-impaired children may show performance well below that of children of the same chronological age in the areas of segmental phonology and syntax controlled by the left hemisphere, yet may retain a strong awareness of the affective content of prosody, as both emotion and prosodic phonology appear to be controlled by the right hemisphere.

Some aspects of these hemispheric associations are not unique to humans. Hauser (1993) observes:

> In humans, the left side of the face (right hemisphere of the brain) is dominant in emotional expression. In rhesus monkeys, the left side of

the face begins to display facial expression earlier than the right side and is more expressive. (p. 475)

Measurements from video recordings of rhesus monkeys showed that the left side of the face began to move into a particular expression before the right side did. In addition, pictures produced by pairing the right side of a rhesus face with its mirror-image duplicate were uniformly judged as more expressive by human informants than a real (two-sided) picture of the monkey's face or a picture based on two left side images. Ujhelyi (1998) argues that face processing is also lateralized to the right hemisphere in macaques and chimps; but there is some evidence of left-hemisphere specialization for the processing of species-specific vocal calls in some non-human primates (Deacon, 1997; Ujhelyi, 1998), including Japanese macaques (Hauser, 1993).

Non-human primates do not appear to display the degree of left-hemispheric specialization for vocal communication found in the modern human brain. According to Pinker (1994):

> The vocal calls of primates are controlled not by their cerebral cortex but by phylogenetically older neural structures in the brain stem and limbic system, structures that are heavily involved in emotion. Human vocalizations other than language, like sobbing, laughing, moaning, and shouting in pain, are also controlled subcortically. Subcortical structures even control the swearing that follows the arrival of a hammer on a thumb, that emerges as an involuntary tic in Tourette's syndrome, and that can survive as Broca's aphasics' only speech. (p. 334)

Vocalization in non-human primates does not rely on specific language areas in the way that human language does (Lieberman, 1991). As we saw earlier, however, there are clear affinities between human and non-human primate vocalizations in terms of: (i) the contribution of prosody to communication and comprehension; and (ii) the association of prosody with emotion, gesture, and facial expression. These affinities support a view that intonation in particular, and arguably prosody in general, have remained in the right hemisphere in the evolution of modern humans, and are therefore predictably still associated with paralinguistic affect and gesture. Both intonation and prosody more generally may also be dissociated from left-hemisphere controlled language production and perception, and this dissociation is evidenced in aphasia and developmental language impairment.

plural phonology and language evolution

Prosody and segmentals may be different, but where did they come from? Accepting that prosody is controlled primarily by the right hemisphere and connected with gesture and emotion does not of course commit us to a theory seeking to derive language from song (Jespersen, 1922) or from gesture (Corballis, 1992). Nor need the affinities between prosody and non-human primate communication systems, and with emotion and gesture, mean that prosody is unchangeable. If prosody involves innate constraints (or parameters), these must be genetically prespecified, but they can still interact to produce a range of possible output forms. Mutation, variation, and natural selection provide a pathway for gradual, and typically minor, change in genetics. As a result of such natural processes, the modern human prosodic system may differ underlyingly from that of other primates.

More crucially, whatever the sources of prosody, it operates as part of a more complex and more highly differentiated linguistic system in modern humans. We may have reasonable precursors for prosody; but how, when, and why did segmental phonology evolve? There is no space here to review the various current alternative theories of language evolution. Useful cross-sections of current opinion are provided by Hurford, Studdert-Kennedy, and Knight (1998); Knight, Studdert-Kennedy, and Hurford (2000); and Christiansen and Kirby (2003). Carstairs-McCarthy (1999) develops a rather different view from the one outlined here, and attempts to bring together phonology and syntax in a novel way; see also Tallerman (in press) for some counterarguments.

There seem to be two main physical differences relevant to language which set humans apart from other primates. First, our brains are considerably larger than one would expect in a mammal of human size and seem to contain areas specialized for language functions, especially, though not exclusively, in the left hemisphere. Second, the human supralaryngeal vocal tract has a characteristic right-angle bend between the pharynx and the oral cavity. This distinctive anatomy seems to allow adult humans to produce the range of consonants, and especially steady-state vowels, which provide the flexibility required for segmental phonology and the construction of a lexicon of the required size for linguistic communication. Some non-human primates, like gelada monkeys (Richman, 1976), produce a subset of vowel- and consonant-like sounds in their calls; but the consistency and range of human segmentals go orders of magnitude beyond the closest system observed in other primates. Nonetheless, the use of some vocal features, along with the observation that some non-human primates show left-lateralization for the processing of species-specific vocal calls, shows that aspects of early primate and hominid vocal communication could have been built on as human spoken language developed a more varied segmental repertoire, and more strongly left-lateralized control. Evolution does not generally build entirely new structures, but redeploys systems and mechanisms which are in existence already.

Dunbar (1996) suggests that the key to evolutionary changes in vocal tract anatomy and brain size lies in the function of language, in association with environmental changes encountered by our early ape ancestors. As Aiello and Dunbar (1993) show, there is a strong and significant correlation between relative neocortex size and social group size in primates; and as group size increases, so does the percentage of the day which animals spend grooming. Grooming in non-human primates acts as a kind of "social cement" maintaining cohesion in groups by demonstrating the willingness of group members to invest energy in their relationships; but since only one group member can be groomed at a time, this limits the effective population size if enough time is to be left in the day for other occupations like sleep and foraging. The abnormally large human neocortex size suggests that we should live in groups of approximately 150; but to maintain social groupings of 150, early hominids would have had to spend 40% of the day engaged in mutual grooming, an entirely unrealistic figure. Dunbar therefore argues that vocal communication became increasingly important in maintaining social cohesion, given its inherent advantage of allowing more than one other group member to be "groomed" at a time. Even larger social groups could be maintained if news could be exchanged of other group members not immediately present (hence Dunbar's invocation of "gossip" as key to language evolution).

These hypotheses may also provide an evolutionary account for Cruttenden's (1986) observation that greetings, farewells, and social formulas represent the most typical cases of atypical intonation. As group size increases, there is a bigger risk that one population member will not know if an unknown individual is a group member or not, potentially allowing cheats, who will gain the benefits of group membership but not share the risks or effort, to thrive. In such cases, some sort of "badge" of membership is needed, and Dunbar argues that dialect divisions may have begun to provide just these indications of group membership. If this is the case, then Cruttenden's observation that greetings and social formulas are particularly susceptible to prosodic divergence seems straightforwardly explicable: where better for groups of hominids to develop specific signals showing whether a newcomer is a group member than right at the beginning of the interaction?

Aiello and Dunbar (1993) suggest that group size may have increased in the first place: (i) for greater protection against predators; (ii) as the result of an "arms race" between early human groups; (iii) or because the nomadic lifestyles of early humans would benefit from social interactions with neighboring groups, since information on water and food sources could then be shared (another function of vocal communication). In turn, brain size may have expanded to allow these larger social groups to be maintained. Larger brains do not in themselves entail changes in the vocal tract. However, without a larger brain, flexible segmental phonology could not have developed, and the lexicon would have been seriously limited in size, constituting a challenge to perception. These changes may also follow from the shift in early hominids towards bipedality, which is likely to have been motivated by an early change in primate habitat, dating back 5 million years. Wheeler (1991a, 1991b) notes that bipedality would have been greatly advantageous to early hominids, providing protection for the large and important hominid brain in open, unprotected environments.

Of course, bipedality does not automatically cause a right-angle bend in the vocal tract; but it would have affected respiration, and control of respiration, which paved the way for volitional control of vocalization. Since hominids were habitually bipedal approximately 3 million years BP (Wheeler, 1991b), there is easily sufficient evolutionary time for the vocal tract modifications to evolve by natural selection, especially since the benefits of "vocal grooming" would, according to Dunbar, have been vital in hominid social groups, which were increasing rapidly by 250,000 years BP. It is also hard from a physiological point of view to find sound reasons for the development of the supralaryngeal vocal tract outside of a possible advantage to speech, since the modern configuration is actually detrimental to the aerodynamics of respiration. However, mutations which allowed clearer and more consistent vocalization would potentially have conferred a distinct social advantage, and hence spread through the population.

As the brain grew in size, and began to incorporate new specializations, the left hemisphere, which is dedicated to analytical operations, would have been the natural home for the developing segmental phonology; the more so since, as Deacon (1997) notes:

[L]anguage production and analysis effectively require that we implement two different modes of phonetic analysis and vocal control simultaneously: prosodic and phonemic processes. These tasks would tend to compete for recruitment of the same brain structures...and as a result would probably interfere with each other.... (p. 316)

Specialization from the earlier midbrain location of vocalization into the right hemisphere for prosody, and the left for the more strongly analytical melody, would have been the natural result.

conclusion

The conclusion to which these various types of evidence cumulatively lead is that prosodic and segmental phonology are separate components neurologically, acquisitionally, and in terms of their relationship with non-human primate vocal communication, where precursors can be found straightforwardly for prosody, but only in a far more rudimentary form for segmentals. In addition, universals of prosody are much easier to find, and there are many suggestions in the literature that features of stress, syllabification, and intonation are constant cross-linguistically, or can at least be treated parametrically. Modern humans maintain this differentiation; and we should not be surprised, but rather encouraged, if individual linguists and linguistic theories reflect it in focusing on either prosodic or segmental phonology. We should also not be surprised, but rather encouraged, to see phonologists working in either area taking a growing interest in language history and human evolution as relevant to their respective fields.

notes

1. Some of the material included here has been presented in the First Annual Lecture of the North-West Centre for Linguistics, February 2001, and in talks at the Ninth Manchester Phonology Meeting, May 2001; the Linguistics Association of Great Britain Autumn Meeting 2001; Triangle 2001; the Cambridge University Department of Classics; the conference on English Phonology at Toulouse, July 2002. I am grateful to audiences at these meetings for helpful comments, which have improved the chapter considerably, and owe special thanks to Ricardo-Bermúdez-Otero, Heinz Giegerich, Patrick Honeybone, Andrew Linn, Rob McMahon, and Marilyn Vihman.
2. These are not perfect, either. On the one hand, *segmentals* suggests a preoccupation with only the segments themselves, although segmentally-inclined phonologists may in fact be more interested in the features of which segments are composed. On the other hand, *prosody* would traditionally include stress and intonation but arguably not syllables. However, this term avoids the implication in the alternative term *suprasegmentals* that only organization

above segment level can be included. This exclusion rules out quantity, which is strongly implicated in syllabification and stress assignment, and clearly prosodic.

3. For example, vowel harmony involves segmental features, governed and delimited by particular suprasegmental, or prosodic, units. Similarly, phonotactic restrictions which determine the appearance of particular segments within specific prosodic domains indicate that prosody conditions segmentals in certain circumstances. In Jakobson's terms, we sometimes need to refer to the *framework* to determine the *content*.

4. Editor's note: a point also made in Chapter 4, this volume.

5. Editor's note: for further discussion of the learning mechanisms involved, see Chapter 2, this volume.

6. Editor's note: as also argued in Chapter 6, this volume, where extensive evidence of linkage between auditory and visual information in language processing is provided.

7. A pitch fall is confirmatory and a pitch rise is questioning.

8. Editor's note: this discussion of prosodic impairment in language disorder can be viewed as complementary to that of Chapter 10, this volume, which focuses on segmentals.

9. The right side of the body is, of course, controlled by the left hemisphere, and vice versa.

references

Aiello, L., & Dunbar, R. I. M. (1993). Neocortex size, group size, and the evolution of language. *Current Anthropology, 34,* 184–93.

Altmann, G. (1997). *The ascent of babel.* Oxford: Oxford University Press.

Barbujani, G., Magagni, A., Minch, E., & Cavalli-Sforza, L. L. (1997). An apportionment of human DNA diversity. *Proceedings of the National Academy of Sciences of the USA, 94,* 4516–19.

Bever, T. G., & Chiarello, R. J. (1974). Cerebral dominance in musicians and nonmusicians. *Science, 185,* 537–9.

Bloom, L. (1973). *One word at a time: The use of single-word utterances before syntax.* The Hague: Mouton.

Blumstein, S. & Cooper, W. E. (1974). Hemispheric processing of intonation contours. *Cortex, 10,* 146–58.

Bolinger, D. (1978). Intonation across languages. In J. H. Greenberg, C. A. Ferguson, & E. A. Moravcsik (Eds.), *Universals of human language: Volume 4, Phonology* (pp. 471–524). Stanford: Stanford University Press.

Bolinger, D. (1983). Intonation and gesture. *American Speech, 58,* 156–74.

Browman, C., & Goldstein, L. (1989). Articulatory gestures as phonological units. *Phonology, 6,* 201–51.

Browman, C., & Goldstein, L. (1992). Articulatory Phonology – An overview. *Phonetica, 49,* 155–180, 222–34.

Carr, P. (1999). *English phonetics and phonology: An introduction.* Oxford: Blackwell.

Carr, P. (2000). Scientific realism, sociophonetic variation, and innate endowments in phonology. In N. Burton-Roberts, P. Carr, and G. Docherty (Eds.), *Phonological knowledge: Conceptual and empirical issues* (pp. 67–104). Oxford: Oxford University Press.

Carstairs-McCarthy, A. (1999). *The origins of complex language: An inquiry into the evolutionary beginnings of sentences, syllables and truth.* Oxford: Oxford University Press.

Christiansen, M. H., & Kirby, S. (Eds.) (2003). *Language evolution.* Oxford: Oxford University Press.

Colantoni, L., & Gurlekian, J. (2004). Convergence and intonation: Historical evidence from Buenos Aires Spanish. *Bilingualism: Language and Cognition, 7,* 107–19.

Corballis, M. C. (1992). On the evolution of language and generativity. *Cognition, 44,* 197–226.

Cruttenden, A. (1986). *Intonation.* Cambridge: Cambridge University Press.

Crystal, D. (1979). Prosodic development. In P. Fletcher & M. Garman (Eds.), *Language acquisition* (pp. 33–48*).* Cambridge: Cambridge University Press.

Davenport, M., & Hannahs, S. J. (1998). *Introducing phonetics and phonology.* London: Arnold.

Davies, P. C. W., & Brown, J. (Eds.) (1988). *Superstrings: A theory of everything?* Cambridge: Cambridge University Press.

Deacon, T. (1997). *The Symbolic Species.* London: Penguin.

Dresher, E., & Kaye, J. (1990). A computational learning model for metrical phonology. *Cognition,* 34, 137–95.

Dunbar, R. (1996). *Grooming, gossip, and the evolution of language.* New York: Faber and Faber.

Giegerich, H. J. (1985). *Metrical Phonology and phonological structure: German and English.* Cambridge: Cambridge University Press.

Giegerich, H. J. (1992). *English phonology: An introduction.* Cambridge: Cambridge University Press.

Giegerich, H. J. (1999). *Lexical strata in English: Morphological causes, phonological effects.* Cambridge: Cambridge University Press.

Goodall, J. (1986). *The chimpanzees of Gombe: Patterns of behavior.* Boston: Harvard University Press.

Halle, M., & Vergnaud, J.-R. (1980). Three-dimensional phonology. *Journal of Linguistic Research, 1,* 83–105.

Harris, J., Watson, J., & Bates, S. (1999). Prosody and melody in vowel disorder. *Journal of Linguistics, 35,* 489–525.

Hauser, M. D. (1993). Right hemisphere dominance for the production of facial expression in monkeys. *Science, 261,* 475–7.

Hauser, M. D., & Fowler, C.A. (1992). Fundamental frequency declination is not unique to human speech: Evidence from nonhuman primates. *Journal of the Acoustical Society of America, 91,* 363–69.

Hirst, D., & Di Cristo, A. (1998). A survey of intonation systems. In D. Hirst & A. Di Cristo (Eds.), *Intonation systems: A survey of twenty languages* (pp. 1–4). Cambridge: Cambridge University Press.

Hock, H. H. (1986). *Principles of historical linguistics.* The Hague: Mouton de Gruyter.

Hogg, R., & McCully, C. (1998). *Metrical Phonology: A coursebook.* Cambridge: Cambridge University Press.

Hurford, J. R., Studdert-Kennedy, M., & Knight, C. (Eds.) (1998). *Approaches to the evolution of language*. Cambridge: Cambridge University Press.
Jakobson, R. (1971). *Studies in child language and aphasia*. The Hague: Mouton.
Jespersen, O. (1922). *Language: Its nature, development, and origin*. Allen & Unwin.
Kager, R. (1999). *Optimality Theory*. Cambridge: Cambridge University Press.
Knight, C., Studdert-Kennedy, M., & Hurford, J. R. (Eds.) (2000). *The evolutionary emergence of language: Social function and the origins of linguistic form*. Cambridge: Cambridge University Press.
Ladd, D. R. (1996). *Intonational phonology*. Cambridge: Cambridge University Press.
Lieberman, P. (1991). *Uniquely human: The evolution of speech, thought, and selfless behavior*. Boston: Harvard University Press.
Locke, J. L. (1998). Social sound-making as a precursor to language. In J. R. Hurford, M. Studdert-Kennedy, & C. Knight (Eds.), *Approaches to the evolution of language* (pp. 190–201). Cambridge: Cambridge University Press.
McCarthy, J. J. (2002). *A thematic guide to Optimality Theory*. Cambridge: Cambridge University Press.
McMahon, A. (2000a). *Lexical Phonology and the history of English*. Cambridge: Cambridge University Press.
McMahon, A. (2000b). *Change, chance, and optimality*. Oxford: Oxford University Press.
McMahon, A. (2001). *An introduction to English phonology*. Edinburgh: Edinburgh University Press (Edinburgh Textbooks on the English Language).
McMahon, A. (2005). Heads I win, tails you lose. In P. Carr, J. Durand, & C. J. Ewen (Eds.), *Headhood, elements, specification and contrastivity: Phonological papers in honor of John Anderson* (pp. 255–75). Amsterdam and Philadelphia: John Benjamins.
Mohanan, K. P. (1986). *The theory of Lexical Phonology*. Reidel.
Pinker, S. (1994). *The language instinct*. New York: Penguin.
Prince, A., & Smolensky, P. (2004). *Optimality Theory: Constraint interaction in Generative Grammar*. Oxford: Blackwell.
Richman, B. (1976). Some vocal distinctive features used by gelada monkeys. *Journal of the Acoustical Society of America, 60*, 718–24.
Schirmer, A., Alter, K., Kotz, S. A., & Friederici, A. D. (2001). Lateralization of prosody during language production: A lesion study. *Brain and Language, 76*, 1–17.
Sininger, Y. S., & Cone-Wesson, B. (2004). Asymmetric cochlear processing mimics hemispheric specialization. *Science, 305*, 1581.
Snow, D. (1994). Phrase-final syllable lengthening and intonation in early child speech. *Journal of Communication Disorders, 23*, 325–36.
Snow, D. (1998). Prosodic markers of syntactic boundaries in the speech of 4-year-old children with normal and disordered language development. *Journal of Speech, Language, and Hearing Research, 41*, 1158–70.
Snow, D. (2001). Imitation of intonation contours by children with normal and disordered language development. *Clinical Linguistics and Phonetics, 15*, 567–84.
Stringer, C., & McKie, R. (1997). *African exodus: The origins of modern humanity*. London: Pimlico.

Tallerman, M. (in press). Did our ancestors speak a holistic protolanguage? To appear in *Lingua*, 2006.

Tesar, B., & Smolensky, P. (2000). *Learnability in Optimality Theory*. Cambridge, MA: MIT Press.

Ujhelyi, M. (1998). Long-call structure in apes as a possible precursor to language. In J. R. Hurford, M. Studdert-Kennedy, & C. Knight (Eds.), *Approaches to the evolution of language* (pp. 177–89). Cambridge: Cambridge University Press.

Ultan, R. (1978). Some general characteristics of interrogative systems. In J. H. Greenberg, C. A. Ferguson, & E. A. Moravcsik (Eds.), *Universals of human language*, Volume 2, *Syntax* (pp. 211–48). Stanford: Stanford University Press.

van der Meulen, S., Janssen, P., & Den Os, E. (1997). Prosodic abilities in children with specific language impairment. *Journal of Communication Disorders, 30*, 155–70.

Vihman, M. M. (1996). *Phonological development: The origins of language in the child*. Oxford: Blackwell.

Wells, W., & Peppé, S. (2003). Intonation abilities of children with speech and language impairments. *Journal of Speech Language and Hearing Research, 46*, 5–20.

Wheeler, P. E. (1991a). The thermoregulatory advantages of hominid bipedalism in open equatorial environments: The contribution of increased convective heat loss and cutaneous evaporative cooling. *Journal of Human Evolution, 21*,107–15.

Wheeler, P. E. (1991b). The influence of bipedalism on the energy and water budgets of early hominids. *Journal of Human Evolution, 21*, 117–36.

8

situated phonologies: patterns of phonology in discourse contexts

elizabeth couper-kuhlen

introduction

A consideration of phonology in discourse contexts raises fundamental questions concerning the domain of phonology, the nature of phonological units and features, and the nature of discourse. In this section I outline assumptions that have previously been made with respect to these issues and contrast them with new ways of thinking about sound patterns in situated language use.

What is the domain of phonology? For some early structural linguists, phonology encompassed only individual consonant and vowel phonemes, i.e., the *segmentable* aspects of the sound continuum. Such linguists argued that *suprasegmental* (or *prosodic*) aspects of language – particularly, intonation – were gradient and therefore defied systematicity (e.g., Martinet, 1962). Other structuralists assigned phonemic status to a limited set of suprasegmental features including stress, pitch level, and clause-final intonation, or *terminal juncture* (e.g., Trager and Smith, 1957). Today there is wide consensus among scholars that both segmental and suprasegmental aspects of language pattern systematically and therefore deserve the label *phonological* – as labels such as *Autosegmental Phonology* (e.g., Goldsmith, 1990), *Metrical Phonology* (Hogg and McCully, 1987), *Intonational Phonology* (e.g., Ladd, 1996), and *Prosodic Phonology* (e.g., Nespor and Vogel, 1986) attest. Exactly *which* suprasegmental or prosodic aspects should be included within phonology, however, is still debated. Is rhythm a component of phonology, or is it outside phonology proper, within the domain of what has been termed *paralanguage*? Are pitch range, or pitch register and other aspects of a speaker's voice quality within or outside the scope of phonology? Scholars can and do disagree on how to categorize these and numerous other auditorily distinguishable features of speech.

What is the nature of phonological units and/or features? All of the approaches to phonology mentioned above have in common that their units and features are predicated on the general principle of contrast, or *context-free distinctivity* (see also Couper-Kuhlen and Selting, 1996). A phonological segment such as a particular consonant or vowel phoneme distinguishes one word or morpheme from another regardless of its phonetic or other context; a phonological feature such as voicing distinguishes one natural class of sounds (those produced with vibrating vocal cords) from another (those produced without vocal cord vibration) under any and all conditions. Similarly, one metrical phonological structure (stress grid or tree) is assumed to contribute to a meaning which is distinct from another regardless of the string of syllables it is applied to; one tone pattern creates a meaning different from that of every other type of tone pattern when aligned with no matter what lexical or grammatical content. In this perspective, any variation (variance from the norm, or standard form) encountered, whether at the segmental or the suprasegmental level, is recognized as significant only if it can be systematically related to the surrounding phonetic context. All other variation is considered "free," i.e., random or unpredictable and therefore of little linguistic interest.

Yet in the context of naturally occurring discourse – whether scripted or spontaneous, monologic or dialogic – many putative phonological distinctions disappear. *Will* and *well* sound alike if they appear in an unstressed position in a spoken utterance. The phrase *white house* is indistinguishable from *White House* if it occurs in a context of narrow focus (e.g., a focus on a particular house by its color), and a specific tone pattern (e.g., rising pitch) may convey quite a different meaning with a different carrier word or phrase embedded in a different context. Moreover, many so-called *free variants* in discourse – for instance, English fully released, aspirated stops in word-final position (e.g., *hip* [hɪpʰ], *hit* [hɪtʰ], *hick* [hɪkʰ]) or English nasalized vowels in non-nasal contexts (e.g., *beg* [bẽg], *law* [lɔ̃ː] – turn out to pattern quite consistently in the service of rhetorical and interactional goals. For instance, final aspiration may occur when speakers are attempting to be forceful, nasalization when speakers are lamenting or complaining.[1]

What role does discourse play in phonology, and what do we mean by *discourse*? Working from the bottom up, i.e., from smaller units of language to larger ones, as many linguists do, it is tempting to call discourse anything larger than a sentence. On this interpretation, examining a given sentence as a coherent follow-up to some prior sentence is treating it *in a discourse context*. Yet for socially minded linguists, discourse is more than just a string of sentences. It is situated language use, language deployed dynamically and in real time for communicative purposes. It follows that discourse on this understanding must be studied in natural, real-life situations. Such a perspective is more top-down than bottom-up, although one can of course "zoom in" to a microscopic level of naturally occurring discourse for analytic purposes.

towards a discourse explanation for phonetic and prosodic variation

Scholars who investigate naturally occurring discourse face a dilemma with respect to phonology, and, on the other side, phonologists have a problem with naturally occurring discourse. How can phonological claims developed on the basis of individual words and isolated forms be reconciled with the contextually rich reality of language in use? How are phonologists to account for the observable patterning of so-called "free variants" in specifiable discourse contexts?[2] Some phonologists have sought a way out of the dilemma posed by context by limiting discourse to a manageable size, such as question-answer pairs, and to an experimentally controllable form, as in the constructed example: *What about Anna? Who did she come with? – Anna came with Manny* (Pierrehumbert, 1980). Yet such a procedure produces artificially simplified claims about phonological form and function which have little relation to the contingencies of real discourse. Other scholars have begun to acknowledge the relevance of what some have termed *paralinguistic* dimensions of speech for language in use (Yule, 1995). It should be noted, however, that the very term *paralinguistic* perpetuates a traditional view of the domain of linguistics based on a structuralist notion of distinctivity as the criterion for what is considered to be *linguistic*.

Perhaps the most innovative response to the dilemma posed by traditional phonology for students of natural discourse – one which embraces the complexity of situated speech rather than trying to reduce or ignore it – is the *doing phonology* approach of Kelly and Local (1989). Taking their inspiration from Firthian linguists, Kelly and Local claim that traditional phoneme-based approaches to phonetics and phonology bring a number of unwarranted assumptions with them, such as that the speech continuum is segmentable into discrete units, that these units are neatly sequenced in the stream of speech with little or no overlap, and that allophonic variance in phonemes is uniquely determined by phonetic context. They conclude that the phoneme – a unit originally developed in relation to written language – is poorly conceived to handle the most common form of language use, everyday discourse, which is far removed from the written standard. In addition, as they point out, so-called "suprasegmental" analysis as practiced so far has a written-language bias. Attention is paid above all to features which are capable of orthographic representation, such as via italics (stress), dashes (pause), and clause- or sentence-final punctuation (final pitch movement). Kelly and Local argue that these and other putative suprasegmental categories (e.g., *nuclear tone*) have been hypostasized based on idealized language use: they are derived from an examination of simple sentences read aloud ("spoken prose," as Abercrombie, 1965, calls it), rather than from an analysis of genuine utterances in naturally occurring discourse.

Instead of relying on phonetic and phonological categories determined a priori, Kelly and Local advocate close listening to real speech in actual situations of language use and *impressionistic recording*. By the latter they mean attending to and notating every phonetic detail which a trained phonetician's ear can perceive in natural speech, including its long-domain properties such as pitch, volume (loudness), tempo, syllable rhythm, articulatory and phonatory settings, resonance, and variability. Only once a careful impressionistic record has been made of speech (or of a selected utterance therein) can functional analysis, involving data *interpretation*, follow. The latter means looking for sound patterns and relationships and setting them in relation to empirically discoverable *tasks* which speakers can be shown to be dealing with in discourse. If a speaker is engaged in that most common and widespread form of discourse, everyday conversation, then those tasks are likely to be both actional and interactional in nature (Schegloff, 1982). That is, a conversationalist is likely to be carrying out verbal actions (*actional tasks*) and doing so in coordinated fashion with one or more co-participants (*interactional tasks*). A linking of actional and interactional tasks with phonological patterns and relationships leads to a *phonology of talk-in-interaction*, which Local (see, e.g., Local, 2003), among others, has been instrumental in developing.

Because talk-in-interaction involves turn-taking and sequential organization, both of which unfold in real time, the analyst needs a thorough understanding and appreciation of the interactional structure of conversation as a foundation for phonetic and phonological analysis. This methodological requirement goes hand in hand with two further tenets: (i) the examination of naturally occurring data in an essentially data-driven or inductive process, and (ii) the validation of analytic categories as *participant categories* via the observable behavior of the interactants themselves. Categories and hypotheses in this approach are both *generated by* the data and *warranted in* the data showing that participants orient their behavior according to those categories. Although in practice these ethnomethodological principles are sometimes difficult to apply when the focus of attention is on phonetic detail,[3] they remain the fundamental goals of a phonology of discourse, or *interactional phonology*.[4]

The following sections are framed from the perspective of interactional phonology and review some of the major findings resulting from doing phonology in natural discourse contexts. The phonological *units* invoked in the discussion are ones which current research has shown to be relevant for a given interactional task in a given language; they should not necessarily be assumed to transfer across dialects or languages. The phonological *features* invoked range from very local or phonetic (segment-based) ones to rather long-range or prosodic ones: syllable structure, stress, timing and rhythm, pitch and loudness configuration, and phonatory and articulatory settings. These phonological features are likewise invoked only if research has shown that they are relevant for a specific interactional task in a specific speech community.

The discussion will be organized around four types of conversational task management for which phonetic detail has been shown to be relevant:

(i)   building turn-constructional units and coordinating turns at talk;
(ii)   joining and separating adjacent units of talk;
(iii) accomplishing actions and building sequences in the pursuit of courses of action; and
(iv)   marking stance and affiliation with respect to talk and co-participants.

It should be noted from the outset that in contrast to traditional phonology, the phonetic/prosodic features identified for interactional tasks do not determine semantic meaning. Rather, because sense-making in situated interaction is always inference-based, they provide a context which cues pragmatic meaning and guides the listener's process of inter-pretation (see also Auer, 1992; Couper-Kuhlen, 2000).

the phonology of building turn-constructional units and coordinating turns at talk

A *turn-constructional unit*, or TCU, is a minimal unit for the construction of a turn at talk. Sacks, Schegloff, and Jefferson (1974) describe its syntactic properties as follows:

> Unit-types for English include sentential, clausal, phrasal, and lexical constructions.... Instances of the unit-types so usable allow a projection of the unit-type under way, and what, roughly, it will take for an instance of that unit-type to be completed. (p. 702)

Whether a given word (e.g., English *how*), as it emerges in talk, is taken to be a lexical TCU and to create a unit on its own, or is taken instead to be part of a phrasal TCU (e.g., *how much*) or a clausal TCU (e.g., *how did you do it*), can only be judged by attending to its phonetic/prosodic characteristics. Does it form a prosodic unit of its own, or is it part of a larger unit? Answering this question requires holistically assessing a tone pattern as to whether it forms a possibly complete contour or not (Auer, 1996; Selting, 1996b, 2000). Precisely which phonetic and/or prosodic features contribute to the impression of a possibly complete or whole contour can vary from language to language. In order for a sequence of tones to sound like a complete intonation phrase in English and German, for instance, at least one syllable must be prosodically prominent. Line 12 in the conversational excerpt below illustrates this point:[5]

(1) Golf date

```
1   Guy:  .hh.hh.hhh ↑hey uh,hhwhhkhh
2         my ↑son-in-law's down an:d
3         I:↓::,hh thought we might play a little golf::
4         ↓either this afternoon or tomorrow
5         would you like to (0.3).hhh (0.3) get out? uhh
6         (.)
7   Jon:  well this afternoon'd be alright
8         but I don't think I'd better tomorrow,
9         (0.6)
10  Guy:  we:ll?
11        (0.6)
```

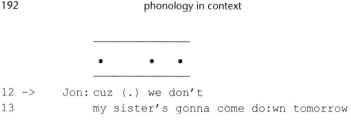

```
12 ->     Jon: cuz (.) we don't
13             my sister's gonna come do:wn tomorrow
```

Although *cuz we don't* in line 12 might easily be delivered as a whole intonational contour and form a turn-constructional unit on its own in another context, in this context and with this prosody, in which none of the three words is prominent (as shown by the three black dots of the same size and at the same level in the intonation diagram above them), it will be interpreted as a fragment of an intonation phrase and an incomplete turn-constructional unit (see also Selting, 2001).

On the other hand, under the proper circumstances, even a syntactic fragment can be produced as a whole intonation phrase if spoken with the appropriate prosody. Line 5 of the following conversational excerpt demonstrates this:

(2) Irishman in Germany

```
1    ALLIE:    yeah but it's ↑NOT even twElve;
2              (1.3)
3    TED:      it's not even TWELVE?
4              0.5)
5 ->GERRI:     °o'CLOCK.°
6              (0.2)
7    ALLIE:    HIH heh!
8              (0.2)
9    TED:      YEAH,
```

Ted is unable to process Allie's remark in line 1 until Gerri, in line 5, provides a disambiguating cue. The cue is provided by Gerri's contribution of *o'clock* spoken with prosodic prominence and forming a complete unit, which makes it clear that Allie is referring to the time.

In other languages, quite different phonetic and prosodic features may be used in the construction of a whole prosodic contour. Nevertheless, participants from whatever language background must make judgments concerning the completion of units when they interact with one another, whether each string of words/morphemes is a turn-constructional unit or is merely a fragment of one yet to be completed. Judgments of this kind affect the meaning which a listener attributes to what is being said, and they have important implications for the projection of not only the possible end of a unit but also the possible end of a turn. The task of judging whether or not a stretch of speech counts as a complete turn is thus a central one for interaction, and for this purpose, phonetic/ prosodic information is crucial. The signaling of turn structure by means of phonological cues can therefore be considered a first important dimension of interactional phonology.

A second task which participants face as they engage in interaction is deciding whether a given turn-constructional unit is *transition-ready*, i.e., permits a legitimate change of speaker, or not. If it is, a current recipient may be expected to produce some kind of response next. If not, the recipient may be expected to withhold a response until a possible turn ending has been reached by the current speaker. Turns-at-talk may be single-unit or multi-unit. In the latter case, they may be planned as such from the outset or they may evolve to become multi-unit over time (Schegloff, 1982). There is an action-related dimension to the shape a turn has: some actions can be completed in a single unit (e.g., a greeting such as *Hello!*), while others require a sequence of units (e.g., listing or telling a story). In addition to lexical and grammatical cues, there are phonetic and prosodic cues as to whether a turn is transition-ready or not, i.e., whether or not the talk has reached a *transition-relevance place* (TRP).This is a point where another participant to a conversation may legitimately take the floor.

In English, for instance, it has been claimed that a certain type of prosody projects that a TRP is upcoming, in contrast to other types which do not (Wells and Macfarlane, 1998). The specific prosodic features involved may vary from dialect to dialect, including not only pitch configuration but also syllable lengthening, volume, and vowel quality, as for the U.K. West Midlands dialect that Wells and Macfarlane (1998) describe and for Tyneside English as described by Local, Kelly, and Wells (1986). For example:

(3) TRP-projecting accent, Type I (Wells and Macfarlane, 1998, p. 285)

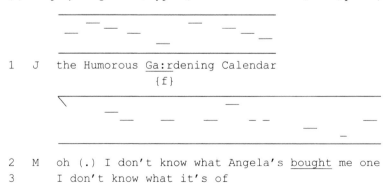

```
1   J    the Humorous Ga:rdening Calendar
                        {f}


2   M    oh (.) I don't know what Angela's bought me one
3        I don't know what it's of
```

The accented syllable (*Gar-*) in line 1, in addition to having centering vowel quality, is lower, louder, and longer than the surrounding syllables and is TRP-projecting, thus signaling that a next speaker may come in. In contrast, the accented syllable *bought* in line 2 lacks either of these sets of features and is non-TRP projecting, signaling that M still has the conversational floor. Needless to say, the phonetic and prosodic cues to a potential turn change in other languages may not be the same or even similar as these examples taken from British English. In Finnish, for instance, it has been argued that non-modal voice quality (especially creaky voice) cues TRPs (Ogden, 2001, 2003, 2004).

Multi-unit turns which are planned from the outset may be formatted lexically in a way which projects that they will have more than one TCU. Among the strategies which have been identified here are discourse markers such as *first of all* and prefaces such as *There are three things I'd like to say* (see, e.g., Schegloff, 1982). There are also phonetic and prosodic cues which speakers use to suppress possible turn transition at the end of what would otherwise be a possibly complete unit so that they can produce a multi-unit turn. One set of features identified for this task has been called a *rush-through* (Schegloff, 1982), in which the speaker "speeds up the pace of talk, withholds a dropping pitch or the intake of breath, and phrases the talk to bridge what would otherwise be the juncture at the end of a unit" (p. 76). A related type is the so-called *abrupt-join* (Local and Walker, 2004). Here is an example:

(4) Ann Percy
Lesley and Robin, both substitute teachers, are comparing educational philosophies at the schools where they teach.

```
1   Robin:   I just fee::l:- (0.4)
2            if they're going to go the wa::y: of the
             modern schoo:ls
3            there's an awf:ul-
4            they're ↑caught. between the two.
5            that's their pro[blem.
6   Lesley:                  [that's ri:ght.
7            (0.3)
8   Robin:   an' they've got to go:: (.)
9            you know really get their finger (out).
10->         =↑what d'you think of Ann Percy
11           (.)
12  Lesley:  .hhhhh ↑WE::LL d'you kno:w e-I wuh-
```

13   I: ↑have a↑ certain ↓sneaking respect for
          her.↓
14 Robin: mm::?

((Conversation continues on topic of Ann Percy and other changes in the organization of the school which mean that Robbie will not get a permanent post there))

In lines 8–9, Robin moves to close down the topic with her summary assessment *they've got to go:: (.) you know really get their finger (out).* Normally, a change of speaker would be expected next, with the new speaker offering an expression of agreement and signaling his or her own readiness to close down the topic (Drew and Holt, 1998). Yet Robin temporally compresses the last syllable of her unit and moves immediately into the next unit, which turns out to be a rather abrupt change of topic. Abrupt-joins, as Local and Walker (2004) describe them, have both disjunctive and integrative phonetic properties: there is often a step-up in pitch and/or volume on the second unit, yet selected phonetic features (articulatory settings) may encroach from the end of the first unit onto the second, thus subtly linking them.

The signaling of readiness or non-readiness to yield the conversational floor is another task which participants must manage in interaction – speakers, in order to give up or retain the floor as they wish, and recipients, in order to know whether they are expected to speak next or not. Waiting until after a unit has been completed or a next unit begun is not a realistic option, given the time pressure of speech production and processing in natural conversation. Because phonetic and prosodic cues to coordinating turn transition can be produced and processed *simultaneously* with other aspects of ongoing talk, they allow talk-in-interaction to retain its tightly interwoven texture despite the non-scripted, spontaneous conditions of its origin. This coordination of turn transitions by means of phonological cues is a second important dimension of interactional phonology.

the phonology of linking adjacent and non-adjacent units

Although talk is produced in a linear fashion over time, its parts do not always relate to one another like beads on a string. Instead, some parts belong together more closely than others; and some parts, although they may be adjacent, do not belong together at all. There are countless "invisible" linkages and hierarchies in talk, whose nature may be syntactic, rhetorical, and/or interactional. These different kinds of hierarchy will be conceptualized here as corresponding to different levels of structure in talk-in-interaction: the turn-unit, the turn, and the sequence. At each of these levels of interactional structure, phonetic and prosodic features can cue which linguistic units belong together (i.e., as a turn-unit, a turn, or a sequence) and which do not. In what follows, I present some of the more striking findings from recent interactional phonological research on phonetically and prosodically cued cohesion and coherence in talk-in-interaction.

Because talk is often produced with minimal preplanning and a high degree of spontaneity, it comes as no surprise that it sometimes needs *repair* – i.e., restarting, recycling, revising, and/or correcting. Since time is irreversible, repair must be executed in the context of managing other aspects of talk. This means that during the ongoing production of talk, participants must know whether an about-to-be-produced word or syllable is a legitimate extension or continuation of prior talk or a repair of it. One of the more important phonetic cues to the fact that repair is about to be initiated in a stretch of talk is the *cut-off* (Jasperson, 2002). A cut-off involves abruptly curtailing what would be the normal delivery of a word by aborting its full production or by shortening the articulation of its final sound(s). In the environment of *continuant* sounds (vowels, fricatives, and approximants), typically a glottal closure is the mechanism speakers use to accomplish a cut-off of talk. Alternatively, an abrupt oral closure made in conjunction with the initial sound of a projected next stop consonant may be used to effect a cut-off.[6] Here are examples of each of these techniques from Jasperson's data:

(5) ML2CC (Jasperson, 2002, p. 262)

```
1  M:    ... and to my sih%  ← glottalized vowel [i]
2         <my nie:ce in
3         William an' Mary:,
```

(6) SA2CO (ibid, p. 265)

```
1  S:    Because usually the
2         kind of bo:dies are b-  ← bilabial stop cut-off
                                     (built?)
3         <ar:e the >spindly< ...
```

Phonetic cut-offs such as these signal that whatever was in the process of being said has been abruptly interrupted because it needs repair. What immediately follows is thus open to interpretation as a replacement, revision, or reworking of the word or words that preceded the cut-off. In the case of so-called *opportunistic cut-off* as in (6) – when the closure of a next stop consonant is preempted for the initiation of self-repair –listeners may be able to anticipate what the projected word was going to be. The closure cut-off signals that the speaker intends *not* to produce this word but will make another (more considered) choice instead.

In producing talk spontaneously and in real time, speakers may also find themselves in need of "breaking" talk temporarily, not to repair something already said but rather to plan what to say next or to find an appropriate way of saying it. For this the *pause* is useful. Interlocutors, however, must be able to judge whether a current speaker is making a turn-internal pause with the intent to continue talking or is instead yielding the floor for someone else to speak. Local and Kelly (1986) show that speakers have two sets of phonetic cues which distinctively display what they are doing when they pause:

(i)   *holding silence* – speakers can make a glottal closure at the end of their suspended talk and hold it, without breathing, over a period of silence until they resume speaking;

(ii) *trail-off silence* - speakers can reduce volume or loudness, slow their speech, use creaky voice, and/or lax voice (which may have a somewhat breathy or whispered quality) towards the end of their talk, avoiding a glottal hold and producing an audible outbreath during the ensuing silence.

A *holding silence* signals unmistakably that the current speaker intends to continue talking, whereas a *trail-off silence* suggests that the floor could (and perhaps should) switch to another speaker. Local and Kelly (1986) give the following examples (the symbol /ʔ/ stands for glottal closure):

(7) NB IV:10:R:18

```
-> Lottie:   S:o uh̲ʔ(.)ʔ I leftʔ, and then I (0.2) e::u
              well
              I stopped on the way to ↓ea:t °'n then°
```

(8) NB IV:3:R6

```
    Lottie:   Yeh I'll see what she says a↓bout it↓ you
              kno:w
->            and uhʔ (.)
    Emma:     ↑Yeah ↓wear it for ↑Christ↓mas again
              God you hate to just wear it once
```

In example (7), the glottal hold following Lottie's *uh* signals her intent to continue talking and thus works as a floor holding cue. By contrast, the lack of a glottal hold *uh* in (8) signals, in a way which is perhaps iconic, that Lottie is releasing her hold on the floor. Not surprisingly, the floor shifts to Emma immediately thereafter.

At the level of multi-unit turns and sequences, speakers face a similar task of signaling that the unit currently being produced is or is not related to the unit which preceded it. Typically, if a turn-constructional unit is to be interpreted as following on from the one which preceded it, it will continue the (gradually declining) pitch and volume settings of the prior unit(s), while a turn-constructional unit which is to be understood as initiating a new course of action will have a "resetting" of pitch and volume (Couper-Kuhlen, 2001, 2003, 2004). Here is an example demonstrating such resetting in a multi-unit turn to initiate a new course of action:[7]

(9) Gulf War I (16A, 227)
((From a radio phone-in broadcast in Berkeley, California, during the first Gulf War))

```
1    Leo:    FRANK on the li:ne;
2            from Walnut CREEK;
3            you're on the GIant sixty eight K-N-B-R.
             135
4    Frank:  hi LEo,
             159
5            HOW you doing.
6    Leo:    HI Frank,
7            I'm GOOD.
8            THANKS for calling.
             152
9 ->         Frank:   I'LL be really quick. uh (.)
             192
10 =>        ↑NUMber one is-
11           I don't THINK uh;
12           a lot of the AMERican uh;
13           ARMy men and,
14           NAvy and,
15           maRINES and,
16           AIR force,
```

```
17        would be there FIGHTing right now if they
                                   didn't, .hh
18        beLIEVE in the fact that;
19        they don't WANT no more TERRorists.
```

((turn continues))

Following the exchange of greetings in this phone call, Frank (the caller) begins his turn in line 9 with *I'll be really quick*. This unit is not marked prosodically as beginning anything new. Rather, because its pitch and volume are no greater than in his prior turn (lines 4–5), it is heard as continuing on from what went before. The next unit, however, has a sudden surge in pitch and loudness on the first accented syllable ↑*NUMber*. Under the circumstances, this prosodic resetting is heard as marking the beginning of Frank's reason for the call. Because it starts with prosodic parameters set high and loud, it makes possible the addition of further units within those settings. The high settings in effect "make room for" an indefinite number of units which will follow and thus herald in the start of a large discourse unit – a "big package" (Couper-Kuhlen, 2001; also 2003, 2004).

On other occasions, speakers may wish to signal that a unit which they are just initiating links back to an earlier turn of theirs, one perhaps discontinued due to an interruption or other contingency. Local (1992) describes how prosodic resources can be used to display that speakers are indeed harking back to an earlier point in their talk rather than starting anew. This distinction is interactionally important because in turn resumption a speaker's prior talk is registered as having been interrupted and as now being resumed, whereas in beginning anew the interruption is not registered as such and consequently "disappears" from the record, so that there is no implication that the other has come in illegitimately. Here are two of Local's examples to demonstrate the distinction:

(10) NB IV 11 4

```
1 ->a  Emma:    °p°t°hh well GLA:D[YS i]f yo-
2      Gladys:                  [But ] thanks ever so:
                                        an:d um
3 ->b  Emma:    IF you NEED US? or want uh WANT anything
                                        ((pitch & volume
                                        matching end of line 1))
4               you know we're right he:r[e ↓so:
5      Gladys:                           [Well
```

In this extract, Emma's turn unit beginning *Well Gladys if yo-* (line 1)
is broken off when Gladys comes in in overlap (line 2). When Emma
resumes her turn (line 3), she marks the resumption as just that, by
picking up prosodically where she left off. The pitch and volume levels
of *IF you* in line 3 are exactly matched to those of the discontinued *if
yo-* in line 1. By contrast, in the following extract, Emma discontinues
an overlapped turn but then later starts anew:

(11) NB IV 13 22

```
1      Emma:    You know and I'm a big ↓m:eat eater
2 ->a           Lo[ttie.] We: come]          do:wn]
3      Lottie:    [I: kn]ow it  an]d you know I n]ever
                ea:t me[at
4      Emma:            [°hh
5 ->b           We come down here and my God we buy-
                (0.4) ((pitch & volume reset vis-à-vis line 2))
6               we'll eat about (.) three dollars worth
                of stea:k.
7               The (b)two of us one ni:ght you know
```

Emma's *We come down* in line 2 is discontinued due to overlap from
Lottie, yet her *We come down* in line 5 is heard as starting anew because
it does not orient to the earlier pitch and loudness levels but instead
adopts new prosodic parameters.

In sum, at both local (turn-constructional unit) and more global (turn
and sequence) levels, speakers face the task of cueing the elements or
units they are about to produce as being related or not to what went
before. In the one case, speakers are heard as carrying on their line of
talk, in the other, to be producing or starting a new unit of talk. At a
very local level, the new material may be a repair or revision of what
went before; at a more global level, it is likely to be the initiation of a
new course of action. Such messages can of course be conveyed meta-
linguistically, by saying explicitly that what follows is related or is not
related to what came before. However, they are most efficiently conveyed
when they are produced simultaneously with the talk, and it is phonetic
and prosodic cues which serve as resources for this job. This linking
of parts of a speaker's talk through phonology is a third dimension of
interactional phonology.

the phonology of accomplishing actions in interaction

In addition to constructing and coordinating turns at talk, and to marking cohesion and coherence within and among them, one of interactants' main jobs is to figure out what their co-participants are trying to do, and are actually doing, with their turns. The simple dichotomy "Are you asking me or telling me?" suggests, in a nutshell, the interpretive work needed. Of course, the set of conversational actions is much larger than just asking or telling, and the job of interpreting these actions in specific contexts is a great deal more complex than one dichotomous choice. Actions in conversation are always context-bound. A particular sequence of words may accomplish one thing in one context but something quite different in another. Conversely, different words may accomplish the same thing in different contexts.

Of importance here are at least two kinds of context: (i) the larger setting (institutional or non-institutional) in which talk takes place, and (ii) the more local sequential context in which a turn is embedded. Both of these types of context impact upon what a specific sequence of words will be understood to be doing. If, however, context is held constant, phonetic and prosodic features can be shown to function distinctly and systematically to cue the action that a given sequence of words is accomplishing. In the following examples, I review three studies which demonstrate this. All deal with other-speaker turn repetition, and each presents the case for a phonology of action in interaction.

One of the earliest studies to show the relevance of phonetic and prosodic characteristics of speech for implementing actions in interaction is Kelly and Local's (1989) analysis of word repetitions in interviews. Informants in these interviews, which were carried out as part of the Tyneside (U.K.) Dialect Survey, were asked if they recognized or used a particular dialect word. Kelly and Local showed that if interviewees repeated the word in question, the word-repeat turn could be interpreted as one of the following three actions: (i) a display of recognition, (ii) an understanding check, or (iii) a "mulling over." For each of these different actions, distinct clusters of phonetic events recurrently accompanied the repeated word. For instance, if the interviewee was displaying recognition of the word, it was said with rising pitch; but if a confirmation of understanding was needed, the word was said loud with pitch quickly falling from high to low. If the interviewee was repeating the word in order to mull it over, the word was said with decreasing volume and with pitch slowly falling from mid to low, often accompanied by breathy voice. Here are examples of each of these three distinct actions:

(12) Display of recognition (Kelly and Local, 1989, p. 272)

```
        McN:    er (0.5) bait
                (0.5)
->      EiR:    bait (.) yes      ((rising pitch))
                (.)
=>      McN:    yes
```

(13) Understanding check (ibid., p. 269)

```
        McN:    er: (1.5) hoy
->      DWi:    hoy            ((loud, quickly falling pitch
                                 from high to low))
=>      McN:    hoy it across: (.) uhu
                (0.7)
        DWi:    uhum
```

(14) Mulling over (ibid., p. 274)

```
        McN:    er (0.8) varnigh
                (0.9)
->      GSh:    varnigh      ((decreasing volume, slowly falling
                               pitch from mid to low, breathy))
=>      MCN:    (1.0)
        GSh:    oh yes I've sometimes said varnigh
        McN:    aye (.) uh (.) yeah
```

Kelly and Local argue that it is the accompanying phonetic patterns which steer the interviewer's interpretation of the turn in each case (as indicated by the double arrows) and prompt him/her in the next turn either (i) to acknowledge the recognition as in (12), (ii) to repeat or gloss the word in case of an understanding check as in (13), or (iii) to withhold talk in the case of mulling over as in (14).

Kelly and Local's study is revealing in a number of ways. For one, it provides an empirical reminder of the fact that what are interaction- ally statements are not invariably delivered with falling intonation nor are what are interactionally questions invariably delivered with rising intonation in English: in the Tyneside dialect precisely the opposite is the case. More generally, Kelly and Local's study makes the important point that the sound patterns identified are sensitive to dialect, situation, sequence, and turn type. The specific recurrent clusters of phonetic features

patterns of phonology in discourse contexts   203

have their described effect only in the Tyneside variety (dialect), in a survey interview (situation), following a word inquiry by the interviewer (sequence), and in a turn by the interviewee formatted as a word-repeat (turn type). In a different context, with a different constellation of contextual features, the same phonetic clusters might have a different import and different phonetic clusters might have the same import (see also Ford and Couper-Kuhlen, 2004).

A second interactional phonological study which makes a similar point concerning prosodic features and the implementation of conversational actions, though for a different set of features and in a quite different setting, involves the analysis of guessing sequences on a Manchester (U.K.) radio program entitled *Brain Teaser*. On this program, listeners call in to the studio and try to solve a weekly riddle (Couper-Kuhlen, 1996). Routinely, once callers have made their guess, the studio moderator repeats the proffered answer before announcing whether it is right or wrong. The prosodic characteristics of the repeat – in particular, its relative pitch in the moderator's voice range – are telling with respect to whether the moderator is checking his understanding of the proposed answer or is rather mimicking the caller and thereby negatively assessing the caller's guess. For instance:

(15) *Brain Teaser*, Radio Manchester

```
      1   Moderator:   It is comPLETE,
      2                though it seems it ISn't.
      3                WHAT do you reckon.
      4   Caller:      well I think I've GOT this one;
      5                and I got it as you were reading it
                       OU:T.
                       301          144
->    6                Is the answer HOLE.
                       (0.6)
                       167          89
=>    8   Moderator:   Is the answer HOLE.
      9   Caller:      YES.
     10   Moderator:   er: NO.
```

In this instance, the caller's guess is framed as an inquiry: *Is the answer "hole"?* (line 6). Following a brief pause, the moderator now repeats this proffered answer (line 8), and in doing so he repeats not only its words but also its prosodic configuration: the same syllables are accented, and the pitch pattern and the syllable lengths are roughly comparable. Although the moderator's voice is naturally lower than his female caller's, he places the repeated contour at approximately the same level in his voice range (slightly above mid) as it is in her voice range (also slightly above mid). The effect of these prosodic characteristics on the turn repetition is to cue it as an understanding check meaning, "Is this what you said?" The caller then confirms in the next turn that it is. Now compare:

(16) *Brain Teaser*, Radio Manchester

```
      1  Moderator:  you can find REFerence in any Latin
      2              dictionary to a briGA:DE.
                                 379
->    3  Caller:     .h .h TROOPS.
      4              (0.5)
                     379
=>    5  Moderator:  TROOPS.
      6              Erm,
      7              TROOPS
      8              is WRONG.
      9  Caller:     Oh:
```

In this instance, although the moderator also repeats the words and the prosodic contour of the caller's proposed answer, *Troops*, in line 5, he does not place his repetition at the same relative position in his voice range but instead he matches – exactly – the (female) caller's absolute pitch values. Since the moderator's voice is naturally much lower than hers, this means that his repetition sounds very high pitched; in fact, he must shift into falsetto to reach the caller's absolute pitch values. The interactional effect of such prosodic cueing is radically different from that in example (15). In example (16), the moderator comes off as mimicking the caller and thereby implying that her answer is in some way inadequate or silly. The caller also interprets his action this way, as is reflected in her lack of audible response: teased parties are known to respond, initially at least, by ignoring, rejecting, or correcting the suggestion made in the tease (Drew, 1987). In this context then, the relevant prosodic cues relate to pitch register, and they cue actions which are in part specific to this special type of interaction.

A third study which examines repetition in another set of circumstances focuses on adult–child interaction during the activity of looking at picture books together (Tarplee, 1996). On such occasions, very young

children are often prompted to label the objects and activities by adult
questions such as "What's that?" or "What's the monkey doing?" As
Tarplee (1996) points out, this exercise presents children with two tasks:
(i) identifying the object or activity correctly ("getting the right word")
and (ii) articulating the word properly ("getting the word right") (p. 408).
Her study shows that adult repetition of the child's labeling attempt
can be interpreted either as inviting reparative work on the label or as
simply affirming the child's choice. Children are quite capable of distinguishing these two actions: in the former case they engage in repair,
sometimes with prompting from the adult; in the latter case, they move
on to the next picture. Here are examples illustrating the different types
of sequences:

(17) Tarplee (1996, p. 420)

1   Child: [tʰa̰dr̰ə̰θ]

=>

2   Adult: [tʰḭːə̰θ]

3   Child: [t̬ḭːjə^h]
4   (.)
5   Adult: where's th<u>o</u>mas' t<u>ee</u>:th

(18) Tarplee (ibid., p. 423f)

1   Child: [p'ḛ̃ḛ̃ʔːt∫'i]
2 =>   (1.2)

3   Adult: [pʰḛ̃n·s·ə̰θ̩]

4   (.)

_____
                        ⟋
            —
_____

5   Child: [pǽə̨s'ǫ̈ʷ]
                     (.)
6   Adult: good boy

(19) Tarplee (ibid., p. 413)

1   Child: [ʔʲa̧ˈɪðę̈ˈ]
2 => Adult: [lɐ·də˙ˋ]
3   (0.8) ((sound of turning pages))
4   Child: [dę̧ˈgɪ]

Tarplee argues that the distinction between affirming a label and inviting repair on that label is cued by the prosodic and phonetic details of the delivery of the repetition. An adult repetition which invites repair is marked by making a deliberate phonological contrast with respect to the child's label, typically in terms of pitch, as in example (17). Alternatively, the adult repetition is temporarily delayed, as in example (18). In this case, although the adult pitch contour may be rather similar to the child's, it is the lengthy pause which works to cue a re-elicitation, thereby encouraging the child to try again. In the absence of these specific prosodic cues, the adult repetition will be taken as a confirmation of the child's choice of label. Despite the fact that the child's version may need repair, no repair will be forthcoming, as seen in example (19).

A comparison of these three studies of other-speaker turn repetition makes it clear that in each case a different set of phonetic and prosodic features are relevant. The initiation of a repair is in all three instances one of the relevant interpretive options, yet it is cued in each case by different phonetic and prosodic properties. Repetition is thus not a monolithic phenomenon, nor is there a single "phonology of repetition." Instead, depending on situational and sequential circumstances there are many different kinds of repetition and a variety of "phonologies" which relate to them.[8]

It is perhaps no coincidence that so many studies of interactional phonetics and prosody focusing on action have dealt with repetition.[9] Given the large number of factors involved, repetitive turns have the advantage for the analyst of holding the factor of wording constant. In each of the contexts discussed above, for instance, repair initiation (to take one action out of many) could also be accomplished by turns such as *What did you say?* or *Would you mind repeating what you just said?* These wordings introduce an added syntactic factor (e.g., *wh*-interrogative, *yes–no* interrogative), which in turn can impact upon phonetic and prosodic realization and thereby add complexity to the analyst's task. Constant wording by contrast reduces the number of variables in a domain where context-sensitivity is high. Yet despite the extreme context-sensitivity of action implementation by the speaker and of interpretation by the recipient in interaction, the contribution of phonetic and prosodic cueing to the task is both patterned and systematic. The accomplishment of actions through phonological means is a fourth dimension of interactional phonology.

the phonology of marking stance and affiliation

The conversational tasks examined so far have all had in common that they are primarily speaker-oriented, in the sense that it is the speaker's turn which is being (self-)constructed and coordinated and the speaker's action which is being (self-)implemented. The task to be considered now is by contrast other-oriented, in that speakers are indicating in one way or another various sorts of affiliation or disaffiliation with the other participant(s) to the interaction or their actions. Talk involves not only the implementation of actions in interaction but also the conveying of stance-related messages such as: "I'm on the same wave-length as you," "There's a problem with what you just said (did)," or, more generally, "I'm (momentarily) aligning with/disaligning myself from you." As Heritage (1984) and others have argued, alignment and disalignment in talk are closely tied to a system of preference which organizes priorities when there are multiple ways of responding to a given initiating move in conversation. Cutting across the system of preferences are non-verbal dimensions of talk which color the import of responses with messages signifying "I'm (not) OK/you're (not) OK." Phonetic and prosodic features of turn construction and coordination are instrumental in conveying these (dis)affiliative messages.

An examination of the coordinated pacing of talk, using English as a case in point (Couper-Kuhlen, 1993), will illustrate how stance and affiliation can be marked phonologically.[10] As is well known, English is a stress-timed language, with speakers tending to produce accented (stressed) syllables at regular intervals in time. English conversationalists appear to capitalize on this "natural" tendency when they talk with one another by coordinating their turns such that a shared rhythmic pattern, or beat, will be established and maintained across turn transitions. This is achieved by a current speaker, shortly before yielding the floor, setting up a rhythmic pattern with two or more accented syllables placed at a regular interval of time,[11] and a next speaker timing their incoming contribution to talk in such a way that the first accented syllable picks up the beat of the prior talk and continues its rhythmic pattern. Slight tempo variations (e.g., "dragging" or "pushing" the beat) can be tolerated, but may also be exploited for specific purposes, e.g., to propose a subtle slowing down or speeding up of the pace of interaction. For example:

(20) Hey Cutie Pie, CSAE Part II

```
1    JILL:    (TSK) What have you been up to.
2    JEFF:    .. Nothing.
3    JILL:    .. Nothing?
4    JEFF:    .. Just homework.
```

The accented syllables in this short sequence have been underlined. Most of the accented syllables come at roughly equal intervals in time and create a regular beat in talk, as shown in (21), where slashes before each accented syllable have been aligned to give an iconic representation of regularity):[12]

(21) Rhythmic analysis of (20)

```
JILL:     /What have you been    /
          /up to.                /
JEFF:     /Nothing. ..           /
JILL:     /Nothing?
JEFF:                  .. Just   /
          /homework.
```

The regular beat towards the end of a current speaker's turn thus establishes a metric according to which a next speaker can time an incoming contribution to talk. Delayed and late incoming talk appears to be judged according to this rhythmic metric (Couper-Kuhlen, 1991). For instance, in the following sequence Jeff is telling Jill about a new discovery in astronomy he has just read about. Jill checks her understanding in the next turn by proffering a guess about what Jeff has just told her:

(22) Hey Cutie Pie, CSAE Part II

```
1        JEFF:   A=nd,
2                .. they think that there's not,
3                (Hx) it can't,
4                .. those planets can't sustain life.
5 ->     JILL:   ... Oh=,
6 ->             just from the distance from it?
7 =>     JEFF:   ... (H) ... % ... No.
8 =>             From .. um,
9                .. like,
10               .. from their surface?
11               .. The .. the planet's surface?
12       JILL:   (H) (TSK) Oh=
```

Based on the beat established in Jill's inquiry (lines 5–6), the onset of Jeff's response is delayed, as the rhythmic analysis in (23) demonstrates:[13]

(23) Rhythmic analysis of lines 4–8 in (22)

```
    JEFF:                 those
            /planets can't sus-        /
            /tain life. ...            /
    JILL:   /Oh=, just from the        /
            /distance from it?         /
    JEFF:   /^ ... (H)                 /
            /^ ... %        ...        /
            /No. From ... um,
```

The delayed onset of Jeff's reply, prefaced by audible inbreathing and glottal constriction, is congruent with its status as a dispreferred response to Jill's comprehension check, which she has constructed as a question expecting an affirmative answer. Because of its phonological features, Jeff's reply signals that Jill's understanding check is misguided.

As the following extract shows, dispreferred responses are not always delayed. In this sequence, Jill is telling Jeff about a friend of theirs who is about to take her medical school exams:

(24) Hey Cutie Pie, CSAE Part II

```
1        JILL:   and then she has .. off,
2                and,
```

```
3              (H) she has vacation,
4              and,
5              .. Oh,
6              it just sounded so good.
7      JEFF:   (TSK) What's she --
8 ->           Oh=.
9 ->           She must be so excited though.
10=>   JILL:   .. Well she sounded really .. bummed.
11=>           .. Actually,
12             just cause school is so tough right now?
13     JEFF:   [Unhunh].
```

Following Jill's story, the latter part of which is shown in lines 1–6, Jeff's reply of *Oh=*. *She must be so excited though* (lines 9–10) is built to expect an affirmative agreement response. In fact, Jill disconfirms Jeff's assumption in her next turn: their friend is not excited, she's "bummed" instead. Despite the fact that it is dispreferred, Jill's "correction" is not rhythmically delayed, as the representation of example (25) shows:

(25) Rhythmic analysis of lines 8–11 of (24)

```
JEFF:   /Oh=. She must be so ex-   /
        /cited though. ..          /
JILL:   /Well she sounded really.. /
        /bummed. .. Actually,
```

The rhythm of Jill's dispreferred response camouflages rather than exposes its corrective nature (Jefferson, 1983). Instead of implying "there's a problem here" – as Jeff's timing did in (23) – the timing in (25) suggests "nothing out of the ordinary" (Couper-Kuhlen, 1992, 1993). Thus, although this turn corrects and thereby disaffiliates,with the message of the other party on the verbal level, it affiliates on the non-verbal level. Maintaining a rhythmic pattern across a turn transition, especially when the incoming turn is a corrective one, contributes to sustaining social solidarity.

There are further ways in which phonetic and prosodic resources can be arrayed congruently with the verbal message or not to convey affiliation or disaffiliation. Many of these have been described by Szczepek (2001, 2003) under the general label of *prosodic orientation*. *Prosodic orientation* describes a situation in which a second speaker noticeably matches (or departs from) one or more of the prosodic characteristics of a prior

speaker's utterance. The orientation may involve pitch contour, pitch
register, syllable lengthening, volume, speech rate, and/or voice quality.[14]
For instance:

(26) Who the heck (Szczepek, 2003, p. 99)
MA, the caller to this radio phone-in, has just reported hearing that
the putative Nazi prisoner Rudolf Hess being held at the Spandau jail is
actually not who he is thought to be.

```
1     DH:  well -
2          YEAH;
3          AlRIGHT then.
4          let me ASK you.
5          if it Isn't HESS,
6  ->      <<h> ↑who the `heck ↑IS `it.>
7  =>  MA: <<h> ↑i've `no ´I´↑DE`A.>
8          (0.5)
9      MA: [well you sEE-
10     DH: [but I mean how HOW can you persuADE somebody;
11         to spend dOnkey's years (.) in PRIson;
```

Subsequent to MA's report that a doctor has confirmed that the Spandau
prisoner is *not* Rudolf Hess (prior to the illustrative stretch of speech
shown here), the moderator DH rather reluctantly expresses (mock)
acceptance (*well yeah; alright then*), followed by the ostensibly innocently
framed question, *Let me ask you. If it isn't Hess, who the heck is it?!* In fact,
the moderator's question is a rhetorical one and arguably intended to
hint at the implausibility of the rumor and at his own incredulity. Yet
the caller does not treat the moderator's action as a statement countering
and potentially discrediting his own position but instead as a genuine
question, which he disingenuously answers with *I've no idea!*, thereby in
effect disarming his opponent's argumentative position.[15] How is this
effect achieved? First of all, by timing his response to be immediate,
MA signals that he sees nothing problematic about DH's question or its
answer. At the same time, by formulating his answer prosodically such
that it echoes the pitch accents and pitch register of DH's *who the heck is
it?!*, MA signals affiliation with his would-be opponent. Although MA's
answer is verbally compatible with the oppositional position he has
assumed so far, on a non-verbal level he conveys agreement with DH
by matching his tone of voice so closely. Prosodic orientation can thus

strategically convey affiliation concurrently with words which may be doing something quite different.

In addition to the general messages of "I'm affiliating with you" or "I'm disaffiliating from you" discussed above, there are more specific affective messages conveyed by the phonetic and prosodic details of turn-constructional units implementing specific actions in specific conversational sequences. A range of stances and affect-related messages have been shown to depend on phonetic and prosodic cues, such as astonishment in repair initiation (Selting, 1996a), extra strong agreement in assessing sequences (Uhmann, 1996), and casting news as good or bad in informing sequences (Freese and Maynard, 1998). Yet in each case, the nature of the stance or affect is specific to the actions being implemented and the way in which turns are constructed to implement those actions, including by means of phonetic/prosodic cues which are themselves highly context-sensitive. Although no one set of cues will transfer perfectly from one sequentially embedded action to another, there is a definite patterning in context which makes use of phonological properties to mark stance and affiliation. This is a fourth and final dimension of interactional phonology.

outlook and directions for future research

Compared to the more established phonologies mentioned at the outset of this chapter, the research direction described here, phonology for talk-in-interaction, is still in its infancy. It is clear from the studies carried out so far that this is an extremely fruitful line of inquiry and that there is a great deal yet to be discovered. Not only is very little known about, e.g., turn construction and coordination across speakers in English and related languages, there is even less known about these matters in non-Indo-European languages.[16] The phonetic and prosodic details of a wealth of conversational actions and action-specific stances have yet to be described for English and other languages, as do techniques for signaling cohesion and coherence within and between turns, which may not be the same across languages. Work on such a program, initiated by Couper-Kuhlen and Selting (1996), has just begun (e.g., Local, 2003; papers in Couper-Kuhlen and Ford, 2004).

Just as importantly, from the interactional phonological studies carried out so far, we know not only what needs investigating, but also how to proceed methodologically in doing so. The basic requirement of an interactional phonological study is data in the form of a collection of naturally occurring conversations. The sounds and prosodies in this material, or in selected parts of this material, must be impressionistically transcribed with as little reference as possible to preconceived (often written-language) categories. Recurrent patterns must then be sought in the impressionistic record, with careful attention being paid to factors such as lexical and syntactic structure, action type, position in the turn-constructional unit, position in the turn, position in the sequence, type of sequence or activity, and situational context – factors which have proved relevant in previous studies of interactional phonology. Functional explanations must be related to the tasks which participants can be shown to be addressing in conjunction with other related interactional demands and goals. Moreover, both formal categories and functional accounts must be not only plausible to the investigator, but also demonstrably relevant to the interactants themselves.

Investigations of this kind come with a strong warranty. Although they do not pretend to account for all phonological structure in a context-free fashion, they offer a persuasive account of phonological patterning in one particular environment on one or several specific occasions. This is the hallmark of interactional phonology. An understanding of the phonology of talk-in-interaction as a whole can only be achieved through a slow but steady accretion of single studies describing the *situated phonologies* with which real interactants can be shown to operate.

transcription conventions

h, hh	Outbreath
.h, .hh	Inbreath
↑	Step up in pitch
↓	Step down in pitch
,	Final low rising pitch
?	Final high rising pitch
;	Final mid falling pitch
.	Final low falling pitch
..	Medium pause
...	Longish pause
%	Closure cut-off with glottalization
<	Rapid resumption of phonation after previous cut-off (a so-called "left push")
< >	Rapid articulation
=	Lengthening
–	Abrupt cut-off
––	Incomplete intonation unit

(0.5)	Pause measured in seconds
(.)	Micropause (≥ 0.2)
TWELVE	Primary accent
twElve	Secondary accent
:, ::, :::	Syllable or sound stretching
f	Forte or increased volume
°	Low audibility
[	Overlapping turns
[	
( )	Doubtful transcription

notes

1. Editor's note: for common associations of nasalization and other types of voice, see Figure 4.6, p. 158, and following discussion in chapter 4 of M. C. Pennington (1996), *Phonology in English language teaching: An international approach* (London: Addison-Wesley Longman).
2. Editor's note: Chaper 3, this volume, addresses the treatment of variation within different schools of phonology.
3. A main difficulty is that speakers rarely talk about phonetic details explicitly in conversation. See, however, Couper-Kuhlen and Selting (1996) for ways to overcome obstacles in validating analytic categories in terms of participants' own categories.
4. This is to be understood as a superordinate term for the various context-sensitive phonologies discussed below.
5. In the conversational excerpts of this chapter, data taken from a published source is referenced in the heading for the excerpt. Otherwise, the excerpt is taken from the author's own data. A consolidated list of the transcription conventions used in the examples is given following the concluding section of the chapter.
6. A pulmonic cut-off of air can also be used to halt articulation. Jasperson finds that this occurs most often when speakers are abandoning talk or recycling prior talk due to overlap with another speaker.
7. The italicized numbers above selected words in the transcript refer to the corresponding frequency values (in Hertz) extracted through acoustic analysis.
8. The argument here runs parallel to the one Schegloff (1996) makes for grammar: there is not one single grammar but instead multiple, contextually specific grammars.
   Editor's note: a point made earlier by certain formalists, e.g., Zellig Harris, who spoke of sublanguages – particularly, of science – with (partially) unique grammars; see, for instance, the discussion in *Mathematical structures of language* (New York: John Wiley & Sons, 1968, p. 154ff).
9. Other studies of prosody and action in interaction which are not restricted to repetition include a study by Freese and Maynard (1998) on good versus bad news deliveries in English and a number of investigations of German,

including studies of conversational questions (Selting, 1992), astonished questions in repair initiation (Selting, 1996a), reproaches cast as *why* questions (Günthner, 1996), and rhythm in assessments (Uhmann, 1996).

10. See also Auer, Couper-Kuhlen, and Mueller (1999), who treat German and Italian as well.
11. Average interval durations in English tend to be between 0.5 and 0.6 seconds, but range between 0.3 (fast) and 1.2 seconds (slow).
12. As the rhythmic representation shows, not every accented syllable (e.g., *you* in the first line) need create a beat in talk (Auer, Couper-Kuhlen, and Mueller, 1999).
13. The symbol /^, represents a silent beat (Auer, Couper-Kuhlen, & Mueller, 1999; Auer, Couper-Kuhlen, 1993).
14. In addition, Szczepek cites one example of matching of vowel quality, an indication that not only strictly prosodic features, but also phonetic or articulatory features lend themselves to orientation and thus are part of interactional phonology.
15. Note that the moderator comes back in the next turn to clarify his intended meaning: *but I mean how how can you persuade somebody to spend donkey's years in prison...* (lines 10–11) (see Schegloff, 1992, on third-position repair).
16. The work of Tanaka (1999, 2000) and Hayashi (1999, 2003) is producing promising insights into turn construction and coordination in Japanese, as is that of Ogden (2001, 2003, 2004) for Finnish.

references

Abercrombie, D. (1965). *Studies in phonetics and linguistics*. London: Oxford University Press.

Auer, P. (1992). Introduction: John Gumperz' approach to contextualization. In P. Auer & A. di Luzio (Eds.), *The contextualization of language* (pp. 1–37). Amsterdam: John Benjamins.

Auer, P. (1996). On the prosody and syntax of turn-continuations. In E. Couper-Kuhlen & M. Selting (Eds.), *Prosody in conversation* (pp. 57–100). Cambridge: Cambridge University Press.

Auer, P., Couper-Kuhlen, E., & Mueller, F. (1999). *Language in time: The rhythm and tempo of spoken interaction*. New York: Oxford University Press.

Couper-Kuhlen, E. (1991). A rhythm-based metric for turn-taking. *Proceedings of the 12th International Congress of Phonetic Sciences*, Volume 1 (pp. 275–8). Aix-en-Provence.

Couper-Kuhlen, E. (1992). Contextualizing discourse: The prosody of interactive repair. In P. Auer & A. di Luzio (Eds.), *The contextualization of language* (pp. 337–64). Amsterdam: John Benjamins.

Couper-Kuhlen, E. (1993). *English speech rhythm: Form and function in everyday verbal interaction*. Amsterdam: John Benjamins.

Couper-Kuhlen, E. (1996). The prosody of repetition: On quoting and mimicry. In E. Couper-Kuhlen & M. Selting (Eds.), *Prosody in conversation: Interactional studies* (pp. 366–405). Cambridge: Cambridge University Press.

Couper-Kuhlen, E. (2000). Prosody. In J. Verschueren, J.-O. Östman, J. Blommaert, & C. Bulcaen (Eds.), *Handbook of pragmatics* (pp. 1–19). Amsterdam: John Benjamins.

Couper-Kuhlen, E. (2001). Interactional prosody: High onsets in reason-for-the-call turns. *Language in Society, 30,* 29–53.

Couper-Kuhlen, E. (2003). On initial boundary tones in English conversation. In M. J. Solé, D. Recasens, & J. Romero (Eds.), *Proceedings of the 15th International Congress of Phonetic Sciences* (pp. 119–122). Barcelona: Universitat Antònoma de Barcelona.

Couper-Kuhlen, E. (2004). Prosody and sequence organization in English conversation: The case of new beginnings. In E. Couper-Kuhlen & C. E. Ford (Eds.), *Sound Patterns in interaction* (pp. 335–76). Amsterdam: John Benjamins.

Couper-Kuhlen, E., & Ford, C.E. (Eds.) (2004). *Sound patterns in interaction.* Amsterdam: John Benjamins.

Couper-Kuhlen, E., & Selting, M. (1996). Towards an interactional perspective on prosody and a prosodic perspective on interaction. In E. Couper-Kuhlen & M. Selting (Eds.), *Prosody in conversation: Interactional studies* (pp. 11–56). Cambridge: Cambridge University Press.

Drew, P. (1987). Po-faced receipts of teases. *Linguistics, 25,* 219–53.

Drew, P., & Holt, E. (1998). Figures of speech: Figurative expressions and the management of topic transition in conversation. *Language in Society, 27,* 495–522.

Ford, C. E., & Couper-Kuhlen, E. (2004). Conversation and phonetics: Essential connections. In E. Couper-Kuhlen & C. E. Ford (Eds.), *Sound patterns in interaction* (pp. 3–25). Amsterdam: John Benjamins.

Freese, J., & Maynard, D. W. (1998). Prosodic features of bad news and good news in conversation. *Language in Society, 27,* 195–219.

Goldsmith, J. (1990). *Autosegmental and metrical phonology.* Oxford: Blackwell.

Günthner, S. (1996). The prosodic contextualization of moral work: An analysis of reproaches in 'why'-formats. In E. Couper-Kuhlen & M. Selting (Eds.), *Prosody in conversation: Interactional studies* (pp. 271–302). Cambridge: Cambridge University Press.

Hayashi, M. (1999). Where grammar and interaction meet: A study of co-participant completion in Japanese conversation. *Human Studies, 22,* 475–99.

Hayashi, M. (2003). *Joint utterance construction in Japanese conversation.* Amsterdam: John Benjamins.

Heritage, J. (1984). *Garfinkel and ethnomethodology.* London: Polity Press.

Hogg, R., & McCully, C. B. (1987). *Metrical phonology: A coursebook.* Cambridge: Cambridge University Press.

Jasperson, R. (2002). Some linguistic aspects of closure cut-off. In C. E. Ford, B. A. Fox, & S. A. Thompson (Eds.), *The language of turn and sequence* (pp. 257–86). Oxford: Oxford University Press.

Jefferson, G. (1983). On exposed and embedded correction in conversation. *Studium Linguistik, 14,* 58–68.

Kelly, J., & Local, J. (1989). *Doing phonology.* Manchester: Manchester University Press.

Ladd, D. R. (1996). *Intonational phonology.* Cambridge: Cambridge University Press.

Local, J. (1992). Continuing and restarting. In P. Auer & A. di Luzio (Eds.), *The contextualization of language* (pp. 273–96). Amsterdam: John Benjamins.

Local, J. (2003). Phonetics and talk-in-interaction. *Proceedings, 15th International Congress of Phonetic Sciences* (pp. 115–18). Barcelona: Universitat Antònoma de Barcelona.

Local, J., & Kelly, J. (1986). Projection and "silences": Notes on phonetic and conversational structure. *Human Studies, 9*, 185–204.

Local, J. K., Kelly, J., & Wells, B. (1986). Towards a phonology of conversation: Turn-taking in Tyneside English. *Journal of Linguistics, 22*, 411–37.

Local, J. K., & Walker, G. (2004). Abrupt-joins as a resource for the production of multi-unit, multi-action turns. *Journal of Pragmatics, 36*, 1375–1402.

Martinet, A. (1962). *A functional view of language.* Oxford: Clarendon.

Nespor, M., & Vogel, I. (1986). *Prosodic phonology.* Dordrecht: Foris.

Ogden, R. (2001). Turn transition, creak and glottal stop in Finnish talk-in-interaction. *Journal of the International Phonetic Association, 31*, 139–52.

Ogden, R. (2003). Voice quality as a resource for the management of turn-taking in Finnish talk-in-interaction. *Proceedings, 15th International Congress of Phonetic Sciences* (pp. 123–6). Barcelona: Universitat Antònoma de Barcelona.

Ogden, R. (2004). Non-modal voice quality and turn-taking in Finnish. In E. Couper-Kuhlen & C. E. Ford (Eds.), *Sounds patterns in interaction* (pp. 29–62). Amsterdam: John Benjamins.

Pierrehumbert, J. (1980). *The phonology and phonetics of English intonation.* Doctoral dissertation, MIT. (published by Indiana University Linguistics Club, 1988).

Sacks, H., Schegloff, E., & Jefferson, G. (1974). A simplest systematics for the organization of turn-taking for conversation. *Language, 50*, 696–735.

Schegloff, E. (1982). Discourse as an interactional achievement: Some uses of "uh huh" and other things that come between sentences. In D. Tannen (Ed.), *Analyzing discourse: Text and talk* (pp. 71–93). Washington, DC: Georgetown University Press.

Schegloff, E. (1992). Repair after next turn. The last structurally provided defense of intersubjectivity in conversation. *American Journal of Sociology, 97*, 1295–1345.

Schegloff, E. A. (1996). Turn organization: One intersection of grammar and interaction. In E. Ochs, E. A. Schegloff, & S. A. Thompson (Eds.), *Interaction and grammar* (pp. 52–133). Cambridge: Cambridge University Press.

Selting, M. (1992). Prosody in conversational questions. *Journal of Pragmatics, 17*, 315–45.

Selting, M. (1996a). Prosody as an activity-type distinctive cue in conversation: The case of so-called "astonished" questions in repair initiation. In E. Couper-Kuhlen & M. Selting (Eds.), *Prosody in conversation: Interactional studies* (pp. 231–70). Cambridge: Cambridge University Press.

Selting, M. (1996b). On the interplay of syntax and prosody in the constitution of turn-constructional units and turns in conversation. *Pragmatics, 6*(3), 357–88.

Selting, M. (2000). The construction of units in conversational talk. *Language in Society, 29*, 477–517.

Selting, M. (2001). Fragments of units as deviant cases of unit production in conversational talk. In M. Selting & E. Couper-Kuhlen (Eds.), *Studies in interactional linguistics* (pp. 229–58). Amsterdam: John Benjamins.

Szczepek, B. (2001). Prosodic orientation in spoken interaction. *InLiSt (Interaction and Linguistic Structures)* No. 27. Retrieved January 31, 2006, from <http://www.uni-potsdam.de/u/inlist>.

Szczepek, B. (2003). Practices for prosodic collaboration in English talk-in-interaction. Doctoral dissertation, University of Potsdam.

Tanaka, H. (1999). *Turn-taking in Japanese conversation: A study in grammar and interaction*. Amsterdam: John Benjamins.

Tanaka, H. (2000). Turn-projection in Japanese talk-in-interaction. *Research on Language and Social Interaction, 33*(1), 1–38.

Tarplee, C. (1996). Working on young children's utterances: Prosodic aspects of repetition during picture labelling. In E. Couper-Kuhlen & M. Selting (Eds.), *Prosody in conversation: Interactional studies* (pp. 406–35). Cambridge: Cambridge University Press.

Trager, G., & Smith, H. L. J. (1957). *An outline of English structure*. Washington, DC: American Council of Learned Societies.

Uhmann, S. (1996). On rhythm in everyday German conversation: Beat clashes in assessment utterances. In E. Couper-Kuhlen & M. Selting (Eds.), *Prosody in conversation: Interactional studies* (pp. 303–65). Cambridge: Cambridge University Press.

Wells, B., & Macfarlane, S. (1998). Prosody as an interactional resource: Turn-projection and overlap. *Language and Speech, 41*, 265–94.

Yule, G. (1995). The paralinguistics of reference: Representation in reported discourse. In G. Cook & B. Seidlhofer (Eds.), *Principle and practice in applied linguistics* (pp. 185–96). Oxford: Oxford University Press.

9
phonology and literacy
keiko koda

introduction

This chapter describes the functional roles of phonology in literacy learning and processing among first-language (L1) and second-language (L2) learners. Reading research consistently demonstrates that poor readers are inept at a multitude of phonological tasks and, more critically, that their deficiencies are restricted primarily to the phonological domain and are usually not attributable to non-phonological factors, such as general intelligence, semantic information retrieval, or visual processing (Share and Stanovich, 1995). Many specialists agree that learning to read depends upon children's understanding that print relates to spoken language. Inevitably, therefore, phonology plays a pivotal role in a learner's process of establishing systematic linkages between spoken language elements and graphic symbols. Phonology continues to be essential in reading and the processing of printed text, well beyond the initial stages in the acquisition of literacy, because visually presented information must be converted into its phonological form in order to be stored and processed efficiently in working memory. Since virtually all of the sub-component processes of comprehension rely on working memory, phonological processing remains critical in text understanding at all stages of reading development. Thus, phonology is essential in acquiring literacy, supporting and promoting it in many ways.

The chapter defines a range of phonological skills directly related to reading acquisition, fluency, and comprehension, and, in so doing, clarifies the specific contributions of phonology to literacy. Additionally, cross-linguistic variation in phonological processing – the operations involved in accessing, extracting, storing, and manipulating phonological information from visual word input – are illustrated. Based on cross-linguistic examination, the chapter also explores the long-term impacts of literacy experience in one language on learning to read in another language.

roles of phonology in learning to read

phonological awareness

In recent times, interest in *metalinguistic awareness* – which includes the abilities to identify, analyze, and manipulate language forms – has risen sharply among reading researchers. The current consensus is that learning to read is fundamentally metalinguistic, because it involves recognition of functionally important elements in spoken language and their relations to the writing system (Fowler and Liberman, 1995; Goswami and Bryant, 1992; Nagy and Anderson, 1999). The facilitative benefits of metalinguistic awareness in learning to read can be illustrated in two ways. First, in order for literacy to develop, the learner must recognize that written symbols correspond to speech units. This insight motivates further efforts on the part of the learner to discover how spoken language elements are mapped onto graphic symbols, and then to discover structural regularities inherent in both the language and the writing system. In the absence of this basic metalinguistic insight, written symbols are viewed simply as nonsense scribbles, and their mastery is problematic. Second, an understanding that words can be segmented into smaller units promotes analytical approaches to lexical learning and processing, which enables a learner to extract partial information from an unknown string of symbols. Without such analytical competence, reading capacity is likely to be restricted to words previously encountered and recalled. Although metalinguistic awareness consists of multiple facets, each relating to a particular linguistic level or feature (phonology, morphology, syntax, or discourse), the discussion here is limited to phonological awareness and its contributions to the acquisition of literacy.

The roles of phonological awareness in alphabetic literacy – of English, in particular – have been extensively studied. Evidence from a large number of studies has led to the widely-endorsed conviction that to master an alphabetic script, the child must (i) recognize that words can be divided into sequences of phonemes, and (ii) acquire the capability to analyze a word's internal structure in order to identify its phonemic constituents. Studies of reading in the early stages show that:

- children's sensitivity to the structure of spoken sounds is directly related to their ability to read and spell words (Stahl and Murray,

1994; Stanovitch, 2000; Stanovich, Cunningham, and Cramer, 1984; Yopp, 1988);
- phonological segmentation capability is a powerful predictor of reading success among early and middle-grade students (Bryant, MacLean, and Bradley, 1990; Juel, Griffith, and Gough, 1986); and
- reading progress is significantly enhanced by phonological awareness training (Bradley and Bryant, 1991).

It is generally accepted that phonological awareness is a by-product of the child's increasing understanding of the segmental nature of spoken sounds (Stahl and Murray, 1994; Stanovich, Cunningham, & Cramer, 1984; Yopp, 1988), involving a constellation of sequentially acquired abilities. Adams (1990), for example, describes five ability clusters:

(i)   *basic perceptual capability* (remembering familiar rhymes – e.g., *pie* and *eye*);
(ii)   *analytical perceptual capacity* (recognizing and sorting patterns of rhymes and alliterations – e.g., while *five* and *fun* start with the same sound, *pie* and *eye* end with the same sound);
(iii) *intra-syllabic awareness and analysis competencies* (segmenting a syllable into its onset and rime – e.g., *pie* → /p/ + /ai/);
(iv)   *phonemic analysis skills* (conducting full phonemic segmentation – e.g., *pie* →/p/+/a/+/i/); and
(v)   *phonemic manipulation ability* (generating words by deleting, inserting, or relocating phonemes – e.g., *school* /sku:l/ minus /s/ → *cool* /ku:l/).

Similarly, by comparing the relative difficulty, reliability, and validity of ten frequently-used phonological awareness measures, Yopp (1988) categorized two interrelated dimensions: *simple awareness* (recognizing intra-syllabic, or onset-rime, speech units, corresponding to Adam's intra-syllabic awareness); and *compound awareness* (analyzing and manipulating multiple phonemes in sequence, roughly equivalent to Adam's last two ability clusters).

These distinct capacities, moreover, develop disparately and on their own timetables. In a well-designed experiment, using a word comparison task that required determining whether orally presented paired-words have any common sounds, Treiman and Zukowski (1991) found that pre-readers and beginning readers were equally adept at tasks requiring both intra-syllabic and inter-syllabic segmentation, but they differed significantly in those necessitating phonemic manipulation. Thus, for example, beginning readers could recognize both shared syllables (e.g., *hammer* and *hammock*) and phonemes (e.g., *steak* and *sponge*), but pre-readers had difficulty in detecting shared phonemes. While the achievement of beginning readers remained constant in tasks involving both syllable- and phoneme-level analysis, pre-readers' performance declined considerably in the phonemic analysis. The researchers concluded that pre-reading children have little difficulty distinguishing syllables, and are capable of making phonological judgments based on the intra-syllabic, onset-rime distinction (the differentiation between the initial phoneme and the remainder within a syllable). More critically, however, children do not become capable of breaking intra-syllabic units into smaller, phonemic, segments until they start reading independently. Clearly, while a basic understanding of the phonological structure of spoken words is a precursor of learning to read, more sophisticated awareness, involving phonemic analysis and manipulation, develops through grapheme-phoneme mapping experience in word reading and spelling. Alphabetic literacy, in short, necessitates phonological segmentation within a word through sequential letter-pattern analysis in addition to integration of the segmental phonological information.

decoding

Phonological decoding is a critical component in reading, because it facilitates the extraction and assembly of a word's phonological information. There is general agreement that achieving decoding efficiency should be the dominant goal of early reading development because a critical task in learning to read is connecting written words with oral vocabulary acquired prior to literacy learning. The significance of decoding in early reading development lies in its capacity to enable the child to use oral language competence in deciphering print. Since oral vocabulary is stored in phonological form, the ability to convert graphic symbols into their corresponding sounds affords ready access to information stored in long-term memory. In fact, ability to pronounce printed words and nonsense words is a reliable predictor of subsequent reading success in children (Bowers, Golden, Kennedy, and Young, 1994; Share and Stanovich, 1995; Torgesen and Burgess, 1998; Wagner, Torgesen, and Rashotte, 1994).

Similarly, in what is referred to as the "simple view of reading," Gough and associates (Gough and Tunmer, 1986; Hoover and Gough, 1990) explain how decoding contributes to literacy learning. According to these researchers, reading consists of two major components, *decoding* and *comprehension*, each developing on its own timetable. While decoding printed words uniquely involves visual information processing, much of comprehension involves shared competencies for both reading and listening. Although comprehension skills develop through oral interaction well before reading instruction commences, they cannot automatically be used in reading until sufficient decoding competence is achieved. Hence, a reader's decoding efficiency establishes a kind of threshold which must be attained in order to take advantage of previously acquired comprehension skills.

Multiple methods are used to decode words. Ehri (1998, p. 7), for example, suggests five ways of reading words aloud in English:

- assembling letters into a blend of sounds;
- pronouncing and blending familiar spelling patterns;
- retrieving the pronunciation of sight words from memory;
- analogizing to words already known by sight;
- using context cues to predict words.

Ehri believes that children learn to use all five methods as they develop reading proficiency. Good readers are adept in all five, as well as capable of selecting the method best suited to the orthographic composition of a given word. Thus, diversity in decoding tactics is associated with neither developmental stages nor reading ability differences. Instead, decoding competence can be characterized as a diverse tactical repertoire, which, in turn, is closely tied with orthographic knowledge.

Although in casual observations, good readers appear to recognize many words instantly and access their meanings and sounds without letter-by-letter analysis, word recognition studies have repeatedly demonstrated that skilled readers are capable of analyzing and manipulating word-internal elements – such as letters and letter clusters (Ehri, 1998; Shankweiler and Liberman, 1972). Competent readers, furthermore, are adept at pronouncing both individual letters and nonsense letter-strings (Hogaboam and Perfetti, 1978; Siegel and Ryan, 1988; Wagner, Torgesen, and Rashotte, 1994). In essence, what seems like seamless and holistic performance is not attributable to whole-word retrievals, but rather to the child's accumulated knowledge of the writing system – sound–symbol relationships, in particular (Adams, 1990; Ehri, 1994, 1998; Seidenberg and McClelland, 1989).

roles of phonology in comprehension

the role of phonology and working memory in reading

One might wonder why speedy access to phonology is critical in silent reading – where overt vocalization is not required. The best answer, perhaps, lies in the ways phonology facilitates integration of various types of information during comprehension. Once extracted from print, lexical information must be consolidated into larger, meaningful chunks such as phrases, sentences, and paragraphs. Working memory plays a pivotal role in this critical process, and virtually every operation in reading, beyond word recognition, relies upon working memory. Critically, the *phonological loop* – a major component of working memory – mediates the formation and retention of phonological representations in mind while processing linguistic material (Gathercole and Baddeley, 1993). Phonological encoding enhances information storage and processing in working memory, by providing durable representations which can be referenced and cross-referenced for information integration (Kleiman, 1975; Levy, 1975).

A principal hurdle in complex cognitive activities is that the number of mental resources which can be simultaneously activated is limited (LaBerge and Samuels, 1974; Schneider and Shiffrin, 1977). Inasmuch as reading requires the continuous integration of what is extracted from print with what is stored in long-term memory at varying processing levels (phonological, morphological, lexical, syntactic, and discourse levels), a number of interlinked cognitive processors must become operative at the same time. To accomplish this within cognitive capacity limitations, several components must become automated (Daneman, 1991; Daneman and Carpenter, 1980, 1983; Perfetti, 1985). Automaticity, however, is not easily accomplished in high-order processes involving meaning construction, since these necessitate deliberate attention rather than simple repetitive operations at each processing step. Hence, it is all the more essential that phonological decoding be automated – in particular, because it depends primarily on repeated computational procedures, or mappings, between finite sets of features (Adams, 1994; LaBerge and Samuels, 1974; Perfetti and Lesgold, 1977, 1979). In an attempt to explore the roles of phonology in comprehension, the sections that follow describe the precise ways in which sentence-level and discourse-level comprehension relies upon working memory.

sentence comprehension

Sentence comprehension necessitates incremental integration of lexical information in such a way that the integrated sequence, or "chunk," of language reflects not only the meaning of the individual words but the correct meaning of the whole sentence. The integration process, often referred to as "syntactic parsing," involves two major operations: (i) creating phrases through integration of lexical information and (ii) assigning functions, or "case-roles," to the created phrases. Parsing simple, canonical, sentences – wherein all sentential elements appear in expected positions – occurs rapidly and at no cost to working memory (Mitchell, 1994). However, sentences vary in their structural complexity and ambiguity. Parsing structurally complex, or ambiguous, sentences is considerably more resource demanding, and thus known to strain working-memory capacity. Presumably, then, efficiency in phonological decoding should be a strong predictor of complex sentence processing.

Sentences containing center-embedded relative clauses, such as *The student whom the teacher praised received a perfect score on the math test*, serve as an example. Inasmuch as the embedded clause, *whom the teacher praised*, interrupts syntactic parsing of the main clause, the initial noun phrase, *the student*, must be retained in working memory until the embedded clause has been processed. Working-memory capacity therefore determines, at least in part, how well structurally complex sentences are understood. King and Just (1991) demonstrated that the sentence comprehension of readers with low working-memory capacity is far more severely impaired by structural complexity than that of high-capacity readers. A subsequent analysis of word-by-word reading times further revealed that low-capacity readers slowed down considerably when they encountered critical syntactic information (i.e., the verb of the main clause, *received*, in the example sentence above). This finding was interpreted as suggesting that the initial noun phrase, *the student*, was not retained in the working memory of low-capacity readers, seriously disrupting their syntactic parsing. The researchers concluded that working-memory constraints become more evident when resources are depleted by increased processing demands, particularly in low-capacity readers.

Another structural factor, ambiguity, is vulnerable to working-memory limitations, because it lends itself to multiple interpretations. Low-capacity readers are therefore likely to have greater difficulty coping with the demands of retaining multiple interpretations in mind when processing structurally ambiguous sentences. As an illustration, the sentence, *The cautious shopper warned about the coming supply shortage rushed to the store*, is (disregarding the last five words) structurally ambiguous, allowing two interpretations: one taking the initial noun phrase, *the cautious shopper*, as the agent/subject of the verb, *warned*; and the other interpreting the same phrase as the patient or object of *warned* in a reduced relative clause construction, *(who had been) warned*. In parsing this sentence, therefore, both interpretations must be retained in working memory until the disambiguating word *rushed* is encountered. Studies demonstrate that low-capacity readers are indeed handicapped to a far greater extent than their high-capacity counterparts in resolving ambiguity during sentence comprehension (MacDonald, Just, and Carpenter, 1992; Pearlmutter and MacDonald, 1995).

Although it is widely acknowledged that phonology is essential for integrating information in working memory, the causal linkage between decoding competence and syntactic parsing remains largely untested. Empirical explorations of this significant, but unsubstantiated, connection would be highly desirable.

discourse comprehension

Text is not a collection of randomly ordered sentences. It is organized in ways that facilitate message transmission. To form coherent textual representations in mind, therefore, the reader must understand the specific ways in which logical relationships among textual elements are signaled both explicitly and implicitly. Inasmuch as textual coherence and interpretation are achieved through connecting local information, it is reasonable to assume that the underlying operations of comprehending texts rely heavily upon working memory. Considering the trade-off between the memory's dual functions – storage and computation – everything affecting extraction of information from print (e.g., orthographic processing, meaning access, vocabulary and syntactic knowledge) contributes to determining how much capacity is left available for storage. Further, given that phonological encoding is necessary in producing durable memory traces for integration of information across sentences, decoding efficiency should also be essential for successful coherence-building in progressively comprehending a text.

A number of studies with both adults and children have investigated individual differences in coherence-building and its relation to discourse comprehension. The outcomes suggest that individual differences exist in knowledge of linguistic and discourse devices signaling textual coherence (Danner, 1976; Garner, Alexander, Slater, Hare, Smith, and Reis, 1986); efforts to increase the structural salience of a text generally facilitate comprehension (Anderson and Davison, 1988; Beck and Dole, 1992); and explicit training on signals of textual coherence frequently improves text comprehension and memory (Pearson and Fielding, 1991). It is important to note, however, that an understanding of how textual coherence is conveyed is a necessary, but not a sufficient, requisite for successful comprehension. To connect text elements beyond sentence boundaries, the information to be linked must be kept active in working memory. Therefore, the ability to manipulate phonological information should play a critical role in building textual coherence. However, a dearth of empirical data disallows further speculations regarding the connections among phonological processing, working memory, and the integration of information across individual sentences during reading comprehension.

Inference is another method of connecting textual elements. Because texts usually do not provide the necessary relational information for the required linking operations, prior knowledge can be activated and used to link text information where relational gaps occur. The information to be connected must be stored in working memory as inferences are made and until logical connections are clarified. Empirical evidence suggests that working memory capacity is directly associated with the ability to generate inferences about meaning and possible interpretation – particularly when the information that needs to be linked appears in non-adjacent sentences (Daneman and Carpenter, 1980; Ehrlich and Johnson-Laird, 1982; Hayth-Roth and Thorndyke, 1979; Singer, Halldorson, Lear, and Andrusiak, 1992).

In sum, the available text comprehension studies focus on the relationship between working-memory capacity and the building of textual coherence. Their implicit underlying assumption is that any variance in decoding efficiency becomes largely inconsequential after the initial learning-to-read stages. However, decoding studies among adult native speakers verify significant individual differences – in both speed and accuracy – in extracting phonological information during word recognition (Jackson and McClelland, 1979; Perfetti, 1985). Consequently, systematic investigations to determine the extent and ways in which decoding ability is associated with text comprehension are warranted.

cross-linguistic variation in phonological decoding

the universal importance of phonology in reading

Certain aspects of reading do not vary from language to language. According to Perfetti (2003), reading is grounded in two interrelated systems: a language and a writing system. Learning to read can be characterized as learning to map between the language (phonemes and morphemes) and the writing system. In this regard, metalinguistic understanding of how sound units correspond to graphic symbols should be critical for reading acquisition in alphabetic and non-alphabetic languages alike, and the significance of phonology is viewed as universal in literacy learning and processing. Moreover, the ultimate goal of reading – which is construction of meaning through uncovering the author's intended message – is also invariant, unaffected by properties of either the language or the writing system. Accordingly, the major operations of reading, determined by what is to be accomplished, are unlikely to vary across languages. Logically, then, the heavy reliance on working memory as the reader attempts to integrate information from a variety of sources, as well as the durability of phonologically encoded information in working memory, should both remain constant irrespective of the language or the writing system of material that is being read.

   Cross-linguistic studies repeatedly suggest that phonological skill deficits are a common attribute of weak readers in typologically diverse languages such as Arabic (Abu Rabia, 1995), Portuguese (Da Fontoura and Siegel, 1995), Chinese (Ho and Bryant, 1999; Li, Anderson, Nagy, and Zhang, 2002; So and Siegel, 1997; Zhang and Perfetti, 1993), and Japanese (Kuhara-Kojima, Hatano, Saito, and Haebara, 1996). Decoding experiments repeatedly demonstrate that phonological decoding in non-alphabetic languages, such as Japanese and Chinese, is as important in processing print information as it is in alphabetic languages (Perfetti and Zhang, 1995; Sasanuma, 1984; Tzeng and Wang, 1983). Working memory research confirms that for native Chinese readers, phonological transformation and encoding is more efficacious than visual encoding in retaining visually presented (printed text) information in working memory (Mou and Anderson, 1981; Yik, 1978; Zhang and Simon, 1985). All in all, it seems reasonable to conclude that in all languages, phonological decoding is an indispensable competence for reading acquisition and comprehension.

orthography-specific demands

Inasmuch as no language has perfect one-to-one symbol-to-sound correspondences, we can logically assume that multiple methods are employed in decoding words in all languages. Although the range of the methods employed by readers is unlikely to vary widely across languages, readers tend to form different preferences for particular methods in accordance with the way phonology relates to the grapheme.

   Writing systems vary on two dimensions: orthographic representation and orthographic depth. *Orthographic representation* refers to the linguistic unit each graphic symbol denotes. For example, in alphabetic systems such as English and Spanish, each letter represents a phoneme – either a single consonant or a single vowel. A string of letters, each carrying a segmental sound, constitutes a word. Although the Korean *Hangul* system is also alphabetic, its representational property is unique in that individual symbols must be packaged into syllable blocks, which serve as the basic graphic unit used to form words (Taylor and Taylor,

1995). In Arabic and Hebrew, vowels are represented within consonantal graphemes by diacritic marks. Since these marks rarely appear in adult texts, children must learn to supply missing vowels to identify what word a string of consonants represents based on contextual and other available information. Finally, in non-alphabetic systems, such as Chinese characters and Japanese *kanji*, each symbol corresponds with a morpheme. For example, the character 空 represents one whole morpheme, 'sky,' embodying its meaning and pronunciation. Since individual morphemes often constitute a single word, lexical information – both sound and meaning – is assigned holistically to a single graphic symbol.

The second dimension, *orthographic depth*, refers to the degree of regularity in symbol–sound correspondences. In "shallow" orthographies, the symbol–sound relationships are regular, and thus transparent. Spanish and Serbo-Croatian, for example, have a highly consistent and reliable set of grapheme-to-phoneme correspondences, in which each letter generally corresponds to only one phoneme. English orthography, in contrast, is a phonologically "deep" system – that is, while governed by phonemic constraints, it tends to preserve morphological information at the expense of phonological transparency. Reflecting this tendency, many spelling irregularities in English are more readily explained by morphological, rather than phonological, regularities. To illustrate, the past tense morpheme -*ed* is pronounced in three different ways, as in *talked* ([t]), *visited* ([ɪd]), and *called* ([d]). Preserving the grapheme -*ed* in one form in order to exhibit its underlying morphological information creates a violation of one-to-one sound–symbol correspondences.

To explain how orthographic depth affects phonological decoding procedures across writing systems, Katz and Frost (1992) proposed the Orthographic Depth Hypothesis (ODH). According to the ODH, in "shallow" (transparent) orthographies, phonological information is assembled in working memory primarily through one-to-one, letter-by-letter decoding and symbol-to-sound translation. Conversely, in "deep" (less transparent) orthographies, phonological information is obtained only after a word has been identified, based on the learner's stored knowledge of the word. The major contention of the ODH is that orthographic depth is directly related to the degree that phonological decoding necessitates lexical information. Transparent sound-symbol relationships in shallow orthographies allow rule-based computational procedures. In such languages, therefore, decoding is not dependent upon particular word information retrieved from lexical memory. In support of this contention, Frost, Katz, and Bentin (1987) successfully demonstrated the differential impacts of word frequency on word naming speed in three writing systems with varying orthographic depths: *unvoweled* (i.e., without diacritic marks representing vowels) Hebrew (deepest), English (deep), and Serbo-Croatian (shallow). Naming is the commonly-used technique to measure decoding efficiency, wherein participants are asked to pronounce visually presented words or nonsense letter strings. Frost et al. reported that Hebrew readers were most affected in their ability to name words and letter strings by word frequency, followed by English and Serbo-Croatian readers. The differential impacts of frequency highlight the varying extent to which readers rely upon lexical information during phonological processing in writing systems of different depths.

Supporting evidence is also available from experimental and clinical studies of Japanese readers. The multiple orthographies of Japanese (logographic *kanji* and syllabic *kana*), for example, make possible comparisons of the processing mechanisms used by people in reading the two scripts. Experimental studies have indicated that interference with phonological processing has differential effects in *kanji* and *kana* processing (Saito, 1981; Saito, Inoue, and Nomura, 1979). Mann (1985) also found that recall of *kanji* words correlated with both linguistic memory (of spoken nonsense words) and non-linguistic memory (of visual "nonsense" designs), while recall of alphabetic (English) and syllabary (*kana*) words related only to linguistic memory. Further, clinical observations revealed that two kinds of Japanese aphasic patients – with either a *kana* or a *kanji* impairment – have lesions in different areas of the brain (Hayashi, Ulatowska, and Sasanuma, 1985; Sasanuma, 1975, 1984). Collectively, these findings provide solid empirical reinforcement for the hypotheses that (i) all reading involves linguistic processing and specifically phonological processing and, more generally, that (ii) reading a particular writing system entails a command of the cognitive mechanisms specifically designed for dealing with its structural and representational properties.

phonology in second-language reading

concerns of second-language reading

L2 reading differs from L1 reading in that it involves two, or more than two, languages. The fundamental questions are to what extent, and in what ways, dual-language involvement alters the progressive course of L2 reading development. As noted above, the roles of phonology in literacy are universally constrained. There is no basis to assume that the utility of phonology differs in L1 and L2 reading. However, considerable variation exists in the way phonology is represented graphically in typologically diverse languages. Since L1 decoding skills transfer to reading in an L2, phonological processing by L2 learners should vary according to their L1 backgrounds. In conceptualizing phonology in L2 reading, it is therefore essential to consider both universal constraints and cross-linguistic variation. In the sections that follow, phonological awareness is reviewed as a universal requisite for learning to read, and then the factors explaining variations in L2 phonological decoding are discussed.

phonological awareness in second-language reading acquisition

Given the irrefutable contribution of phonological awareness to early reading development, the issue in L2 research is how the learning-to-read process of school-aged L2 learners differs from that of their native-speaking counterparts. Presumably, young L2 learners are handicapped within a double bind. First, unlike native-speaking children, they may not have an adequate command of oral language at the time when they begin literacy learning in a second language. Second, unlike adult L2 learners, they do not have well-developed reading skills from prior literacy experience that can be transferred to the task of learning to read in the L2.

How can development of decoding skills be facilitated in these children who are learning to read without a sufficient basis in oral language or literacy-related metalinguistic awareness? The answer may lie in helping them develop phonological awareness. L1 research has demonstrated that phonological awareness is a by-product of a child's growing understanding of the structure of spoken sounds and that this awareness precedes and supports the task of linking speech and graphic elements in the initial development of literacy. The procedures involved in phonological segmentation, once developed in one language, should facilitate learning to read another language. Research on the development of literacy in two languages (biliteracy) demonstrates that L1 phonological awareness is closely related to L2 decoding ability in English language learners with diverse L1 backgrounds (August, Calderon, and Carlo, 2001; Carlisle and Beeman, 2000; Chiappe, Siegel, and Wade-Woolley, 2002; Durgunoglu, Nagy, and Hancin, 1993; Gottardo, 2002). Similar results have been reported in a study involving Grades 2 and 3 native Mandarin-speaking children learning to read in English as a second language and Chinese as a heritage language (Wang, Perfetti, and Liu, 2005).

Chiappe, Siegel, and Wade-Woolley (2002), as an illustration, compared early reading development of Grade 1 monolingual and bilingual children. The researchers found that phonological skills and word-reading ability were correlated similarly among bilingual and monolingual children, and that letter knowledge and phonological skills both contributed significantly to early reading development. Gottardo (2002) examined the relationships between oral language proficiency and reading skills among Spanish-English bilingual Grade 1 children in their first and second languages. Her data indicated that word-reading ability was closely related to phonological processing skills within and across languages.

In sum, the acquisition of L2 reading relies on underlying competencies similar to those promoting L1 literacy. Hence, the prerequisite competencies enabling the processes of learning to read do not differ substantially in monolingual and bilingual literacy development. It therefore seems reasonable to conclude that phonological awareness, as a major prerequisite to learning to read, once developed in one language offers substantial facilitation in literacy development in another.

factors explaining differences in second language decoding

reading skills transfer

Inasmuch as cross-language transfer occurs in virtually every aspect of L2 learning (Gass and Selinker, 1983; Kellerman and Sharwood Smith, 1986), a logical assumption would be that adult L2 learners who are literate in their native language rely upon their well-developed L1 reading abilities during L2 processing. Logically, decoding is one such component. A group of experimental studies have shown that L2 readers utilize a variety of skills in extracting phonological information from L2 visual (print) input, and the observed variation in strategies used systematically corresponds with differences in L1 orthographic properties (Brown and Haynes, 1985; Gairns, 1992; Koda 1989b, 1990; Koda, Enright, and Park, 2000; Hamada, 2003).

Koda (1990), for example, compared phonological decoding procedures of adult learners of English with alphabetic (Arabic and Spanish) and logographic (Japanese) L1 backgrounds. Participants read two linguistically matched texts – one describing a variety of cocktails and the other depicting different types of fish – in two phonological conditions: accessible versus inaccessible. In the phonologically accessible condition, nonsensical but pronounceable letter-strings (e.g., *mermo*) were used as names for either the cocktails or the fish described. In the phonologically inaccessible condition, Sanskrit symbols were inserted as names of the items depicted. Because the participants did not know how to pronounce these symbols, they served as phonologically inaccessible elements. While the alphabetic readers were seriously impaired by the Sanskrit symbols, they had virtually no effect on the logographic participants' reading performance. The contrast in reading performance indicates that

L2 learners from different L1 backgrounds use qualitatively different procedures for phonological decoding in processing L2 texts.

Analogous results were obtained through a cross-linguistic experiment involving logographic (Chinese) and non-Roman alphabetic (Arabic) learners of English (Gairns, 1992). Under two conditions (orthographic and phonological), lexical decision performance between the two groups was compared. In the orthographic condition, participants were presented with two phonologically identical letter-strings (e.g., *snow*, *snoe*), and asked to determine which of the two was a real English word. In the phonological condition, contrastingly, the task was to choose, which of two orthographically legal letter-strings (e.g., *rane*, *tane*) sounded like a real English word. Gairns found, first, that both groups did better when orthographic, rather than phonological, information was available; and, second, the performance of Chinese participants declined far more sharply than that of Arabic learners when orthographic cues were unavailable. The clear implication is that the extent to which phonological and orthographic cues are used differs among English as a second language (ESL) learners with contrasting L1 backgrounds. The fact that alphabetic readers depend on phonological information to a much greater degree than logographic readers provides still further support for cross-language transfer of decoding skills in L2 reading development.

Approaching L2 reading from another perspective, Brown and Haynes (1985) examined the effects of L1 reading experience on L2 reading development in Arabic, Spanish, and Japanese learners of English. Although the Japanese participants were superior to other groups in visual discrimination, the superiority vanished in decoding which required symbol-to-sound translation, further confirming the significant influence of L1 experience on L2 reading development. Interestingly, they also found that listening and reading comprehension abilities correlated differently in logographic (Japanese) and alphabetic (Arabic and Spanish) groups. While reading and listening skills were closely related for the Arabic and Spanish participants, the correlation was negligible for their Japanese counterparts – suggesting that L1 orthographic experience and its resulting competencies may induce different strategic approaches to various processing tasks imposing different cognitive and linguistic demands.

To summarize, reading transfer studies collectively demonstrate that L1 orthographic experience has clearly detectable and long-lasting impacts on the formation of decoding skills in the L2, and thus constitutes a major source of performance variation in phonological processing among L2 readers.

cross-linguistic interactions

Given that transferred L1 skills are a source of variance in L2 decoding, the next step is to clarify precisely how transferred skills operate in the processing of print information in a second language. The central issues are how, and to what degree, transferred L1 skills interact with visual input in L2 reading. Such cross-linguistic interactions have just begun to command attention. A handful of studies demonstrate the conjoint impacts of prior processing experiences in both first and second languages on the development of L2 decoding skill.

Koda (1998, 1999), for example, compared phonological awareness and orthographic sensitivity among proficiency-matched Korean and Chinese learners of English. Since intra-word segmentation is central to phonological processing in alphabetic systems, but not mandatory in logographic orthographies, it was hypothesized that alphabetic experience among Korean learners would promote their acquisition of competence in analyzing and manipulating segmental phonological information in English. It was further hypothesized that accelerated phonological awareness among Korean learners would enhance their development of decoding skills in the L2. Results yielded a far more complex picture than had been anticipated. Contrary to prediction, the groups differed neither in phonological awareness nor in decoding ability. However, a clear contrast existed in the extent to which phonological awareness and decoding skill were related to reading comprehension. In the Korean group, the two variables were closely related to reading performance, but no such relationships were observed in the Chinese group. The contrast was interpreted as suggesting that graphemic similarity in the two languages seems to induce a strong preference for use of particular processing procedures while reading. However, the study did not confirm the predicted advantage in L2 metalinguistic awareness and the subsequent development of decoding skills for Korean learners. Since Korean employs a typologically similar (alphabetic) yet unrelated (non-Roman) writing system, the similarity in type of writing system does not in and of itself ensure an advantage in the acquisition of L2 decoding skills. Given that the groups were matched for English proficiency, it was speculated that experience of processing print in the target language may have a stronger impact than L1 background, overriding differences associated with prior literacy experiences.

Subsequent studies more directly compared the impacts of L1 and L2 processing experiences, by incorporating efficiency (speed) measures for proficiency-matched Chinese and Korean learners of English (Hamada, 2003; Koda, 1999, 2000; Koda, Takahashi, and Fender, 1998; Wang and Koda, 2005; Wang, Koda, and Perfetti, 2003). These investigations consistently demonstrate that although both groups are equally sensitive to the properties of the target language, Korean learners are significantly faster and more accurate than Chinese in extracting lexical information from English words displayed visually, and the two groups respond differently to phonological and graphic interference when this is introduced into the task.

Hamada (2003) examined the impact of L1 literacy experience on L2 decoding efficiency and the relationship of decoding efficiency to word learning and retention. Participants were presented with nonsense letter strings, and asked to read them aloud. Word reading speed was compared between two proficiency-matched ESL groups (Korean versus Chinese), as well as between two regularity conditions (regularly-spelled versus irregularly-spelled strings) within each language group. A subset of letter strings was then paired with pictures and a series of string-picture pairs was presented one at a time for associative learning. Paired associative learning was then tested through a variety of production and recognition tasks. Hamada's data demonstrated that:

- both ESL groups were significantly faster when pronouncing regular than irregular letter strings;
- the Korean learners were considerably more efficient than the Chinese learners in pronouncing both regular and irregular strings;
- decoding speed was positively correlated with word learning performance; and
- the Korean group outperformed the Chinese on all of the word learning/retention tasks.

Taken together, these findings suggest that L2 decoding efficiency is seriously affected by both the L1 factor of orthographic similarity and the L2 factor of spelling regularity. They further suggest that decoding competence is crucial to efficient word learning by adult L2 learners.

Viewed collectively, these studies seem to indicate that structural insights evolving from L1 and L2 experiences are *both* operative in the development of L2 phonological awareness and decoding competence. All in all, research evidence suggests that L2 input and processing experience seem to have the primary impact on learners' developing phonological awareness and decoding competence, but L1 influence has continuing importance as well. Hence, both L1 background and L2 proficiency jointly explain individual differences in the development of L2 decoding skills

– both qualitative (procedural or process differences) and quantitative (differences in efficiency).

orthographic similarity

Orthographic similarity or dissimilarity between the languages involved is another possible factor explaining variation in L2 decoding efficiency. In learning to read in a second language, skills transferred from L1 reading continue to develop through cumulative experience with visual input from the written form of the target language. The degree of similarity between L1 and L2 visual (i.e., orthographic) properties may dictate the degree of accommodation necessary for transferred skills to become functional in the L2. If so, when the two writing systems are unrelated, skills used for processing printed words in the L1 will not be efficient for decoding in the L2 but will require substantial modification to be functional. Conversely, when the first and second languages share orthographic similarities (e.g., both use largely the same method of representing sounds with their graphic symbols), L1 skills can be utilized in L2 processing with minimum adjustment. By logical extension, we can postulate that the degree of orthographic similarity can predict the extent to which L1 transfer will facilitate phonological processing in an L2 .

As a case in point, using a homophone detection task, Koda and Park (2002) compared decoding efficiency and its relation to reading comprehension among proficiency-matched ESL learners with orthographically unrelated (Chinese) and orthographically related (Spanish) L1 backgrounds. Despite the two groups' similarity in English language learning experience and proficiency, the Spanish learners were significantly more efficient in detecting letter strings whose pronunciation could be identical to real English words (e.g., *snoe* for *snow*). Moreover, decoding efficiency was differentially correlated with comprehension performance in the groups. While decoding and comprehension scores were closely related in the Spanish group, the two abilities formed no systematic relationship in the Chinese group. Given that the groups did not differ in measured reading comprehension, the findings would seem to indicate that orthographic similarity significantly enhances L2 decoding. However, the restricted efficiency in L2 decoding that is experienced by those familiar with an unrelated orthographic system from their L1 does not appear to impede their ability ultimately to comprehend textual material in the L2.

The critical questions as to what extent, and how, L1 and L2 orthographic similarity facilitates decoding and overall processing in L2 reading remain to be definitively answered. Muljani, Koda, and Moates (1998) have shed significant light on the issue in a study comparing lexical-decision performance by ESL learners with either a similar, i.e., Roman-alphabetic, orthographic background (Indonesian) or a dissimilar one (Chinese). The researchers manipulated two word-related variables: word frequency and syllable structure consistency. Syllable structure consistency has to do with whether the syllable structure of the test words were permissible in both English and Indonesian (consistent), or in English but not in Indonesian (inconsistent). Since Chinese characters primarily represent morphemes, each of which, in turn, corresponds with a single syllable holistically, syllable structure consistency was predicted to have no impact on the performance of the Chinese learners. Although the Indonesian participants outperformed the Chinese in all conditions, syllable structure consistency differentially affected the two groups. As expected, structural consistency benefited the Indonesian participants, who performed better on the structurally consistent items, but not the Chinese, who had no advantage for these items. However, the performance difference between the two groups was far less pronounced on items whose syllable structures were not shared with Indonesian. The researchers surmised that the performance superiority was attributable to the accelerated efficiency stemming from the common processing requirements shared by the two alphabetic languages. In sum, orthographic similarity not only explains overall performance differences among L2 learners with orthographically related and unrelated L1 backgrounds, but also underscores the ways in which L1 experience facilitates decoding and the processing of print information in an L2 more generally.

research horizons

These findings regarding the role of phonology in L2 reading have raised a number of interesting questions to be addressed in future research. Given the universal constraints on the functions of phonology and cross-linguistic variation in the extraction of phonological information from printed words, two issues seem particularly significant. First, a causal linkage between decoding efficiency and higher-order operations during comprehension is highly plausible because of their reliance on working memory and the central role of phonology in working memory. Despite its plausibility, the connection has yet to be tested empirically. Over the past decade, a variety of approaches to instructing reading comprehension have been proposed and implemented, but their effectiveness has not been consistent across readers, nor across different contexts (National Reading Panel, 2000). If, indeed, decoding efficiency is a prerequisite to effective comprehension, providing training in decoding skills may help to assure desired outcomes. Empirical investigation of techniques for training decoding skills and of the causal connection between decoding and comprehension will be critical in ensuring students' readiness for benefiting from comprehension training.

Second, cross-language decoding skills transfer has been well-established in second-language research. However, we know little about how transferred skills affect L2 reading development. Studies generally indicate that transferred decoding skills substantially facilitate phonological processing when the two languages involved are closely related. The findings also attest to the differential relationship between decoding and comprehension among learners with unrelated first-language backgrounds. It is well within the realm of plausibility that contrasting degrees of facilitation of L2 phonological decoding brought about by transferred L1 skills explains both varying rates of development of decoding skill and varying degrees of decoding utility in comprehension. The longitudinal tracking of the development of L2 decoding skill will elucidate the specific ways in which learners who have limited linguistic proficiency cope with the universal requirements of phonological processing.

conclusion

At base, learning to read is essentially a matter of mapping spoken language elements onto graphic symbols. As a major spoken language component, phonology plays a central role in the acquisition of reading skills. In particular, phonological awareness – the abilities to analyze and manipulate the phonological structure of spoken words – is a strong predictor of the successful acquisition of such mappings. Beyond initial learning, moreover, phonology is particularly significant because it establishes a durable representation in working memory, where segmental information extracted from printed text is integrated. Thus, skills for extraction of phonological information are critical in both reading acquisition and comprehension. Since the roles of phonology in reading are dictated by universal constraints on literacy learning and processing – and are not specific to any particular language – the significance of phonology for literacy remains constant across languages.

Languages vary, however, in their ways of representing phonology in their writing systems. Inasmuch as decoding competence evolves through experience with symbol-to-sound mappings, the optimal procedure in any particular language reflects the peculiarities of its writing system, and thus varies systematically across languages. These cross-linguistic variations also have significant implications for the development of L2 decoding. First, since L1 decoding skills transfer to L2 reading, they serve as a major source of procedural variations in phonological processing among learners with diverse L1 orthographic backgrounds. Second, once transferred, L1 skills continue to mature through cumulative experience with processing print in the L2. Consequently, the resultant competence is an amalgamation of cross-linguistic interactions between transferred L1 skills and L2 visual input. Finally, not all L2 learners benefit from transferred skills to the same extent nor in the same manner, simply because the extent of L1-induced facilitation may vary according to the extent to which the two writing systems share similar properties. When the two systems are closely related, they have similar processing requirements for extracting phonological information. In such cases, transferred skills are functional without substantial modification. On the other hand, when the two systems share little in common, transferred skills are likely to be somewhat inefficient until sufficient modifications of processing strategies evolve through cumulative experience processing print in the target language. In short, L2 decoding skills are jointly shaped through L1 and L2 print processing experiences.

references

Abu Rabia, S. (1995). Learning to read in Arabic: Reading, syntactic, orthographic and working memory skills in normally achieving and poor Arabic readers. *Reading Psychology*, 16, 351–94.

Adams, M. J. (1990). *Beginning to read*. Cambridge: MIT Press.

Adams, M. J. (1994). Modeling the connections between word recognition and reading. In R. B. Ruddell, M. R. Ruddell, H. Singer (Eds.), *Theoretical models and processes of reading* (pp. 830–63). Fourth edition. Newark, DE: International Reading Association.

Anderson, R. C., & Davison, A. (1988). Conceptual and empirical bases of readability formulas. In A. Davison & G. M. Green (Eds.), *Linguistic complexity and text comprehension* (pp. 23–54). Hillsdale, NJ: Erlbaum.

August, D., Calderon, M., & Carlo, M. (2001). *Transfer of skills from Spanish to English: A study of young learners*. NABE News, March/April 2001. Retrieved January 16, 2006, from <http://www.cal.org/pubs/articles/skillstransfer-nabe.html>.

Beck, I. L., & Dole, J. A. (1992). Reading and thinking with history and science text. In C. Collins & J. M. Mangieri (Eds.), *Teaching thinking: An agenda for the twenty-first century* (pp. 1–22). Hillsdale, NJ: Erlbaum.

Bowers, P., Golden, J., Kennedy, A., & Young, A. (1994). Limits upon orthographic knowledge due to processes indexed by naming speed. In V. W. Berninger (Ed.), *The varieties of orthographic knowledge I: Theoretical and developmental issues* (pp. 173–218). Dordrecht: Kluwer.

Bradley, L., & Bryant, P. (1991). Phonological skills before and after learning to read. In S. A. Brady & D. P. Shankweiler (Eds.), *Phonological processing in literacy* (pp. 37–45). Hillsdale, NJ: Erlbaum.

Brown, T. & Haynes, M. (1985). Literacy background and reading development in a second language. In T. H. Carr (Ed.), *The development of reading skills* (pp. 19–34). San Francisco, CA: Jossey-Bass.

Bryant, P., MacLean, M., & Bradley, L. (1990). Rhyme, language, and children's reading. *Applied Psycholinguistics, 11*, 237–252.

Carlisle, J. F & Beeman, M. M (2000). The effects of language of instruction on the reading and writing achievement of first-grade Hispanic children. *Scientific Studies of Reading, 4*, 331–53.

Chiappe, P., Siegel, L. S., & Wade-Woolley, L. (2002). Linguistic diversity and the development of reading skills: A longitudinal study. *Scientific Studies of Reading, 6*, 369–400.

Da Fontoura, H. A., & Siegel, L. S. (1995). Reading, syntactic, and working memory skills of bilingual Portuguese-English Canadian children. *Reading and Writing, 7*(1), 139–53.

Daneman, M. (1991). Individual differences in reading skills. In R. Barr, M. L. Kamil, P. Mosenthal, & P. D. Pearson (Eds.), *Handbook of reading research*, Volume II (pp. 512–38). New York: Longman.

Daneman, M., & Carpenter, P. A. (1980). Individual differences in working memory and reading. *Journal of Verbal Learning and Verbal Behavior, 19*, 450–66.

Daneman, M., & Carpenter, P. A. (1983). Individual differences in integrating information between and within sentences. *Journal of Experimental Psychology: Learning, Memory, and Cognition, 9*, 561–83.

Danner, F. W. (1976). Children's understanding of intersentence organization in the recall of short descriptive passages. *Journal of Educational Psychology, 68*, 174–83.

Durgunoglu, A. Y., Nagy, W. E., & Hancin, B. J. (1993). Cross-language transfer of phonemic awareness. *Journal of Educational Psychology, 85*, 453–65.

Ehri, L. C. (1994). Development of the ability to read words: Update. In R. Ruddell, M. Ruddell, & H. Singer (Eds.), *Theoretical models and processes of reading* (pp. 323–58). Fourth edition. Hillsdale, NJ: Erlbaum.

Ehri, L. C. (1998). Grapheme-phoneme knowledge is essential to learning to read words in English. In J. L. Metsala & L. C. Ehri (Eds.), *Word recognition in beginning literacy* (pp. 3–40). Mahwah, NJ: Erlbaum.

Ehrlich, K., & Johnson-Laird, P. N. (1982). Spatial descriptions and referential continuity. *Journal of Verbal Leaning and Verbal Behavior, 22*, 75–87.

Fowler, A. E., & Liberman, I. Y. (1995). The role of phonology and orthography in morphological awareness. In L. B. Feldman (Ed.), *Morphological aspects of language processing* (pp. 157–88). Hillsdale, NJ: Erlbaum.

Frost, R., Katz, L., & Bentin, S. (1987). Strategies for visual word recognition and orthographic depth: A multilingual comparison. *Journal of Experimental Psychology: Human Perception and Performance, 13*, 104–15.

Gairns, B. (1992). Cognitive processing in ESL reading. Master's thesis, Ohio University.

Garner, R., Alexander, P., Slater, W., Hare, V. C., Smith, T., & Reis, R. (1986). Children's knowledge of structural properties of expository text. *Journal of Educational Psychology, 78*, 411–16.

Gass, S., & Selinker, L. (1983). Introduction. S. Gass & L. Selinker (Eds.), *Language transfer in language learning* (pp. 1–20). Rowley, MA: Newbury House.

Gathercole, S., & Baddeley, D. (1993). *Working memory and language.* Hove, U.K.: Erlbaum.

Goswami, U., & Bryant, P. (1992). Rhyme, analogy, and children's reading. In P. B. Gough, L. C. Ehri, & R. Treiman (Eds.), *Reading acquisition* (pp. 49–64). Hillsdale, NJ: Erlbaum.

Gottardo, A. (2002). The relationship between language and reading skills in bilingual Spanish-English speakers. *Topics in Language Disorders, 22,* 46–90.

Gough, P., & Tunmer, W. (1986). Decoding, reading, and reading disability. *RASE: Remedial & Special Education, 7,* 6–10.

Hamada, M. (2003). Second language printed vocabulary acquisition: Influence of first language orthographic experience on decoding and lexical memory. Master's thesis, Carnegie Mellon University.

Hayashi, M., Ulatowska, H. K., Sasanuma, S. (1985). Subcortical aphasia with deep dyslexia: A case study of a Japanese patient. *Brain & Language, 25,* 293–313.

Hayth-Roth, B., & Thorndyke, P. W. (1979). Integration of knowledge from text. *Journal of Verbal Learning and Verbal Behavior, 18,* 91–108.

Ho, C. S.-H. & Bryant, P. (1999). Different visual skills are important in learning to read English and Chinese. *Educational and Child Psychology, 16,* 4–14.

Hogaboam, T. W., & Perfetti, C. A. (1978). Reading skill and the role of verbal experience in decoding. *Journal of Educational Psychology, 70,* 717–29.

Hoover, W. A., & Gough, P. B. (1990). The simple view of reading. *Reading and Writing: An Interdisciplinary Journal, 2,* 127–60.

Jackson, M. D., & McClelland, J. L. (1979). Processing determinants of reading speed. *Journal of Experimental Psychology: General, 108,* 151–81.

Juel, C., Griffith, P. L., & Gough, P. B. (1986). Acquisition of literacy: A longitudinal study of children in first and second grade. *Journal of Educational Psychology, 78,* 243–55.

Katz, L., & Frost, R. (1992). Reading in different orthographies: The orthographic depth hypothesis. In R. Frost & L. Katz (Eds.), *Orthography, phonology, morphology, and meaning* (pp. 67–84). Amsterdam: Elsevier.

Kellerman, E. & M. Sharwood Smith (Eds.). (1986). *Crosslinguistic influence in second language acquisition.* Oxford: Pergamon Press.

King. J., & Just, M. A. (1991). Individual differences in syntactic processing: The role of working memory. *Journal of Memory and Language, 30,* 580–602.

Kleiman, G. M. (1975). Speech recording in reading. *Journal of Verbal Learning and Verbal Behavior, 14,* 323–39.

Koda, K. (1989). The effects of transferred vocabulary knowledge on the development of L2 reading proficiency. *Foreign Language Annals, 22,* 529–42.

Koda, K. (1990). The use of L1 reading strategies in L2 reading. *Studies in Second Language Acquisition, 12,* 393–410.

Koda, K. (1998). The role of phonemic awareness in L2 reading. *Second Language Research, 14,* 194–215.

Koda, K. (1999). Development of L2 intraword structural sensitivity and decoding skills. *Modern Language Journal, 83,* 51–64.

Koda, K. (2000). Cross-linguistic variations in L2 morphological awareness. *Applied Psycholinguistics, 21,* 297–320.

Koda, K., Enright, M., Park, E. (2000). *The relationship between verbal processing and reading comprehension.* Internal Report. Princeton, NJ: ETS Research Board.

Koda, K., & Park, E. C. (2002). Development of L2 morphological awareness. Paper presented at the 13th World Congress of Applied Linguistics, Singapore, December.

Koda, K., Takahashi, E., & Fender, M. (1998). Effects of L1 processing experience on L2 morphological awareness. *Ilha do Desterro*, 35, 59–87.

Kuhara-Kojima, K., Hatano, G., Saito, H., & Haebara, T. (1996). Vocalization latencies of skilled and less skilled comprehenders for words written in hiragana and kanji. *Reading Research Quarterly*, *31*, 158–71.

LaBerge, P., & Samuels, S. J. (1974). Toward a theory of automatic information processing in reading. *Cognitive Psychology*, *6*, 293–323.

Levy, B. A. (1975). Vocalization and suppression effects in sentence memory. *Journal of Verbal Learning and Verbal Behavior*, *14*, 304–16.

Li, W., Anderson, R. C., Nagy, W., & Zhang, H. (2002). Facets of metalinguistic awareness that contribute to Chinese literacy. In W. Li, J. S. Gaffiney, & J. L. Packard (Eds.), *Chinese children's reading acquisition: Theoretical and pedagogical issues* (pp. 87–106). Boston: Kluwer Academic.

MacDonald, M. C., Just, M. A., & Carpenter, P. A. (1992). Working memory constraints on the processing of syntactic ambiguity. *Cognitive Psychology*, *24*, 56–98.

Mann, V. A. (1985). A cross-linguistic perspective on the relation between temporary memory skills and early reading ability. *Remedial and Special Education*, *6*, 37–42.

Mitchell, D. C. (1994). Sentence parsing. In M. A. Gernsbacher (Ed.), *Handbook of psycholinguistics* (pp. 375–410). New York: Academic Press.

Mou, L. C., & Anderson, N. S. (1981). Graphemic and phonemic codings of Chinese characters in short-term retention. *Bulletin of the Psychonomic Society*, *17*, 255–8.

Muljani, M., Koda, K., & Moates, D. (1998). Development of L2 word recognition: A Connectionist approach. *Applied Psycholinguistics*, *19*, 99–114.

Nagy, W. E., & Anderson, R. C. (1999). Metalinguistic awareness and literacy acquisition in different languages. In D. Wagner, R. Venezky, & B. Street (Eds.), *Literacy: An international handbook* (pp. 155–60). Boulder, CO: Westview Press.

National Reading Panel (2000). *Teaching children to read: An evidence-based assessment of the scientific research on reading and its development for reading instruction.* Washington, DC: National Institute of Child Health and Human Development.

Pearlmutter, N. J., & MacDonald, M. C. (1995). Individual differences and probabilistic constraints in syntactic ambiguity resolution. *Journal of Memory and Language*, *34*, 521–42.

Pearson, P. D., & Fielding, L. (1991). Comprehension instruction. In R. Barr, M. L. Kamil, P. Mosenthal, & P. D. Pearson (Eds.), *Handbook of reading research*, Volume II (pp. 815–60). New York: Longman.

Perfetti, C. A. (1985). *Reading ability.* New York: Oxford University Press.

Perfetti, C. A. (2003). The universal grammar of reading. *Scientific Studies of Reading*, *7*, 3–24.

Perfetti, C. A., & Lesgold, A. M. (1977). Discourse comprehension and source of individual differences. In M. A. Just & P. A. Carpenter (Eds.), *Cognitive process in comprehension* (pp. 141–84). Hillsdale, NJ: Erlbaum.

Perfetti, C. A., & Lesgold, A. M. (1979). Coding and comprehension in skilled reading and implications for reading instruction. In L. B. Resnick & P. Weaver (Eds.), *Theory and practice of early reading* (pp. 57–84). Hillsdale, NJ: Erlbaum.

Perfetti, C. A., & Zhang, S. (1995). Very early phonological activation in Chinese reading. *Journal of Experimental Psychology: Learning, Memory, and Cognition, 21*, 24–33.

Saito, H. (1981). Use of graphemic and phonemic encoding in reading Kanji and Kana. *Japanese Journal of Psychology, 52*, 266–73.

Saito, H., Inoue, M., & Nomura, Y. (1979). Information processing of Kanji (Chinese characters) and Kana (Japanese characters): The close relationship among graphemic, phonemic, and semantic aspects. *Psychologia, 22*, 195–206.

Sasanuma, S. (1975). Kana and Kanji processing in Japanese aphasics. *Brain and Language, 2*, 369–83.

Sasanuma, S. (1984). Can surface dyslexia occur in Japanese? In Henderson, L. (Ed.), *Orthographies and reading: Perspectives from cognitive psychology, neuropsychology and linguistics* (pp. 43–56). Hillsdale, NJ: Erlbaum.

Schneider W., & Shiffrin, R. M. (1977). Controlled and automatic human information processing: Detection, search, and attention. *Psychological Review, 84*, 1–66.

Seidenberg, M. S., & McClelland, J. L. (1989). A distributed, developmental model of word recognition and naming. *Psychological Review, 96*, 523–68.

Shankweiler, D., & Liberman, I. Y. (1972). Misreading: A search for causes. In J. F. Kavanaugh & I. G. Mattingly (Eds.), *Language by eye and by ear* (pp. 293–317). Cambridge: MIT Press.

Share, D., & Stanovich, K. E. (1995). Cognitive processes in early reading development: Accommodating individual differences into a model of acquisition. In J. S. Carlson (Ed.), *Issues in education: Contributions from psychology* (Vol. 1, pp. 1–57). Greenwich, CT: JAI.

Siegel, L. S., & Ryan, E. B. (1988). Development of grammatical sensitivity, phonological, and short-term memory in normally achieving and learning disabled children. *Developmental Psychology, 24*, 28–37.

Singer, M., Halldorson, M., Lear, J. C., & Andrusiak, P. (1992). Validation of causal bridging inferences in discourse understanding. *Journal of Memory and Language, 31*, 507–24.

So, D., & Siegel, L. S. (1997). Learning to read Chinese: Semantic, syntactic, phonological and short-term memory skills in normally achieving and poor Chinese readers. *Reading and Writing: An International Journal, 9*, 1–21.

Stahl, S. A., & Murray, B. A. (1994). Defining phonological awareness and its relationship to early reading. *Journal of Educational Psychology, 86*, 221–34.

Stanovich, K. E. (2000). Progress in understanding reading: Scientific foundations and new frontiers. New York: Guilford Press.

Stanovich, K. E., Cunningham, A. E., & Cramer, B. B. (1984). Assessing phonological awareness of kindergarten children: Issues of task comparability. *Journal of Experimental Psychology, 38*, 175–90.

Taylor, I., & Taylor, M. M. (1995). *Writing and literacy in Chinese, Korean, and Japanese*. Philadelphia: John Benjamins.

Torgesen, J. K., & Burgess, S. R. (1998). Consistency of reading-related phonological processes throughout early childhood: Evidence from longitudinal-correlational and instructional studies. In J. L. Metsala & L. C. Ehri (Eds.), *Word recognition in beginning literacy* (pp. 161–88). Mahwah, NJ: Erlbaum.

Treiman, R., & Zukowski, A. (1991). Levels of phonological awareness. In S. A. Brady & D. P. Shankweiler (Eds.), *Phonological processes in literacy* (pp. 67–83). Hillsdale, NJ: Erlbaum.

Tzeng, O. J. L., & Wang, W. S.-Y. (1983). The first two R's: The way different languages reduce speech to script affects how visual information is processed in the brain. *American Scientist, 71,* 238–243.

Wagner, R. K., Torgesen, J. K., & Rashotte, C. A. (1994). The development of reading-related phonological processing abilities: New evidence of bi-directional causality from a latent variable longitudinal study. *Developmental Psychology, 30,* 73–87.

Wang, M., & Koda, K. (2005). Commonalities and differences in word identification skills among English second language learners. *Language Learning, 55,* 71–98.

Wang, M., Koda, K., & Perfetti, C. A. (2003). Alphabetic and non-alphabetic L1 effects in English semantic processing: A comparison of Korean and Chinese English L2 learners. *Cognition, 87,* 129–49.

Wang, M., Perfetti, C. A., & Liu, Y. (2005). Chinese-English biliteracy acquisition: Cross-language and writing system transfer. *Cognition, 97,* 67–88.

Yik, W. F. (1978). The effect of visual and acoustic similarity on short-term memory for Chinese words. *Quarterly Journal of Experimental Psychology, 30,* 386–494.

Yopp, H. K. (1988). The validity and reliability of phonemic awareness tests. *Reading Research Quarterly, 23,* 159–77.

Zhang, G., & Simon, H. A. (1985). STM capacity for Chinese words and idioms: Chunking and acoustical loop hypothesis. *Memory and Cognition, 13,* 193–201.

Zhang, S., & Perfetti, C. A. (1993). The tongue-twister effect in reading Chinese. *Journal of Experimental Psychology: Learning, Memory and Cognition, 19,* 1–12.

10

research and practice in developmental phonological disorders

fiona e. gibbon

introduction

Children with developmental speech disorders form a large, heterogeneous group. Various conditions, both biological and environmental, place children at risk for speech disorders. These conditions include: sensory deficits (e.g., hearing impairment); cognitive deficits (e.g., learning disabilities, mental retardation); psychiatric and emotional disorders (e.g., autism); neuromotor disorders (e.g., cerebral palsy, Worster-Drought syndrome); and structural abnormalities of the vocal tract (e.g., cleft palate, malocclusion). Developmental phonological disorders – the focus of this chapter – are unlike the disorders listed above because their presence cannot be attributed to any known or detectable condition or cause.

Under normal circumstances, adults can understand most of the speech produced by typically developing 3-year-old children. It has been estimated that 80% of speech in children of this age is intelligible and by the time they are 4 years old, children are highly intelligible even in connected speech (Gard, Gilman, and Gorman, 1993). Children with phonological disorders, in contrast, have major difficulties acquiring clear, intelligible speech and this problem becomes increasingly apparent during the preschool years. Most children's phonological difficulties will resolve before they are 5–6 years old, particularly if there are no associated language or cognitive difficulties (Bishop and Edmundson, 1987) and they receive appropriate and timely speech therapy. A minority have disorders that persist into the primary school years, however, and these children not only have serious communication difficulties, they also often have problems with socializing behavior and self-esteem. They are additionally at risk for problems learning to read and spell, and for overall low school attainment (Felsenfeld, Broen, and McGue, 1992).

Phonological disorders are one of the most frequently encountered communication disorders affecting children, and for parents, speech and language difficulties are the most common single cause of concern about child development. Estimates show that 6–10% of pre-school and school-age children fail to develop intelligible speech in the absence of any identifiable underlying condition, and 80% of this group requires the services of a speech and language therapist (Broomfield and Dodd, 2004; Weiss, Gordon, and Lillywhite, 1987). There is some demographic variation, however, with inner cities having a higher prevalence of children with speech and language disorders than other locations (Law, 1992). Fortunately, phonological disorders are also one of the most responsive to speech therapy. A consistent and robust finding from the extensive research literature is that preschool and school age children benefit from speech therapy, and make greater gains in phonology than those who receive no intervention (Almost and Rosenbaum, 1998; Gierut, 1998).

In a pioneering book published nearly fifty years ago entitled *The Development and Disorders of Speech in Childhood*, Morley (1957) presented a classification of developmental speech disorders, along with brief perceptual descriptions of the speech characteristics found in the different groups. Speech sound errors produced by children were identified and remediated as though they were separate, unrelated phenomena. Attempts to pinpoint the underlying nature of these speech disorders in children produced divergent accounts. Morley's view was that they were phonetic in nature, due specifically to faulty motor learning of articulatory gestures that at a later stage became habitual.

This view persisted throughout the 1960s and 1970s (see McReynolds, 1988, for a summary). At this time, the term *functional articulation disorder* replaced Morley's (1957) original term *dyslalia*, with *functional* indicating that the disorder was not associated with organic pathology, and *articulation* indicating the assumed motoric origin of the speech difficulty.

Since the publication of Morley's work, the most significant single influence on the field of developmental speech disorders has been the application of linguistic frameworks to describe and present clinical speech data. The linguistic influence has had a major impact on views about the fundamental nature and the treatment of speech disorders in children. One effect has been that the speech disorder previously known as dyslalia was renamed *phonological disorder* and another has been that instead of a strictly phonetic disorder, the origin of children's speech difficulties is seen as arising from breakdowns at the cognitive level of linguistic knowledge and phonological organization, and not primarily due to an articulatory or motor difficulty.

The phonological view of children's speech disorders shows the influence of early work by a number of linguists (most notably Jakobson, 1968; Smith, 1973; Stampe, 1969) who introduced linguistic descriptions of child speech patterns. Phonological analyses were later used to characterize clinical speech data (e.g., Compton, 1970; Grunwell, 1981; Ingram, 1976; and see Leonard, 1995, for a review). Phonological analyses of speech data showed that speech errors produced by children were not separate, unrelated phenomena, but systematic and rule-governed. Terminology from the field of phonology was subsequently adopted in order to capture these regularities.

Despite advances in linguistic descriptions of children's surface error patterns, the nature and underlying cause or causes of phonological disorders remain elusive and the subject of ongoing controversy. Recent instrumental studies have led researchers to question the reliability of transcription based analyses of phonological disorders and the causal explanations developed on the basis of these. This chapter reviews the nature of phonological disorders and approaches to their remediation, with attention to underlying causes, theoretical claims, and methodological problems and advances.

speech characteristics associated with phonological disorders

Several texts provide comprehensive overviews of the speech characteristics of children with phonological disorders (Grunwell, 1981; Ingram, 1976; Stoel-Gammon and Dunn, 1985). A number of theoretical frameworks have been used to describe children's phonological error patterns, including *distinctive features* (McReynolds and Engmann, 1975), *Generative Phonology* (Compton, 1970), *Natural Phonology* (Stampe, 1969), *Nonlinear Phonology* (Bernhardt and Stoel-Gammon, 1994), *Gestural Phonology* (Kent, 1997) and *Optimality Theory* (Bernhardt and Stemberger, 1998). Although various analytic frameworks are used to describe disordered phonological systems, one framework remains popular for clinical and research purposes. This is a *phonological process analysis*, which is a particularly useful approach because the patterns produced by children with disorders can be compared with those of children who are developing normally. This makes it possible to define processes from a developmental perspective, identify delayed processes, deviant patterns and co-occurrence of delay and deviance. Gibbon and Grunwell (1990) summarize the phonological characteristics derived from the available literature as involving:

- a reduced system of phonological contrasts
- a restricted phonetic inventory and limited word and syllable shapes
- persisting normal processes
- chronological mismatch
- unusual/idiosyncratic processes
- extensive variability.[1]

These characteristics will be illustrated using speech data from young Scottish boy, Callum, who has a phonological disorder. As the case study shows, his speech can be seen to be idiosyncratic but nevertheless rule-based, and his speech error patterns can be described succinctly in terms of phonological processes.

case study of callum

At 4;06 (years; months), Callum's spontaneous speech is often unintelligible although there are no obvious reasons for his difficulty in learning to speak clearly. He has normal hearing, there are no obvious anatomical or physiological abnormalities of the speech production mechanism, and he has at least average cognitive ability. He also has normal psychosocial development and normal understanding of language, and his expressive skills at the levels of discourse, vocabulary, syntax, and morphology are good. The small speech sample below shows transcribed data recorded when Callum was naming pictures.

(1)

1. cage	[kedʒ]	7. frog	[fʊɒd]	13. penguin	['pendʊɪn]
2. cake	[keⁱt]	8. ghost	[gost]	14. pie	[paˈ]
3. chips	[ʔɪps]	9. guinea pig	['gɪnɪ pɪd]	15. scarf	[sgaˈf]
4. Christmas tree	['ʔɪsməs 'ʔiː]	10. jeep	[ʔiːp]	16. tractor	['ʔæʔtɚ]
5. crab	[klæb]	11. jump	[ʔʌmp]	17. teeth	[tiθ]
6. cucumber	['kjuːkʌmbɚ]	12. kangaroo	['kɪndəʊu]	18. triangle	[ʔaˈjændʊ]

The sample illustrates some typical speech characteristics of children with phonological disorders. First, many of his speech errors can be described in terms of phonological processes, some of which are known to occur in children with normal phonological development, but they have remained in Callum's speech after the age at which they should have disappeared. Examples from the sample include *velar fronting*, which is a process whereby all velar consonants are replaced by sounds located at a more anterior location in the vocal tract, in this case alveolars. Interestingly, Callum only gives evidence of this process in some phonetic contexts, namely syllable final position, and he produces velars normally in other contexts such as at the beginning of words. For example:

(2) cake [keⁱt]   guinea pig ['gɪni pɪd]
     crab [klæb]   ghost [gost]

It seems that Callum can physically produce velar sounds but only does so consistently in word-initial position (other than in a cluster with /r/ as in *Christmas*). In other positions, he often produces alveolars (/t, d/) instead. A similar tendency to produce sounds in some contexts but not others is seen for affricates. Unlike velars, Callum produces affricates accurately in word final position, but either deletes them or substitutes a glottal stop in word initial position. For example:

(3) cage [kedʒ]   jump [ʔʌmp]
     chips [ʔɪps]   jeep [ʔip]

He also substitutes a glottal stop for initial /tr/, as in:

(4) tractor ['ʔæʔtɚ]   Christmas tree ['ʔɪsməs 'ʔiː]
     triangle ['ʔa'jændʊ]

One of the effects of phonological processes is that they neutralize phonological contrasts in Callum's speech, with the result that he produces many words identically (also referred to as homophonous forms). For example, Callum produces both *Kate* and *cake* as [keⁱt] and he says [ʔeⁱt] for *Jake, ate, ache* and *drake*.

A second characteristic of phonological disorders that Callum exhibits is unusual or *idiosyncratic processes*. Idiosyncratic phonological processes occur only rarely (or for short periods) in normal child phonology. Callum's idiosyncratic realization of the affricates /tʃ/ and /dʒ/ and the clusters /tr/ and /dr/ as a glottal stop in initial position is one that is not usually found in children with normal phonological development (Dodd, 1995). A third characteristic that Callum shows is *chronological mismatch*. This term refers to processes usually found at an early stage of phonological development co-occurring with those that are more typical of a later stage of development. In Callum's speech, velar fronting errors (characteristic of early development) occur contemporaneously with correct production of affricates, the dental fricatives /θ/ and /ð/, and clusters – all of which are characteristic of later development – in some contexts. For example:

(5) cage [kedʒ]   cake [keⁱt]   cucumber ['kjuːkʌmbɚ]
     ghost [gost]   scarf [sgarf]   teeth [tiθ]

These data illustrate some typical characteristics of the speech of children with phonological disorders. Callum's speech error patterns are regular or rule-governed, making it possible to predict how he will produce words. In addition, the sample shows that it is not easy to explain his speech difficulty in terms of an articulatory or phonetic difficulty alone, as he demonstrates the ability to produce sounds in some contexts but not in others.

vowel errors

Most of the literature on phonological disorders is concerned with describing patterns of errors that affect consonants, as in Callum's case described in the previous section, although children with phonological disorders may experience difficulties with vowels as well. Vowels are not yet well described in the literature, although a recent book focusing on vowel disorders (Ball and Gibbon, 2002) discusses patterning of vowels in children with disorders and intervention for vowel errors. The percentage of children with abnormal vowel systems is not known for certain. Pollock and Berni (2003) measured the percentage of correct vowels in a group of 149 children aged 2–6 years with delayed/disordered phonology and found that those with moderate to severe consonant errors were at greatest risk for concurrent vowel errors. Some studies show that at least some vowel errors may occur in as many as 50% of children with phonological disorders (Eisenson and Ogilivie, 1977; Pollock and Berni, 2003; Stoel-Gammon and Herrington, 1990). This high frequency indicates that all children with phonological disorders should be screened for vowel errors.

Although vowel errors may be relatively common, speech and language therapists often do not detect them in routine examinations of children's speech (Pollock and Keiser, 1990). There are several possible explanations for vowel errors going undetected in clinical assessments. First, many standard speech assessment procedures do not allow for a full range of vowels to be elicited, so vowel errors are not always recorded. Second, clinicians may not be aware of the types of errors that can affect vowels, and as a result fail to identify vowel error patterns. Third, Stoel-Gammon (1990) suggests that listeners find vowels difficult to transcribe reliably, and that normal dialectal differences existing in vowel systems make listeners more tolerant of abnormal variations in vowel productions. A final difficulty is that we still have a rather incomplete understanding of normal patterns of vowel development in typically developing children, and as a result, it is not always possible to know whether vowel errors reflect normal, delayed, or deviant development.

limitations of transcription data

As illustrated in Callum's speech sample, standard auditory-impression-istic transcription is the most frequently used method for recording the speech of normal and disordered child phonology for both research and clinical purposes. Reasons for the popularity of transcription are clear: it records functionally relevant aspects of production; it is an easily accessible dimension of speech; it requires no complex instrumentation; and there is an extensive literature based on this methodology. The symbol selected by the transcriber carries implicit assumptions about whether a child has:

(i)   produced a sound accurately
      (e.g., /k/ in <u>car</u> → [k]);
(ii) produced an error such as a phonological substitution
      (e.g., /k/ in <u>car</u> → [t]);
(iii) omitted a sound (e.g., /k/ in <u>car</u> → ∅); or
(iv) produced a non-English sound, in other words a phonetic distortion
      (e.g., /k/ in <u>car</u> → [χ]).

Although it is a widespread practice, there are well-recognized problems associated with using transcription data alone for investigating disordered speech generally, and in particular for the purpose of measuring speech motor control (Butcher, 1989; Hardcastle, Morgan Barry, and Clark, 1987). One limitation is that the activity of transcription affords at best an indirect representation of the actions of the articulators, with the result that articulatory information must be inferred by the transcriber from an accumulation of complex cues contained in the acoustic signal. It is also known to be unreliable, with listeners often "hearing" segments in the speech signal where there is no evidence of a segment's existence (Oller and Eilers, 1975).

A less recognized source of valuable data in the field of phonological disorders has come from studies originating largely in the 1980s onwards that have used instruments for the analysis of speech data (Weismer, 1984). Instrumental procedures, particularly acoustic analysis and electro-palatography (EPG), are able to measure objectively aspects of articulation and speech motor control. EPG is one of the few instrumental techniques able to record directly the actions of one of the major articulators involved in speech production, namely the tongue. EPG records details of the location and timing of tongue contacts with the hard palate during speech (Hardcastle and Gibbon, 1997; Hardcastle, Gibbon, and Jones, 1991). Tongue-to-palate contact is registered in normal speakers' productions of sounds such as /t/, /d/, /n/, /k/, /g/, /s/, /z/, /l/, /ʃ/, /tʃ/, /dʒ/, /j/, /ŋ/; EPG data from approximately 20 children with phonological disorders have been reported in the literature (see reviews in Dagenais, 1995; Gibbon, 1999).

Two phenomena, covert contrasts and undifferentiated gestures, are described in the following sections. These two phenomena illustrate very well the contribution that instrumental data can make to our understanding of the underlying nature of phonological disorders.

covert contrasts

An interesting and important phenomenon, as well as a potential difficulty for studies using transcription-based analyses, is the existence of covert contrasts in the speech of children with phonological disorders. The term *covert contrast* was coined by Hewlett (1988) to describe instrumentally measurable differences between target phonemes that are neutralized in listeners' perceptions. In other words, it can be demonstrated by careful instrumental analysis that some children who appear even to a trained listener to neutralize contrasts in reality produce consistent articulatory differences between target phonological categories, though these are difficult to detect by the human ear.

The phenomenon of covert contrast was probably first identified in a paper published by Kornfeld in 1971. In this study, Kornfeld reported spectrographic evidence from children with typical speech development. The data showed that children's productions of *grass* and *glass* sounded the same to adult listeners and both targets were transcribed as [gwas]. Although sounding the same, spectrographic analysis of the utterances showed differences in locus of the second formant and duration of the glide segment between the [w] in the target word *grass* compared with the [w] in the target word *glass*. As Kornfeld concluded, "adults do not always perceive distinctions that children make" (ibid., p. 462), as they are biased to hear children's speech in terms of the distinctions present in the target system. In other words, a biased adult may judge as neutralized two acoustically and articulatorily distinct phonological categories produced by a child. Since Kornfeld's study, it has become evident that covert contrasts are common. In a review of the literature, Gibbon (2002) identified over 20 studies that used either acoustic analysis or EPG to detect covert contrast in typically developing and phonologically disordered children.

Although researchers interpret the presence of covert contrasts in different ways, many view their presence as indicating phonetic (articulatory or motor) rather than phonological (categorization) difficulties. Kent's (1997) view is that covert contrast cannot be explained in any way "except by attributing it to faulty phonetic implementation" (p. 265). Gibbon and Scobbie (1997) argued that the presence of covert contrasts reflects "productive phonological knowledge" of the contrast and are likely to be due to phonetic limitations relating to inadequate motor control for adult-like realizations of the relevant phonetic or articulatory categories. In other words, instrumental analyses reveals that some children produce covert contrasts, which suggests a phonetic deficit rather than a difficulty learning the underlying phonological rules of the language.[2]

undifferentiated gestures

Theories of phonetics and phonology have nearly always involved some notion of place of articulation identifying the location within the oral cavity at which major articulatory events occur. Although place of articulation, most frequently identified impressionistically, retains a pre-eminent status in phonological analysis, recent studies using EPG have shown that children with phonological disorders produce articulations that cannot be described accurately using traditional place of articulation labels. Gibbon (1999) describes an abnormal type of articulation termed "undifferentiated gestures," which occur during productions of lingual consonants (those using the tongue) and are characterized by tongue-palate contact that lacks clear differentiation between the tongue tip/blade, the tongue body, and the lateral margins of the tongue. In normal speech, /t/ and /d/ are produced by a combination of lateral bracing and an upward movement of the tongue tip and blade to the alveolar ridge. In contrast, undifferentiated gestures involve placement that is not confined to the anterior region of the palate but instead extends back into the palatal and even velar regions of the palate. Thus, undifferentiated gestures involve simultaneous alveolar, palatal, and velar placement, a phenomenon not captured using standard transcription symbols and also not seen in the articulation of normal children or adults. These undifferentiated patterns occur quite frequently in children with phonological and articulation disorders. The EPG literature reports 17 school-age children with articulation and phonological disorders, of whom 12 (71%) showed evidence of undifferentiated gestures (Gibbon, 1999).

The undifferentiated pattern that Gibbon (1999) described may explain much of the perceptual variability noted by previous investigators (Grunwell, 1981). These gross, whole-tongue gestures are unstable, in that they can have a different place of articulation at the onset and at the release of closure (Gibbon and Wood, 2002). Gibbon and Wood suggested that an abnormal shift in tongue placement during the production of undifferentiated gestures generates conflicting acoustic cues for place of articulation, which listeners find difficult to interpret in a categorical manner. A final point is that standard transcriptions do not reliably detect undifferentiated gestures, which are transcribed in some contexts as speech errors (e.g., as phonological substitutions or phonetic distortions) but as correct productions in other contexts.

a changing perspective

To summarize so far, the shift of emphasis from articulation to phonology over the past 50 years has been reflected in a change in the diagnostic classification used for speech disorders of unknown origin, with *phonological disorder* becoming the preferred term. This term is now commonly used as a diagnostic label when the underlying origin of the disorder is considered to be due to abnormal organization of the child's system of speech sounds. Grunwell (1990) summarizes this position, stating that "phonological disorders...because they occur in the absence of any known physical or physiological deficits, must result from breakdowns at the cognitive level of linguistic knowledge and organization" (p. 5). However, data from instrumental studies revealing phenomena such as covert contrasts and undifferentiated gestures cast some doubt on these conclusions, suggesting that subtle phonetic difficulties could underlie many of the surface patterns that we hear in the speech of children with phonological disorders.

clinical characteristics of children with phonological disorders

The previous sections have been concerned with the way in which children's phonological disorders are described in terms of their surface behaviors, using linguistic frameworks based on phonological theory or instrumental measurements. In the 1980s and 1990s, researchers studied phonological disorders from a psycholinguistic perspective, investigating skills such as phonological working memory and phonological awareness in order to determine what might underlie these children's difficulties in acquiring intelligible speech. Many researchers have also sought to uncover possible medical causes, such as a link between middle ear infections (*otitis media*) and phonological disorders. Some of these explanations and causes are described in the sections that follow.

speech perception

Perception is in almost all cases stronger than production in children with phonological disorders. Nevertheless, children vary in their speech perception skills, and on careful testing many children can be shown to have at least subtle difficulties in this area. Speech perception refers to children's ability to detect and discriminate between the sound contrasts used in the language. The specific nature of perceptual deficits and their precise relationships to production errors remains controversial, however, and children with phonological disorders vary in their ability to discriminate between phonological contrasts that they do not produce in their expressive phonology.

Phonological discrimination is often tested using pictures representing words that are minimal pairs and the child points to the picture that corresponds to the word or phrase that the clinician says, e.g., *show me fan* and *show me van*. For many children with phonological disorders, this type of task presents no difficulties, even when the minimal pair contains a contrast that is neutralized in their own speech. An alternative approach to assessing discrimination proposed by Locke (1980) is for the child to judge whether the clinician has produced the name of a familiar picture correctly. For example, the clinician shows a child a picture of a dog and asks, *Is this a dod?* The advantage of this assessment method is that it is adaptable for individual children and assesses sound contrasts that individual children are unable to produce. Locke (1980) found that when auditory discrimination focused on children's specific production errors, approximately one-third of children with disorders showed that they could not discriminate between their own error productions and the correct realization. Using a similar methodology, Bird and Bishop (1992) studied 14 children with phonological disorders and 14 normally speaking children. Their results showed that, compared to the control group, children with phonological disorders were poor at discriminating between phonemes although the children's performance varied widely. For example, half of the children achieved nearly perfect scores, and all of them showed some ability to discriminate between phonological contrasts that they were unable to produce.

speech motor deficits

Many researchers have investigated whether children with phonological disorders demonstrate subtle speech motor deficits. As mentioned earlier, the overwhelming majority of studies of speech in children with phonological disorders are based on transcribed data, which is not a suitable methodology for measuring speech motor skill. Fletcher (1992) defined speech motor skill as "spatial and temporal proficiency in executing a motor task" (p. 1). Fletcher views speed, spatial (i.e., positional) accuracy, consistency of articulatory movement, and movement efficiency as hallmarks of motor skill development. None of these characteristics of motor skill development can be measured accurately using a linear notation system such as transcription (Oller and Eilers, 1975).

In the 1980s a number of studies made use of advances in instrumental procedures, such as acoustic analysis, to investigate speech motor control abilities directly. These studies focused largely on the precise timing and variability of articulatory gestures and measured aspects of speech such as vowel duration, consonant closure duration, and voice onset time. These timing measures are taken as relatively sensitive indicators of speech motor control, with more mature control characterized by, for example, shorter durations and reduced variability. Catts and Jensen (1983) measured voice onset times of word-initial and word-final stop consonants and found that some phonologically disordered children had less mature speech timing control compared to typically developing children. Other studies have shown that children with phonological disorders have longer segment durations than typically developing children (Catts and Jensen, 1983; Weismer and Elbert, 1982), once again indicating the presence of subtle speech motor control difficulties.

Towne (1994) used a different methodology to investigate speech motor control in children with phonological disorders. This study investigated whether these children could adjust their tongue movements to compensate when their jaws were artificially stabilized with a bite block under experimental conditions. The children's rapid alternating productions of sounds (known as *diadochokinetic rate*) were measured under two conditions: when the jaw was free and when it was experimentally stabilized. In general, although most of the children with phonological disorders could compensate for the presence of the bite block, the study found that a subgroup of children had no capacity for tongue compensation during this task. The results supported the view that delays in motor speech development – specifically, a lack of independent control of the jaw and tongue – may contribute to phonological disorders in some children. Additional support for the notion that children with phonological disorders have delayed control of functionally independent articulators comes from a study by Edwards, Fourakis, Beckman, and Fox (1999). These researchers used acoustic analysis to examine speech motor control in six preschool-age children with phonological disorders. Their results suggested that, compared to those who were developing normally, children with phonological disorders were less able to maneuver the jaw and tongue body separately and used ballistic (i.e., less controlled) gestures when moving from lingual consonants to vowels.

EPG is another valuable technique for measuring aspects of control, such as speed of articulation, spatial (i.e., positional) accuracy of articulation, timing of tongue movements, consistency of articulatory movement, and coarticulation. The undifferentiated gestures that Gibbon (1999) described using EPG are interpreted as a lack of coordinated control between parts of the tongue – the tip/blade, the (main) tongue body, and the lateral margins – which in normal adult speakers function as independent articulators (Hardcastle, 1976; Stone, Epstein, and Iskarous, 2004). Gibbon (1999) interpreted the presence of undifferentiated gestures as reflecting a speech motor constraint involving either delayed or deviant control of functionally independent regions of the tongue. The results of this EPG study and the other instrumental studies described in this section suggest that some children with phonological disorder have difficulties with speech motor control. These motor difficulties can manifest in subtle ways, however, which means that they are not always detected by standard clinical assessment procedures.

structural abnormalities of the vocal tract

One of the defining characteristics of children with phonological disorders is that they do not have major structural abnormalities of the vocal tract, such as cleft palate. Nevertheless, some studies have investigated the relationship between minor structural abnormalities and phonological (or articulation) disorders. Snow (1961) studied the articulation of 438 children, some of whom had missing or abnormal upper incisor teeth. Although significantly more children with abnormal dentition misarticulated the fricatives /f/, /v/, /θ/, /ð/, /s/, and /z/ compared to those with normal dentition, nevertheless, 75% of children with abnormal dentition did not misarticulate these sounds. In other words, most children with abnormal teeth made these sounds correctly, and some children with normal teeth did not make the sounds correctly. This study therefore did

phonology in context

not show a clear relationship between the presence of abnormal teeth and articulation accuracy.

   To take a second example, some studies have examined the effect of "tongue-tie" (otherwise known as *ankyloglossia*) on speech. Tongue-tie is a condition that involves a restricted lingual frenum, which is the thin, vertical fold of tissue under the tongue that attaches to the under-surface of the tongue and to the floor of the mouth. Individuals with tongue-tie often have limited tongue mobility, with the result that they cannot protrude the tongue tip beyond the edges of the lower teeth, or when it is protruded it forms a characteristic *w* shape. Most young children with tongue-tie do not have any associated speech difficulties and compensate adequately for their decreased lingual mobility. Wright (1995) reviewed a number of cases of tongue-tie and concluded that speech difficulties related to tongue-tie were overstated. On the other hand, other studies have shown that tongue-tie can be related to articulation difficulties in older children and adults. Lalakea and Messner (2003) found that half of the adolescents and adults they studied with uncorrected ankyloglossia had persisting articulation errors.

   The two structural abnormalities described here, abnormal dentition and tongue-tie, illustrate the complex relationships that exist between vocal tract structure, phonology, and articulation. It may be that the presence of structural limitations has an effect on some children who are already at risk for phonological or articulation difficulties, yet in other risk-free children they have a negligible impact on development.

family history

Speech and language therapists have frequently observed a tendency for phonological disorders to run in families and most research studies support these observations. Shriberg and Kwiatkowski (1994) studied a group of 62 children with phonological disorders aged 3–6 years old and found that 56% had one or more family members with a similar communication problem. Lewis, Ekelman, and Aram (1989) also found that families of children with speech disorders reported significantly more members with speech disorders than did families of children without disorders. Felsenfeld and Plomin (1997) used a different methodology to study the familial basis of speech disorders. They studied the speech of adopted and non-adopted children at varying risk for speech disorders based upon self-reported parental speech history. Their results showed that 25% of the children with a genetic background of familial speech disorder displayed features of disordered speech at age 7;0 years, in comparison to 9% of the children with no known genetic history of familial speech disorder. Felsenfeld, McGue, and Broen (1995) found that, compared to a control group, the children of adults with a documented history of phonological disorder performed less well on tests of articulation and expressive language functioning and were significantly more likely to have received articulation treatment. These studies show that genetic factors put children at risk for phonological disorders. In addition, Fox, Dodd, and Howard (2002) investigated the relationship between risk factors and speech disorders and found that a positive family history was one of the few factors that distinguished the speech-disordered group from the normally speaking control population.

otitis media

The ability to hear normally is crucial for children to acquire phonology. Although a diagnosis of phonological disorder excludes severe or permanent hearing loss, many children with phonological disorders experience fluctuating periods of reduced hearing or transient hearing loss due to otitis media, or inflammation of the middle ear. Transient hearing loss presents children with an acoustic signal that is reduced, unstable and difficult to process, and this may hamper early phonological acquisition. The relationship between otitis media and phonological disorders has therefore been the subject of many studies, although its exact role as a causative factor remains unknown. A complicating issue is that a high percentage (77%) of children with normal phonological development also experience episodes of otitis media (Teele, Klein, and Rosner, 1984), suggesting that there is not a straightforward link between this medical condition and phonological disorders.

Although a high percentage of children who experience periods of reduced hearing have normal phonological development, it is possible that severe and frequent episodes of otitis media have a detrimental effect on phonological development, particularly when these episodes occur in infants. Petinou, Schwartz, Gravel, and Raphael (2001) conducted a longitudinal study of a large group of young children. They found that children at the age of 2 years who had experienced frequent episodes of otitis media during the first year of life were more likely to have impaired speech than children who had normal hearing. They also found that at 2 years of age, children with an early history of otitis media had greater difficulty producing consonants at the ends of words and syllables. With respect to grammatical development, these children were also less likely to recognize or perceive morphological markers such as *-ed*, *-ing*, *-s*, and unstressed syllables as well as failing to recognize function words such as articles and prepositions and auxiliary verbs. Miccio, Gallagher,

Grossman, Yont, and Vernon-Feagans (2001) examined longitudinally the influence of otitis media on the range and types of consonants produced by six children with phonological disorders. Their results indicated that depressed hearing levels place children at greater risk for delays in early speech and language development.

The effect of otitis media on language development, and phonological acquisition in particular, is complex and may depend on a number of factors such as the severity, age of onset, and frequency of the hearing loss and other factors such as children's environment and the extent to which their other abilities enable them to compensate for a reduction in hearing levels. Even though the effects of otitis media may vary from child to child, it is nevertheless essential to know when children with phonological disorders are affected so that they can be referred for appropriate audiological assessment.

language skills

Many children with phonological disorders show additional difficulties with other aspects of language development and language use.[3] Almost all studies have found that as a group, children with phonological disorders have lower language scores than their typically developing peers (Grunwell, 1981; Winitz, 1969). In a review of the literature on the relationship of phonological to wider language disorders, Tyler and Watterson (1991) suggested that 60–80% of children who have a disorder of one type will also have a disorder of the other type. Paul and Shriberg (1982) studied a group of children with speech delay and found that two-thirds of them also had delayed syntactic development. Although the remaining children did not show any general difficulty with syntax, some had specific problems with phonologically complex grammatical morphemes. In these children, morphological development was affected by a phonological deficit involving, in particular, final consonants or unstressed syllables. Children in this group made numerous errors involving past tense forms, plurals, possessives, and pronouns – deficits that could be directly attributable to their phonological errors.

Some children with phonological disorders have slow development in lexical as well as syntactic abilities. Although there may be lexical deficits in some children, most children with phonological disorders are nevertheless functioning with much larger vocabularies than younger, typically developing children with similar phonological abilities. As with syntax, lexical deficits may be part of a general language difficulty in some children, but in others the presence of a phonological disorder may play a role in slowing down the process of acquiring new words. Leonard

(1995) has suggested that this may be the case for children with a poor phonological memory. Phonological memory serves to hold new words in the mind until a mental representation can be formed and stored permanently in the lexicon. A poor memory could lead to a more rapid decay in the auditory impression before the representation is fully stored. As a result, children with a limited phonological memory may need to hear a new word many more times than a typically developing child before an adequate representation is laid down in their mental lexicon.

In clinical practice it is important to be aware of the possible interrelationships between children's phonology and other aspects of language development from the point of view of intervention and prognosis. One reason is that the clinician will need to decide whether to focus intervention on developing a child's grammatical, lexical, or phonological skills, or on developing all aspects simultaneously. In terms of prognosis, it is important to identify children with both phonological and other language difficulties because this combination indicates a poorer long-term outcome than difficulties in phonology alone. Children with specific, isolated phonological difficulties have a more favorable prognosis for developing normal speech and may be less vulnerable for later reading and other academic problems than children who have phonological disorders combined with other linguistic and cognitive deficits (Bishop and Adams, 1990; Bishop and Edmundson, 1987).

Studies show that factors such as language performance, severity of phonological disorder, and phonological processing skills all correlate with literacy development, although the impact of these factors on an individual child is difficult to determine. Larrivee and Catts (1999) compared children with phonological disorders with normally developing children on tests of expressive phonology, phonological awareness, and language ability at the end of kindergarten. A year later, the children with expressive phonological disorders performed significantly less well than a control group on tests of reading achievement. Children with phonological disorders and additional deficits in language (vocabulary size and syntax), are particularly at risk for later literacy difficulties. Lewis, Freebairn, and Taylor (2000) studied a group of children aged 4–6 years with moderate to severe phonological disorders, some of whom had additional language disorders. They found that when followed up, the children with a phonological disorder and a language disorder performed more poorly on measures of reading and spelling than those with just a phonological disorder. They also found that the children with just phonological difficulties were also at risk for later literacy difficulties, however.[4]

types of phonological disorder

As many of the studies on speech related abilities (auditory discrimination, language skills, etc.) already described in the previous sections
show, children with phonological disorders are a highly heterogeneous
group. This well-recognized fact has led some researchers to propose
subgroups of phonological disorders. For example, based on a series of
studies over the past 15 years, Dodd and colleagues (Dodd, 1995; Dodd
and Bradford, 2000; Dodd, Leahy, and Hambly, 1989) have proposed
three subgroups of children with phonological disorder based on their
surface errors patterns. The first group have *delayed* phonology. These
children follow the normal developmental path, albeit slowly, due to
factors such as neurological immaturity or cognitive delay. The second
group have *deviant consistent* phonology. Their phonological processes
are consistent but deviant in the sense of not matching normal speech
development. These children are thought to have a deficit at the level of
linguistic organization. Callum, the case described earlier in the chapter,
is an example of a child with deviant consistent phonology. The third
group, *deviant inconsistent* phonology, exhibit a number of apparently
non-rule governed speech errors. These children are often highly unintelligible and their performance on a variety of tasks suggests that they have
a difficulty with motor planning for speech production. A recent study
by Broomfield and Dodd (2004) found that of 320 children with primary
speech impairment, over half (58%) had delayed phonology, with around
a quarter (21%) having deviant consistent phonology, and relatively few
(9%) having deviant inconsistent errors. As this classification suggests,
there may be a number of sources underlying phonological disorders,
each requiring a different approach to intervention. In a clinical setting
the implication is that each child needs a detailed and comprehensive
phonological assessment and an intervention program specifically
tailored to meet the child's individual needs.

approaches to therapy for phonological disorders

Many studies conducted in the 1960s and 1970s focused on treatment for
school age children and tended to utilize a traditional, sound-by-sound
motor approach to articulation therapy. More recent studies have focused
on younger, pre-school children and have adopted a more global linguistic
orientation with the focus of therapy on changing the underlying rule
governed nature of children's phonological errors. In addition, there is
now a greater emphasis on considering children's phonological disorder
in a wider social and academic context, with the result that children's

family, friends and school have a central role in the intervention process (McLeod and Bleile, 2004).

In this section some examples of frequently used approaches to phonological therapy are described. These diverse approaches are not mutually exclusive, and effective management of phonological disorders involves clinicians selecting and sequencing different approaches to meet children's needs as therapy progresses (Dodd and Bradford, 2000). There is some controversy in the literature about whether therapy is most effective when it targets processing deficits directly. In the view of Dodd and Bradford, "intervention targeting the primary area of deficit for children is likely to be more effective than other treatment techniques" (2000, p. 191). Dodd and Bradford might argue that in cases where assessment reveals auditory discrimination deficits, the most effective therapy approach is one that focuses directly on improving auditory discrimination skills. An alternate view is that the most effective therapy approach is one that bypasses children's specific areas of difficulty. Waters (2001) adopted this alternate view in a therapy program that capitalized on input and cognitive processing strengths to overcome a motor/articulatory difficulty in a 5-year-old boy with a severe developmental speech disorder.

Four approaches to intervention for phonological disorders are considered here (for further details of these and other approaches, see Bernthal and Bankson, 2004). The first three approaches focus on developing children's (i) auditory/perceptual skills, (ii) linguistic/ phonological abilities, and (iii) motor/articulatory skills. The final approach uses (iv) computer-based instrumentation to develop children's perceptual skills and to provide visual feedback in the way of acoustic or articulatory information.

auditory/perceptual approach

An example of an auditory/perceptual approach to therapy is *auditory input therapy* (Flynn and Lancaster, 1996) . Flynn and Lancaster state that auditory input therapy "aims to enhance the auditory salience of target speech sounds and structures in a natural context" (p. 51). This approach is also called *structured listening* and does not require children to produce target sounds but focuses only on perception. Flynn and Lancaster's view is that it is not necessary to include production practice because the increased opportunities to hear target speech sounds are sufficient to induce positive changes in output in many children.[5]

Auditory input therapy aims to enhance the auditory salience of target speech sounds through children experiencing increased opportunities to hear well-formed adult productions during naturalistic communicative tasks, such as structured stories and games. The approach maximizes the auditory salience of target speech sounds by placing them in contexts that involve maximally clear productions. For example, target speech sounds are placed in syllables that have primary stress and placed in nouns that occur at the ends of phrases. Because children are not put under pressure to correct their incorrect productions, auditory input therapy is considered an appropriate intervention for parents to carry out in a home-based program.

linguistic/phonological approach

Linguistic/phonological approaches emphasize the importance of phonological contrasts and communicating meaning as integral components of the therapy process. In addition, therapy is typically directed towards targeting whole sound classes, rather than individual segments, in order to maximize generalization. Examples of phonological approaches are *minimal pair contrast therapy* (Weiner, 1981), *maximal oppositions* (Elbert and Gierut, 1986), *multiple oppositions* (Williams, 2000), *cycles* (Hodson and Paden, 1991), *nonlinear-based intervention* (Bernhardt, 1994), *parents and children together* (PACT) (Bowen and Cupples, 1999), and *Metaphon* (Dean and Howell, 1986; Howell and Dean, 1994). The first two of these approaches are described here.

Minimal pair contrast therapy, probably the best known and most researched phonological therapy, typically involves a game format presenting pairs of words that the child produces as identical (i.e., homophonous). Callum, the boy with a phonological disorder described earlier, had many homophonous forms in his speech, such as *Kate* and *cake* judged by listeners as identical [keⁱt]. A game format encourages children to produce the word pairs distinctly in order to communicate a message to the listener. The clinician sets up situations where communication breaks down if children produce what the clinician perceives as homophonous word pairs. In order to repair the breakdown, children attempt to change their habitual incorrect productions in some way in order to get the message across. Through contexts that focus on minimal pair distinctions, children learn the communicative importance of producing contrasts that are sufficiently distinct for listeners to detect.

The maximal opposition approach (Elbert and Gierut, 1986; Gierut, 1989), like the minimal pair approach, presents a conceptual approach to phonological therapy. In minimal pairs, phonological oppositions typically vary in one feature, whereas in the maximal opposition approach, the phonological oppositions vary not just in one but along multiple articulatory dimensions of voice, manner, and place of articulation. Gierut

(1989) suggests that this approach is suitable for children with significant gaps in their phonological systems, or for those who find making the subtle distinctions in minimal pairs difficult. For these children, grosser distinctions may be easier for them to produce, so avoiding frustration particularly in the early stages of therapy. Furthermore, a practical advantage of this approach is that clinicians have a wider choice of vocabulary from which to select words to use in therapy activities. A final important point is that Gierut (1990) has found maximal opposition therapy to be more effective than minimal pair therapy.

motor/articulatory approach

Therapy to develop motor/articulatory skills follows general principles of motor learning, which emphasize the importance of providing repetitive, intensive, and systematic practice drills. These drills are used to establish consistency in articulation and reduce variable performance. Motor approaches emphasize the importance of the child's knowledge of results in the form of verbal, visual, tactile, and/or kinaesthetic feedback on performance. An example of the articulatory approach is the *traditional method* (Van Riper, 1947).

Van Riper's traditional method (Van Riper, 1947; Van Riper and Emerick, 1984) proceeds in four stages:

(i)   *Sensory-perceptual training (ear training)* focuses on identifying the target sound and discriminating it from error productions.
(ii) *Production training* aims to change production of the error sound. The approach introduces different syllable positions throughout therapy, gradually increasing the motor complexity of tasks.
(iii) *Stabilization* strengthens the correct production, helping children to produce newly acquired sound quickly and easily, with what has been termed "articulatory ease".
(iv) *Transfer* ensures carry-over of the newly acquired sound into syllables, words, and ultimately into everyday communicative situations.

The traditional approach focuses on motor learning of individual speech sounds and is therefore suitable for children with phonetic difficulties in articulating a limited number of speech sounds rather than for children with phonological difficulties that affect entire sound classes.

computer-based approaches

Computer technology offers new possibilities for engaging children in auditory discrimination and identification tasks by the use of a variety of types of material, including synthetic speech material, which allows for selective cue manipulation (Hazan, Wilson, Howells, Miller, Abberton, and Fourcin, 1995). Rvachew (1994) described a procedure, the Speech Assessment and Interactive Learning System (SAILS), for children aged 3–9 years to assess and treat phonemic perception in order to improve phoneme identification and to establish appropriate phonemic boundaries. The basis for the program is digitally manipulated auditory stimuli representing correct and incorrect productions of words, and the child identifies whether a production they hear is correct or incorrect. Rvachew found that children who received this auditory/perceptual program in combination with therapy that focused directly on production made significantly better progress than children who received therapy for production only.

   In terms of speech production, visual feedback systems can detect real-time physiological events as they occur and convert this information into a meaningful display, making ambiguous internal cues explicit and enabling conscious control of such cues to develop. In relation to therapy for speech disorders, Shuster, Ruscello, and Smith (1992) suggested that biofeedback is particularly effective when details of target sound production are difficult to describe to clients. Such difficulty of description applies particularly to movement of the visually inaccessible articulators, such as the tongue, velum, and larynx. In the recommended therapy, subconscious cues are made explicit and brought to conscious attention, and through interaction and practice, children can develop control over the position and movement of these articulators. For example, under normal circumstances children are not aware that their anterior tongue needs to be positioned precisely on the alveolar ridge with a delicate groove formed through which the air is channeled during production of sibilant /s/. When undergoing visual feedback therapy with EPG, tongue positioning and grooving can be visualized, bringing these features to children's conscious attention (Hardcastle and Gibbon, 1997). The EPG system offers a direct visual display in real time of lingual contacts as they occur and so can be used as a visual biofeedback aid for correcting abnormal articulatory patterns. The technique has been particularly successful in treating the intractable problems in older children whose articulation or phonological difficulties have resisted previous approaches to therapy.[6]

efficacy of therapy

The past decade has seen increased recognition among clinicians and researchers of the need to examine research evidence when making clinical decisions. An awareness of the principles of evidence-based practice encourages clinicians to seek out high quality research evidence about the outcomes of interventions they adopt in their clinical practice and, when necessary, to change their current practice in the light of this evidence. There is now a substantial literature demonstrating the beneficial effects of speech therapy for children with phonological disorders (Geirut, 1998). Law, Garrett, and Nye (2004) conducted a systematic review of experimental investigations of speech and language therapy interventions for children with developmental speech and language delay/disorder including those with phonological disorders. They concluded that speech and language therapy might be effective for children with phonological disorders. Almost and Rosenbaum (1998) also conducted a meta-analysis of the literature on intervention for preschool children with phonological disorders published during the period 1985–94. The major finding of this review was that, although phonological skills of children improved after intervention, the studies reviewed had methodological limitations. They subsequently conducted a randomized controlled study in order to strengthen the evidence about the effectiveness of intervention. In their study, the children who received intervention made greater gains in phonology than the children who received no treatment over the same period. Almost and Rosenbaum concluded that speech therapy for phonological disorders, as currently practiced in many community settings, is effective.

A wide range of factors can affect the rate of progress in phonological intervention, but we lack knowledge about the most critical variables for predicting and maximizing progress. A range of important variables to do with the child (e.g., age, type and severity of phonological disorder, degree of motivation), treatment (time in therapy) and therapist characteristics (e.g., ability to motivate client, experience in phonological intervention), are discussed by Baker and Bernhardt (2004). As well as these variables, Almost and Rosenbaum (1998) are of the opinion that certain parenting styles and parental motivation and cooperation can have a beneficial impact on the effectiveness of treatment. These positive skills include, for example, good turn-taking skills, eye contact, and frequent corrective feedback as well as regular attendance for speech therapy sessions. Other studies support this finding, adding to the evidence that intervention that includes parents and teaching staff is beneficial (Eiserman, Weber, and McCoun, 1992).

conclusion

While there is still controversy about the nature and processing difficulties that underlie phonological disorders, it is generally agreed that these children essentially have a linguistic difficulty in learning and organizing speech sounds into a system of phonological contrasts. Moreover, the range of effective therapies for phonological disorder and the linkages to perceptual, motor, cognitive, and linguistic capacities underscores the complexity of the disorder as it manifests in individual children. Much more is now known about the long-term outcomes in adolescence and adulthood for children with phonological disorders and there is a greater awareness of the need for ongoing support to ensure children achieve their potential in all aspects of life. Children with phonological disorders are a group for whom we now have effective diagnostic and intervention procedures. The availability of effective therapy procedures underlines the importance of identifying children with phonological disorders at a young age and referring them as soon as possible for speech assessment and appropriate intervention.

notes

1. Editor's note: note that the focus in this chapter is on segmental phonology; for a complementary discussion of phonological disorder in the prosodic dimension, see Chapter 7, this volume. In McMahon's view, some systematic segmental errors may be attributable to "prosodic disorder," e.g., as manifested in an English-speaking child's prosodic constraint disallowing syllables with long vowels and diphthongs.
2. Editor's note: this case is illustrative of some of issues surrounding the classification of phenomena as "belonging" to phonetics or phonology. These difficulties with discriminability of contrasts involve fine detail and thus might be seen as a matter of "phonetics." At the same time, they clearly involve the phonetic realization of contrasting phonological categories and the phonological system overall, since the child must learn how to differentiate categories in a way which is the same as, or sufficiently similar to, that of other speakers, so as to be functional for communication with them.
3. Editor's note: at the same time, McMahon (Chapter 7, this volume) believes that these children may be able to compensate to an extent by use of prosody to improve performance.
4. Editor's note: for a detailed discussion of literacy development, see Chapter 9, this volume.
5. Editor's note: compare the emphasis placed on training perception in second-language learning in Chapters 5 and 6, this volume.
6. Editor's note: compare with visualization techniques used for teaching pronunciation to second-language learners as described in Chapters 6 and 11, this volume, and note applications for deaf speakers in Chapter 6.

references

Almost, D., & Rosenbaum, P. (1998). Effectiveness of speech intervention for phonological disorders: A randomized controlled trial. *Developmental Medicine and Child Neurology, 40*, 319–25.

Baker, E., & Bernhardt, B. (2004). From hindsight to foresight: Working around barriers to success in phonological intervention. *Child Language Teaching and Therapy, 20,* 287–318.

Ball, M. J., & Gibbon, F. E. (Eds.) (2002). *Vowel disorders.* Boston: Butterworth Heinemann.

Bernhardt, B. (1994). Phonological intervention techniques for syllable and word structure development. *Clinics in Communication Disorders,* March, 54–65.

Bernhardt, B., & Stemberger, J. P. (1998). *Handbook of phonological development from the perspective of constraint-based nonlinear phonology.* San Diego: Academic Press.

Bernhardt, B., & Stoel-Gammon, C. (1994). Nonlinear phonology: Introduction and clinical application. *Journal of Speech and Hearing Research, 37,* 123–43.

Bernthal, J., & Bankson, N. (2004). *Articulation and phonological disorders.* Fifth edition. Boston: Allyn and Bacon.

Bird, J., & Bishop, D. (1992). Perception and awareness of phonemes in phonologically impaired children. *European Journal of Disorders of Communication, 27,* 289–311.

Bishop, D. V., & Adams, C. (1990). A prospective study of the relationship between specific language impairment, phonological disorders and reading retardation. *Journal of Child Psychology and Psychiatry, and Allied Disciplines, 31,* 1027–50.

Bishop, D. V., & Edmundson, A. (1987). Language-impaired 4-year-olds: Distinguishing transient from persistent impairment. *Journal of Speech and Hearing Disorders, 52,* 156–73.

Bowen, C., & Cupples, L. (1999). Parents and children together (PACT): A collaborative approach to phonological therapy. *International Journal of Language and Communication Disorders, 34,* 35–55.

Broomfield, J., & Dodd, B. (2004). The nature of referred subtypes of primary speech disability. *Child Language Teaching and Therapy, 20,* 135–51.

Butcher, A. (1989). The uses and abuses of phonological assessment. *Child Language Teaching and Therapy, 3,* 262–76.

Catts, H., & Jensen, P. J. (1983). Speech timing of phonologically disordered children: Voicing contrasts of initial and final stop consonants. *Journal of Speech and Hearing Research, 26,* 501–9.

Compton, A. J. (1970). Generative studies of children's phonological disorders. *Journal of Speech and Hearing Disorders, 35,* 315–40.

Dagenais, P. A. (1995). Electropalatography in the treatment of articulation/phonological disorders. *Journal of Disorders of Communication, 28,* 303–29.

Dean, E., & Howell, J. (1986). Developing linguistic awareness: A theoretically based approach to phonological disorders. *British Journal of Disorders of Communication, 21,* 223–38.

Dodd, B. (1995). *The differential diagnosis and treatment of children with speech disorder.* London: Whurr Publishers.

Dodd, B., & Bradford, A. (2000). A comparison of three therapy methods for children with different types of developmental phonological disorder. *International Journal of Language and Communication Disorders, 35,* 189–209.

Dodd, B., Leahy, J., & Hambly, G. (1989). Phonological disorders in children: Underlying cognitive deficits. *British Journal of Developmental Psychology, 7,* 55–71.

Edwards, J., Fourakis, M., Beckman, M. E., & Fox, R. A. (1999). Characterizing knowledge deficits in phonological disorders. *Journal of Speech, Language, and Hearing Research, 42*, 169–86.

Eisenson, J., & Ogilvie, M. (1977). *Speech correction in the schools*. Fourth edition. New York: Macmillan.

Eiserman, W. D., Weber, C., & McCoun, M. (1992). Two alternative program models for serving speech-disordered preschoolers: A second year follow-up. *Journal of Communication Disorders, 25*, 77–106.

Elbert, M., & Gierut, J. (1986). *Handbook of clinical phonology: Approaches to assessment and treatment*. San Diego: College Hill Press.

Felsenfeld, S., Broen, P. A., & McGue, M. (1992). A 28-year follow-up of adults with a history of moderate phonological disorder: Linguistic and personality results. *Journal of Speech and Hearing Research, 35*, 1114–25.

Felsenfeld, S., McGue, M., & Broen, P.A. (1995). Familial aggregation of phonological disorders: Results from a 28-year follow-up. *Journal of Speech and Hearing Research, 38*, 1091–107.

Felsenfeld, S., & Plomin, R. (1997). Epidemiological and offspring analyses of developmental speech disorders using data from the Colorado Adoption Project. *Journal of Speech, Language, and Hearing Research, 40*, 778–91.

Fletcher, S. G. (1992). *Articulation: A physiological approach*. San Diego: Singular Publishing Group.

Flynn, L., & Lancaster, G. (1996). *Children's phonology sourcebook*. Bicester, England: Winslow.

Fox, A. V., Dodd, B., & Howard, D. (2002). Risk factors for speech disorders in children. *International Journal of Language and Communication Disorders, 37*, 117–31.

Gard, A., Gilman, L., & Gorman, J. (1993). *Speech and Language Development Chart*. Second edition. Austin: Pro-ED.

Gibbon, F. E. (1999). Undifferentiated lingual gestures in children with articulation/ phonological disorders. *Journal of Speech Language and Hearing Research, 42*, 382–97.

Gibbon, F. (2002). Features of impaired motor control in children with articulation / phonological disorders. In F. Windsor, L. Kelly, & N. Hewlett (Eds.), *Investigations in clinical linguistics and phonetics* (pp. 299–309). London: Erlbaum.

Gibbon, F., & Grunwell, P. (1990). Specific developmental language learning disabilities – clinical and special educational management. In P. Grunwell (Ed.), *Developmental speech disorders* (pp. 135–61). Edinburgh: Churchill Livingstone.

Gibbon, F. E., & Scobbie, J. M. (1997). Covert contrasts in children with phonological disorder. *Australian Communication Quarterly*, Autumn 1997, 13–16.

Gibbon, F. E., & Wood, S. E. (2002). Articulatory drift in the speech of children with articulation/phonological disorders. *Perceptual and Motor Skills, 95*, 295–307.

Gierut, J. A. (1989). Maximal opposition approach to phonological treatment. *Journal of Speech and Hearing Disorders, 54*, 9–19.

Gierut, J. A. (1990). Differential learning of phonological oppositions. *Journal of Speech and Hearing Research, 33*, 540–9.

Gierut, J. A. (1998). Treatment efficacy: Functional phonological disorders in children. *Journal of Speech, Language, and Hearing Research, 41*, 85–100.

Grunwell, P. (1981). *The nature of phonological disability in children.* London: Academic Press.

Grunwell, P. (Ed.) (1990). *Developmental speech disorders.* Edinburgh: Churchill Livingstone.

Hardcastle, W. J. (1976). *Physiology of speech production.* London: Academic Press.

Hardcastle, W. J., & Gibbon, F. E. (1997). Electropalatography and its clinical applications. In M. J. Ball & C. Code (Eds.), *Instrumental clinical phonetics* (pp. 151–95). London: Whurr Publishers.

Hardcastle, W. J., Gibbon, F. E., & Jones, W. (1991). Visual display of tongue-palate contact: Electropalatography in the assessment and remediation of speech disorders. *British Journal of Disorders of Communication, 26,* 41–74.

Hardcastle, W. J., Morgan Barry, R. A., & Clark, C. (1987). An instrumental phonetic study of lingual activity in articulation disordered children. *Journal of Speech and Hearing Research, 30,* 171–84.

Hazan, V., Wilson, G., Howells, D., Miller, D., Abberton, E. R., & Fourcin, A. (1995). Speech pattern audiometry for clinical use. *European Journal of Disorders of Communication, 30,* 116–23.

Hewlett, N. (1988). Acoustic properties of /k/ and /t/ in normal and phonologically disordered speech. *Clinical Linguistics and Phonetics, 2,* 29–45.

Hodson, B., & Paden, E. (1991). *Targeting intelligible speech: A phonological approach to remediation.* Second edition. San Diego: College Hill Press.

Howell, J., & Dean, E. (1994). *Treating phonological disorders in children: Metaphon – theory to practice.* Second edition. London: Whurr Publishers.

Ingram, D. (1976). *Phonological disability in children.* London: Edward Arnold.

Jakobson, R. (1968). *Child language, aphasia and phonological universals.* The Hague: Mouton.

Kent, R. D. (1997). Gestural phonology: Basic concepts and applications in speech-language pathology. In M. J. Ball & R. D. Kent (Eds.), *The new phonologies: Developments in clinical linguistics* (pp. 247–68). London: Singular.

Kornfeld, J. R. (1971). Theoretical issues in child phonology. *Papers of the 7th Regional Meeting, Chicago Linguistic Society,* 454–68.

Lalakea, M. L., & Messner, A. H (2003). Ankyloglossia: The adolescent and adult perspective. *Otolaryngology – Head and Neck Surgery, 128,* 746–52.

Larrivee, L. S., & Catts, H. W. (1999). Early reading achievement in children with expressive phonological disorders. *American Journal of Speech-Language Pathology, 8,* 118–28.

Law, J. (1992). *The early identification of language impairment in children.* London: Chapman and Hall.

Law, J., Garrett, Z., & Nye, C. (2004). *Speech and language therapy interventions for children with primary speech and language delay or disorder.* Oxford: The Cochrane Library.

Leonard, L. B. (1995). Phonological impairment. In P. Fletcher, & B. MacWhinney (Eds.), *The handbook of child language* (pp. 573–602). Oxford: Blackwell.

Lewis, B. A., Ekelman, B. L., & Aram, D. M. (1989). A familial study of severe phonological disorders. *Journal of Speech and Hearing Research, 32,* 713–24.

Lewis, B. A., Freebairn, L. A., & Taylor, H. G. (2000). Follow-up of children with early expressive phonology disorders. *Journal of Learning Disabilities, 33,* 433–44.

Locke, J. L. (1980). The inference of speech perception in the phonologically disordered child: Parts I and II. *Journal of Speech and Hearing Disorders, 45,* 431–68.

McLeod, S., & Bleile, K. (2004). The ICF: A framework for setting goals for children with speech impairment. *Child Language Teaching and Therapy, 20*, 199–219.

McReynolds, L. (1988). Articulation disorders of unknown aetiology. In N. Lass, L. McReynolds, J. Northern, & D. Yoder (Eds.), *Handbook of speech-language pathology and audiology* (pp. 419–41). Toronto: B. C. Decker.

McReynolds, L. V., & Engmann, D. (1975). *Distinctive feature analysis of misarticulations*. Baltimore: University Park Press.

Miccio, A. W., Gallagher, E., Grossman, C. B., Yont, K. M., & Vernon-Feagans, L. (2001). Influence of chronic otitis media on phonological acquisition. *Clinical Linguistics and Phonetics, 15*, 47–51.

Morley, M. (1957). *The development and disorders of speech in childhood*. Edinburgh: Churchill Livingstone.

Oller, D. K., & Eilers, R. E. (1975). Phonetic expectation and transcription validity. *Phonetica, 31*, 288–304.

Paul, R., & Shriberg, L. D. (1982). Associations between phonology and syntax in speech-delayed children. *Journal of Speech and Hearing Research, 25*, 536–47.

Petinou, K. C., Schwartz, R. G., Gravel, J. S., & Raphael, L. J. (2001). A preliminary account of phonological and morphophonological perception in young children with and without otitis media. *International Journal of Language and Communication Disorders, 36*, 21–42.

Pollock, K. E., & Berni, M. C. (2003). Incidence of non-rhotic vowel errors in children: Data from the Memphis Vowel Project. *Clinical Linguistics and Phonetics, 17*, 393–401.

Pollock, K., & Keiser, N. (1990). An examination of vowel errors in phonologically disordered children. *Clinical Linguistics and Phonetics, 4*, 161–78.

Rvachew, S. (1994). Speech perception training can facilitate sound production learning. *Journal of Speech and Hearing Research, 37*, 347–57.

Shriberg, L .D., & Kwiatkowski, J. (1994). Developmental phonological disorders, I: A clinical profile. *Journal of Speech and Hearing Research, 37*, 1100–26.

Shuster, L. I., Ruscello, D. M., & Smith, K. D. (1992). Evoking [r] using visual feedback. *American Journal of Speech-Language Pathology, 1*, 29–34.

Smith, N. V. (1973). *The acquisition of phonology: A case study*. Cambridge: Cambridge University Press.

Snow, K. (1961). Articulation proficiency in relation to certain dental abnormalities. *Journal of Speech and Hearing Disorders, 26*, 209–212.

Stampe, D. (1969). The acquisition of phonetic representation. *Proceedings of the Fifth Regional Meeting of the Chicago Linguistic Society*, 433–44.

Stoel-Gammon, C. (1990). Issues in phonological development and disorders. In J. Miller (Ed.), *Progress in research on child language disorders* (pp. 255–65). Austin: PRO-ED.

Stoel-Gammon, C., & Dunn, C. (1985). *Normal and disordered phonology in children*. Baltimore: University Park Press.

Stoel-Gammon, C., & Herrington, P. (1990). Vowel systems of normally developing and phonologically disordered children. *Clinical Linguistics and Phonetics, 4*, 145–60.

Stone, M., Epstein, M. A., & Iskarous, K. (2004). Functional segments in tongue movement. *Clinical Linguistics and Phonetics, 18*, 507–21.

Teele, D. W., Klein, J. O., & Rosner, B. A. (1984). Otitis media with effusion during the first three years of life and development of speech and language. *Pediatrics, 74*, 282–7.

Towne, R. L. (1994). Effect of mandibular stabilization on the diadochokinetic performance of children with phonological disorder. *Journal of Phonetics, 22,* 317–32.

Tyler, A. A., & Watterson, K. H. (1991). Effects of phonological versus language intervention in preschoolers with both phonological and language impairment. *Child Language Teaching and Therapy, 7,* 141–60.

Van Riper, C. (1947). *Speech correction: Principles and methods.* Second edition. New York: Prentice Hall.

Van Riper, C., & Emerick, L. (1984). *Speech correction: An introduction to speech pathology and audiology.* Englewood Cliffs, NJ: Prentice Hall.

Waters, D. (2001). Using input processing strengths to overcome speech output difficulties. In J. Stackhouse & B. Wells (Eds.), *Children's speech and literacy difficulties 2: Identification and intervention* (pp. 164–203). London: Whurr Publishers.

Weiner, F. (1981). Treatment of phonological disability using the method of meaningful minimal contrast: Two case studies. *Journal of Speech and Hearing Disorders, 46,* 97–103.

Weismer, G. (1984). Acoustic analysis strategies for the refinement of phonological analysis. In M. Elbert, D. A. Dinnsen, & G. Weismer (Eds.), *Phonological theory and the misarticulating child.* American Speech Hearing Association Monographs, *22,* 30–52. Rockville, MD: American Speech and Hearing Association.

Weismer, G., & Elbert, M. (1982). Temporal characteristics of "functionally" misarticulated /s/ in 4- to 6-year-old children. *Journal of Speech and Hearing Research, 25,* 275–86.

Weiss, C. E., Gordon, M. E., & Lillywhite, H. S. (1987). *Clinical management of articulatory and phonologic disorders.* Baltimore: Williams and Wilkins.

Williams, A. L. (2000). Multiple oppositions: Theoretical foundations for an alternative contrastive intervention approach. *American Journal of Speech-Language Pathology, 9,* 282–288.

Winitz, H. (1969). *Articulatory acquisition and behavior.* New York: Appleton-Century-Crofts.

Wright, J. E. (1995). Tongue-tie. *Journal of Paediatrics and Child Health, 31,* 276–8.

11
technological advances in researching and teaching phonology

dorothy m. chun

introduction

Technology has been used for many decades for phonological research as well as for teaching phonetics, phonology, and pronunciation. However, it is only in the last 15 years that the incorporation of speech technology into linguistic and applied linguistic inquiry has begun to yield major results in research and practice. The purpose of this chapter is to examine advances and new directions in acoustic analysis and speech recognition as they relate to issues of phonology, both from a research perspective of quantifying and measuring segmental phonemes and prosody, and from the practical perspective of using technology to teach.

The chapter contains three sections. The first section reviews the technological advances that have been made in linguistics involving acoustic research on the phonological elements and features of spoken language. It includes discussion of projects in speech recognition; text-to-speech synthesis; spoken dialogue systems; and the recording, archiving, tagging, and transcribing of speech corpora. The second section reviews applied linguistic research in which technology is used to manipulate components of second-language phonology in order to determine which of them are the most crucial for listening and speaking competence and should therefore be taught. Research has attempted, for example, to quantify the components of a foreign accent as well as the factors that contribute to comprehensibility of spoken language. Prosody has been shown to play an important role in both perception and production, and must be considered in conjunction with the entire discourse context in which an utterance occurs. The third section reviews the available hardware and software for the teaching of pronunciation, including intonation, as well as the research that has been conducted on the efficacy of these technological tools and programs.

One of the most striking developments of the last decade is that research in both theoretical and applied linguistics is concerned increasingly with authentic, spontaneous speech (e.g., Couper-Kuhlen and Selting, 1996; Jenkins, 2004; Wennerstrom, 2001; Wichmann, 2000) and with the role of discourse-level prosody in interpreting speech (e.g., Brazil, 1997; Chun, 2002; Pickering, 2001). The fact that human interactions can be recorded and analyzed digitally with ease has led linguists and other scientists to collect and study naturally-occurring human speech data, as well as human–computer interactions. Much of the research reported here concerns spontaneous speech, and this augurs well for the future of using technology for researching and teaching phonology in natural context.[1]

technological advances in speech research

digitization of analog speech and corpora

One of the most basic uses of technology today involves digitizing speech samples and speech corpora that had existed previously in analog form (e.g., analog audiotapes or videotapes). The ability to store and process massive quantities of natural data, as well as the current ability to make original recordings digitally, has resulted in extensive speech corpora. These corpora can then be analyzed in many different ways, from a micro-level examination of acoustic phonetic properties to a macro-level examination of discourse features. Efforts to mechanically transcribe corpora of naturally occurring language have been reported by many linguists, including, for example, Du Bois, Schuetze-Coburn, Paolino, and Cumming (1992) on the Santa Barbara Corpus of Spoken American English (CSAE). Du Bois has developed two software tools for discourse transcription, *VoiceWalker* and *SoundWriter*,[2] the second of which allows the transcriber to align transcripts with sound files. Another example is research at the University of Hamburg Research Center on Multilingualism to develop theory-independent and platform-independent tools for creating, analyzing, and transcribing spoken language corpora.[3]

speech technology

There is an ever-growing body of research in the field of *Human Language Technology* (HLT; Gupta and Schulze, 2000). Key areas of HLT include *Natural Language Processing* (NLP), *Machine Translation* (MT) and *Speech*

Technologies (ST). *HLTCentral* <http://www.hltcentral.org>, launched in 1999, provides on-line access to language technology resources. For the purposes of this chapter on technology and phonology, the focus will be on spoken rather than written language and thus on speech technology.

In its broadest sense, speech technology spans many disciplines, including, but not limited to, computer science, electrical engineering, linguistics, phonetics, psychology, speech communication, physics, and acoustics. At the beginning of the twenty-first century, Greenberg (2005) laments the historic tension between science and technology with respect to spoken language, but he is hopeful that "over the coming decades this tension is likely to dissolve into a collaborative relationship melding linguistic knowledge with machine-learning and statistical methods" (p. 1). Greenberg deals with corpora that consist of hundreds of brief (5–10 minute) telephone dialogues representative of casual conversation. Approximately five hours of this material has been phonetically annotated at his institute (ICSI, described below), and a one-hour subset of the material has also been labeled with respect to prosodic features. These two annotated corpora provide a means with which to characterize spoken language and thereby serve to link linguistic analysis and computer-based technology. This expressed need to develop such linkage appears to be gaining increasing recognition by speech technology groups.

Among the numerous speech technology groups is one located at the International Computer Science Institute (ICSI) at the University of California at Berkeley, where Greenberg worked. This is The Speech Group, which currently lists three main projects, all of which are of interest to linguists. The first project, EARS (Effective Affordable Reusable Speech), is a major DARPA (Defense Advanced Research Projects Agency) speech initiative, one of whose components, called Rich Transcription of Conversational Speech, is being developed in collaboration with the Stanford Research Institute (SRI) and the University of Washington. The goal is to generate readable transcriptions of conversational speech in multiple languages. The Meeting Recorder project seeks to develop speech recognizers that would be useful in conventional meeting contexts. SpeechCorder is a portable digital tape recorder that uses robust speech recognition to create a word stream for archiving meetings that can be indexed and annotated. The third project is generically termed Speaker Recognition, with a goal of using a variety of higher-level features (such as word usage, prosodic characteristics, pronunciation patterns, idiosyncratic laughs or other non-speech events) to improve speaker recognition <http://www.icsi.berkeley.edu/Speech/projects.html>.

The Technology and Information Processing section of the Department of Language and Speech at the University of Nijmegen is one of four units of the Center for Language Studies. Researchers there investigate the contribution that language and speech technology can make to automatic processing of information encoded in written and spoken language. In particular, the focus is on improving automatic speech recognition and the application of speech technology in multimodal human–machine interaction and computer-assisted language learning. There are plans to start a new line of research addressing the contribution that non-verbal (mainly prosodic) information in the speech signal can make to the recognition and interpretation of the verbal message. Ongoing projects include robust automatic speech recognition, multimodality, pronunciation variation, speaker verification and identification, text-to-speech systems, corpora, and computational linguistics (see <http://lands.let.kun.nl/research/programme.html>).

The Language Technologies Institute at Carnegie Mellon University is part of the School of Computer Science and pursues research in machine translation, natural language processing, speech, information retrieval, and knowledge acquisition. Among their speech projects is a program entitled FLUENCY, which uses speech recognition to help users perfect their accents in a foreign language by detecting pronunciation errors, such as duration errors and incorrect phones. The system offers visual and aural input as to how to correct the errors (see discussion below of Eskenazi, 1999). Also under development is *TalkBank*, a project funded by the U.S. National Science Foundation and hosted by Carnegie Mellon University and the University of Pennsylvania, which will house a database of hundreds of hours of audio linked to transcripts, including the CHILDES (Child Language Data Exchange System) database and the CSAE (Corpus of Spoken American English) mentioned above.

speech synthesis

Today, hardware devices and computer programs for processing spoken data are commonplace – in fact, standard – on personal computers. Spoken input can be analyzed according to a wide variety of parameters, and such acoustic analyses of speech have proven valuable for speech synthesis and speech recognition. Speech synthesis is often equated with the conversion of text to speech, though it can also involve creating or synthesizing sounds that resemble human speech. Currently, speech synthesis is far more advanced than speech recognition, and there is even software available as freeware or shareware that achieves reasonable results in terms of generating spoken renditions of text. Such text-to-speech translation is, of course, more complicated than simply matching characters to sounds in any given language because in most languages, the relationship between them is not one-to-one.[4] In order to produce natural human-sounding speech, one has to consider intonation, rhythm, and the other prosodic elements that are part and parcel of human speech.

For the purposes of language learning, text-to-speech synthesis may be relevant for rudimentary listening comprehension and for learning sound–symbol (phoneme–grapheme) correspondences. To be sure, for the ultimate test of listening comprehension, i.e., understanding native speakers of a language, one would need to have access to authentic speech (see the description of the *Streaming Speech* software in the final section). Nevertheless, there are some speech synthesis projects worthy of mention. For example, a dissertation by Marsi (2001) investigated intonation in spoken language generation. Commercially, Nuance's Realspeak (formerly ScanSoft) claims to provide "expressive, natural, multi-lingual text-to-speech" capabilities <http://www.nuance.com/realspeak/>.

speech recognition

One of the functions of speech recognition (SR) is to convert an acoustic signal of human speech to a set of words, and this aspect of SR has not reached as high a level of performance as speech synthesis. Speech recognition is far more complex and challenging than speech synthesis, not only because of external, speaker-independent factors such as background noise, but also because of speaker-dependent factors such as idiosyncratic pronunciation features. The problem is compounded by the fact that words are normally not produced in isolation but are uttered in connected speech, i.e., the pronunciation of preceding and following words influence a given word through co-articulatory effects, and the intonation and rhythm of a stretch of speech will also have a bearing on how a single word is pronounced.

Some are quite optimistic about SR technology. According to Alwang (1999):

> The accuracy of past generations of speech recognition topped out at a little more than 90 percent (nearly one error every ten words)....The good news about the latest speech software is that most of the products provide recognition accuracy above 95 percent.... (p. 167)

In the view of Harris (2000):

> Speech recognition technology has finally come of age – at least for language training purposes for young adults and adults. Computer programs that truly 'understand' natural speech, the Holy Grail of

artificial intelligence researchers, may be a decade or more away, and today's SR programs may be merely pattern-matching devices, still incapable of parsing real language, of achieving anything like 'understanding,' but, nonetheless, they can now provide language students with realistic, highly effective, and motivating speech practice. (p. 1)

It must be noted that Harris is promoting a commercial product, and the reviews of commercial and non-commercial software discussed below will prove to be more realistic in the extent to which automatic speech recognition can or does improve pronunciation.

focus on prosody

Current research on speech recognition is focusing increasingly on prosody. Chang (2002), for example, refutes the assumption in many automatic speech recognition (ASR) systems that words are readily decomposable into constituent phonetic components (phonemes). Rather, the conventional phonemic "beads-on-a-string" approach is thought to be of limited utility, particularly with respect to informal, conversational material. Chang's study shows that there is a significant gap between authentic speech data and the pronunciation models of current ASR systems and therefore analyzes spontaneous speech with respect to three important, but often neglected, components of speech: articulatory-acoustic features, the syllable, and stress accent (location of primary and weak stresses). The alternative approach to speech modeling proposed is one in which the syllable assumes preeminent status and is linked to the lower as well as higher tiers of linguistic representation through the incorporation of prosodic information such as stress accent. One specific finding was that, "in contrast to the traditional linguistic framework [for ASR], the most salient features for stress accent are related to energy, duration and vocalic identity. Pitch-related features were found to play only a minor role" (Chang, 2002, p. 131). These findings can inform future phonological descriptions and practical applications to pronunciation teaching programs.

Using computer-based techniques, Hirschberg (2002) examined areas of prosodic variation and some of their functions in human-human communication. She confirms that "interest in the contribution prosodic information makes to human communication has led to increasing expectations that such information could be of use in text-to-speech and speech understanding systems, and in application of these technologies to spoken dialogue systems" (p. 31). Hirschberg notes that linguists, computational linguists, and speech engineers have increasingly looked to intonation as an important component in language processing. New software and schemes for prosodic description, such as the ToBI system (Pitrelli, Beckman, & Hirschberg, 1994; Silverman, Beckman, Pitrelli, Ostendorf, Wightman, Price, Pierrehumbert, and Hirschberg, 1992, <http://ling.ohio-state.edu/~tobi>), allow researchers to compare their findings within and across languages more easily, and facilitate the construction of very large labeled speech corpora. Corpus-based prosodic research has become an active area for speech technologists and other linguists.[5]

This attention to prosody is echoed in other work using conversational speech as the basis for speech technology research. Galley, McKeown, Hirschberg, and Shriberg (2004) propose a statistical approach for modeling agreements and disagreements in authentic conversational interaction. The approach first identifies adjacency pairs in a digitized speech corpus, then automatically classifies utterances as agreement or disagreement using these adjacency pairs and features that represent various pragmatic influences of previously occurring examples of agreement or disagreement. The features are defined from a set of lexical, durational, and structural features that look both forward and backward in the discourse.

Shriberg and Stolcke (2004a, 2004b) propose a "direct modeling" approach to analyzing prosody and applying the results in the classification of linguistic features using speech technology. Prosodic features are extracted directly from the speech signal and from the output of an automatic speech recognizer. In order to provide an indication of how their speech technology performs on real-world data, they focus on spontaneous (rather than read or acted) speech from a variety of contexts – including human-human telephone conversations, game-playing, human-computer dialog, and multi-party meetings. Shriberg and Stolcke's research covers four general application areas which set the stage for current and future work: (i) *structural tagging* (e.g., finding sentence boundaries and disfluencies); (ii) *pragmatic and paralinguistic tagging* (e.g., classifying dialog acts and emotions); (iii) *speaker recognition*; and (iv) *word recognition*.

The above-cited sources indicate that exciting work is being done in linguistic technology and computational linguistics, particularly with natural speech and in the area of prosody using digital samples and computer-based technologies of analysis. In order to develop effective analytical and pedagogical tools and uses of these, applied linguists will need to continue to collaborate with technologists in ways that are not always encouraged in our increasingly specialized world.

acoustic research on segmentals

In the realm of acoustic phonetic research, Peter Ladefoged, arguably the world's pre-eminent phonetician, has relied for decades on technology to record and describe the sounds of human languages. His most recent publications include: (1) the second edition of *Elements of Acoustic Phonetics* (Ladefoged, 1996), which presents information on computer speech processing (including FFT [Fast Fourier Transform] and LPC [Linear Predictive Coding] analysis); (2) the second edition of *Vowels and Consonants* (Ladefoged, 2001), which is accompanied by a CD-ROM on which the sounds of a wide variety of languages are reproduced, and in which Ladefoged discusses computers and text-to-speech systems and speech recognition systems; and (3) *Phonetic Data Analysis* (Ladefoged, 2004), which presents the procedures involved in describing the sounds of a language and illustrates the basic techniques of experimental phonetics, using technologies such as a tape recorder, a video camera, and a computer.

Virtually all acoustic phonetic research today involves the use of computer technology to record, synthesize, and analyze speech. Examination of acoustic phonetic research in the last 10–15 years in two of the premier journals on this subject, *Journal of Phonetics* and *Journal of the Acoustical Society of America*, reveals that studies continue to investigate acoustic correlates of segmental phonology, often using experimentally produced speech or constructed tasks rather than natural data. In the articles on phonology or pronunciation that appeared in the *Journal of the Acoustical Society of America* between 1990 and 2005, approximately 90% involved research done with some form of technology, e.g., digitized speech that was analyzed acoustically; by use of ultrasound, magnetic resonance imaging (MRI) and X-ray films to analyze articulation; and by means of electroglottographic (EGG) and electromyographic (EMG) technologies to study different aspects of prosody. In addition, there is much reported research on speech recognition, text-to-speech systems, speech perception, and speech synthesis.

In a different use of electronic technology, computer programs for statistical analyses are being used with increasing frequency in linguistics. The most commonly used analytical tool in sociolinguistic variationist studies, VARBRUL, is a multiple regression computer program developed based on Labov's (1969) notion of the variable rule. In the subfield of phonology, VARBRUL (Cedergren and Sankoff, 1974) can be used, for example, in analyses of variation of English phonology, as shown by Bayley and Preston (1996) or in analyses of probabilistic phonology, as done by Pierrehumbert (2003), in which she shows that probability can be found at all levels of linguistic representation, e.g., in probability distribution over the phonetic space (p. 182). She also suggests that speech perception, production, and well-formedness are affected by frequency and that phonetic learning requires continuous updating of probability distributions.

technology in applied linguistics research

research on second-language speech

The recent focus on prosody in speech technology research is mirrored in second-language (L2) research on certain key areas, namely, foreign accent, comprehensibility, fluency, and discourse intonation. In this section, L2 research studies using technology that have implications for how technology can be used to teach phonology will be discussed. In the section which follows, advanced software created expressly to teach pronunciation will be described and critiqued.

With regard to the issue of foreign accent and comprehensibility, Munro and Derwing (2001) used speech compression-expansion software to manipulate speaking rates of L2 speakers and found that the relationship between speaking rates and judgments of accentedness and comprehensibility was attributable to the rate differences themselves, rather than to other differences in L2 performance that might co-vary with rate. In a related study, Derwing and Munro (2001) conducted an experiment in which two groups of speakers of English as a second language assessed the appropriateness of the speech rate of narratives read by native English speakers and Mandarin learners of English. The narratives were played to listeners at their original, unmodified rates and at three computer-manipulated rates. In general, the modifications did not result in improvements in the assessments of appropriateness of speech rate, though the listeners did tend to assign better ratings to the mechanically accelerated speech of the slowest Mandarin speakers. This type of L2 research using technology to manipulate speech in order to gain empirical evidence of comprehensibility is valuable for linguists, practitioners, and software developers.

In a study of L2 fluency, Kormos and Dénes (2004) used computer technology to record and process speech samples in order to explore the variables that predict native and non-native speaking teachers perceptions of fluency in L2 learners. The speech samples of L2 Hungarian learners were analyzed acoustically, and the speech rate, mean length of utterance, phonation time ratio (that is, time speaking as a percentage of the time taken to produce the speech sample), and number of stressed words produced per minute were found to be the best predictors of fluency scores.

technology in discourse intonation research

As a number of researchers have long claimed, prosody in general and intonation in particular are critical to interpreting speech. Increasingly, the search for intonational meaning has focused on discourse, as seen in the latest speech technology research described above as well as in other applied linguistics research. Uses of technology in discourse intonation research have been described by Chun (1998, 2002) and by Chun, Hardison, and Pennington (2004). In this section, selected studies by Wennerstrom and Pickering will illustrate recent L2 research conducted with computers.

Wennerstrom has carried out a number of studies analyzing speech by computer means. Her dissertation (Wennerstrom, 1997) showed that L2 speakers' intonation was a significant factor contributing to better scores on an exam of overall comprehensibility in English. Several measures of intonation from the speech samples of L2 speakers (Mandarin Chinese-speakers speaking English) were computed, including pitch range of initial and final utterances on a topic. The significant result was that the greater a learner's average pitch increase to signal topic shift, the higher the score indicating comprehensibility. The ability to quantify this prosodic marker of topic shift is facilitated greatly by acoustic (computer) analysis of pitch range. Wennerstrom (2000) reported on a conversation analysis of naturally occurring dialogues using computerized speech analysis of L2 speakers' pitch patterns and showing that intonation is one of the important variables contributing to fluent speech in English. Wennerstrom (2001), based on computer analysis of digitized samples of various types of speech, demonstrated the centrality of prosody in the interpretation of spoken texts. The role of prosody was considered in such discourse genres as casual conversation, oral narratives, courtroom testimony, lectures, and second-language discourse. The studies established a framework for transcribing and analyzing prosody in discourse and provided a wealth of data illustrating a wide range of intonational phenomena measured and quantified by acoustic analysis software.

Pickering (2001, 2002) examined data from naturally occurring university classroom interactions, focusing specifically on the contribution of prosodic cues to exchanges between Teaching Assistants (TAs) and students. Her focus on prosody in the broader context of classroom interaction led to the quantitative measurement by computer of tone choice (e.g., rising or falling tone) and represents an important direction for future research in L2 phonology. In related work, Pickering (2004) used computer-based acoustic analyses of prosody – in terms of pitch prominence, length of pauses, and pitch range – to describe differences in intonation between native speaker and L2 speaker groups. By quantifying the phonological (prosodic) criteria that are used to mark paragraphs, she is able to make concrete suggestions about how non-native speakers can improve their comprehensibility when speaking an L2.

The above studies suggest natural pedagogical applications, based on computer representations and measurements, for highlighting and teaching speaking rate, placement of primary stress, the number of prominent syllables in a tone unit, the use of pitch to signal topic shifts, and appropriate length and location of pauses. Such pedagogical applications will be explored in the next section.

technological advances in teaching phonology

the state of the art

Near the end of the twentieth century, Jager, Nerbonne, and Van Essen (1998) published a volume, *Language Teaching and Language Technology*, that argued for an increased focus on the capabilities and use of language technologies in second-language teaching. Their lament was that "existing CALL [computer-assisted language learning] programs and packages seemed to make little use of language technologies" (p. 1). They distinguished between (i) *language technology*, or technology specifically designed for language-related tasks (speech recognition and synthesis, lexical and syntactic analysis, and text generation); and (ii) *non-language technology* (hypertext, digital audio and video, database technology, and network communication). Pennington (1999) presented an overview of the promises, limitations, and directions of computer-aided pronunciation [CAP] pedagogy, arguing the need for more ambitious goals. In the most recent *Annual Review of Applied Linguistics*, Jenkins (2004) stated that "of the recent findings of pronunciation research, the most influential in terms of pedagogic developments fall into two main groupings: those concerned with issues of context and those that relate to technological advances" (pp. 109–10). For the remainder of this chapter, I will focus only on published research on pronunciation teaching and attempt to determine whether progress has been made since the assessment of the state of the art by Jager, Nerbonne, and Van Essen (1998).

speech recognition

In the same year that *Language Teaching and Language Technology* appeared, Ehsani and Knodt (1998) published a discussion on the suitability of deploying speech technology for teaching foreign-language-speaking skills. They noted that a number of techniques had been suggested for automatic recognition and scoring of segmental phonemes in L2 speech (Bernstein, 1997; Franco, Neumeyer, Kim, and Ronen, 1997; Kim, Franco, and Neumeyer, 1997; Witt and Young, 1997). The procedure generally consists of building native-speaker pronunciation models and then measuring the L2 speech data. Machine scores are calculated from statistics derived by comparing the L2 speakers' values for these variables to the native-speaker models. Reliability and accuracy of the computer recognition of phonemes is checked by correlating the machine scores for the phoneme targets against human judgments of the phonemes produced.

A system for the teaching of Japanese long vowels and double-mora nasals and obstruents was reported by Kawai and Hirose (1997, 2000). Learners read minimal pairs, and the duration of each phone is measured by speech recognition technology. The system informs the learner of the likelihood of native Japanese speakers understanding the learner's utterance. Learners' intelligibility scores are based on perception experiments in which native speakers of Japanese judged the discriminability of minimal pairs containing phones with various synthesized durations. The system further instructs the learner to either shorten or lengthen the pronunciation of phones for which native-speaker judgments would indicate an insufficient length distinction. Results of the experiments demonstrate that learners "quickly capture the relevant duration cues" (2000, p. 131).

Franco and Neumeyer (1996) and Neumeyer, Franco, Digalakis, and Weintraub (2000) presented a paradigm for the automatic assessment of pronunciation quality by machine. In their scoring paradigm, both native and L2 speech data were collected, and a database of human-expert ratings of the speech of these two groups was created as a foundation for developing a variety of machine scores. The researchers addressed pronunciation evaluation as a prediction problem, creating statistical models which aim to predict the rating a human expert would assign to a particular component of pronunciation, such as segment duration. The machine scoring routines seek to predict the human-expert judgment of the speaker's pronunciation as native or non-native by using machine scores, or predictor variables. The researchers validated the machine scores on the Voice Interactive Language Training System (VILTS) corpus, evaluating the pronunciation of American speakers speaking French on a native-French-speaker model, and showed that machine scores in some cases achieved correlation with the human scores, for example, for duration. However, and not surprisingly, the correlation of these machine scores with human scores still did not match the correlations of human raters with each other in all cases, for example, at the sentence level.

In 1999, *CALICO Journal* published a special issue, "Tutors that Listen: Speech Recognition for Language Learning." The articles in that issue which are relevant to pronunciation training will be discussed here. These articles describe interesting work being conducted at universities and research institutes, lamenting the fact that commercialized ASR (generally for business applications) does not fully meet the needs of language learners.

Wachowicz and Scott (1999) review learning activities in selected commercial products. Of the ones using ASR for pronunciation practice, the activities fall into three categories: (i) minimal pair exercises, (ii) pronunciation scoring as part of vocabulary games and conversational practice, and (iii) word boundary and phrase segmentation practice. In the pronunciation scoring products, such scoring is secondary to a vocabulary game or dialogue exercise, and the technology, in their view, is not even as good as "the rather superficial integration of ASR that appears typical of commercial products" (p. 269). Wachowicz and Scott conclude that among commercial offerings, minimal pair exercises and acoustic wave form comparisons appear to be the most promising kinds of activities to aid pronunciation. However, these uses of computer technologies do not exploit them to their full potential but only elevate them to high-tech tape recorders. This observation is in line with the conclusion of LaRocca, Morgan, and Bellinger (1999): "Unfortunately, the best ASR technology is not yet available off the shelf with all the adaptations needed to support language learning" (p. 302).

Egan (1999) devotes a section of an article on speaking skills to the challenges of developing ASR for computer-aided language learning. Her article and several of the other papers in the same issue of *CALICO Journal* describe closed-response designs, i.e., systems in which there are a small number of restricted utterance choices for learner responses. These include: the *ECHOS* version by Rypa and Price (1999) of the VILTS system described below; the *Virtual Conversations* program of Harless, Zier, and Duncan (1999); the minimal pair exercise (for "tiny two-word vocabularies") described by LaRocca, Morgan, and Bellinger (1999, p. 300); and the minimal pair drills in the Pronto system reported by

Dalby and Kewley-Port (1999) for native speakers of American English learning Spanish and for native speakers of Mandarin Chinese learning English. A review of a CD-ROM that is part of the *Virtual Conversations* program optimistically notes: "The program's accent evaluation features and the intelligent prompting could provide useful tools for computer-based language learning, especially if they were integrated into a clearly articulated language pedagogy" (Blake, 2000, p. 35).

Delmonte (2000) argues that "the use of Automatic Speech Recognition (ASR) as Teaching Aid should be *under*-utilized [emphasis added] and should be targeted to narrowly focused spoken exercises, disallowing open-ended dialogues, in order to ensure consistency of evaluation" (p. 145). He proposes a prosodic module of a computer-assisted language learning program, SLIM (Multimedia Interactive Linguistic Software) developed at the University of Venice. The goal of the software is to improve a student's performance both in the perception and the production of prosodic aspects of spoken language. Delmonte argues that ASR alone cannot be used to gauge "goodness of pronunciation" (GOP), and is in fact inherently inadequate for that goal. He supports the use of ASR technology together with prosodic tools to produce GOP measures usable for linguistically consistent and adequate feedback to the student. Because it tackles the important issue of assessment of learner performance, Delmonte's SLIM appears to be a promising project.

Eskenazi (1998, 1999) discusses the FLUENCY system developed at Carnegie Mellon University which uses ASR for accent improvement in a foreign language. A feature that distinguishes Eskenazi's system from many others is that it is based on the principle of trying to foster as many characteristics of total immersion in a real speech context as possible. The FLUENCY system emphasizes both prosody and phonetics, and techniques for eliciting freely constructed yet specifically targeted utterances are suggested. Carefully constructed exercises can elicit from one to three distinct responses, so despite the goal of freely constructed utterances, this is a closed response program. Given that it can be predicted what will be said, FLUENCY uses the method of "forced alignment," by which the system automatically aligns the predicted text to the incoming speech signal.

In addition to specific pedagogic recommendations based on immersion, Eskenazi (1999) provides insights into whether and how different types of learner errors can be detected successfully, and what methods are effective in giving students feedback on errors and showing them how to make corrections. The SPHINX II automatic speech recognizer which she describes detects errors in phones produced by L2 learners and compares them with native speakers' utterances. In addition, a pilot study attempting to detect errors in prosody (in duration, pitch, and intensity) is also described. Eskenazi (1999) states that how the speech recognition results are best interpreted for instruction differs for correction of errors at the level of phones and prosody. In her view: "Whereas students must be guided as to tongue and teeth placement for a new phone, they don't need instruction on how to increase pitch if they have normal hearing: They only need to be shown when to increase and decrease it, and by how much" (p. 463). She proposes that the visual display, more than specific instructions, is critical to correction of a learner's inaccurate prosody. The key is for learners to see where the curve representing their intonation differs from the native speaker's intonation curve.

Since they do not restrict learners' utterances, open-response systems, as opposed to closed-response designs, require much more complex processing capabilities. An example is an extension of VILTS called SOLVIT (Special Operations Language Voice Interactive Training) described by Rypa and Price (1999). In SOLVIT, students are coached through lessons involving successively more independent spoken interactions in French to a level of free-form utterances bounded only by the types of grammatical constructions and vocabulary introduced in the lesson. Students produce these utterances without text support and without reading utterance choices from the screen. In terms of general L2 pedagogy, this type of courseware is a step in the right direction, but it remains to be seen how much the technological capabilities of ASR can be improved so that freely formed, open responses can be recognized and evaluated.

Rypa and Price (1999) reported that the best sentence-level result using the automatic pronunciation scoring of the VILTS system was a correlation of .609 of the computer's pronunciation score with that of human raters, close to the average .68 correlation found between human raters. The key, however, to deploying this technology successfully is to include useful feedback to the learners as to exactly how they need to modify their pronunciation. As the authors observe:

> Pronunciation scoring…has the potential of being even more useful if we can devise ways to provide more detailed feedback, diagnosis, and repair strategies. In selecting feedback, it is important to understand both technical challenges and pedagogical validity. (p. 401)

Derwing, Munro, and Carbonaro (2000) also investigated popular ASR packages for teaching pronunciation in English as a second language and found that these packages are still not able to perform as well as human listeners with regard to L2 speech. They conclude that there is potential for improving this type of software; however, it must be carefully developed and evaluated to ensure that it recognizes speech with reasonable accuracy so as to avoid unnecessary correction and frustration, and to also be effective in providing the kind of feedback that human teachers provide.

To summarize this discussion of ASR for L2 pronunciation training, based on the research to date, it appears that the most theoretically and pedagogically promising projects are the non-commercial ones being developed at universities and research institutes. Commercial products are generally too ambitious and all-encompassing, purporting to teach all aspects of a language, from pronunciation to syntax. Neri, Cucchiarini, Strik, and Boves (2002) arrived at the same conclusion in their review of available literature and various computer-assisted pronunciation training systems. They show that "many commercial systems tend to prefer technological novelties to the detriment of pedagogical criteria that could benefit the learner more" (p. 441).

Verhofstadt (2002) reviewed the pronunciation training capabilities of 17 programs[6] aimed at teaching English as a foreign language to beginners and found them wanting: "[T]here is still a lot of room for improvement, both with regard to the technological and the pedagogical design" (p. 182). Specifically with respect to ASR and assessments, Verhofstadt found that "not one program was able to perform its assessments satisfactorily. Furthermore, we have raised objections against the mere use of assessments as a didactic method in itself, especially because the learners are largely left in the dark about on which criteria their pronunciation is judged" (ibid.).[7] The same can be said about most commercial programs. In the *Tell Me More* program (Auralog), users can view their waveform and pitch curve immediately below the waveform and pitch curve of a native speaker. Simply displaying waveforms and pitch curves is not necessarily helpful unless one is an expert at interpreting these graphic representations, which the average language learner surely is not. In addition, some programs are effective only for learners at certain levels of proficiency. A study by Hincks (2003) of Swedish learners who had unlimited access to *Talk to Me* software (also by Auralog) found that "practice with the program was beneficial to those students who began the course with a strong foreign accent but was of limited value for students who began the course with better pronunciation" (p. 3).[8]

visual and audio feedback

In the conclusion to her dissertation in which 17 programs for improving pronunciation were reviewed, Verhofstadt (2002) singles out a particular aspect of such programs that shows promise:

> It has been shown that the use of speech visualizations can help the didactic process, provided that the phonetic material is carefully selected so that it best serves the didactic goal, and that there is enough explicit phonological advice and theoretical guidance about how to interpret the display. This is very rarely the case with commercial CALL/CAP programs...[and] there is still a long way to go before the expertise of the human language teacher will be equaled. (p. 182)

Although commercial software in general is largely inadequate for computer-aided pronunciation training, there is a growing body of research and development in this area. In this section, some of the excellent software in development at universities and research institutes will be described. Some of these programs are available as freeware; others are being introduced for sale.

For a historical overview of research on the use of technology for pronunciation, and in particular, on the effectiveness of audio and visual feedback, see Chun (2002). Studies of note include those by Anderson-Hsieh (1992, 1994), de Bot (1983), Pennington and Esling (1996), and Weltens and de Bot (1984). Recent work includes studies by Carey (2004); Cosi, Cohen, and Massaro (2002); de la Vaux and Massaro (2004); several studies by Hardison (1999, 2003, 2004); Hew and Ohki (2004); and Pennington, Ellis, Lee, and Lau (1999), to name a few.

Two recent studies reporting on the effectiveness of computer-based visual feedback dealt with the segmental and word levels. Hew and Ohki (2004) examined the effectiveness of imagery and electronic visual feedback in facilitating students' acquisition of the pronunciation of specific Japanese word pairs. They found that students who viewed animated graphic annotations or received immediate visual feedback and also heard an audio file in which the words were pronounced had better pronunciation than those who only heard the audio files. Carey (2004) reported on a study using *Kay Sona-Match*, which displays a user's vowel space in real time and has the capacity to display individual productions in the vowel space using different phonetic fonts. He conducted an intervention experiment in which learners viewed their own vowel production in real time as displayed on a vowel space chart and also viewed a video clip of native-speaker models showing tongue position, lip shape, and jaw lowering for the same vowel. A significant lasting improvement was achieved for one of the target vowels when it was produced in citation form, but not in continuous speech.[9]

At the sentence and discourse levels, research is being conducted on prosody and intonation training with technology. Pennington, Ellis, Lee, and Lau (1999) investigated the learning of intonation on computer, comparing seven different pedagogical orientations. Two treatments which showed some significant pre/post improvements in intonation were a treatment combining repetition and a visual representation of the intonation contour and a treatment combining repetition and an extracted auditory pitch contour. In general, the Pennington, Ellis, Lee, and Lau results for prosody are consistent with those of Carey (2004) and of Hew and Ohki (2004) for segmentals, demonstrating that focused training in a computer-mediated learning environment can improve pronunciation in a second language.

Hardison (2004) found that visual feedback provided in a computer-assisted program was effective in the acquisition of French prosody by foreign-language learners (L1 English), and demonstrated generalization to novel sentences and improved segmental production accuracy – hallmarks of successful training. In addition, questionnaire responses indicated a positive evaluation of computer-assisted training. Respondents also noted increased confidence in their oral production of French and heightened awareness of the elements that make up speech.

Another study by Hardison (2005) was conducted with L1 speakers of Mandarin Chinese who were advanced L2 speakers of English and graduate students at an American university. Their pre-training difficulties with English prosody are captured in the category described by Chun (2002) as discourse functions of intonation that contribute to cohesion in speech, including the marking of thought groups with appropriate pausing and pitch movement, and the use of stress and intonation to mark information focus. The study investigated the effects on the production of discourse-level English prosody of different types of contextualized training using segments from the participants' own oral presentations on familiar topics. Two computer-based tools were used to compare two weeks of training with and without the visual context of the speech event, and with discourse-level input versus isolated sentences. The tools were (i) web-based *Anvil* (Kipp, 2001),[10] which provides a screen display integrating the audio and video components of a speech event with the associated pitch contour created in Praat,[11] a public domain phonetic tool; and (ii) Kay Elemetrics *Real-Time Pitch* (RTP) program in conjunction with the *Computerized Speech Lab*, which produces a pitch contour in real-time and allows on-screen comparison of a learner's utterance with that of a native speaker, including overlay of one contour on another.[12] Results showed that the presence of video was helpful, more so with discourse-level input than with individual sentences, strongly suggesting that meaningful contextualized input, as provided, for example, by video, is valuable in prosody training.

Research on speech perception includes examination of factors influencing the integration of auditory and visual information in speech perception (e.g., Hardison, 1999). The findings of this research point to the need to incorporate into perceptual training for L2 learners the enhancement of the information value of visual cues as a second channel of input. In a study on the acquisition of L2 speech, Hardison (2003) proposed that, given the beneficial role of the presence of visual cues from a talker's face in the improvement of L2 perceptual accuracy, one might focus attention on the talker's lip movements in improving speech and pronunciation, such as by uses of video within computer-based pronunciation training. This focus on facial information in movements and gestures has also been key to the work of Massaro and his colleagues developing: (i) research procedures for systematically manipulating the amount of visual information presented to a listener in testing and training word and phoneme recognition (e.g., de La Vaux and Massaro, 2004) and (ii) computer-animated conversational agents (*Baldi* and *Baldini*) with potential applications to tutoring second-language speakers, deaf children, and children with phonological disorders (e.g., Cosi, Cohen, and Massaro, 2002; Massaro and Light, 2003).[13]

commercial software for computer-assisted pronunciation

Although, as stated above, commercial products in general have pedagogical shortcomings, three commercial software packages developed initially at universities and research institutes have attempted to incorporate principles of discourse intonation and contextualized speech into their programs: *In Tune with English* (reported in Kaltenboeck, 2001); *Connected Speech* (available from Protea Textware; <http://www.proteatextware.com.au>);[14] and *Streaming Speech: Listening and Pronunciation for Advanced Learners of English* (produced by Richard Cauldwell; <http://www.speechinaction.com>. Cauldwell's (2002) software is based on Brazil's (1997) theory of discourse intonation, which is endorsed by a number of contemporary applied linguists, e.g., Chun (2002), Jenkins (2004), Levis (1999), and Levis and Pickering (2004), and Pickering (2001, 2004). To date there are no published empirical studies to my knowledge on the effectiveness of these programs.[15]

In *Streaming Speech*, all of the recordings are of natural spontaneous speech. The speech samples are analyzed in terms of a discourse syllabus focused on the choices speakers make in conveying meaning through pitch and stress and the strategies they use to communicate effectively in real time. *Streaming Speech* represents a worthwhile use of multimedia technology coupled with authentic, discourse-level speech in the service of teaching pronunciation and listening comprehension. The use of authentic speech is in stark contrast to the vast majority of programs for pronunciation which use stilted, unnatural-sounding recordings. At the same time, the program does not promise automatic speech recognition and pronunciation evaluation, as so many other commercial packages offer but fail to deliver.

conclusion

These are exciting times for researching language with speech technology and developing applications for teaching pronunciation, including prosody, based on naturally occurring speech. The hardware is generally not the stumbling block that it once was, and in general, most of the focus today is on software. One enduring dilemma is reconciling automatic speech recognition with the desire for unscripted speech and open-response discourse activities in instruction. Commercial products aiming to teach pronunciation will continue to be inadequate unless they focus on designing better didactic activities, and most critically, on providing more useful feedback to learners about where and how segmental and prosodic aspects of speech can be modified and improved.

As this review makes clear, there have been many advances in technologies for researching and teaching phonology in the recent past, but there is still much more to do. There is a continuing need for theoretical and applied linguists to collaborate with speech technologists, especially in the areas of: acoustic analysis; visual presentation of intonation, rhythm, and stress; speech synthesis; and the challenging area of speech recognition. Assuming such collaborations, we can hope to see the continuation of major advances in phonological research and practice that impact linguistic theory and description as well as remediation and pedagogy in very positive ways.

notes

1. Editor's note: see Chapter 8, this volume, for further discussion.
2. Both of these software tools are available for free download at <http://www. linguistics.ucsb.edu/resources/computing/download/download.htm>.

3. Their system, EXMARaLDA, is available free of charge at <http://www.rrz. uni-hamburg.de/exmaralda>.
4. Editor's note: see Chapter 9, this volume, for discussion.
5. Editor's note: e.g., Couper-Kuhlen (Chapter 8, this volume).
6. A number of these programs for English are produced by companies that market programs for other languages as well, including: DynEd (*New Dynamic English, Clear Speech Works*), Fairfield Language Technologies (*Rosetta Stone*), and Auralog (*Talk to Me/Tell Me More*).
7. A potentially promising authorware system is *EduSpeak®*, a speech recognition system that, through its Software Development Kit, enables developers of multimedia applications to incorporate continuous speaker-independent speech recognition into their applications. It was developed in the Speech Technology and Research (STAR) Laboratory of the Information and Computing Sciences Division at SRI International, an independent research institute in California, and was designed for use in educational software by developers of applications for language learning, reading development, assessment, and corporate training <http://www.speechatsri.com/products/ eduspeak.shtml>. To date, however, no reviews or research documenting its use could be found.
8. A useful websites for teachers discussing the available technology are "Information and Communications Technology for Language Teachers" <http://www.ict4lt.org> and "Computer Assisted Pronunciation Teaching References" (see Llisterri, 2004).
9. Carey (2004) examined 23 commercial pronunciation software packages and found only six products that provide learners with visual feedback: (1) Technologically Enhanced Accent Modification (TEAM), 1999 Version 2.0 (Erlbaum), retrieved January 31, 2006, from <http://www.ed.gov/about/offices/list/ope/ fipse/lessons4/cleveland.html>; (2) Accent Lab (Accent Technologies); (3) Protrain (Avaaz Innovations, Inc.); (4) Dr. Speech (Tiger DRS, Inc.), which comes in two product versions, Real Analysis and Speech Training; (5) Video Voice (Micro Video Corporation); and (6) Sona-Match (KayPENTAX, formerly Kay Elemetrics).
10. See <http://www.dfki.de/~kipp/anvil>. At this site, there is a link to a demo screen shot. Directions are given for those who wish to obtain the address for downloading the files, and it is free for research purposes.
11. Created by Boersma (2001) and Weenink. Available free of charge at <http:// www.fon.hum.uva.nl/praat>.
12. Another highly-regarded program, *Winpitch LTL*, was created by Philippe Martin (University of Toronto, <http://www.winpitch.com/index.htm> and is a Windows-based program that is a real time speech analyzer, visualizer, and synthesizer. Weinberg and Knoerr (2003) state that "students can visualize exactly what they have pronounced through a sonogram and intonation indicator. The teacher can redesign a student's incorrect prosodic pattern to synthesize correct prosodic pattern[s] in the student's own voice for direct feedback." Thus, the "feedback capabilities substantially exceed those of its most widely used predecessor, Kay Elemetrics' *VisiPitch*, which allowed learners to record utterances, play them back, and see a visual display of their intonation curve but did not allow for explanations or monitoring" (p. 316).

13. Editor's note: for a detailed discussion of this area of research, see Chapter 6, this volume.
14. *Connected Speech* was reviewed by Darhower (2002), <http://calico.org/CALICO_Review/review/conspeech.htm> and Egbert (2004) <http://llt.msu.edu/vol8num1/review2/default.html>.
15. *Streaming Speech* has however received positive reviews by Chun (2005), Lian (2004) <http://llt.msu.edu/vol8num2/review2/default.html>, Petrie (2003) <http://calico.org/CALICO_Review/review/streaming.htm>, Rixon (2004), Setter (2003), and Wilson (2004).

references

Alwang G. (1999). Speech recognition. *PC Magazine*, 10 November 1999. Cited in Gupta & Schulze (2000).

Anderson-Hsieh, J. (1992). Using electronic visual feedback to teach suprasegmentals. *System, 20*, 51–62.

Anderson-Hsieh, J. (1994). Interpreting visual feedback on suprasegmentals in computer assisted pronunciation instruction. *CALICO Journal, 11*, 5–22.

Bayley, R., & Preston, D.R. (1996). *Second language acquisition and linguistic variation.* Amsterdam: John Benjamins.

Bernstein, J. (1997). Automatic spoken language assessment by telephone (Technical Report No. 5–97), Menlo Park, CA: Entropic, Inc.

Blake, R. (2000). Review of *Roberto's Restaurant* CD-ROM. *Language Learning and Technology, 4* (2), 31–6.

Boersma, P. (2001). PRAAT, a system for doing phonetics by computer. *Glot International, 5*(9/10), 341–345.

Brazil, D. (1997). *The communicative value of intonation in English.* Cambridge, U.K.: Cambridge University Press.

Browman, C. P., & Goldstein, L. (1986). Towards an articulatory phonology. *Phonology Yearbook, 3*, 219–252.

Browman, C. P., & Goldstein, L. (1989). Articulatory gestures as phonological units. *Phonology, 6*, 201–251.

Carey, M. (2004). Visual feedback for pronunciation of vowels: Kay Sona-Match. *CALICO Journal, 21*, 571–601.

Cauldwell, R. (2002). Streaming speech: Listening and pronunciation for advanced learners of English. In D. Teeler (Ed.), *Talking computers* (pp. 18–22). Whitstable, U.K.: IATEFL.

Cedergren, H. J. & Sankoff, D. (1974). Variable rules: Performance as a statistical reflection of competence. *Language, 50*, 333–55.

Chang, S. (2002). A syllable, articulatory-feature, and stress-accent model of speech recognition. Doctoral dissertation, University of California at Berkeley.

Chun, D. M. (1998). Signal analysis software for teaching discourse intonation. *Language Learning & Technology, 2*, 61–77. Retrieved January 31, 2006, from <http://llt.msu.edu/vol2num1/article4>.

Chun, D. M. (2002). *Discourse intonation in L2: From theory and research to practice.* Amsterdam: John Benjamins.

Chun, D. M. (2005). Review of *Streaming Speech.* TESOL Quarterly 39, 559–62.

Chun, D. M., Hardison, D. M., & Pennington, M. C. (2004). Technologies for prosody in context: Past and future of L2 research and practice. Paper presented

269

296   phonology in context

in the Colloquium on the State-of-the-Art of L2 Phonology Research at the Annual Conference of the American Association of Applied Linguistics. Portland, Oregon.

Cosi, P., Cohen, M. A., & Massaro, D. W. (2002). Baldini: Baldi speaks Italian! In J. H. L. Hansen, & B. Pellom (Eds.), *International Conference on Spoken Language Processing 2002* (pp. 2349–52). Sydney, Australia: Causal Productions PTY, Ltd.

Couper-Kuhlen, E., & Selting, M. (Eds.) (1996). *Prosody in conversation.* Cambridge: Cambridge University Press.

Dalby, J. and Kewley-Port, D. (1999). Explicit pronunciation training using automatic speech recognition technology. *CALICO Journal, 16,* 425–45.

Darhower, M. (2003). Review of *Connected Speech, CALICO Journal, 20* (3), 603–12.

de Bot, K. (1983). Visual feedback of intonation I: Effectiveness and induced practice behavior. *Language and Speech, 26,* 331–50.

de la Vaux, S. K., & Massaro, D. W. (2004). Audiovisual speech gating: Examining information and information processing. *Cognitive Process, 5,* 106–12.

Delmonte, R. (2000). SLIM prosodic automatic tools for self-learning instruction. *Speech Communication, 30,* 145–66.

Derwing, T., & Munro, M. J. (2001). What speaking rates do non-native listeners prefer? *Applied Linguistics, 22,* 324–37.

Derwing, T., Munro, M., & Carbonaro, M. (2000). Does popular speech recognition software work with ESL speech? *TESOL Quarterly, 34,* 592–603.

Du Bois, J. W., Schuetze-Coburn, S., Paolino, D., & Cumming, S. (1992). Discourse transcription. *Santa Barbara Papers in Linguistics, 4.* Santa Barbara: Department of Linguistics, University of California at Santa Barbara.

Egan, K. B. (1999). Speaking: A critical skill and a challenge. *CALICO Journal, 16,* 277–93.

Egbert, J. (2004). Review of *Connected Speech, Language Learning and Technology, 8* (1), 24–8.

Ehsani, F., & Knodt, E. (1998). Speech technology in computer-aided language learning: Strengths and limitations of a new CALL paradigm. *Language Learning and Technology, 2*(1), 45–60.

Eskenazi, M. (1998). Using automatic speech processing for foreign language pronunciation tutoring: Some issues and a prototype. *Language Learning and Technology 2*(2), 62–76.

Eskenazi, M. (1999). Using a computer in foreign language pronunciation training: What advantages? *CALICO Journal, 16,* 447–69.

Franco, H., & Neumeyer, L. (1996). Automatic scoring of pronunciation quality for language instruction. *Journal of the Acoustical Society of America 100,* 2763.

Franco, H., Neumeyer, L., Kim, Y., & Ronen, O. (1997). Automatic pronunciation scoring for language instruction. *Proceedings of the International Conference on Acoustics, Speech, and Signal Processing,* Volume 2, pp. 1471–74. Munich.

Galley, M., McKeown, K., Hirschberg, J., & Shriberg, E. (2004). Identifying agreement and disagreement in conversational speech: Use of Bayesian networks to model pragmatic dependencies. To appear in *Proceedings of the 42nd Meeting of the ACL,* Barcelona.

Greenberg, S. (2005). From here to utility – Melding phonetic insight with speech technology. In W. Barry and W. van Dommelen (Eds.), *The integration of phonetic knowledge in speech technology* (pp. 107–32). Dordrecht: Kluwer.

Gupta, P., & Schulze, M. (2000). Human language technologies. Retrieved January 31, 2006, from <http://www.ict4lt.org/en/en_mod3-5.htm>.

Hardison, D. M. (1999). Bimodal speech perception by native and nonnative speakers of English: Factors influencing the McGurk effect. *Language Learning*, *49*, 213–83.

Hardison, D. M. (2003). Acquisition of second-language speech: Effects of visual cues, context and talker variability. *Applied Psycholinguistics*, *24*, 495–522.

Hardison, D. M. (2004). Generalization of computer-assisted prosody training: Quantitative and qualitative findings. *Language Learning & Technology*, *8*, 34–52. Retrieved January 31, 2006, from <http://llt.msu.edu/vol8num1/hardison>.

Hardison, D. M. (2005). Contextualized computer-based L2 prosody training: Evaluating the effects of discourse context and video input. *CALICO Journal*, *22*, 175–90.

Harless, W. G., Zier, M. A. & Duncan, R. C. (1999). Virtual dialogues with native speakers: The evaluation of an interactive multimedia method. *CALICO Journal*, *16*, 313–37.

Harris, N. (2000). Considerations for use in language training. Retrieved January 31, 2006, from <http://www.dyned.com/about/speech.shtml>.

Hew, S.-H., & Ohki, M. (2004). Effect of animated graphic annotations and immediate visual feedback in aiding Japanese pronunciation learning: A comparative study. *CALICO Journal*, *21*, 397–420.

Hincks, R. (2003). Speech technologies for pronunciation feedback and evaluation. *ReCALL 15*(1), 3–20.

Hirschberg, J. (2002). Communication and prosody: Functional aspects of prosody. *Speech Communication*, *36*, 31–43.

Jager, S., Nerbonne, J., & Van Essen, A. (Eds.) (1998). *Language teaching and language technology*. Lisse: Swets & Zeitlinger.

Jenkins, J. (2004). Research in teaching pronunciation and intonation. *Annual Review of Applied Linguistics*, *24*, 109–25.

Kaltenboeck, G. (2001). A multimedia approach to suprasegmentals: Using a CD-ROM for English intonation teaching. *Phonetics Teaching and Learning Conference Proceedings* (pp. 19–22). London. Retrieved January 31, 2006 from <http://www.phon.ucl.ac.uk/home/johnm/ptlc2001/pdf/kaltenboeck.pdf>.

Kawai, G., & Hirose, K. (1997). A CALL system using speech recognition to train the pronunciation of Japanese long vowels, the mora nasal and mora obstruents. *Proceedings of Eurospeech, the 3rd European Conference on Speech Communication and Technology, 2* (pp. 657–60). Rhodes.

Kawai, G., & Hirose, K. (2000). Teaching the pronunciation of Japanese double-mora phonemes using speech recognition technology. *Speech Communication*, *30*, 131–43.

Kim, Y., Franco, H., & Neumeyer, L. (1997). Automatic pronunciation scoring of specific phone segments for language instruction. *Proceedings of Eurospeech, the 3rd European Conference on Speech Communication and Technology*, Volume 2 (pp. 645–8). Rhodes.

Kipp, M. (2001). Anvil – A generic annotation tool for multimodal dialogue. *Proceedings of Eurospeech, the 7th European Conference on Speech Communication and Technology* (pp. 1367–70). Aalborg, Denmark.

Kormos, J., & Dénes, M. (2004). Exploring measures and perceptions of fluency in the speech of second language learners. *System 32*, 145–64.

Labov, W. (1969). Contraction, deletion and inherent variability of the English copula. *Language 45*, 715–62.

Ladefoged, P. (1996). *Elements of acoustic phonetics*. Chicago: University of Chicago Press.

Ladefoged, P. (2001). *Vowels and consonants*. Oxford: Blackwell.

Ladefoged, P. (2004). *Phonetic data analysis: An introduction to phonetic fieldwork and instrumental techniques*. Oxford: Blackwell.

LaRocca, S., Morgan, J., & Bellinger, S. (1999). On the path to 2X learning: Exploring the possibilities of advanced speech recognition. *CALICO Journal, 16*, 295–310.

Levis, J. M. (1999). Intonation in theory and practice, revisited. *TESOL Quarterly, 33*(1), 37–63.

Levis, J. M. and Pickering, L. (2004). Teaching intonation in discourse using speech visualization technology. *System, 32*, 505–24.

Lion, A. (2004). Review of *Streaming Speech, Language Learning and Technology, 8* (2), 23–32.

Llisterri, J. (2004). Computer assisted pronunciation teaching references. Retrieved January 31, 2006, from http://liceu.uab.es/~joaquim/applied_linguistics/L2_phonetics/CALL_Pron_Bib.html.

Marsi, E. (2001). Intonation in spoken language generation. Doctoral dissertation, University of Nijmegen.

Massaro, D. W. & Light, R. (2003). Read my tongue movements: Bimodal learning to perceive and produce non-native speech /r/ and /l/. *Proceedings of Eurospeech (Interspeech), 8th European Conference on Speech Communication and Technology*. Geneva.

Munro, M. J., & Derwing, T. M. (2001). Modeling perceptions of the accentedness and comprehensibility of L2 speech: The role of speaking rate. *Studies in Second Language Acquisition, 23*, 451–68.

Neri, A., Cucchiarini, C., Strik, H., & Boves, L. (2002). The pedagogy-technology interface in computer assisted pronunciation training. *CALL Journal, 15*, 441–67.

Neumeyer, L., Franco, H., Digalakis, V., & Weintraub, M. (2000). Automatic scoring of pronunciation quality. *Speech Communication, 30*, 83–93.

Pennington, M. C. (1999). Computer-aided pronunciation pedagogy: Promise, limitations, directions. *Computer Assisted Language Learning, 12*, 427–40.

Pennington, M. C., Ellis, N. C., Lee, Y. P., & Lau, L. (1999). Instructing intonation in a second language: Lessons from a study with Hong Kong Cantonese undergraduate English majors. Unpublished manuscript.

Pennington, M. C. & Esling, J. H. (1996). Computer-assisted development of spoken language skills. In M. C. Pennington (Ed.), *The power of CALL* (pp. 153–89). Houston: Athelstan.

Petrie, G. M. (2005). Review of *Streaming speech: Listening and pronunciation for advanced learners of English, CALICO Journal, 22*, 731–40.

Pickering, L. (2001). The role of tone choice in improving ITA communication in the classroom. *TESOL Quarterly, 35*, 233–55.

Pickering, L. (2002). Patterns of intonation in cross-cultural communication exchange structure in NS TA and ITA classroom discourse. *Proceedings of the Seventh Annual Conference on Language, Interaction and Culture* (pp. 1–17). University of California at Santa Barbara.

Pickering, L. (2004). The structure and function of intonational paragraphs in native and nonnative instructional discourse. *English for Specific Purposes, 23,* 19–43.

Pierrehumbert, J. B. (2003), Probabilistic phonology: Discrimination and robustness. In R. Bod, J. Hay & S. Jannedy (Eds.), *Probability theory in linguistics* (pp. 177–228). Cambridge: MIT Press.

Pitrelli, J. F., Beckman, M. E., & Hirschberg, J. (1994). Evaluation of prosodic transcription labeling reliability in the ToBI framework. *International Conference on Spoken Language Processing,* Volume 1 (pp. 123–6). Yokohama.

Rixon, S. (2004). Review of *Streaming Speech. Modern English Teacher,* 77–8.

Rypa, M. E., & Price, P. (1999). VILTS: A tale of two technologies. *CALICO Journal, 16* (3), 385–404.

Setter, J. (2003). Review of *Streaming Speech: Listening and pronunciation for advanced learners of English. Journal of the International Phonetic Association, 33,* 240–44.

Shriberg, E., & Stolcke, A. (2004a). Direct modeling of prosody: An overview of applications in automatic speech processing. *Proceedings of the International Conference on Speech Prosody* (pp. 1–8). Nara, Japan.

Shriberg, E., & Stolcke, A. (2004b). Prosody modeling for automatic speech recognition and understanding. In M. Johnson, M. Ostendorf, S. Khudanpur, & R. Rosenfeld (Eds.), *Mathematical foundations of speech and language modeling,* Volume 138 in IMA Volumes in Mathematics and its Applications (pp. 105–14). New York: Springer-Verlag.

Silverman, K., Beckman, M., Pitrelli, J., Ostendorf, M., Wightman, C., Price, P., Pierrehumbert, J., and Hirschberg, J. (1992). ToBI: A standard for labeling English prosody. *Proceedings of International Conference on Spoken Language Processing,* Volume 2 (pp. 867–70). Banff.

Verhofstadt, K. (2002). A critical analysis of commercial computer-assisted pronunciation materials. Doctoral dissertation, University of Ghent. Retrieved January 31, 2006, from <http://members.tripod.com/katrienverhofstadt/>.

Wachowicz, K. A., and Scott, B. (1999). Software that listens: It's not a question of whether, it's a question of how. *CALICO Journal, 16,* 253–76.

Weinberg, A., and Knoerr, H. (2003). Learning French pronunciation: Audiocassettes or multimedia? *CALICO Journal, 20*(2), 315–36.

Weltens, B., & de Bot, K. (1984). Visual feedback of intonation II: Feedback delay and quality of feedback. *Language and Speech, 27,* 79–88.

Wennerstrom, A. (1997). Discourse intonation and second language acquisition: Three genre-based studies. Doctoral dissertation, University of Washington at Seattle.

Wennerstrom, A. (2000). The role of intonation in second language fluency. In H. Riggenbach (Ed.), *Perspectives on fluency* (pp. 102–27). Ann Arbor, MI: University of Michigan Press.

Wennerstrom, A. (2001). *The music of everyday speech.* Oxford: Oxford University Press.

Wichmann, A. (2000). *Intonation in text and discourse.* Harlow: Longman.

Wilson, D. (2004). Review of *Streaming Speech. English Teaching Professional, 32,* 46.

Witt, S., & Young, S. (1997). Language learning based on non-native speech recognition. *Proceedings of Eurospeech, the 3rd European Conference on Speech Communication and Technology* (pp. 633–6). Rhodes.

subject index

abstract categories, 120, 122
abstract representations, 2, 7, 126
abstraction
  see processing
abstractness, 2, 7, 11, 34, 35, 38–40,
  44, 48, 55, 57, 66, 120, 125
accent
  foreign, 109–10, 129, 274, 277, 282,
    287, 289
  regional/social, 61, 66, 162
  prosodic, 31, 87, 100–2, 105, 107,
    163, 193–4, 199, 203, 207–8, 211,
    214–15, 279
accuracy
  production (articulation), 39,
    256–8, 291
  perception (discrimination/
    identification), 120, 123, 128–9,
    144, 289, 292
  automatic speech recognition, 278,
    285
affect
  see emotion
affiliation/disaffiliation, 207–12
alphabetic literacy, 220, 222, 228,
  230, 232, 233, 234, 237
ambient language, 5, 19, 25, 27,
  28, 30, 31, 32, 35, 37, 43, 113,
  120–1, 126
  see also input
Anvil, 152–3, 291, 294
aphasia, 174, 176–7, 230
applied linguistics, 3, 12, 129, 274–5,
  282–4
areal influence, 6, 77, 78, 83–9
articulatory ease, 26, 31, 42, 265
Articulatory Phonology, 54, 119, 160
assimilation, 33, 37, 60, 64, 120, 124,
  127, 163

associative network
  see under cognition
auditory cue
  see under cue
auditory feedback
  see under feedback
auditory input
  see under input
auditory trace
  see under trace
autistic children, 8, 151, 245
automatic speech recognition (ASR),
  12, 277, 279, 287, 293
Autosegmental Phonology, 45, 163,
  186

babble/babbling, 25, 26, 30–1, 32, 34
  of blind infants, 130
Baldi/Baldini, 151, 292
bilingualism/multilingualism, 13, 18,
  20, 76, 78, 84, 97, 100, 111, 115,
  116, 121, 122, 124, 128–9, 231–2,
  275
borrowing, 6, 77, 79–84, 99–100, 101,
  102
brain, 35–7, 44, 178–9
  Broca's area, 113, 141, 152, 177
  cortex, 142, 177
    auditory, 8, 139–40
    neocortex size, 179
  hemispheres/lateralization, 9, 113,
    167, 174–9, 180–1, 182
  size, 178–80
  see also cognition

casual speech, 53, 56, 57, 69, 276, 283
categoricity, 6, 30, 52, 53, 59, 254
categorization, 14, 15, 19, 118–20,
  122–4, 127–8, 131–2, 164

language index

author index

LaVergne, TN USA
25 September 2009
159008LV00001B/25/P